T0318397

Ethnic Marketing

Together with the development of transformative technologies that epitomize globalization, the ongoing movements of people across borders and other socio-economic pressures are creating a fast-changing business environment that is difficult for business to understand, let alone control. Dominant social expectations that immigrants should seek to adopt an assimilationist socialization path towards the host country's mainstream are contradicted by minority ethnic group resilience. There is no evidence that these groups naturally disappear within the cultural and behavioural contexts of their adopted countries. Since ethnic minority consumers cannot be expected to assimilate, then they maintain some significant degree of unique ethnicity-related consumer characteristics that convert into threats and opportunities for business. The inherent socialization process also provides opportunities for ethnic entrepreneurship and for proliferation of ethnic minority business.

Following from the extensive examination of scholarly perspectives of ethnic marketing theory, there is an acknowledged and marked divide between theoretical exhortations and what is done in practice, a relative oversight of the implications of mixed embedded markets and a propinquity to overlook the crucial role played by ethnic entrepreneurship and ethnic networks. Opportunity valuations are difficult to enact due to a lack of intelligence about ethnic markets. Variable sentiment about the future of ethnic marketing links to different predictions on how the drivers of globalization will impact the acculturation paths of ethnic minorities.

Keeping a focus on the ethnic group as the unit of analysis, combining ethnic marketing and ethnic entrepreneurship theories provides intelligence about contemporary ethnic marketing and practice perspectives. The ultimate objective is to reduce the theory-practice divide through the development of a collaborative framework between business and scholars that converts into theory-in-use.

Guilherme D. Pires, PhD, is Associate Professor at the Newcastle Business School, Faculty of Business and Law at University of Newcastle, Australia. He is a Trustee for the Business and Economics Society International and serves on the editorial boards of various scholarly journals.

John Stanton, PhD, is Adjunct Associate Professor (Marketing) in the School of Business, Western Sydney University, Australia.

Routledge Studies in Marketing

This series welcomes proposals for original research projects that are either single or multi-authored or an edited collection from both established and emerging scholars working on any aspect of marketing theory and practice and provides an outlet for studies dealing with elements of marketing theory, thought, pedagogy and practice.

It aims to reflect the evolving role of marketing and bring together the most innovative work across all aspects of the marketing "mix"—from product development, consumer behaviour, marketing analysis, branding, and customer relationships, to sustainability, ethics and the new opportunities and challenges presented by digital and online marketing.

Ethnic Marketing
Theory, Practice and Entrepreneurship

Guilherme D. Pires and John Stanton

Routledge
Taylor & Francis Group

NEW YORK AND LONDON

First published 2019
by Routledge
605 Third Avenue, New York, NY 10017

and by Routledge
2 Park Square, Milton Park, Abingdon, Oxon, OX14 4RN

First issued in paperback 2020

*Routledge is an imprint of the Taylor & Francis Group,
an informa business*

Library of Congress Cataloging-in-Publication Data
Names: Pires, Guilherme D., author. | Stanton, John L., author.
Title: Ethnic marketing : theory, practice and entrepreneurship /
    Guilherme D. Pires and John Stanton.
Description: New York : Routledge, 2019. | Series: Routledge
    studies in marketing | Includes bibliographical references
    and index.
Identifiers: LCCN 2018046827| ISBN 9781138210608 (hardback) |
    ISBN 9781315454894 (ebook)
Subjects: LCSH: Minority consumers. | Market segmentation. |
    Marketing—Cross-cultural studies.
Classification: LCC HF5415.332.M56 P57 2017 |
    DDC 658.8/12089—dc23
LC record available at https://lccn.loc.gov/2018046827

ISBN 13: 978-0-367-73217-2 (pbk)
ISBN 13: 978-1-138-21060-8 (hbk)

Typeset in Sabon
by Apex CoVantage, LLC

Guilherme D. Pires: To my wife, Maria Clara, for years and years of unlimited patience and support. To the other women in my life, my daughter Dianne and my grand-daughters Catarina, Lara and Sara.

John Stanton: To Patricia, whose forbearance knows no bounds, and to Eloise and Louis, who give us hope for a kinder and more tolerant world.

Contents

Tables

Figures

Acknowledgements

We would like to thank the many marketing scholars and practitioners whose wisdom contributed to this research.

We would also like to thank the Business & Economics Society International (B&ESI), the delegates to its conferences for their insights into the matters discussed in this text, and its leaders, Helen and Demetri Kantarelis, for their encouragement.

Finally, we would like to thank Routledge, David Varley and Mary Del Plato for their patience and assistance in making this book possible.

Foreword

Over more than two decades of researching and writing about cultural diversity and marketing to ethnic minorities within nation-states, we have sought to capture the ongoing changes in approaches to ethnic marketing and the largely environmental drivers of those changes that have been occurring. Over this period, we have observed growing differences between theory and practice as well as growing differences between countries in how practitioners appear to treat marketing to ethnic minorities. In this text we have sought to explain the causes of these differences while still advancing the theoretical underpinnings for ethnic marketing to be successful.

A major innovation in this text is to recognize that ethnic markets are incubators for ethnic entrepreneurship and ethnic minority business, which strengthens the value of ethnic networks for new arrivals and for entrepreneurs, adding to the resilience of the minority ethnic group even in the face of strong environmental constraints. Ultimately, success in ethnic entrepreneurship is entwined with successful ethnic marketing, hence our dual focus.

1 Issues in Ethnic Marketing Theory, Practice and Entrepreneurship

Several decades of large migrant flows into many advanced economies, often from culturally dissimilar sources to the host country, combined with a reawakening of ethnic identity among groups already resident, have stimulated large and often conflicting marketing and entrepreneurship literatures discussing whether, when and how to target consumers based on their ethnicity. The diversity of this body of work spans differences in both theoretical and practical perspectives. This book examines these different views of ethnic marketing, its practice and its future, with particular attention given to ethnic entrepreneurship.

The development of ethnic marketing requires understanding the sources of the differences, as well as the drivers of ethnic group resilience over time, as a prerequisite to reconciling the different perspectives. For this reason, a large portion of this text focusses on the process of creation, development and growth or demise of ethnic minority businesses, as a mainstay in minority ethnic group resilience.

This chapter explains how conceptual ambiguity in the development of ethnic marketing is causing a gap between theory and practitioners. To obtain a perspective of differences in ethnic marketing, the explanation draws on the ethnic marketing literature as well as an analysis of interviews with marketing scholars from several countries, some practitioners, on their understanding of ethnic marketing theory and practice and of how ethnic marketing may develop over time. The need for theory-in-use and a framework to achieve better theory that is also pragmatic enough for adoption by business is offered as a way of reconciling theory and practice.

Conceptual Ambiguity

Ethnic marketing research is hampered by different notions of ethnicity drawn from anthropology, ethnography, psychology, sociology and marketing (Weber, 1961; Cohen, 1978; Barth, 1998; Gjerde, 2014). Further discussion of these different notions and their implications will be discussed in Chapter 2. At this early stage of the discussion, we follow Weber's (1961) view of ethnicity as

> a shared sense of common descent extending beyond kinship, political solidarity vis-a-vis other groups, and common customs, language, religion, values, morality, and etiquette, providing "a set of sociocultural features that differentiate ethnic groups from one another".
>
> (cited in Cohen, 1978, p. 385)

Applying this view of ethnicity can arguably delimit ethnic marketing and contributions identifiable as ethnic marketing research; however, ethnic marketing is a field where different views of ethnicity exist and ethnic marketing theory and practice often reflects these differences.

A lack of definitional clarity permits divergent claims to the field of study and in practice, allowing for disagreement on what a minority ethnic group is and on what is ethnic marketing research. As a consequence, the divergent claims also sustain varying estimates of market size and related assessments of the substantiality of a minority ethnic group, crucially complicating incremental learning about ethnic marketing and decisions about where its application is justified. Lack of definitional clarity is an important ethnic marketing concern. As acknowledged by Phinney (1990),

> in order for ethnic identity to develop as a methodologically sound area of . . . research, there needs to be agreement on the meaning of concepts and valid measures that can be used across groups and settings.
>
> (p. 5)

But the importance of definitional clarity has also been noted as a point of concern in marketing covering both the discipline in general and specific fields of research. Without agreed definitions, scientific discussion can descend into babble (Gilliam and Voss, 2013). In the context of social marketing, Andreasen (1994) lamented that the lack of consensus in the definition resulted in varied research agendas and in "talking at cross purposes". Definitional differences caused disagreement about the particular domain of social marketing and how it differed from related fields, hindering its theoretical advancement by fuelling incorrect application by practitioners of research findings emerging under the social marketing heading, which justified the likely disaffection by practitioners with the findings of social marketing researchers. In the context of advertising, Richards and Curran (2002) argued the need for an agreed common definition to ensure general understanding and to delimit the profession.

What Is Ethnic Marketing? Definitional Differences

Currently, ethnic marketing has no agreed upon definition. What is asserted to be ethnic marketing varies widely in terms of both theory and practice, being very much dependent on users' or practitioners' understanding of ethnicity, of ethnic identity and of the role of acculturation, as well as on the need by practitioners to often be pragmatic in the application of any chosen definition. Further confusion arises from the use of terms other than ethnic marketing, apparently covering the same field.

We discuss these differences in terminology first, followed by an examination of differences in views about ethnic marketing. If ethnic marketing is referred to as marketing focussed on ethnic minority consumers or ethnic minorities (Jamal, 2003; Cui, 2001, 1997), competing terms include multicultural marketing, diaspora marketing, international marketing at home, domestic cross-cultural marketing, ethno-marketing and intercultural marketing. Each of these is briefly explained and their differences noted in the following paragraphs.

"Multicultural marketing" is a term widely used by theorists and practitioners to describe strategies developed to target consumers from different ethnic minority groups within a country. As cultural diversity within a country consists of more than its ethnic diversity, multicultural marketing's scope is wider than addressing ethnic diversity through marketing strategies. This is reflected in Burton's (2002) research, who interprets multiculturalism in a wide context of all possible subcultures within a country whether they be based on ethnic differences or not. Different variants of its practice will emerge dependent on political and social conditions. As such, ethnic marketing involves a narrower focus than multicultural marketing.

Cui and Choudhury (2002) provide a contrasting approach, using the term "Ethnic Marketing" in a generic way, to refer to marketing using distinctive marketing programs targeting an ethnic minority within a country, with "Multicultural Marketing" having a more specific meaning. Ethnic marketing embraces a framework of strategies to market to ethnic minorities that encompasses approaches with minimal adaptation (cross-cultural) to the needs of an ethnic minority to the development of specific tailored programs intended to build loyalty and long-term relationships with a minority ethnic group. Which strategy is applied will depend on both demand and supply conditions. In this case, multicultural marketing is more feasible in a country with many *ethnic* subcultures each requiring a "unique" marketing mix to realize the "sales potential" of that minority group. Multicultural marketing is distinguished from "*ethnic niche marketing*" by the degree of focus on cultural diversity within a country.

In the Cui and Choudhury schema, fewer ethnic groups enable more focus on their distinctive needs, with ethnic niche marketing potentially enabling marketers to develop a customized offer that can build loyalty and a long-term relationship. Clearly, multicultural marketing based on recognizing each subculture's unique needs can achieve similar outcomes but the implications of a changed environment consisting of a greater number of diverse ethnic groups is that, for cost/benefit reasons, commonalities and adaptations across groups may be sought to reduce the cost of excessive differentiation. Of course, any behaviour that is ethnicity focused is not taken into account.

"Multicultural marketing" is also used interchangeably with the term "ethnic marketing" by Chan and Ahmed (2006), while Makgosa (2012)'s view of multicultural marketing as targeting and communicating with ethnic minority groups within culturally diverse societies could also be interchanged with ethnic marketing, which Makgosa does in the context of marketing to a particular ethnic minority.

Makgosa (2012) considers that heterogeneity within ethnic groups residing in the UK may require intra-group as well as between group differences in ethnic marketing strategies, adding another layer of complexity in terms of defining either multicultural or ethnic marketing. His study groups of African Blacks and Indians residing in the UK are broadly specified minorities, heterogeneous not only in terms of acculturation and strength of ethnic identity, but also in terms of key subculture elements such as language and religion. Effectively, Makgosa (2012) is embracing the concept of "panethnicity", borrowed from the USA where multiple ethnicities have been labelled as Asian, Latino or African-American; the creation of pan ethnic groups for a variety of social and economic purposes is discussed by Okamoto and Mora (2014).

Other terms that capture to varying degrees the focus of ethnic marketing in marketing to ethnic minorities include "International Marketing at Home", "Domestic Cross-Cultural marketing", "Diaspora Marketing", "Ethno-Marketing" and "Intercultural Marketing". Diaspora marketing (Kumar and Steenkamp, 2013) is directed at targeting first generation immigrants in a host country based on meeting their home country developed preferences for particular brands. As such, it is similar to what has been called International Marketing at Home (Wilkinson and Cheng) and domestic cross-cultural marketing (Pires, 1999), all being narrower in their focus than most forms of ethnic marketing because they appear to ignore possible acculturation effects as well as subsequent generations that may still retain varying strengths of ethnic identity.

Ethno-marketing and Intercultural marketing appear more closely related to ethnic marketing in their specific focus and approach. Szillat and Betov (2015) use ethnic marketing and intercultural marketing interchangeably, both referring to the orientation of marketing activities towards target groups with particular ethnic characteristics. This similarity is evident in Ethno-marketing, defined by Waldeck and von Gosen (2006) as differentiated marketing with respect to the cultural origin of the target groups. Cultural minorities that live in a certain country will be targeted with a tailored marketing mix.

Following Cui and Choudhury (2002), the term "Ethnic Marketing", as currently used, can include a variety of approaches that need consideration. In their framework "Ethnic Marketing" may consist of "Ethnic Niche Marketing" if a culturally diverse country has only a few ethnic minority groups and each warrants a targeted approach. "Multicultural marketing" is used when a country has many ethnic minority groups and the heterogeneity encourages a targeted approach tempered by looking for commonalities.

For Makgosa (2012) ethnic marketing to an ethnic minority may require further segmentation and adjustments in marketing to that group depending on its heterogeneity, where the researcher's focus is on differences arising from acculturation patterns and strength of ethnic identification rather than more traditional variables used to assess a group's ethnic homogeneity.

A French view is offered by Blanchard (2003) who distinguishes different forms of "ethnic marketing", ranging from the tokenistic use of iconic ethnic characters to attract attention, to what he describes as "hard line ethnic marketing" which recognizes differences between ethnic groups within France and the consequent need for targeting based on recognizing those differences. Multicultural marketing focusses on changing marketing communications to an ethnic group's preferences, a more superficial approach to adaptation than that instituted through ethnic marketing.

Further insight into the focus of ethnic marketing and some key issues comes from interviews conducted by Pires with a panel of prominent marketing academics (Pires and Stanton, 2015). Four of the more detailed responses to the request for a definition of ethnic marketing elicited the following responses. The first two were chosen because of their focus on the ethnic group as well as the potential scope of ethnic marketing:

> It's targeting to a small group, an ethnic group of people. For example, in Malaysia, especially in the East Malaysia, there are various ethnic groups, such as the Ibans, Kadazans, Bajaus, Muruts and so on. These are groups of people and when you start marketing to them, you don't do it as to any ordinary general consumers. They have their own specific values, customs, religious beliefs and such, so you have to take into consideration these characteristics in order to reach them, so they can associate with what you are trying to communicate to them, with their belief.
>
> (Kim Fam)

It's anything that is focused on some ethnic segments, because of the nature of the demand of the segment. It is different to generic marketing. It's more focused towards the ethnic community, taking their background and their culture into account. It's both about how ethnic entrepreneurs target their own communities and about how anybody markets to particular segments defined by ethnicity.

(Kamal Ghose)

Ethnic marketing is target marketing based on ethnicity and more specifically, ethnic groups or communities distinguished by their differences from the mainstream or other groups. However, in both definitions, ethnic marketing is a response to differences, seeking to better communicate with, and understand the differences in order to improve the value offer. Ghose's definition also draws attention to ethnic entrepreneurs as a part of the marketing system targeting ethnic communities, a neglected role in the marketing literature that is discussed in later chapters.

While the above quotes indicate the focus of ethnic marketing, the following two allude to the possible issues of implementation that can arise, reflected in the variants of ethnic marketing outlined earlier. The first reflects on how standardization encourages the seeking of commonalities in consumer behaviour across cultural and subcultural groups when developing marketing strategies and seeking to apply these common approaches across groups where possible, whereas ethnic marketing focusses on eliciting the differences between ethnic groups and assessing their significance for consumer decision-making. Many issues reflected in the heterogeneity of approaches in marketing to ethnic groups can be linked to the assessment of which differences between groups are of sufficient importance to the consumer decision-making process to warrant changes as seen through the lens of the marketer, with an eye on the benefits and costs of any changes. Drilling down the "T" into group differences can also reveal intra-group heterogeneity, such differences needing assessment as to their relevance for ethnic marketing strategies.

In essence, as the second quote suggests, the concept of ethnicity is not a straightforward matter of using demographics to identify a group, resting very much on the sociology of the group and the context of its existence with other subcultures. This is a dynamic relationship both for a particular group as well as for members within a group which suggests that ethnic marketing requires ongoing, in-depth research into ethnic groups in order to gain the necessary understanding to develop relevant marketing strategies.

It's understanding the similarities and differences of marketing to groups of consumers defined by their ethnicity as compared to marketing to the general population. I see it as the shape of a T. There are commonalities in the way that we market to ethnic groups as well as to the majority of the population. That goes across the T, the horizontal. The vertical is where there are differences. I think that extant research is mainly focused on the differences. This is because that's how you tend to publish work. It is to say: here's what we thing about everybody, but here is a group of people that behave somewhat differently. Then the theoretical part is the possible explanation for why those differences exist. I think that's the general domain of ethnic marketing.

(Rohit Deshpandé)

On the surface it sounds like a very simple question . . . but it does tend to be quite complicated. I guess, for me, it's a convention of tailoring marketing campaigns for goods and services—so there's certainly an aspect of it that's designed to generate business—and that convention is targeting a group of people that are designated by what we now recognise as ethnicity. Which begs another definition but, for me, I think of it more in cultural terms, and I mean that as much sociologically as geographically in that sense. So we're talking about a group of people that typically is identified in terms of—some kind of geography, language, often a belief system, sometimes a form of religion, sometimes not, as well as physical characteristics like color, race, as well as coming back to the sociological social class. So there's a kind of a composite.

(Lisa Peñaloza)

Reconciliation of the various approaches to ethnic marketing is problematic but necessary if ethnic market is to develop as a coherent field of study. Figure 1.1 provides a snapshot of the complexity that surrounds ethnic marketing.

At a minimum, ethnic marketing requires a marketing focus on an ethnic minority. The basis for identifying an ethnic minority, the geographic and product scope of any focus and the depth of adaptation to meet the wants of an identified group, appear to vary considerably in terms of theory and practice. Using this minimalist approach, ethnic marketing, ethno-marketing and intercultural marketing (alternative names favoured by some European researchers) are interchangeable terms, while multicultural marketing focusses on subcultures of all kinds, rather than subcultures identified by their ethnicity differences. Terms such as diversity marketing and international marketing at home have a narrower subset than an ethnic minority as a whole, as well as more of a product orientation rather than a market orientation focus.

Bringing together the different viewpoints, ethnic marketing treats ethnic minority consumers (or the ethnic community they are a part of) as markets distinguishable from a broader, more heterogeneous market.

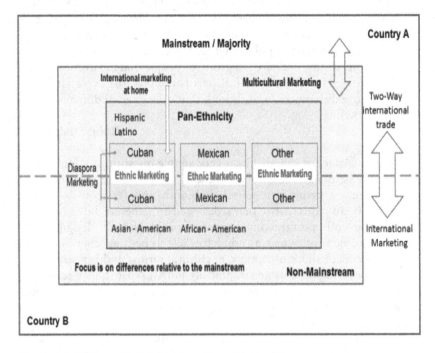

Figure 1.1 Different Definitions in a Two Country Context

(*) Multicultural Marketing—An aggregation of minority ethnic groups is involved, with one marketing strategy being deployed for all groups making up the aggregate. Several combinations may apply:

1. A multicultural marketing strategy independent of any one of the aggregated groups is devised and deployed to all minority ethnic groups in the aggregate—e.g. McDonald's;
2. The group aggregate is profiled based on marketing significant similarities between the minority ethnic groups in the aggregate. A marketing strategy is devised based on the profile derived for the aggregate, subsequently deployed to aggregated groups;
3. As per point 2 above, but minimal adaptations are allowed to cater for particular uniqueness in particular constituent groups. For example, a Hispanic general store may reserve some shelf space for specific ethnic products demanded by one of the groups in the aggregate.

Recognizing and seeking to act on this distinctiveness requires using segmentation. Contrasting the then dominant approach of product differentiation with segmentation as a strategy, Smith (1956) wrote,

> Segmentation is based on development of the demand side of the market and represents a rational and more precise adjustment of product and marketing effort to consumer or user requirements.
>
> (p. 5)

This focus can be incorporated into the American Marketing Association's (AMA) definition of for marketing such that the definition of ethnic marketing conveyed in this book is:

the activity, set of institutions, and processes for creating, communicating, delivering, and exchanging offerings that have value for ethnic identified customers, clients, partners and communities, and for society at large.

Consistent with this definition, decisions and situations inherent to exchanges in the business to consumer (B2C), government to consumer (G2C), business-to-business (B2B) and consumer-to-consumer (C2C) environments are part of ethnic marketing.

Ethnic Marketing Issues

Differences in the conceptualization of ethnic marketing give rise to differences in practice. If a particular practice is not successful, the value of ethnic marketing as whole tends to be debased as that particular "form" of ethnic marketing is wound back. Some of the key issues challenging a common understanding of ethnic marketing include the following:

- Aggregation: Recurring observation of self-titled ethnic marketing strategy by practitioners, particularly in the USA, provides tangible evidence that cultural or ethnic groups are aggregated for marketing purposes. Ethnic marketing based on definitions of an individual groups' unique characteristics (Engel, Fiorillo and Cayley, 1971) contrasts with different levels of aggregation of ethnic minority groups into aggregates such as Blacks and Whites, Hispanics, Latinos and Asians. In such broad categorizations, race, language, geographic origin and specific sets of cultural values may be conflated (incorrectly) with ethnicity. The aggregation of ethnic minority groups to achieve critical mass and economies of scale may prove advantageous for marketers (Pires and Stanton, 2005, p. 81) but challenge narrower concepts of ethnic marketing.
- Uncertainties and limitations in the universal application of a racial/ethnic segmentation and targeting approach suggest that it can become problematic over time (Makgosa, 2012; Koeman, Jaubin and Stesmans, 2010). Technologically empowered consumers may not conform to any one specific segment or category, either individually or as a group (Pires, Stanton and Rita, 2006; Jamal, 2003).
- A long held, dominant assumption that the acculturation process follows a linear pattern towards cultural assimilation has tended to be unchallenged until the 1980's with growing recognition that acculturation may take various paths (O'Guinn, Lee and Faber, 1986). Luedicke (2011), reviewing research findings and shifts in thinking since then, argues consumer acculturation is a circular system of mutual observation and socio-cultural adaptation within complex networks. The assumption of a linear acculturation process can lead

marketers to neglect ethnic groups long resident in a host country and to overlook within-group differences.

- Without excluding ethnic consumers' identification with a minority ethnic group, ethnic consumers' acculturation to a global consumer culture (cosmopolitanism) may also be important (Cleveland, Laroche and Hallab, 2013; Cleveland, Papadopoulos and Laroche, 2011; Cleveland and Laroche, 2007), although it can be questioned whether targeting ethnic consumers by their global dimension or affiliative identity (Jiménez, 2010) can/should be seen as ethnic marketing.
- Ethnic minority consumers, such as Mexicans in the USA, may resist the pulls of both the dominant and their minority ethnic group (Lerman, Maldonado and Luna, 2009; Peñaloza, 1994).
- An aggregate of consumers with diverse ethnicities who share particular preferences for the attributes of a product is sometimes identified as an ethnic marketing segment, although ethnicity is not the consumer behaviour determinant. For example, geographical proximity (e.g. the Portuguese and Spanish markets in Southern Europe) or language similarity (e.g. Portuguese and Brazilian) may provide sufficient critical mass and cost savings for marketing Corona beer in those countries, justifying the segmentation approach (Deshpandé, 2010). But the congruency of such an approach with ethnic marketing theory based on one ethnicity is difficult to establish.

Other Ethnic Marketing Issues Identified by Researchers

In pursuing the objective of understanding what is ethnic marketing and where it is headed, in-depth interviews with established marketing scholars were undertaken. Consistent with judgmental convenience sampling (Malhotra et al., 1996), the sampling frame first required selection for their expertise in the marketing discipline and then for their status as ethnic marketing specialists indicated by scholarly publications. It was important to include reputable marketing scholars who had no research interest in ethnic marketing. Including specialist and non-specialist academics reduces potential bias from a recognized shared interest in the topical area. An active ethnic marketing researcher is unlikely to advocate against the importance of this type of marketing. That is, ethnic marketing is allowed to be seen as unimportant in this research.

While the sample for this study is not large, it is sufficient to highlight principal schools of thought in ethnic marketing research. The geographical dispersion of the sample was not a consideration. Starting from a short list of potential participants with 16 names, an introductory email communication was then sent to the scholars, detailing the research purpose, providing an interview guide outlining the themes that could/

would be raised, and inviting their participation in an in-depth interview. Five invited scholars (from China, England and Germany) were unable to take part in the interviews during the period of time allocated for data collection.

Eleven scholars[1] (from Canada, Finland, Hungary, Japan, New Zealand, Portugal and the USA) participated in a pre-arranged in-depth interview, conducted during 2013. Two interviews were conducted via Skype. All other interviews were conducted face-to-face. The duration of the interviews varied between 1 and 2 hours (seven interviews), between 2 and 3 hours (three interviews), with one interview involving more hours.

Each interview took place at the time and place agreed with interviewees. Upon restating the purpose of the study, each interviewee was first asked to define/explain the concept of ethnic marketing. This provided clarity on what was discussed and was particularly important given the lack of a universally accepted definition and its conceptualization. The interview guide sought to develop a conversation around the standing of ethnic marketing in terms of its scope and importance; ethnic marketing theory and its development over recent years; opportunities and issues for ethnic marketing in the scholar's respective country of residence; globalization perspectives for ethnic marketing; and the future development of ethnic marketing.

All interviews were taped (voice and video or voice only) and transcribed by the researcher.[2] Comments made during the interviews that were unrelated to the topic were omitted. The transcripts were made available to the relevant interviewees for checking and endorsement. The transcripts were then processed using Nvivo (Veal, 2005), leading to the identification of recurring themes (see Table 1.1).

The 37 themes are wide-ranging, from the very general to the specific. In line with seeking better understanding of the interviewees' perceived domain of ethnic marketing and their concerns, our approach was to classify the themes as to whether they were predominantly macro (of the wider economy and political/social environment) or micro (markets, firms or consumers); predominantly theory issues or practice issues; or theory related to practice.

Sixteen of the themes identified (numbered 1 to 15) are predominantly concerned with theory issues, many of which are closely linked to macro or economy—wide considerations, hence the need for more research to understand the effects of ethnic marketing. Understanding the causes and effects of acculturation and its various possible paths is a prominent concern while another is how the onward march of information-communication-distribution technologies and globalization may impact both on ethnic consumers and hence how ethnic marketing needs to be change.

Themes 16–27 pertain to the conditions or context for ethnic marketing to develop, as well as to the political, social and economic conditions

Table 1.1 Output from Thematic Analysis of Interview Transcripts

---

Theory Issues (Scope and Effects)

1. EM definitional issues.
2. EM can be B2C, B2B, A2C and C2C.
3. Potential disadvantages for host country arising from EM.
4. Potential disadvantages for home country arising from EM.
5. Potential disadvantages for MEGs arising from EM.
6. Extent to which the importance of EM is reflected in the marketing discipline.
7. Barriers to acculturation by EMCs.
8. Inverse link between the acculturation process and the need/justification for EM.
9. 2nd generation EMC's and their familiarity with mainstream behaviour.
10. Is EM relevant for 2nd and higher generation minorities?
11. The role of information, communications and technology in EM.
12. The future of EM.
13. Impact of tangibility on EM.
14. EM and ethnic entrepreneurship.
15. Ethnic marketing as a buzz word.

Conditions for Ethnic Marketing—Environmental Issues

16. Characteristics of a multicultural society.
17. What makes a MEG weak or strong?
18. Implication of mainstream expectations that migrants assimilate.
19. Can EMCs adapt, integrate or assimilate into the mainstream if the mainstream wants them out (e.g. the case of MEGs recognized by religion).
20. Politics and EM.
21. The relationship between EM and social order.
22. Leaving EM to the invisible hand market forces.
23. Environmental conditions for resilient MEGs.
24. Justification for EM in specific countries.
25. Socialization issues for new EMCs.
26. The link between MEGS and their home country: Push and pull factors.
27. Host country support for MEGs.

Theory to Practice

28. Operationalization of ethnicity.
29. Justifying the targeting of large, aggregated ethnic groups or smaller, single groups using the same EM theory.
30. When are MEGs important for marketing?
31. The importance of context for EM. Ethics and social responsibility issues in EM.
32. Using EM perspective to justify Hispanics, Latinos and Asian-American for segmentation purposes.
33. The role of geography and distance in EM.
34. The role of language in EM.
35. Markets might be fragmenting, but marketers globalize.

Micro/Practitioner Issues

36. The relevance of targeting by neighbourhood for EM.
37. Segmenting MEGs by extent of acculturation.

EM: Ethnic Marketing; EMC: Ethnic minority consumer; MEG: Minority ethnic group, A2C: agency to consumer; B2B: business-to-business; B2C: business-to-consumer; C2C: consumer-to-consumer.

(the macro-environment), and to the potential negative effects arising from ethnic marketing practice. Themes 28–35 deal with the interrelationship of the theory with practice, while only two (36–37) are micro focused, direct practice issues.

Consistent with the noted definitional ambiguity, the interviewees articulated widely different views on the scope and domain of ethnic marketing. Their focus was predominantly on the "big picture" (the environment for ethnic marketing and the benefits and cost of ethnic marketing), on theoretical issues and, to a lesser extent, on theory related to practice issues. A micro and practitioner focus was generally absent, arguably supporting Baker's (2001) observation of the lack of interest in practice.

While the vast majority of interviewees supported the continued development of a rigorous theory of ethnic marketing based on deductive and inductive principles, the desirability for practical utility advocated by Corley and Gioia (2011), or Brennan's (2008) theory-in-use, was conspicuous for its omission.

The divide was largely explained in two ways, both of which focused more on practice capabilities and competencies. One was that current practices of focusing on aggregates of minority ethnic groups may be perceived by practitioners as having been successful to date, providing grounds for questioning the need to incur unnecessary and possibly unjustified risks related to focusing on narrowly defined minority ethnic groups. The other is that practitioners may face a lack of capabilities and competencies, including those related to knowledge about narrowly defined minority ethnic groups, also fueled by a continued lack of relevant and appropriate statistical reporting with many groups remaining invisible (Simon, 2008; Ghaill, 2000), an overall lack of strategic information making decision-making difficult and onerous.

More than any philosophical distance between ethnic marketing theory and practice, reconciliation appears to be impeded by what is perceived as possible and practical, given different interests and priorities by theorists and by practitioners (Kerin, 1996). One way to reduce the theory-practice divide is the adoption of a pragmatic approach to developing ethnic marketing sensitive theory and practice, as articulated below.

These examples suggest different reasons why ethnic marketing theory and practice have diverged. The challenge is to appraise the root causes of divergence and to reconcile the theoretical and practical perspectives, whilst recognizing the need for close interdependence between perspectives and the irrelevance of theory if it cannot explain, or is not applied in practice (Brownlie et al., 2008). Mostly untouched in the ethnic marketing context, this is a challenge that has arisen intermittently in various disciplines, the subsequent literature providing guidance as to the generic causes and possible solutions for the ethnic marketing context.

Causes of a Gap and Approaches to Reconciliation

Dewey (1904) addressed the relation of theory to practice in education, noting that:

> (the) present divorce between scholarship and method is as harmful upon one side as upon the other—as detrimental to the best interests of higher academic instruction as it is to the training of teachers.
>
> (p. 24)

Recognizing that differences in viewpoints of teachers and practitioners must be reconcilable (Coutant, 1938), special issues of highly ranked journals in marketing and management have devoted attention to a similar focus (Baker, 2001; Brownlie et al., 2008), while nursing (Baxter, 2007) and information technology (IT) (Martin, 2004) also appear concerned with such a gap.

In addressing the gap, the common approach is to question the relationship between theory and practice and to identify the possible causes for the gap, with some follow-up on how reconciliation can be achieved. The brief discussion below identifies general points of relevance that can be drawn relative to the gap in the ethnic marketing context.

Recognizing the Gap

Recognition of a gap between theory and practice, as well as its importance from the viewpoint of discipline development depends on how theory is conceptualized and how the need for a relationship between theory and practice is assessed.

In the case of marketing and consumer research, Holbrook (2008) espouses an extreme viewpoint that achieving a reconciliation of the differences between scholarly inquiry and managerial relevance "constitutes an undesirable or even deplorable form of compromise" (p. 570). The rationale is that generalization depends on contextual abstraction (Serrão, 1977). The bulk of the literature, however, is more concerned with understanding the nature of the gap and its likely causes.

Management theorists have debated different interpretations of theory (Corley and Gioia, 2011; Sutton and Staw, 1995; Di Maggio, 1995), focusing on the need of a theory to have relevance. Even noting variations in interpretations of relevance, Brownlie et al. (2008) argue that,

> (t)he construct "relevance" offers a convenient "prism" through which to understand perennial debates about the balance between putting theory into practice and practice into theory in management and business subjects.
>
> (p. 64)

Corley and Gioia (2011) recognize contribution in terms of theory origi-
nality and scientific and practical utility, to be achieved by a renewed
emphasis on "practice oriented utility as a focus for future theorising"
(p. 12). This is an effective call for pragmatism.

On the Need for Pragmatism or Theory-in-Use

Focused on the gap between information technology (IT) theory and
practice, Martin (2004) placed the reconciliation issues in general terms
of how they interact with each other, theory learning from practice and
vice-versa. Accordingly, by the nature of the learning, process gaps may
be seen as inevitable and also variable, depending on the degree of interaction occurring between theorists and practitioners. Reviewing the cause
of the gap in the discipline areas of nursing, economics and marketing,
Brennan (2008) suggests that inefficient mechanisms and poor resourc-
ing explain the slow introduction of best evidence-based practice into
nursing theory; in the cases of economics and marketing, the gap is more
about practitioners allegedly harbouring a perception of theory as irrelevant. Marketing attributes the generation of theory irrelevance to the
promotional incentive structures for academic research, given research
funding requirements that often fail to cater for the practical aspects of
the research. This appears to echo the assertion that marketing academics
are "not really interested in its practice" (Baker, 2001, p. 24).

Drawing from a small survey of academic researchers and interviews with
ten practitioners and eight marketing academics in a business-to-business
context, Brennan and Ankers (2004) posited that closer interaction depends
on both imaginary and real impediments. The imagined impediments dwell
on the perception of different communities, each with a different focus. The
real impediments pertain to practitioners' seemingly dismissive attitude of
academic research and of its relevance to their practice. Arguably,

> (p)ractitioners need theory-in-use that is directly applicable to context-
> specific, unique marketing problems; academics strive for more gen-
> eral, higher-order theory that necessarily abstracts from day-to-day
> reality. The reason that academic theory is largely irrelevant to mar-
> keting practitioners is that it is intentionally made that way.
>
> (Brennan, 2008, p. 525)

Hence, while differences may ensue from the incentive structures for
academic research, the rationale supports Coutant (1938)'s view that
the intention to bring theory and practice closer together is achievable,
provided that is the intention of stakeholders.

Fendt, Kaminska-Labbé and Sachs (2008) also contest the notion that a
gap between theory and practice is inevitable, arguing that the gap derives
from the philosophical approach underlying much of management and, by

extension given the close relationship, marketing research. Their claim is that dominant management theory follows ontological assumptions "similar to the natural sciences" (p. 477), a process that leads to generic theory remaining almost always in need of further refinement or extension, in order to be used by an organization. Their alternative, also espoused by Martin (2004), is to introduce pragmatism into theory building. Essentially, the argument in both cases is that scientific orthodoxy leads to irrelevant theory and to a divorce between theory and management practice, and that pragmatism is an approach that can achieve reconciliation.

An overview of the philosophy of pragmatism and a detailed advocacy of the need for pragmatism in Operations Research (OR) was provided by Ormerod (2006). On the premise that OR ought to be practical and instrumental, Ormerod offered 12 reasons why a pragmatic approach in OR theory should be attractive to practitioners by meeting their needs. Many of the reasons relate to beliefs underlying the pragmatic approach, but some have strong resonance with complaints about relevance raised by marketing practitioners (Brennan, 2008; Brennan and Ankers, 2004). Ormerod (2006) posits that pragmatism engenders a focus on the practical significance of a proposition; that it supports an empirical or evidence-based approach; that it recognizes science as fallible and subject to social contexts and associated uncertainty and change; that, because inquiry is social, it requires the whole of community of practice to be involved; and that "pragmatism places theory in the service of practice" (p. 906).

Pragmatism is a philosophical mindset that assists theorists in understanding the needs of practitioners and their views on the irrelevance of theory in various disciplines. Nevertheless, how to use pragmatism to make theory more relevant to practitioners is given less attention, being limited to possible connotations with action research and contingency theory. Perry and Gummesson (2004) draw together contributions to a special issue devoted to action research, suggesting that marketing action research needs to be complemented with case research so as to account for the importance of the diversity of customers and competitors to marketing management, and for the external environment of the marketplace. Fendt, Kaminska-Labbé and Sachs (2008) see this as converting action research into a research method compatible with pragmatism, because it is based on collaboration between researchers and research subjects. Arguably, extending action research to ethnic marketing may deliver theory suitable to the circumstances of practitioners targeting a particular group in one country, even if a universal approach or solution applicable to another group in that country or other countries is not possible.

A more general approach to addressing the theory-practice gap, arguably applicable to ethnic marketing research, is offered by Martin (2004, p. 31) in the IT context. Much of the gap results from the failure of theory to recognize changes over time that reduce its applicability (including local influence factors that restrict usefulness elsewhere), and pragmatic considerations considered important (presumably by practitioners) that are perceived (presumably by theorists) to add little to the theory's value (and may in some cases reduce its value). To address these concerns Martin proposes a contingency theory approach, essentially adapting the environmental scanning tool of PESTLE analysis (Aguilar, 1967) to list and classify pragmatic considerations that contribute to the theory and practice gap. The specific aim is to acknowledge and, where possible, to include pragmatic considerations in the theory.

Pragmatism in Ethnic Marketing Theory

The possibly substantial implications of different scopes of ethnic marketing research and practice created by diverging definitions and conceptualizations early in this chapter can be explained, to some extent, by the recognition of the need to reconcile theory with practice.

Recommendations for using environmental scanning and contingency theory to deliver theory-in-use, rather than theories aiming at universal application (Martin, 2004), were followed by calls in the specialist literature for theory to recognize the place of pragmatism in theory building (Brennan, 2008), thus reducing the theory-practice divide.

Figure 1.2 offers a conceptual framework for a process that, arguably, can contribute to reducing the theory-practice divide. Since focus is on

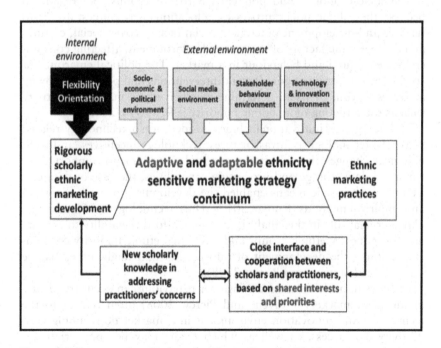

Figure 1.2 Framework to Reduce the Theory-Practice Divide

process and not on the development of any one particular strategy in a particular context, the problem of generalization may not be an issue that needs consideration.

The framework starts from the premise that the internal environment underpinning research, the researcher's viewing lense, can be changed, such that ethnic marketing thinking can adopt a flexibility orientation. Flexibility refers to the degree to which a business has actual or potential procedures, and how fast those procedures can be implemented to increase management's effective control of the outside environment (De Leeuw and Volberda, 1996). Adapted to ethnic marketing thinking, the flexibility philosophy is borrowed from the relational contracting literature (Noordewier, John and Nevin, 1990), whereby stakeholders accept to approach ethnic marketing problems from a perspective that is responsive to context (Ivens, 2005). Flexibility is considered in the management and IT literatures as giving *"an organization the ability to control outside environments effectively"* (Byrd and Turner, 2000, p. 170), hence to account for context.

Underpinned by PESTLE but reaching significantly further, context is deemed to be determined by four environmental conditions (the socio-economic and political environment, the social media environment, the stakeholder behaviour environment, and the technology and innovation environment).

The socio-economic and political environments must be considered because they shape policy processes, allocation of resources, access to services and development outcomes. Social factors cover social, cultural and demographic factors of the external environment, affecting consumers' state of mind and behaviour in a market. The political environment covers various forms of government interventions and political lobbying activities; it can, by itself, determine whether ethnic marketing activity such as the targeting of an ethnic minority is legal (Ho, 2014).

Technology and innovation include consideration of technology-related activities, technological infrastructures, technology incentives, and technological changes that affect the external environment. Supported by enhanced data storage and processing capabilities, the ease of data collection by electronic means enabled the development of new analytical and empirical methods (Kumar, 2015). Thus, technology innovation may play a crucial role in this analysis as it may afford the ability to capture data on minority ethnic groups and individual ethnic minority consumers, enabling the development of information that might otherwise be unavailable (Cravens and Piercy, 2008).

Changes in practitioner and consumer behaviour can occur frequently in turbulent markets (Cravens and Piercy, 2008) often related to the technology and innovation environment in a market determining connectivity and access, as well as which media may be appropriate for reaching particular consumer groups. Intertwining the effects of changes in consumers' behaviour with technology and innovation determines the need for ethnic marketers to take social media into account. As noted by Kumar (2015), practitioners and consumers

> "use social networks to communicate with (and within) one another", and "the merging of social networks and mobile devices has made it extremely easy and compelling for people to stay connected and, thus, influence one another's purchase decisions".
>
> (p. 5)

While there appears to be no difference in the use of technology based on ethnicity (Schradie, 2012; Lenhart et al., 2010), this also reveals the importance of social media and social networks for ethnic marketing and for minority ethnic group resilience.

The external environments facing practitioners are subject to dynamic turbulence, explaining why theories that account for context may need to change over time. The implication here is that, in addition to flexibility, theories are needed that are either adaptive, with flexibility being assured by the theories themselves (Oppermann, 1994), or adaptable, requiring theories to be adapted by scholars (Hallen, Johanson and Seyed-Mohamed, 1991) and/or by practitioners in a co-creation process. This is shown in the framework (Figure 1.1) by the closer interface and cooperation between scholars and practitioners, necessarily guided by the perception of shared interests and priorities. This cooperation leads to new scholarly knowledge addressing practitioners' concerns, which impacts both the stakeholders' interface and the generation of rigorous but flexible ethnic marketing theory.

Overall, the framework to reduce the theory-practice divide does not offer either a prescription of concrete actions to be taken every time by researchers and practitioners, or a quick-fix solution for the divide, but reaches further than simply explaining the divide. The claim is that the pragmatization of ethnic marketing theory is supported by an adaptive and adaptable ethnicity-sensitive marketing strategy continuum whereby differences between theory and practice may exist concomitantly, depending on context and on the objective in hand. Rather than prescribing a theory to be applied to problem solving, focus needs to be in a gradual reduction of the gap.

Under a pragmatic orientation, understanding practitioners' objections to adopting a theory leads to the formulation of theory-in-use, capable of contributing to the alleviation of ethnic marketing practitioners' perceptions that ethnic marketing theory is irrelevant to ethnic marketing practice, motivating an adaptation effort by practitioners. The outcome is an improvement in the theory-practice gap that, nevertheless, needs to be seen as transient, as it becomes the starting point for further improvement on the theory and further adaptation, in a continuous co-creation process. While the theory-practice gap may persist over time, the closer cooperative interface underlining the co-creation process becomes the promoter of new knowledge and more applicable theory.

Summary

In the consideration of ethnic marketing theory and its relationship to practice, one perspective is that the alleged need for "adjustments for the real world" might be too big and may steer too far from ethnic marketing theory, for what is done by practitioners to be considered as ethnic marketing. But the view resulting from the extensive interviews with marketing experts purposely conducted for this research is that the greatest challenge is to promote an effective articulation between theory and practice. Hence, this chapter primarily advocates the need for agreement on the definition of ethnic marketing, and thus its research domain, as well as to take into account the identification of the type of stakeholder involved, including three main types: co-ethnic minority businesses, non-co-ethnic minority businesses, and mainstream businesses. Once this is done, the development or co-creation of culturally sensitive marketing strategies to make an effective connection between theory and practice can then follow.

Ethnic marketing needs to be refined/extended to be able to explain what is done in practice and who does it. Why marketers do what they do, and how this can be reconciled with ethnic marketing theory, is a required focus. A continuation of theory that fails to acknowledge and to take advantage of the practitioner requirements for pragmatic solutions to ethnic marketing problems is unlikely to bridge the theory-practice divide.

New awareness about how the workings of inner-group networks promote a group's critical mass together with the much advanced targeting capabilities allowed by micro-targeting technologies (Kumar, 2015) can be expected to herald opportunities offered by targeting narrowly defined minority ethnic groups and, when justified, ethnic minority consumers.

This chapter identifies many areas for further research, many of which are listed in Table 1.1. A priority is to deepen researchers' understanding of the difference between an aggregate of consumers involving a variety of ethnicities, and aggregates of consumers with one single shared ethnicity—the essence of ethnic marketing. There is also an opportunity to examine the need for researchers' and practitioners' ambidexterity, encompassing the skills of taking advantage of the sameness across groups, while focusing narrowly when this is justified by real differences. Under emerging evidence of bi-cultural behaviour, businesses considering targeting ethnic markets may need to develop ambidextrous tactical capabilities in ways that can recognize and take into account how to respond to both similarities and differences in distinct environments.

The Path Ahead

Chapter 2 deals with the meaning and relevance of ethnicity; the meaning and centrality of ethnic groups; ethnic groups as social networks; the development of ethnic identity and the interlinking of ethnic identity with the ethnic group; and the relationship between ethnic identity, consumer behaviour and the ethnic group.

Chapter 3 deals with the dynamics of ethnicity: In order to pave the way to a better understanding of when and how to implement an ethnic marketing strategy, we use the concept of acculturation, considering how acculturation patterns can impact on a person's ethnic identity and thus the ethnic group. From the perspective of group stability and whether groups may converge, perhaps enabling pan ethnic groups for marketing purposes, it is necessary to know how individual acculturation affects the consumer behaviour of each generation of consumers from the same ethnic group background and whether the individual acculturation paths of consumers from different ethnic backgrounds are likely to differ.

Chapter 4 develops the rationale for an ethnic marketing focus on minority ethnic groups. The chapter discusses the reasons and potential shortcomings for seeking group size through the aggregation of one or more minority ethnic groups but grounds this discussion in the need to meet the requirements for effective market segmentation. Findings from the growth of panethnicity are then discussed and linked to the marketing reasons for aggregating ethnic groups. The nature of homophily in ethnic group formation is linked to the need for an emic approach to creating panethnic segments. A framework for assessing panethnic groups is offered.

The focus of Chapter 5 is to discuss ethnic loyalty as a major factor to take into account in examining ethnic marketing, as well as providing the grounding for the discussion of ethnic marketing in general and, in particular, for the justification of the deployment of ethnic-sensitive tactics that are focused on developing loyalty advantages, discussed in later chapters of this text. Drawing on Oliver (1999)'s four-step loyalty development process, the discussion accounts for loyalty drivers and for switching drivers.

Chapter 6 marks the transition in the text into a more holistically supported analysis of market-related cultural diversity issues, via the introduction of substantial management literature, particularly the extensive literature dealing with ethnic entrepreneurship and ethnic minority business.

Drawing from relevant ethnography/cultural, entrepreneurship/economics, and sociology literatures, Chapter 7 seeks to understand the inner-workings of ethnic entrepreneurship, exploring the close link between minority ethnic groups and ethnic minority businesses during the latter's creation and consolidation phases. The chapter explains that the entrepreneur's minority ethnic group of affiliation is the business incubator that supports enterprise consolidation, the principal market and the natural habitat for ethnic minority businesses, whereas a lack of access to the minority ethnic group is likely to justify declining sales and loss of business. Conversely, focus on the cultural side of minority ethnic groups suggests that entrepreneurship has more of an influence on the development of a minority ethnic group's economic stability than through the process of assimilation.

Chapter 8 continues the examination of the role played by minority ethnic groups for the development of ethnic entrepreneurship, with a focus on the breakout strategies that are likely to underpin an ethnic minority business' growth potential.

Chapter 9 offers a cognitive relational perspective that elaborates on the importance of the promotion of suppliers to a minority ethnic group to a perceived "preferred supplier" status, as a factor in the generation of affiliated ethnic minority consumers' loyalty to the supplier and to the group.

Based on the discussion and evidence provided in previous chapters emphasizing loyalty and the importance of networks, Chapter 10 examines the development of relational marketing strategies. Chapter 11 reviews tactical activities deployed by ethnic minority businesses, namely place, process, physical evidence, product and price. The focus of Chapter 12 is on promotion and personalization tactical activities, and Chapter 13 discusses the importance of people-related tactical activities and ethnic minority businesses' ethical behaviour.

Finally, Chapter 14 provides a conclusion to the text. The host country environmental conditions that are most conducive to the growth of ethnic marketing are discussed, focusing on variables in the two categories most relevant to society of settlement and moderating factors during acculturation. The interaction between these two sets of variables is highlighted since they create the environment within which ethnic marketing must work.

Notes

1. Each held a full professorial position at their respective institutions
2. The transcription of all interviews is available in Pires and Stanton (2015).

References

Aguilar, F. (1967). *Scanning the Business Environment*. London: Macmillan.
Andreasen, A. (1994). Social marketing: Its definition and domain. *Journal of Public Policy & Marketing*, 13(11), 108–114.
Baker, M. (2001). Commentary: Bridging the divide. *European Journal of Marketing*, 35(1/2), 24–27.

Barth, F. (1998). *Ethnic Groups and Boundaries: The Social Organization of Culture Difference.* Long Grove, IL: Waveland Press.

Baxter, P. (2007). The CCARE model of clinical supervision: Bridging the theory: Practice gap. *Nurse Education in Practice,* 7, 103–111.

Blanchard, P. (2003). Ethnic marketing is here! *Africultures.* Accessed 2/2017 at http://africultures.com/

Brennan, R. (2008). Theory and practice across disciplines: Implications for the field of management. *European Business Review,* 20(6), 515–528.

Brennan, R. and Ankers, P. (2004). In search of relevance: Is there an academic-practitioner divide in business-to-business marketing? *Marketing Intelligence & Planning,* 22(5), 511–519.

Brownlie, D., Hewer, P., Wagner, B. and Svensson, G. (2008). Management theory and practice: Bridging the gap through multidisciplinary lenses. *European Business Review,* 20(6), 461–470.

Burton, D. (2002). Towards a critical multicultural marketing theory. *Marketing Theory,* 2(2), 207–236.

Byrd, T. and Turner, D. (2000). Measuring the flexibility of information technology infrastructure: Exploratory analysis of a construct. *Journal of Management Information Systems,* 17(1), 167–208.

Chan, A. and Ahmed, F. (2006). Ethnic marketing in Australia. *International Review of Business Research Papers,* 2(4), 10–21.

Cleveland, M. and Laroche, M. (2007). Acculturation to the global consumer culture: Scale development and research paradigm. *Journal of Business Research,* 60(3), 249–259.

Cleveland, M., Laroche, M. and Hallab, R. (2013). Globalization, culture, religion, and values: Comparing consumption patterns of Lebanese Muslims and Christians. *Journal of Business Research,* 66(8), 958–967.

Cleveland, M., Papadopoulos, N. and Laroche, M. (2011). Identity, demographics, and consumer behaviors: International market segmentation across product categories. *International Marketing Review,* 28(3), 244–266.

Cohen, R. (1978). Ethnicity: Problem and focus in anthropology. *Annual Review of Anthropology,* 7(1), 379–403.

Corley, K. and Gioia, D. (2011). Building theory about theory building: What constitutes a theoretical contribution? *Academy of Management Review,* 36(1), 12–32.

Coutant, F. (1938). President's annual report. *Journal of Marketing,* 2(April), 269–271.

Cravens, D. and Piercy, N. (2008). *Strategic Marketing.* New York: McGraw-Hill Irwin.

Cui, G. (2001). Marketing to ethnic minority consumers: A historical journey (1932–1997). *Journal of Macromarketing,* 21(1), 23–31.

Cui, G. (1997). Marketing strategies in a multi-ethnic environment. *Journal of Marketing Theory and Practice,* 5(4), 122–134.

Cui, G. and Choudhury, P. (2002). Marketplace diversity and cost-effective marketing strategies. *Journal of Consumer Marketing,* 19(1), 54–73.

De Leeuw, A. and Volberda, H. (1996). On the concept of flexibility: A dual control perspective. *Omega,* 24(2), 121–139.

Deshpandé, R. (2010). Why you aren't buying Venezuelan chocolate. *Harvard Business Review,* 88(12), 25–27.

Dewey, J. (1904). The relation of theory to practice in education. In C. McMurry (eds.), *The Third Yearbook of the National Society for the Scientific Study of Education*, Part 1. Bloomington, IL: Public School Publishing Company, pp. 9–30.

Di Maggio, P. (1995). Comments on "what theory is not". *Administrative Science Quarterly*, 40(3), 391–397.

Engel, J., Fiorillo, H. and Cayley, M. (1971). *Marketing segmentation: Concepts and applications*. New York: Holt, Rinehart & Winston.

Fendt, J., Kaminska-Labbé, R. and Sachs, W. (2008). Producing and socializing relevant management knowledge: Re-turn to pragmatism. *European Business Review*, 20(6), 471–491.

Ghaill, M. (2000). The Irish in Britain: The invisibility of ethnicity and anti-Irish racism. *Journal of Ethnic and Migration Studies*, 26(1), 137–147.

Gilliam, D. and Voss, K. (2013). A proposed procedure for construct definition in marketing. *European Journal of Marketing*, 47(1/2), 5–26.

Gjerde, P. (2014). An evaluation of ethnicity research in developmental psychology: Critiques and recommendations. *Human Development*, 57, 176–205.

Hallen, L., Johanson, J. and Seyed-Mohamed, N. (1991). Interfirm adaptation in business relationships. *Journal of Marketing*, 29–37.

Ho, J. (2014). Formulation of a systemic PEST analysis for strategic analysis. *European Academic Research*, 2(5), 6478–6492.

Holbrook, M. (2008). Compromise is so . . . compromised: Goldilocks, go home. *European Business Review*, 20(6), 570–578.

Ivens, B. (2005). Flexibility in industrial service relationships: The construct, antecedents, and performance outcomes. *Industrial Marketing Management*, 34(6), 566–576.

Jamal, A. (2003). Marketing in a multicultural world: The interplay of marketing, ethnicity and consumption. *European Journal of Marketing*, 37(11/12), 1599–1620.

Jiménez, T. (2010). Affiliative ethnic identity: A more elastic link between ethnic ancestry and culture. *Ethnic and Racial Studies*, 33(10), 1756–1775.

Kerin, R. (1996). In pursuit of an ideal: The editorial and literary history of the Journal of Marketing. *Journal of Marketing*, 60(1), 1.

Koeman, J., Jaubin, K. and Stesmans, A. (2010). Standardization or adaptation? Ethnic marketing strategies through the eyes of practitioners and consumers in Flanders. *Communications*, 35, 165–185.

Kumar, N. and Steenkamp, J. (2013). Diaspora marketing. *Harvard Business Review*, 91(10), 127.

Kumar, V. (2015). Evolution of marketing as a discipline: What has happened and what to look out for. *Journal of Marketing*, 79(1), 1–9.

Lenhart, A., Purcell, K., Smith, A. and Zickuhr, K. (2010). Social media & mobile internet use among teens and young adults: Millennials. *Pew Internet & American Life Project*. http://pewinternet.org

Lerman, D., Maldonado, R. and Luna, D. (2009). A theory-based measure of acculturation: The shortened cultural life style inventory. *Journal of Business Research*, 62(4), 399–406.

Luedicke, M. (2011). Consumer acculturation theory: (Crossing) conceptual boundaries. *Consumption Markets & Culture*, 14(3), 223–244.

Makgosa, R. (2012). Ethnic diversity in Britain: A stimulus for multicultural marketing. *Marketing Intelligence & Planning*, 30(3), 358–378.

Malhotra, N., Hall, J., Shaw, M. and Crisp, M. (1996). *Marketing Research: An Applied Orientation.* Sydney: Prentice Hall.

Martin, A. (2004). Addressing the gap between theory and practice: IT project design. *Journal of Information Technology Theory and Application,* 6(2), 23–42.

Noordewier, T., John, G. and Nevin, J. (1990). Performance outcomes of purchasing arrangements in industrial buyer-vendor relationships. *Journal of Marketing,* 80–93.

O'Guinn, T., Lee, W. and Faber, R. (1986). Acculturation: The impact of divergent paths on buyer behavior. *ACR North American Advances.* www.acrwebsite.org/volumes/6558/volumes/v13/NA-13

Okamoto, D. and Mora, G. (2014). Pan-ethnicity. *Annual Review of Sociology,* 40, 219–239.

Oppermann, R. (ed.) (1994). *Adaptive User Support: Ergonomic Design of Manually and Automatically Adaptable Software.* London: CRC Press.

Ormerod, R. (2006). The history and ideas of pragmatism. *Journal of the Operational Research Society,* 57, 892–909.

Peñaloza, L. (1994). Atravesando fronteras/border crossings: A critical ethnographic exploration of the consumer acculturation of Mexican immigrants. *Journal of Consumer Research,* 21, 32–54.

Perry, C. and Gummesson, E. (2004). Action research in marketing. *European Journal of Marketing,* 38(3/4), 310–320.

Phinney, J. (1990). Ethnic identity in adolescents and adults: Review of research. *Psychological Bulletin,* 108, 499–514.

Pires, G. (1999). Domestic cross cultural marketing in Australia: A critique of the segmentation rationale. *Journal of Marketing Theory and Practice,* 7(4), 33–44.

Pires, G. and Stanton, J. (2005). *Ethnic Marketing: Accepting the Challenge of Cultural Diversity.* London: Thomson Learning.

Pires, G. and Stanton, J. (2015). *Ethnic Marketing: Culturally Sensitive Theory and Practice.* New York City, NY, USA: Taylor and Francis.

Pires, G., Stanton, J. and Rita, P. (2006). The Internet, consumer empowerment and marketing strategies. *European Journal of Marketing,* 40(9/10), 936–949.

Richards, J. and Curran, C. (2002). Oracles on "advertising": Searching for a definition. *Journal of Advertising,* 31(2), 63–77.

Schradie, J. (2012). The trend of class, race, and ethnicity in social media inequality: Who still cannot afford to blog? *Information, Communication & Society,* 15(4), 555–571.

Serrão, J. (1977). *A emigração Portuguesa,* 3rd ed. Lisbon: Livros Horizonte.

Simon, P. (2008). The choice of ignorance: The debate on ethnic and racial statistics in France. *French Politics, Culture & Society,* 26(1), 7–31.

Smith, W. (1956). Product differentiation and market segmentation as alternative marketing strategies. *Journal of Marketing,* 21(1), 3–8.

Sutton, R. and Staw, B. (1995). What theory is not. *Administrative Science Quarterly,* 40(3), 371–384.

Szillat, P. and Betov, A. (2015). Marketing to multicultural audiences-ethnic marketing for Turks in the German automotive and telecommunications industries. *International Journal of Business and Management,* 3(2), 85–95.

Veal, A. (2005). *Business Research Methods: A Managerial Approach,* 2nd ed. French Forest: Pearson Addison Wesley.

Waldeck, B. and von Gosen, C. (2006). Ethno marketing in Germany. *The 1st International Conference on Strategic Development of the Baltic Sea Region (BSR)*, Tallinn, Estonia, February 25–27. Accessed 31/07/2018 at www.fh-kiel. de/fileadmin/Data/wirtschaft/Dozenten/Waldeck_Bernd/Ethno_Marketing. pdf

Weber, M. (1961). Ethnic groups. In T. Parsons, E. Shils, K. Naegele and J. Pitts (eds.), *Theories of Society*, Vol. 1, pp. 305–309.

Wilkinson, I. and Cheng, C. (1999). Multicultural marketing in Australia: Synergy in diversity. *Journal of International Marketing*, 106–125.

2   Ethnicity, Ethnic Groups and Ethnic Identity

The purpose of this chapter is to review three critical concepts that under-pin ethnic marketing and its potential value as a marketing strategy. The order of consideration is to address meanings of ethnicity in terms of the various points of view used by different researchers and a consensus that appears to be emerging. Ethnic groups are then introduced because ethnicity is often used to identify the boundaries of such groups. A per-ceived ethnic group is also the likely target of any marketing strategy using ethnic identifiers. However, the link between individual ethnicity and an ascribed ethnic group for market purposes requires closer exami-nation because of the role of ethnic identity, another concept undergoing re-evaluation as to its behavioural importance. While an ethnic group's coherence and dynamics may be influenced by the varying strengths of ethnic identities of its members, the ethnic identity self-ascribed by the individual may be influenced by the ethnic group to which the person chooses to belong.

The Meaning and Relevance of Ethnicity

A succinct dictionary definition of ethnicity such as a *"state of belong-ing to a social group that has a common national or cultural tradition"* (Stevenson, 2010) obscures differences in schools of thought about the concept and how the concept has developed to the point of the definition currently used (Wimmer, 2008; Gjerde, 2014). One perspective, used in this book, is that

> the concept of ethnicity depends on the meaning of several other concepts, particularly those of ethnic group and ethnic identity. The concept of ethnic group is the most basic, from which the others are derivative.
>
> (Isajiw, 1980, p. 5)

However, this essentially constructivist perspective is at odds with other interpretations that still are current. As given in Table 2.1 below, they

Table 2.1 The Source of Ethnicity

Perspective	Origins
Primordialist theories	Ethnicity is fixed at birth. Ethnic identification is based on deep, "primordial" attachments to a group or culture.
Instrumental theories	Ethnicity, based on people's "historical" and "symbolic" memory, is something created and used and exploited by leaders and others in the pragmatic pursuit of their own interests.
Constructivist theories	Ethnic identity is not something people "possess" but something they "construct" in specific social and historical contexts to further their own interests. It is therefore fluid and subjective.

(Adapted from Wan and Vanderwerf, 2010).

can be classed as "primordial"; instrumental, and the most recent and increasingly dominant, the social-constructivist perspective.

The social construction of ethnicity is still relatively recent (Bath, 1969), competing with a primordial view that

> there are bounded natural ethnicities, stable, and unique in their own right, that maintain a fixed nature over time and generations.
>
> (Gjerde, 2014)

The elements of what constitutes a common national, or cultural, tradition also tends to become a diverse list of elements for arbitrary inclusion for exclusion. Common reference is made to ancestry, race, shared biological or genetic makeup, ethnic origin, religion, language, values, customs and self-identification.

Depending on the variables included in the definition of ethnicity, such as an individual's genetic make-up or ethnic origin, ones ethnicity can be considered fixed, not changing despite migration to a new country or citizenship from the host culture (Lee and DeVos, 1981). As noted by Phinney and Ong (2007), "ethnicity cannot be chosen by the individual, but rather it is determined at birth or assigned to one by others on the basis of ethnic background or phenotype" (p. 275).

Basis for Defining Ethnicity

The basis for defining ethnicity is riddled with difficulties. Lee and DeVos (1981) include racial uniqueness, territoriality, economic bases, religion, aesthetic cultural patterns and language. Each identifier alone is itself riddled with ambiguity, as noted below.

- *Racial uniqueness* refers to the genetic features, qualities or characteristics that are unique to a specific group—whether real or as perceived by those outside the group—but leaves hanging the faulty premise of uniqueness.

- *Territoriality* refers to national boundaries or one's nationality, but territoriality is not confined to physical boundaries. An individual of Chinese background may be born elsewhere and yet may still identify and also be perceived as "Chinese" by nationality whilst national boundaries can be, and are, variable.
- *Economic bases* refer to the economic development or economic level of an ethnic group that influences their status and/or identity.
- *Religion* is also considered important because of the common values and associated practices it can instil, although it is sufficient to think of India to understand than an Indian ethnic group is unlikely to have one single religion.
- *Aesthetic cultural patterns* refer to the food, costumes, dances, hair styles, jewellery and communication styles considered unique and pleasing to a specific group of people.
- *Language* is considered important to one's ethnicity for such reasons, but its overall impact may be weakened as an indicator when it crosses national boundaries. For example, English is widely spoken in many different countries but may be the preferred language of persons with different ethnicities, and sometimes treated as the lingua franca, adopted as a common language used for communication between groups of people who speak different languages (Seidlhofer, 2010; Canagarajah, 2007). In turn, variations in the use of a mother tongue may strengthen a sense of ethnicity.

Other definitions of ethnicity can also be noted: Peñaloza (2006) described ethnicity as both mainstream and as sub-groups of people including their history and geography, their physical characteristics, their relationship with members from their own ethnic group and other groups and how they and their group are treated by other groups in the workforce, education system and by their government. Costa and Bamossy (1995) define ethnicity as "an involuntary group of people who share the same culture" (p. 73). Phinney (1992) defined ethnicity as an "objective group membership as determined by parents' ethnic heritage" (p. 158).

"Ethnicity", "race" and "membership of an ethnic group" are often loosely used interchangeably, as evidenced by Cui and Choudhury (2000). In their perusal of primarily American studies of ethnic consumer behaviour they observe an overwhelming focus on major racial minority groups in the United States, consistent with the use of *"ethnic [as] a broad term that refers to race, nationality, religion, language and customs"* (p. 6).

In short, ethnicity is essentially an ascribed (by others or by self) label assigning a person to a group without any connotation as to how strongly an individual thus ascribed may share either traits, common beliefs and/ or engage in common practices (ABS, 2000).

We Are All Ethnic—Or Are We?

The Australian Bureau of Statistics or ABS (2000, p. 3) offers an attempt at inclusiveness referring to ethnicity as the shared similarity of a group of people on the basis of one or more of the following factors: cultural tradition, including family and social customs; a common geographic origin; a common language; a common literature (written or oral); a common religion; being a minority; or being racially conspicuous. It is a more inclusive definition of ethnicity than some (Peñaloza, 2006; Costa and Bamossy, 1995) and also tends to be more straightforward than Lee and DeVos' (1981).

Notwithstanding, the inclusion of "being a minority" is, by itself, a confounding factor. As noted by Peñaloza (2006), ethnicity is also being mainstream, the invited implication being that we are all ethnic. However, preserving the right to self-ascription, it is conceivable that an individual might chose to socially construct by self-ascription to a state of non-ethnicity. A similar example is that of acculturation outliers (such as marginalization or exclusion) where an individual may choose to distance her/himself from any minority or mainstream group (Berry and Sabatier, 2011; Pfafferott and Brown, 2006; Van Oudenhoven and Hofstra, 2006).

The literature shows that ethnicity is often used as a label to pigeon-hole individuals into *categories* based on an individual's country of birth, parentage or some combination of attributes associated with the definition of ethnicity, and these are then called "ethnic groups". However, it is disputable whether such ethnic categories have much marketing relevance unless it can be shown the category meets segmentation criteria (discussed in Chapter 4) in which case it can be termed an ethnic group, having connections and a sense of commonality that identify some collective set of values and behaviours that marketers can focus on.

The marketing problem can be seen in terms of Hugo's (1995) reference to an ethnic group as a cluster of people who are identified as a community due to commonalities in cultural heritage and customs, birthplace and language, although customs and language may be special cases. These commonalities alone do not necessarily lead to social interactions and group behaviours and, when applied to identifiable immigrant groups by any of the above labels, the diversity encompassed within each of these variables may create a degree of heterogeneity that may defy marketing relevance.

This is a consideration that raises important issues, particularly when it is common practice for certain groups of individuals to be targeted mostly, if not solely, based on language—such as the Hispanic group in the United States (Therrien and Ramirez, 2001; Rodriguez, 1997).

Meaning and Centrality of Ethnic Groups

If a person's ethnicity derives from belonging to an ethnic group, then a group needs to be distinguished from an ethnic category (Gjerde, 2014). The latter is commonly associated with a collection of individuals, often defined by an external categorizer. In contrast, a group is defined by the nature of the relations between its members. This is a subtle but important change for marketing purposes, compared to earlier definitions such as by Yinger (1976), where categorization by other is possible:

> a segment of a larger society whose members are thought, by themselves and/or others, to have a common origin and to share important segments of a common culture and who, in addition, participate in shared activities in which the common origin and culture are significant ingredients.
>
> (p. 200)

A social construction view of an ethnic group (Béji-Bécheur, Özçağlar-Toulouse and Zouaghi, 2012; Chaudhari and Pizzolato, 2008; Phinney, 1992, 1990; Ting-Toomey, 1981) is that ethnicity is only present in social situations and in social engagements where the individual displays conformity to group norms. Béji-Bécheur, Özçağlar-Toulouse and Zouaghi (2012, p. 506) argue that ethnicity extends beyond "the process of acculturation or the balancing or negotiation of identity" and incorporates both the process of acculturation and the awareness, development and acceptance of one's ethnic identity. The social interactions within a category determine whether it constitutes an ethnic group or simply an ethnic category. Specifically, Gjerde (2014) argues that a group

> is dense with interactions and has a sense of itself as a distinct entity based on the perceived interdependence among its members . . . an ethnic category . . . can be viewed as a collection of individuals who share at least one common feature (such as being of Asian descent) but not characterized by close interdependence.
>
> (p. 183)

An example that strongly tells about this category vs group distinction is the unlikely inclusion of Chinese and Japanese individuals in the same group, at least for marketing purposes (Sun, Horn and Merritt, 2004).

The Australian Bureau of Statistics (ABS, 2000) proceeds from its definition of ethnicity to the definition of an ethnic group as a group that considers itself and in turn is considered by others as a separate community due to the group's discernible characteristics. These characteristics include, amongst others, having the commonalities of common origin, language, food, religion and geographic location (Yinger, 1985). What are missing from such "group" definitions, rendering them less effective for marketing purposes, are the interactions and perceived interdependence characteristic of group behaviour.

The influence of the ethnic group is evident in the use of specific businesses highly recommended by influential members of the community. Ethnic group members have a tendency to frequent businesses owned and frequented by other members of their ethnic group especially if word-of-mouth and personal experience have been positive (Huang, Oppewal and Mavondo, 2013). This is also an important driver of ethnic group resilience, a matter discussed in-depth in Chapters 7 to 9. In a study on consumers of Hispanic heritage, it also was found that Hispanics like to frequent businesses owned by other Hispanics or where customer service personnel are fluent in Spanish (Berkowitz, Bao and Allaway, 2005).

Ethnic Groups as Social Networks

Acceptable group norms are established by the members of each ethnic group by informal processes and remain unwritten. These group norms, which include religion, cultural values, cultural customs and traits that are characteristic of the ethnic group, have a significant impact on which ethnic group an individual identifies with (Frideres and Goldenberg, 1982). However, ethnic groups are not the same as cultural groups. While there may be the commonality of cultural practices, the historical, social and situational context shapes the ethnic group (Gjerde, 2014).

Largely absent from studies of ethnic marketing theory and practice is any focus on the social network of ethnic consumers that presumably shapes their distinctive (from other groups) consumer behaviour and which warrants a distinctive strategy for reaching them. In arguing that social networks are a key determinant of economic action, Granovetter (1985) urged a focus on the social context to explain individual economic behaviour:

> Actors do not behave or decide as atoms outside a social context, nor do they adhere slavishly to a script written for them by the particular intersection of social categories that they happen to occupy. Their attempts at purposive action are instead embedded in concrete, ongoing systems of social relations.
>
> (p. 486)

Because of the social structure and varying ties between members of an ethnic group, social networks impact on individual economic behaviour primarily through the flow and quality of information, rewards and punishments, and the trust engendered through the ties (Granovetter, 2005). The importance of these elements in shaping economic decisions will vary between networks according to fairly standard network principles (Barney, 2004).

Apart from embeddedness, a characteristic that implies that behaviour is constrained by ongoing social relations, network density, weak ties and structural holes can play varying roles in the collective behaviour of the group. Density, measured by the proportion of possible connections among nodes (people, firms or other social units) plays an important role in maintaining norms, with denser networks more able to enforce such norms. Weak ties between some members of the group exposes the group as a whole to more novel information, while individuals with ties to multiple networks not only facilitate such information flows but act as bridges (Granovetter, 2005). When an ethnic group is a minority, mixed embeddedness connects the ethnic group's social networks to the structures of the host country (Kloosterman, 2010; Kloosterman and Rath, 2001).

The economic value of a social network is dependent on its social capital,

> the resources embedded in a social structure which are accessed and/ or mobilised in purposive action.
> (Lin, Fu and Hsung, 2001, p. 12; also Lin, 2017)

Social capital can be described in terms of a group's structural (network configuration and size), cognitive (the strength of presence of shared codes such as language) and relational (strength of trust and obligation) dimensions (Nahapiet and Ghoshal, 1998). The stock and composition of this capital shapes the economic importance of a group.

The significance of social networks in explaining patterns of economic action and outcomes will be greatest *"in those spheres of economic activity where search and deliberation pertaining to potential exchange partners are important but problematic"* (Rangan, 2000, p. 814) because social capital can reduce such costs. The implications are that social networks and economic activity are more closely interlinked than indicated by an examination of markets in terms of individual buying units, and that the social capital of such networks is amenable to measurement, but there are difficulties because it is an intangible asset and the items used to measure its main components can vary (Field, 2003; Van der Gaag and Snijders, 2005).

Field (2003, p. 124), surveying the measurement issues, suggests that any indicators are likely to be proxies but they should have some clear connection to social capital. Both survey (Van der Gaag and Snijders, 2005) and ethnographic approaches can be used (Schensul et al., 1999).

Sociologists have long recognized that ethnic groups constitute social networks and have sought to identify their boundaries (Wimmer, 2008; Sanders, 2002). Barth (1969) argued that the social spaces within which group interaction occurred defined the boundaries of an ethnic group.

These boundaries create and subsequently reinforce in-group members' self-identification and outsiders' confirmation of group distinctions (Sanders, 2002). The boundaries of an ethnic group, its links with other groups, internal interdependence and the degree and form of social control of members can vary significantly between communities and over time (Bentley, 1981), even to the point of ethnic group switching (Sanders, 2002). Sanders' review of the ethnic boundaries literature found that, for various groups in the USA, ethnic identity is strongly shaped by location of settlement with regional and neighbourhood concentrations facilitating the maintenance of social boundaries and ethnic identity.

Ethnic Group Heterogeneity

Heterogeneity in terms of age, income, education and class is inevitable within any ethnic group, and these differences may qualify how ethnicity is used for particular operational segmentation purposes (Wentz, 2003). Langer (1998) observes class differences within the small Salvadorean community in Australia, differences in the degree of ascription to the community, as well as the creation of a hybrid culture that is neither Salvadorean nor mainstream Australian.

A focus of investigation has therefore been to understand the reasons for the perpetuation of ethnic boundaries. Sanders (2002) emphasizes the social capital provided by such networks, observing that relatively intense feelings of ethnic identity and involvement in an ethnic community are likely to exist when ethnic networks can supply social goods otherwise in short supply. Boundaries are more likely to be maintained because they protect valued forms of association. Continued provision by ethnic networks of valued resources that benefit participants in that community helps to maintain ethnic identity.

The core values approach (Smolicz, Secombe and Hudson, 2001) assists in understanding how ethnic identity is supported by the social capital of a group. Core values are those forming the fundamental components of a group's culture, symbolic of the group. From the perspective of an outsider, it is through core values that social groups can be identified as distinctive cultural communities. Their study examined the relative significance of collective family structure and minority languages as core cultural values among four ethnic groups in Australia (Greek, Italian, Latvian and Chinese). Particular core values were found to act as "markers" of group identity with important variations between groups in aspects of culture regarded as their core values, as well as the number of foci. If social capital maintains and protects the group's core values, the marketing strategies of businesses external to this ethnic group network must either build bridges that can cross these boundaries using the strength of weak ties [using persons who may span more than one group] (Buchanan, 2002, ch.2; Granovetter, 2005) or become a part of the network.

A social network view does not limit the size of an ethnic group, which can range from very large to very small. Further, nothing is said about the extent or intensity of social interaction that occurs within such groups. The potential variability and changes that can occur over time and spatially will require more focus on the beliefs, values and both interactional and independent behaviours that hold the group together, as well as how this may change over time. The role of ethnic identity at an individual level and how it interacts within an ethnic group plays a key role.

The Interlinking of Ethnic Identity With the Ethnic Group

Similar to ethnicity, definitions of ethnic identity are likewise mired in differences. Morimoto and La Ferle (2008) and Parker et al. (1998), for example, would argue for a difference between ethnic identity and ethnic identification, defining ethnic identity as the cultural customs and beliefs that are passed down the generations while ethnic identification is described as "the degree of an individual's sense of belonging and group pride . . . and social behaviors" (Morimoto and La Ferle, 2008, p. 51). However, their ethnic identification is almost universally treated as synonymous with the concept of ethnic identity, the term used here.

Ethnic identity is relevant both in the presence of one's own ethnic group and in the interaction with other ethnic groups (Phinney, 1990). One's ethnicity and ethnic identity is only prevalent when the individual has been exposed to other ethnic groups and to the host group (Béji-Bécheur, Herbert and Özçağlar-Toulouse, 2011; Laroche, Kim and Tomiuk, 1999). It is through this exposure and interaction that the individual develops an awareness of their own ethnicity and the ethnicity of their ethnic group. The premise is that the individual is aware of the ethnicity of other ethnic groups in order to have a perception of their own ethnicity and ethnic identity.

A social identity construction of ethnic identity appears to have gained dominance since the 1990s. The definitions of ethnic identity provided below all share common elements of a social construction, a sense of belonging, a link or a membership to a particular ethnic group or ethnic background: Cohen (1978) and Eriksen (2001) define ethnic identity as the recognition (whether self-ascribed or imposed upon by others) of commonalities in language, religion, culture, cultural practices and customs that links an individual emotionally or in essence to a particular ethnicity. Chaudhari and Pizzolato (2008) define ethnic identity as the dimensions of:

> the shared beliefs, attitudes, and behaviors by a particular ethnic background [and] the extent of importance of and membership to a particular ethnic background.
>
> (p. 444)

Phinney (1990) reviewed prior studies of ethnic identity, pointing to the multiplicity of definitions associated with different approaches to identity development, as well as looseness in terminology. Our interest in ethnic identity is in having some idea of how it forms and develops and how ethnic identity can influence individual and group consumer behaviour. A considerable body of literature on ethnic identity is concerned with the development of a measurement construct (Phinney, 1990, 1992; Phinney and Ong, 2007; Gjerde, 2014). Our interest is not in its measurement but the underlying premises; specifically, the viewpoints of the researchers underlying their measurement approaches and how they see ethnic identity influencing behaviour.

Subsequent long-term research and testing by Phinney and Ong (2007) have led to fairly widespread use of a social identity approach in which ethnic identity is viewed as a part of a person's social identity, an approach that is used in this text. An individual's social identity is tied to their sense of belonging to a social group and the positive self-esteem that this sense of belonging evokes for the individual (Kinket and Verkuyten, 1997). Explained by Tajfel (1981), ethnic identity as a component of a person's social identity is:

> that part of an individual's self-concept which derives from her (or his) knowledge of her (or his) membership of a social group (or groups) together with the value and emotional significance attached to that membership.
>
> (p. 255)

Phinney (1990) conceptualized ethnic identity as a complex construct including a commitment and sense of belonging to one's ethnic group, positive evaluation of the group, interest in and knowledge about the group, and involvement in activities and traditions of the group. Testing of her construct led to some refinement but retention of a self-identified commitment and involvement: "at the core of ethnic identity is a sense of self as a group member that develops over time through an active process of investigation, learning, and commitment". (Phinney and Ong, 2007, p. 479). Ethnic identity changes with time and context; that is, the development of a person's ethnic identity is a process that can be ongoing and very different from others', depending on the life path of the individual.

Development of Ethnic Identity

Whether one's ethnicity can or cannot be chosen (Phinney and Ong, 2007), one's ethnic identity can be. Finding one's ethnic identity entails an initial process of not knowing the community or family-based ethnicity given from birth. Through the process of exploration, an ethnic individual finds her/his social identity. The more nurturing the family environment, the stronger the ethnic identity and sense of belonging an ethnic individual will feel towards her/his ethnic group (Costigan, Su and Hua, 2009). Self-rejection or a challenge to her/his ethnic identity from the wider community will cause the individual to question her/his identity and her/his membership of and sense of belonging towards her/his ethnic group (Phinney, 1992, 1990, 1996; Chaudhari and Pizzolato, 2008; Ting-Toomey, 1981). This can lead to self-disidentification—an active negation of any association with a group (Becker and Tausch, 2014; McCall, 2003), but rejection-identification is also possible—when people perceive that they are rejected because of a group membership, identification with that group can increase (Wiley, 2013).

Yeh and Huang (1996) provide another perspective and assert that the development of ethnic identity is a unique process that is influenced by external factors such as the perceptions of the host culture towards ethnic groups and the social interactions that are encountered. Costa and Bamossy (1995) expand on this view affirming that culture is dynamic, constantly evolving and adapting to external influences.

In characterizing the formation or development of an individual's ethnic identity, Phinney (1990) noted:

- The individual does not identify with any ethnicity;
- The individual explores her/his ethnicity and ethnic identity, and
- The individual accepts her/his ethnicity and ethnic identity.

Phinney and Ong (2007) suggest the process begins in childhood with major changes going into "young adulthood". By adulthood, they argue,

> most people have acquired a relatively stable and secure sense of themselves as ethnic group members, that is, an achieved ethnic identity.
>
> (p. 475)

In the context of an individual growing and residing within the same community, there may be little questioning or exploration of identity issues. Given the contemporary movement of large numbers of migrants from diverse ethnicities to host countries often with very different cultures, ethnic identity for many migrants and their families may be unsettled, adapting and adjusting to influences from other ethnic groups in the new environment, as well as the dominant host group (Isajiw, 1980; Laroche, Pons and Richard, 2009). Because acculturation can influence ethnic minorities towards embracing some if not all the cultural values of the host culture, ethnic identity can be transitional. Individuals will self-ascribe to different identities or labels based on their situation or circumstances although how they label themselves may be challenged by how they are perceived by outsiders, particularly if their physical features are unique to their racial background (Phinney, 1996). The consequences of possible acculturation paths are discussed in the next chapter.

Ethnic Identity, Consumer Behaviour and the Ethnic Group

The definition of ethnic identity used in this book has the parsimony of focusing on self-identification, commitment and involvement with others of similar ethnicity. This commitment and involvement may involve behaviours such as use of the ethnic language, eating the food, as well as other aspects that engender oral satisfaction (Pires and Stanton, 2015), as well as associating with members of one's group, but as Phinney and Ong (2007) note, ethnic identity has an internal structure separate from behaviour. While some measures of ethnic identity have included explicit behavioural measures (Phinney, 1992; Felix-Ortiz, Newcomb and Myers, 1994), Phinney and Ong (2007) recommend the concept of ethnic identity be treated separately from ethnic behaviours, such behaviours being the outcome of a person's ethnic identity, such that it is necessary "to distinguish the implications of identity per se and the associated behaviors" (p. 473).

An ethnic group consists of persons with a common ethnic identity, although the strength of ethnic identity may vary between individuals within the group. Individuals' ethnic identity contribute to their self-perspective (Phinney, 1996). The strength of their ethnic identity and the sense of belonging towards their ethnic group may be reflected by their purchase behaviour for products that are consumed socially. Accordingly, a strong ethnic identity may indicate a preference for ethnic goods and services (Minor-Cooley and Brice, 2007). This can be explained by social consumption being dependent upon the presence of parents or peers who may impact upon the self-awareness and strength of one's ethnicity and ethnic identity.

The influence of ethnicity and ethnic identity on the consumption of certain types of products is confirmed by various studies. The consumption of ethnic clothing, traditional foods and drinks, as well as ethnic performing arts are recurring products (Intharacks, 2017; Xu et al., 2004). Ethnic apparel is a reflection of the individual retaining her/his ethnic identity and affiliation with her/his ethnic group and homeland (Lindridge and Dibb, 2002). It is a display and communication of one's ethnic heritage and identity (Chattaraman and Lennon, 2008; Kim and Arthur, 2003) and a visual revelation of one's ethnicity (Eicher and Sumberg, 1995).

Situational ethnic identity arises when an individual's identity transcends beyond national boundaries; when an individual swaps her/his culture; when an individual moves between their various identities (Öçağlar-Toulouse et al., 2009) or when an individual selectively displays their ethnic identity based on whether they feel more or less ethnic depending upon the circumstances and environment (Morimoto and La Ferle, 2008; Podoshen, 2006; Stayman and Deshpandé, 1989). In her study of ethnic groups in the United States, Oswald (1999) argued that the link between consumer behaviour and ethnicity was one of continual interdependence—ethnic minorities situationally adopted their ethnic identity depending upon how strongly they felt about their ethnicity or towards their ethnic group so the influence on their consumer behaviour was situational.

Because people determine their own identity they may selectively display their ethnic identity during significant milestones, such as "coming of age, marriage and religious holidays" and during social engagements (Cui and Choudhury, 2002, p. 57). Moreover, ethnic minorities are likely to transition between their self-ascribed identities in situations involving food, clothes, music, movies—any product that is linked to their cultural heritage or to that of the host culture (Béji-Bécheur, Herbert and Özçağlar-Toulouse, 2011). Kiang and Fuligni (2009) find an individual's ethnic identity is situational where one may feel more ethnic (ethnic pride) or less ethnic (ethnic shame) when interacting with individuals from their own ethnic background. Their study also found that young adults felt the highest level of ethnic pride and connection to their ethnic heritage when they were engaging with their parents. This can be attributed to the parental role as a source of knowledge about one's ethnic heritage, cultural beliefs, values and traditions. However, there are also contradictory results where ethnic identity is concerned. While some research findings suggest high involvement and engagement with the host culture is not conducive to the retention of a strong ethnic identity, other research findings suggest the opposite holds true, that is, greater participation in the host culture engenders a stronger ethnic identity (Costigan, Su and Hua, 2009).

When trying to understand the influence of ethnic identity on an individual's consumer behaviour it is necessary to look into the ties and interaction within the group due to the "*shared norms and beliefs . . . [that] . . . impact on their dispositions and behaviours . . . as consumers*" (Kwok and Uncles, 2005, p. 171). Ethnic groups consisting of individuals with a strong sense of group ethnic identity (Berry and Sam, 1997) may provide an attractive market opportunity (Schiffman et al., 2008) because of the resources and access provided by the ethnic group to its members and the "*collective shared values and behaviors, expressed through predictable group behavior*" (Pires, Stanton and Stanton (2011, p. 911).

The interaction between the individual and the group in terms of the wider consumption preferences and choices beyond the area of "ethnic products" is less researched although a network approach would suggest a wider impact on consumer behaviour beyond ethnic products. Migrants, in particular those who choose to settle in an environment where the ethnic enclave is already in existence, use their ethnic group's social network to gain access to providers of healthcare, legal, childcare and employment support services in order to lessen their settlement anxieties (Pires and Stanton, 2005; Sharma, 2007). As Sanders (2002,) notes:

> Social networks that provide scarce resources to a wide spectrum of the ethnic community are highly useful to in-group members.
>
> (p. 347)

Word of mouth within the group can lead to preferred suppliers, not only of ethnic products, but also preferred retailers (Badghish, Stanton and Hu, 2015). By associating themselves with their ethnic group instead of the host culture, the ethnic identity of these ethnic migrants is reinforced (Hume, 2008) and their consumption behaviours shaped by the ethnic group.

Summary

The terms ethnicity, ethnic identity and ethnic group are widely perceived and used in very different ways. The lack of definitional clarity impedes the development of a coherent investigation and discussion of the relevance of ethnicity as the focus of a marketing strategy.

Within an ethnically diverse country there is a strong tendency to categorize individuals into "ethnic groups" based on characteristics defining an ethnic group, regardless of an individual's felt affinity with that group. This concept of "ethnicity", we argue, has little usefulness for marketers because such categorization fails to take into account whether this category equates to a social group with shared values and interactions that equates to marketing relevant behaviour. It is the sense and strength of shared ethnic identity that determines the relevance of ethnicity and the ethnic group to marketers.

The ethnic group is discussed next, rather than ethnic identity, because the group is effectively the focus of an ethnic marketing strategy. The ethnic group as a social construct lends itself to a network interpretation that brings out the value of the group in terms of the social capital available to it members, as well as the interactions and ties that can strengthen the importance of the group in influencing individual behaviours.

The ethnic group will consist of individuals with varying strengths of ethnic identity (reflecting how important their ethnic identity is in terms of their social identity) as well as having varying strength of ties to other group members and those external to this ethnic group. Understanding ethnic identity and how it develops and changes is therefore critical to understanding the ethnic group. Understanding how one's ethnicity influences their consumer decision-making thus requires understanding how ethnic identity forms and also perhaps changes over time.

References

Australian Bureau of Statistics (ABS) (2000). *Australian Standard Classification of Cultural and Ethnic Groups.* Catalogue no. 1249. Canberra, Australia: Australian Bureau of Statistics.

Badghish, S., Stanton, J. and Hu, J. (2015). An exploratory study of customer complaint behaviour (CCB) in Saudi Arabia. *Asian Journal of Business Research*, Special, 49–67.

Barney, D. (2004). *The Network Society*, Vol. 2. Polity.

Barth, F. (ed.) (1969). Ethnic Groups and Boundaries: The Social Organization of Culture Difference. Results of a symposium held at the University of Bergen, February 23–26, 1967.

Becker, J. and Tausch, N. (2014). When group memberships are negative: The concept, measurement, and behavioral implications of psychological disidentification. *Self and Identity*, 13(3), 294–321.

Béji-Bécheur, A., Herbert, M. and Özçağlar-Toulouse, N. (2011). Étudier l'ethnique. *Revue française de gestion*, 7, 111–128.

Béji-Bécheur, A., Özçağlar-Toulouse, N. and Zouaghi, S. (2012). Ethnicity introspected: Researchers in search of their identity. *Journal of Business Research*, 65(4), 504–510.

Bentley, G. (1981). *Ethnicity and Nationality: A Bibliographic Guide.* Seattle: University of Washington Press.

Berkowitz, D., Bao, Y. and Allaway, A. (2005). Hispanic consumers, store loyalty and brand preference. *Journal of Targeting, Measurement and Analysis for Marketing*, 14(1), 9–24.

Berry, J. and Sabatier, C. (2011). Variations in the assessment of acculturation attitudes: Their relationships with psychological wellbeing. *International Journal of Intercultural Relations*, 35(5), 658–669.

Berry, J. and Sam, D. (1997). Acculturation and adaptation. *Handbook of Cross-Cultural Psychology*, 3(2), 291–326.

Buchanan, M. (2002). Nexus. In *Small Words and the Groundbreaking Science of Networks*. New York: WW Norton & Company.

Canagarajah, S. (2007). Lingua franca English, multilingual communities, and language acquisition. *The Modern Language Journal*, 91, 923–939.

Chattaraman, V. and Lennon, S. (2008). Ethnic identity, consumption of cultural apparel, and self-perceptions of ethnic consumers. *Journal of Fashion Marketing and Management*, 12, 518–531.

Chaudhari, P. and Pizzolato, J. (2008). Understanding the epistemology of ethnic identity development in multiethnic college students. *Journal of College Student Development*, 49(5), 443–458.

Cohen, R. (1978). Ethnicity: Problem and focus in anthropology. *Annual Review of Anthropology*, 7(1), 379–403.

Costa, J. and Bamossy, G. (1995). *Marketing in a Multicultural World: Ethnicity, Nationalism, and Cultural Identity.* Thousand Oaks, CA: Sage Publications.

Costigan, C., Su, T. and Hua, J. (2009). Ethnic identity among Chinese Canadian youth: A review of the Canadian literature. *Canadian Psychology/Psychologie Canadienne*, 50(4), 261–272.

Cui, G. and Choudhury, P. (2002). Marketplace diversity and cost effective marketing strategies. *Journal of Consumer Marketing*, 19, 54–74.

Cui, G. and Choudhury, P. (2000). Marketing to ethnic consumers. In *An Annotated Bibliography*. Chicago: American Marketing Association.

Eicher, J. and Sumberg, B. (1995). World fashion, ethnic, and national dress. *Dress and Ethnicity: Change across Space and Time*, 295–306.

Eriksen, T. (2001). *Small Places, Large Issues: An Introduction to Social and Cultural Anthropology*. London: Pluto Press.

Felix-Ortiz, M., Newcomb, M. and Myers, H. (1994). A multidimensional measure of cultural identity for Latino and Latina adolescents. *Hispanic Journal of Behavioral Sciences*, 16(2), 99–115.

Field, J. (2003). Civic engagement and lifelong learning: Survey findings on social capital and attitudes towards learning. *Studies in the Education of Adults*, 35(2), 142–156.

Frideres, J. and Goldenberg, S. (1982). Ethnic identity: Myth and reality in Western Canada. *International Journal of Intercultural Relations*, 6, 137–151.

Gjerde, P. (2014). An evaluation of ethnicity research in developmental psychology: Critiques and recommendations. *Human Development*, 57, 176–205.

Granovetter, M. (2005). The impact of social structure on economic outcomes. *Journal of Economic Perspectives*, 19(1), 33–50.

Granovetter, M. (1985). Economic action and social structure: The problem of embeddedness. *American Journal of Sociology*, 91(3), 481–510.

Huang, Y., Oppewal, H. and Mavondo, F. (2013). The influence of ethnic attributes on ethnic consumer choice of service outlet. *European Journal of Marketing*, 47(5/6), 877–898.

Hugo, G. (1995). Understanding where immigrants live. In B. O. Immigration (ed.), *Multicultural and Population Research*. Canberra: Australian Government Publishing Service.

Hume, S. (2008). Ethnic and national identities of Africans in the United States. *Geographical Review*, 98(4), 496–512.

Intharacks, J. (2017). *The Influence of Ethnicity on Consumer Behaviour: A Study of Inter-Generational and Inter-Group Differences*. PhD Thesis, Western Sydney University, Australia. Accessed 3/2018 at https://researchdirect.westernsydney.edu.au/islandora/object/uws%3A43245

Isajiw, W. (1980). *Definitions of ethnicity* cited in Hui, M. K., Laroche, M. & Kim, C. 1998, A typology of consumption based on ethnic origin and media usage. *European Journal of Marketing*, 32, 868–883.

Kiang, L. and Fuligni, A. (2009). Ethnic identity in context: Variations in ethnic exploration and belonging within parent, same-ethnic peer, and different-ethnic peer relationships. *Youth Adolescence*, 38, 732–743.

Kim, S. and Arthur, L. (2003). Asian-American consumers in Hawai'i: The effects of ethnic identification on attitudes toward and ownership of ethnic apparel, importance of product and store-display attributes, and purchase intention. *Clothing and Textiles Research Journal*, 21(1), 8–18.

Kinket, B. and Verkuyten, M. (1997). Levels of ethnic self-identification and social context. *Social Psychology Quarterly*, 338–354.

Kloosterman, R. (2010). Matching opportunities with resources: A framework for analysing (migrant) entrepreneurship from a mixed embeddedness perspective. *Entrepreneurship and Regional Development*, 22(1), 25–45.

Kloosterman, R. and Rath, J. (2001). Immigrant entrepreneurs in advanced economies: Mixed embeddedness further explored. *Journal of Ethnic and Migration Studies*, 27(2), 189–201.

Kwok, S. and Uncles, M. (2005). Sales promotion effectiveness: The impact of consumer differences at an ethnic-group level. *Journal of Product & Brand Management*, 14, 170–186.

Langer, B. (1998). Globalisation and the myth of ethnic community. In D. Bennett (ed.), *Multicultural States*. London: Rutledge, pp. 163–177.

Laroche, M., Kim, C. and Tomiuk, M. (1999). Italian ethnic identity and its relative impact on the consumption of convenience and traditional foods. *British Food Journal*, 101(3), 201–228.

Laroche, M., Pons, F. and Richard, M. (2009). The role of language in ethnic identity measurement: A multitrait-multimethod approach to construct validation. *The Journal of Social Psychology*, 149(4), 513–540.

Lee, C. and Devos, G. (1981). *Koreans in Japan: Ethnic Conflict and Accommodation*. Berkeley, CA, USA: University of California Press.

Lin, N. (2017). Building a network theory of social capital. In *Social Capital*. Abingdon, UK: Routledge, pp. 3–28.

Lin, N., Fu, Y. and Hsung, R. (2001). Measurement techniques for investigations of social capital. In N. Lin and A. Gruyter (eds.), *Social Capital: Theory and Research*. New York: Routledge.

Lindridge, A. and Dibb, S. (2002). Is "culture" a justifiable variable for market segmentation? A cross-cultural example. *Journal of Consumer Behaviour*, 2, 269–286.

McCall, G. (2003). The me and the not-me. In *Advances in Identity Theory and Research*. Boston, MA: Springer, pp. 11–25.

Minor-Cooley, D. and Brice, Jr., J. (2007). Please check the appropriate box: The problems with ethnic identification and its potential in cross-cultural marketing. *Academy of Marketing Science Review*, 2007, 1.

Morimoto, M. and La Ferle, C. (2008). Examining the influence of culture on perceived source credibility of Asian Americans & the mediating role of similarity. *Journal of Current Issues & Research in Advertising*, 30(1), 49–60.

Nahapiet, J. and Ghoshal, S. (1998). Social capital, intellectual capital, and the organizational advantage. *Academy of Management Review*, 23(2), 242–266.

Oswald, L. (1999). Culture swapping: Consumption and the ethnogenesis of middle-class Haitian immigrants. *Journal of Consumer Research*, 25(4), 303–318.

Özçağlar-Toulouse, N., Béji-Bécheur, A., Fosse-Gomez, M., Herbert, M. and Zouaghi, S. (2009). Ethnicity in the study of the consumer: An overview. *Recherche et Applications en Marketing (English Edition)*, 24(4), 57–75.

Parker, V., Sussman, S., Crippens, D., Elder, P. and Scholl, D. (1998). The relation of ethnic identification with cigarette smoking among US urban African American and Latino youth: A pilot study. *Ethnicity & Health*, 3(1–2), 135–143.

Peñaloza, L. (2006). *Handbook of Qualitative Research Methods in Marketing*. Cheltenham, UK: Edward Elgar Publishing Limited.

Pfafferott, I. and Brown, R. (2006). Acculturation preferences of majority and minority adolescents in Germany in the context of society and family. *International Journal of Intercultural Relations*, 30(6), 703–717.

Phinney, J. (1990). Ethnic identity in adolescents and adults: Review of research. *Psychological Bulletin*, 108, 499–514.

Phinney, J. (1992). The multigroup ethnic identity measure: A new scale for use with diverse groups. *Journal of Adolescent Research*, 7, 156–176.

Phinney, J. (1996). Understanding ethnic diversity: The role of ethnic identity. *American Behavioral Scientist*, 40(2), 143–152.

Phinney, J. and Ong, A. (2007). Conceptualization and measurement of ethnic identity: Current status and future directions. *Journal of Counseling Psychology*, 54(3), 271–281.

Pires, G. and Stanton, J. (2015). *Ethnic Marketing: Culturally Sensitive Theory and Practice*. New York City, NY, USA: Taylor and Francis.

Pires, G. and Stanton, J. (2005). *Ethnic Marketing: Accepting the Challenge of Cultural Diversity*. Hong Kong: Thomson Learning.

Pires, G., Stanton, J. and Stanton, P. (2011). Revisiting the substantiality criterion: From ethnic marketing to market segmentation. *Journal of Business Research*, 64(9), 988–996.

Podoshen, J. (2006). Word of mouth, brand loyalty, acculturation and the American Jewish consumer. *Journal of Consumer Marketing*, 23, 266–282.

Rangan, S. (2000). The problem of search and deliberation in economic action: When social networks really matter. *Academy of Management Review*, 25(4), 813–828.

Rodriguez, A. (1997). Commercial ethnicity: Language, class and race in the marketing of the Hispanic audience. *Communication Review (The)*, 2(3), 283–309.

Sanders, J. (2002). Ethnic boundaries and identity in plural societies. *Annual Review of Sociology*, 28(1), 327–357.

Schensul, J., le Compte, M., Trotter, II, R., Cromley, E. and Singer, M. (1999). *Mapping Social Networks, Spatial Data & Hidden Populations*. Walnut Creek, CA: Altamira Press.

Schiffman, L., Bednall, D., O'Cass, A., Paladino, A., Ward, S. and Kanuk, L. (2008). *Consumer Behaviour*. Australia: Pearson Education, Frenchs Forest: Pearson Education Australia.

Seidlhofer, B. (2010). Lingua franca English. *The Routledge Handbook of World Englishes*, 355.

Sharma, S. (2007). Marketing success, defining ethnicity: South Asian print media in the US. *South Asian Popular Culture*, 5, 179–191.

Smolicz, J., Secombe, M. and Hudson, D. (2001). Family collectivism and minority languages as core values of culture among ethnic groups in Australia. *Journal of Multilingual and Multicultural Development*, 2, 152–172.

Stayman, D. and Deshpandé, R. (1989). Situational ethnicity and consumer behavior. *Journal of Consumer Research*, 16(3), 361–371.

Stevenson, A. (ed.) (2010). *Oxford Dictionary of English*. Oxford, USA: Oxford University Press.

Sun, T., Horn, M. and Merritt, D. (2004). Values and lifestyles of individualists and collectivists: A study on Chinese, Japanese, British and US consumers. *Journal of Consumer Marketing*, 21(5), 318–331.

Tajfel, H. (1981). *Human Groups and Social Categories: Studies in Social Psychology*. Cambridge: Cambridge University Press Archive.

Therrien, M. and Ramirez, R. (2001). The Hispanic population in the United States. *Current Population Reports*, 20–535.

Ting-Toomey, S. (1981). Ethnic identity and close friendship in Chinese-American college students. *International Journal of Intercultural Relations*, 5(4), 383–406.

Van Der Gaag, M. and Snijders, T. (2005). The resource generator: Social capital quantification with concrete items. *Social Networks*, 27(1), 1–29.

Van Oudenhoven, J. and Hofstra, J. (2006). Personal reactions to "strange" situations: Attachment styles and acculturation attitudes of immigrants and majority members. *International Journal of Intercultural Relations*, 30(6), 783–798.

Wan, E. and Vanderwerf, M. (2010). A review of the literature on "ethnicity" and "national identity" and related missiological studies. *Global Missiology English*, 3(6).

Wentz, L. (2003). Pepsis puts interests before ethnicity. *Advertising Age*, July 7, 74(27), S24.

Wiley, S. (2013). Rejection-identification among Latino immigrants in the United States. *International Journal of Intercultural Relations*, 37(3), 375–384.

Wimmer, A. (2008). Elementary strategies of ethnic boundary making. *Ethnic and Racial Studies*, 31(6), 1025–1055.

Xu, J., Shim, S., Lotz, S. and Almeida, D. (2004). Ethnic identity socialization factors, and culture-specific consumption behavior. *Psychology & Marketing*, 21, 93–112.

Yeh, C. and Huang, K. (1996). The collectivistic nature of ethnic identity development among Asian-American college students. *Adolescence*, 31(123), 645.

Yinger, J. (1985). Ethnicity. *Annual Review of Sociology*, 11, 151–180.

Yinger, J. (1976). Ethnicity in complex societies. In A. Lewis, et al. (eds.), *The Uses of Controversy in Sociology*. New York: Free Press, pp. 197–216.

3 Acculturation, the Minority Ethnic Group and Ethnic Consumer Behaviour

The previous chapters sought to ascertain the underlying foundations of ethnic marketing, and to some extent to ethnic entrepreneurship, reaching a suitable conceptualization that can be used to assess the requirements for ethnic marketing and its potential effectiveness. Two critical concepts were identified in Chapter 2: the ethnic group and ethnic identity. The two concepts are closely interlinked with the strength of ethnic identity of individual group members, and that strength may influence the coherence and importance of the group to its individual members, as well as these members' dependence on the group, including that of associated ethnic minority businesses.

Even in an economically and socially stable, multicultural society with no population growth through immigration, the group's collective values, beliefs and behaviours can change as a result of changes in the individual ethnic identities of its members as their social identities develop through the acculturation process. If there are large migrant inflows from countries with cultures very different from the dominant host culture, the acculturation processes of the new arrivals and of their children born in the host country are likely to have significant impact on the group that can influence the value that can be expected from the implementation of an ethnic marketing strategy.

In order to pave our way to better understanding when the necessary conditions exist, and how to implement an ethnic marketing strategy, which are issues discussed later in this text, we need to consider how acculturation patterns can impact on a person's ethnic identity and thus on the ethnic group. From the perspective of group stability and whether groups may converge, perhaps stimulating ethnic entrepreneurship and/or enabling pan ethnic groups for marketing purposes, it is necessary to know how individual acculturation affects the consumer behaviour of consumers with a common ethnic background, and whether the individual acculturation paths of consumers from different ethnic backgrounds are likely to differ.

This chapter has a focus on the social construction of ethnic groups and on the dynamics of changes that ensue through group interactions. A summary of the various definitions of acculturation is discussed including the different schools of thought on acculturation and the different acculturation strategies that may be employed by an ethnic individual. Given that there is an acculturation process over time when persons from different cultures interact, the impact of acculturation on an individual's ethnic identity and consumer behaviour is examined to address intergenerational and inter-group differences that may arise.

What Is Acculturation?

There are many definitions for acculturation. The definitions below highlight the varying points of view on how acculturation is perceived by different researchers. A number of researchers discuss acculturation in terms of migration from an old culture to a country or region with a different culture and the processes of either assimilation, adaptation, maintenance or resistance to the new culture or country by the migrating group. Other researchers discuss acculturation in terms of the change in values and behaviours of one group or more, or the sense of belonging and or conformance to the host culture. Table 3.1 compiles alternative perspectives of acculturation covering its conceptualization, what it involves and its consequences.

Considerable diversity is evident in these various definitions, some with troubling implications. For example:

- Levels of acculturation (Kara and Kara, 1996) treat acculturation as both a process and an outcome, with high acculturation implying a continuum of either closer movement to what Berry and Sam (1997) would describe as assimilation or retention of the home culture values, neither which are necessary outcomes.
- Consumer acculturation (Ogden, Ogden and Schau, 2004) separates consumer behaviour from the overall behaviour and social identity of the consumer. It also treats acculturation as a learning process of a new culture, assuming that will be the host culture, as per Gordon (1964), excluding a multicultural environment and thus a wider range of options.

More general definitions are offered by Peñaloza (1994, 2006), referring to acculturation as involving interaction and adaptation, as well as Berry and Sam (1997), who focus on a process of learning about other cultural groups when exposed to each other and the need to interact. But acculturation definitions increasingly reflect a movement to a social constructivist perspective of ethnicity and ethnic identity, referring to acculturation as a process of social and psychological change that arises from intercultural contact both at an individual and group level (Berry et al., 2006), which can arise through migration and/or colonization.

Group and individual processes should be separated, Berry and Sam (1997, p. 298) using the term *psychological acculturation* to refer to an

Table 3.1 Illustrative Perspectives on Acculturation

Acculturation		
Involves	A general term that encompasses intercultural interaction and adaptation and includes assimilation of a new culture, maintenance of the old culture and resistance to both new and old culture.	Peñaloza (1994), Quester, Karunaratna and Chong (2001)
	The exposure of the individual to a new culture through migration or colonization to another culture.	Berry and Sam (1997) and Sam and Berry (1995)
	A sense of self-identification with either the host culture or to their ethnic origin, including the extent of the conformance of the individual to the host culture.	Gordon (1964) Hui, Laroche and Kim (1998) Kim, Laroche and Joy (1990) Yinger (1976)
Is a process	Of adapting to the cultural environment in the host country by an individual from a different country.	Peñaloza (2006)
	Of learning a culture that is different from the one in which a person was raised.	Valencia (1985) Dublish (2001)
Causes	A change in values and behaviours in one or more cultural groups.	Berry (1997, 1980) Dublish (2001) Jamal and Chapman (2000) Laroche, Kim and Hui (1997c) Laroche, Kim and Tomiuk (1998) and Laroche, Pons and Richard (2009) Schiffman et al. (2009)
Can be	High: if an individual has progressed towards the values and attitudes of the host culture. Low: if an individual has maintained the values and attitudes of their ethnic origin.	Kara and Kara (1996)
Applied to consumption	Is a socialization process of learning values, attitudes and behaviours of a culture that is different from the individual's culture of origin.	Ogden, Ogden and Schau (2004)

individual's response resulting from this encounter. For most individuals, adaptation to the new cultural context is dependent upon a variety of factors and can take many different forms ranging from assimilation or integration into the dominant culture to extreme marginalization or segregation. Understanding the process at both individual and group levels is essential if marketers are to develop ethnic marketing strategies based on sound segmentation principles.

Acculturation Phases

Berry (1980) first argued the need to focus on an individual migrant's links to both their culture of origin as well as to their society of settlement to understand the process of acculturation. Likewise, Phinney (1990) has also argued that there are two independent dimensions underlying people's cultural identity. The implication is that an individual can have an independent identity with respect to their culture of origin and to the culture where they have settled. Berry and Sam (1997) have used these two dimensions to construct a framework of four possible alternative acculturation strategies, shown in Table 3.2.

Integration involves individuals seeking to maintain the cultural identity of their ethnic heritage while embracing part of the cultural identity of the host culture. *Assimilation* involves individuals seeking to adopt the cultural identity of the host culture by rejecting the cultural identity of their ethnic heritage. *Separation* or *Rejection* involves individuals seeking to maintain the cultural identity of their ethnic heritage by rejecting the cultural identity of the host culture. *Marginalization* or *de-culturation* involves individuals rejecting the cultural identity of the host culture and also rejecting the cultural identity of their cultural heritage.

Manifestation of these strategies can be expressed in terms of acculturation attitudes, such as preferences for involvement in one or both cultures or none, as well as behaviours engaged in by the individual, including preferred language use, music preferences, food preferences as well as social relationships.

While depicted as a rational choice in terms of an end state, the use of the term strategy is perhaps unfortunate. Berry and Sam (1997) note constraints can be related to context, with the host country conditions influencing the ability to follow a particular path. Further, individuals may explore various options rather than a linear acculturation path. In short, there is no predetermined age or stage in life that these acculturation methods are employed and nor are they employed sequentially. Indeed,

Table 3.2 Alternative Acculturation Strategies

Issue	*Is it considered of value to maintain one's cultural identity and values?*	
	Yes	*No*
Is it considered of value to maintain relationships with the dominant society?	Yes	Integration assimilation
	No	Separation marginalization

Adapted from Berry and Sam (1997).

as discussed in Chapter 2, individuals may opt for a strategy-outcome of self-disidentification—an active negation of any association with a group (Becker and Tausch, 2014; McCall, 2003), and rejection-identification is also possible—when people perceive that they are rejected because of a group membership, identification with that group can increase (Wiley, 2013). Ultimately, different strategies may be tried before an individual decides upon one that works best for her or him.

Ethnic groups, as the collective entity of similar self-ascribed individuals, can therefore follow similar individual acculturation paths (Berry and Sam, 1997, p. 297):

1. Integration: ethnic groups members maintain their cultural identity yet also seek interaction with other cultures;
2. Assimilation: ethnic groups members abandon their cultural identity and seek interaction with other cultures;
3. Separation: ethnic group members maintain their cultural identity and shun interaction with other cultures;
4. Segregation: when the host culture or dominant group rejects the cultural identity of ethnic minority groups and their members and avoid interaction.

Indicators of Acculturation

Acculturation can be observed through *behavioural* and *socio-cultural* changes. *Behavioural* changes include:

1. Culture Learning—learning the host language, trying local foods, dressing like the mainstream population and learning the social norms of the host culture;
2. Culture Shedding—discarding the social norms associated with the culture of origin in favour of the social norms of the host culture; and
3. Culture Conflict—the individual perceives the norms, attitudes and values of the host culture to be incompatible with the norms, attitudes and values of her (or his) culture of origin.

(Berry and Sam, 1997, pp. 301–302)

Behavioural indicators of individual acculturation used by researchers include changing language, music and media and communication preferences, food preferences and participation in cultural events (Laroche, Kim and Tomiuk, 1998; Laroche, Pons and Richard, 2009).

Socio-cultural changes include adapting one's cultural knowledge, social skills and relationships with family, friends and the community to integrate into mainstream culture (Berry and Sam, 1997, pp. 301–302). For example, the ethnic background of an individual's spouse (or partner) and closest friends provides an indication of her (or his) acculturation level (Garcia, 1982; Laroche, Pons and Richard, 2009). A less acculturated individual is more likely to have a social and personal network from within their own ethnic community, whereas a highly acculturated individual is more likely to have a social and personal network of friends from outside their ethnic community, in particular from the mainstream culture (Xu et al., 2004).

Acculturation Forces

Acculturation cannot be investigated in isolation from the influence of home and host country links. From the home country, these may include its language, arts, religion, values, political and economic situation, as well as support and services provided to emigrants. For example, Portugal currently seeks to reinvigorate the actual connection of its citizens living abroad by implementing a variety of measures that may include financial incentives for return migration, advertising online of job opportunities "at home", sponsored tertiary education in the home country for descendants of emigrants and similar appellative tactics (ACM, 2015).

From the host country perspective, the host culture's immigration history and settlement policies, including societal attitudes towards immigration, as well as the contrasts and similarities between home and host countries also influence chosen acculturation paths as do the demographic characteristics (e.g. age, gender, education) of the individual or group undergoing the acculturation process (Berry, 1997).

Clearly, following Aronowitz (1992)'s recommendation, the objective in the present discussion is to understand how these different factors impact upon the migration process to affect how people adapt to their new settlement society. The process of acculturation is potentially influenced and moderated by many possible variables. Berry and Sam (1997) organized these into five categories, identified in Table 3.3.

The diverse influences that shape individual acculturation paths suggest that such paths are basically unpredictable. The link between migrant inflows and the size and growth of ethnic groups, and hence their relevance for ethnic entrepreneurship and for marketing purposes, cannot be based on a person's ethnic origin because of the contextual influences that will shape their ethnic identity and thus their identification, if any, with a particular ethnic group.

Acculturation is also influenced by a number of factors such as a person's age, the age they were when they migrated to the host country, the level of education achieved in their country of origin versus the level of education achieved in the host country, the individual's social and informal business networks and the host country's immigration policy.

All the noted factors affect how individuals adapt to the host country. For example, age at time of migration is relevant because older

Table 3.3 Influencers/Moderators on the Acculturation Process

Sources	Examples of Variables
Society of origin (alias *home country* and *country of provenance*)	*Ethnographic* such as language, values; *Political* such as instability, oppression; *Demographic* such as population pressures; *Economic* such as poverty, inequality.
Society of settlement (alias *host country*)	Immigration policy; Attitudes to immigration; Attitudes to particular ethnic groups or phenotypes.
Group acculturation	Changes occurring in the acculturating group.
Moderating factors prior to acculturation	*Demographic*—age; gender; education; *Economic*—status; expectations; *Personal*—health, motives driving migration; expectations.
Moderating factors during acculturation	Acculturation strategies; Contact and participation; Social support sources.

Adapted from Berry and Sam (1997), Table 8.1.

migrants are assumed to have a stronger sense of the cultural values of their country of origin and therefore may reject, resist, or take time to adapt or adopt the host culture. In comparison, younger migrants are assumed to be too young to have fully embraced the cultural values of their parents' country of origin—exposure to the host culture through school and peers from outside their ethnic group therefore may cause conflicting identity issues (Berry, 1989; Berry and Sam, 1997; Phinney, 1992; Phinney, 1990; Lee and DeVos, 1981). Costigan, Su and Hua (2009) agree saying that children adjust and settle to the host environment and therefore acculturate at a faster rate than their migrant parents.

Yeh and Huang (1996) provide another perspective and assert that the development of ethnic identity is a unique process that is influenced by external factors, such as the perceptions of the host culture towards Asians and the social interactions that are encountered. Costa and Bamossy (1995) expand on this view, affirming that culture is dynamic, constantly evolving and adapting to external influences. Interaction between groups may induce more change in one group than in another.

Choice of Acculturation Path

There are different schools of thought on the direction of acculturation by different groups. One school of thought follows the belief that as ethnic minorities adopt the traits, values and norms of the host culture, aspects of their culture of origin is lost (Keefe and Padilla, 1987; Nwankwo and Lindridge, 1998; Laroche, Kim and Tomiuk, 1998; Phinney, 1990), implying an assimilation or integration path. Acculturation is seen as lessening an individual's ties to his or her ethnic identity (Dublish, 2001; Deshpandé, Hoyer and Donthu, 1986; O'Guinn and Faber, 1985). For example, some American research findings have concluded Asian-Americans were ". . . *well assimilated in the [host] culture*" from their desire to achieve success in mainstream society (Dublish, 2001, p. 26; Delener and Neelankavil, 1990; Faulkner, 1998). These findings imply that, for well-assimilated Asian-Americans, there may be very little disparity between their consumption behaviour and that of individuals from the host culture (Dublish, 2001). Kara and Kara (1996) used the term "highly acculturated" to describe Hispanic-Americans who displayed similar purchase behaviour to Anglo-Americans.

Another school of thought on acculturation proposes the opposite outcomes. Researchers (Jamal and Chapman, 2000; Laroche, Kim and Hui, 1997b) argue that ethnic identity can remain unaltered despite social interactions with, and adoption of the values and norms of the dominant culture—a view supported by Miller's study that ". . . *immigrants are increasingly trying to maintain their cultural identities*" (Miller, 1993; Rajagopalan and Heitmeyer, 2005, p. 84). Solomon (1996) concurs that as a result of progressive learning, ". . . *people gradually learn a new culture as they increasingly come in contact with it*" (p. 479), yet still maintain their ethnic identity. Therefore, it can be conjectured that consumption behaviour for these individuals will remain distinct from those of the host culture.

Both schools of thought support Berry and Sam (1997)'s idea that two independent dimensions influence the acculturation path: the value of maintaining ethnic traditions and the value of learning the traditions and values of the host culture (Dohrenwend and Smith, 1962; Laroche, Kim and Tomiuk, 1998).

Individual Acculturation

Acculturation paths vary between ethnic groups and within these ethnic groups its members also vary in their acculturation paths. For example, although the ethnic group to which the individual identifies with may be integrating the host culture, within the ethnic group itself there may still be some individuals who seek to maintain their ethnic identity by wearing their ethnic dress, conversing in their native tongue, consuming ethnic food and upholding their ethnic customs, traditions and beliefs, some much more strongly than others (Rajagopalan and Heitmeyer, 2005). An individual's acculturation can also be affected by other factors such as the place of residence and the amount of contact the individual has with the host culture. Context impacts on acculturation, thereby accounting for differences within the ethnic group or its heterogeneity (Ogden, Ogden and Schau, 2004).

Other studies support this view that the process of acculturation is individualistic in nature as people ". . . *vary greatly in the degree to which they participate in these community changes*" (Berry and Sam, 1997, p. 294). The behaviour of those who identify strongly with their ethnic group or community will reflect those values and social mores representative of their ethnic group or community such as ". . . *customs, language, dress, foods, religion, product use* . . ." (Appiah, 2004, p. 314). Indeed, the mitigating factor of acculturation on ethnic identity is such that a number of researchers (Berry and Sam, 1997; Laroche, Kim and Tomiuk, 1998; Verbeke and López, 2005) use it to measure the maintenance and/ or retention ". . . *of the culture of origin*" (Verbeke and López, 2005, p. 836). Thus, it can be argued that differences in psychological acculturation impact on the accuracy (Chattalas and Harper, 2007) of measuring the effects of one's ethnicity on her (or his) consumption behaviour. This difference is likely to be evident, especially in the consumption behaviour of the younger generation moving away from the more ". . . *traditional norms of their parents' culture*" (Chattalas and Harper, 2007, p. 353), but following Berry and Sam (1997) this is but one of several possible paths.

A number of researchers agree that language, food, media preferences (O'Guinn and Faber, 1985), participating in cultural events and having friends of various cultural backgrounds, in particular from the mainstream culture (Laroche, Kim and Tomiuk, 1998; Laroche, Pons and Richard, 2009; Phinney, 1990) within an individual's close circle of friends, are good indicators of their acculturation path (Garcia, 1982; Laroche, Kim and Tomiuk, 1998). Further, an individual's acculturation path can also be explained by the ethnic background of their spouse/ partner and their closest friends. An individual less integrated in the host society than another is more likely to have a social and personal network from within their own ethnic community, whereas a more highly integrated (to the host culture) individual is more likely to have a social and personal network of friends from outside their ethnic community (Quester, Karunaratna and Chong, 2001, p. 16; Montero, 1981).

Inter-Generational Differences

Both inter-generational similarities and differences have been found in consumer behaviour. Kim and Kang (2001) found inter-generational *similarities* in consumer behaviour amongst consumers from the same ethnic background in their use of information sources, product selection and in the frequenting of particular stores. However, as a result of the individual nature of the acculturation process, inter-generational *differences* in consumer behaviour between members within an ethnic group are probably more likely (Chung and Fischer, 1999a; Chung and Fischer, 1999b; Rajagopalan and Heitmeyer, 2005; Jimenez et al., 2013;

Kizgin, 2016). These differences may not transpose into consistent directions of acculturation between generations. For example, Kizgin (2016) has found third generations born to original Turkish migrants had a stronger ethnic identity than the second generation. A very large, cross-sectional Canadian survey (Statistics Canada, 2003) across ethnic groups revealed something similar. While the first generation had a much higher percentage of respondents holding a strong sense of belonging to their ethnic group than subsequent generations, the second generation fell away while the third generation was slightly higher.

Inter-generational differences in consumer behaviour cannot be looked at in isolation of the acculturation process because these differences are influenced by the forces of acculturation (Berry, 1997; Berry, 1980; Chae and Foley, 2010). Each individual within the ethnic group may have a different acculturation path, or may have undertaken different acculturation strategies (Ozcaglar-Toulouse et al., 2009) which may influence their consumer behaviour accordingly. Following Quester, Karunaratna and Chong, 2001), differences in inter-generational consumer behaviour may be attributed to:

- an individual's country of birth,
- language,
- amount of time spent overseas versus in the host country,
- ethnic identity,
- the frequency of travels to the homeland,
- the ethnicity or ethnic background of the individual's spouse and three closest friends and
- the individual's residential status in the host country.

But other influencers have been identified. Also observed is the important role of the family unit (Huijnk, Verkuyten and Coenders, 2013) with family life in the country of residence and in the host country either encouraging socio-cultural maintenance or influencing attitudes towards social-cultural adaptation. For example, Myers and Lumbers' (2008, p. 297) study of older shoppers found "inherent differences across [and within] generations" that impact upon the generation's consumer behaviour. Other supporting literature from various researchers (Lumpkin, 1985; Lumpkin and Greenberg, 1982; Martin, 1976; Pingol and Miyazaki, 2005; Seock and Bailey, 2009) highlight notable differences between age groups in terms of their preferred information source. The younger generation displayed a preference for friends as their main information source for service and product choices in comparison to the older generation who relied on family, relatives and respected members of their community as their main information source. Inter-generational differences in acculturation paths therefore reflect consumer choices.

Acculturation and Ethnic Identity

Acculturation influences an individual's ethnic identity. A number of researchers concur that ethnic identity varies ". . . *with development and experience, and with changes in the social and historical context*" (Phinney, 1992. p. 160). Due to the dynamic nature of ethnic identity, the process and impact of acculturation may influence decision-making and therefore consumer behaviour. Studies of Asian-Americans revealed a circular link between an individual's cultural adjustment and the strength of their ethnic identity (Chae and Foley, 2010). Moreover, Ogden, Ogden and Schau (2004) state that the strength of an individual's feelings towards their ethnic identity may influence their acculturation level, thus shaping their ethnic identity.

Studies show that children and young adults of parents less acculturated to the host culture have a stronger sense of their ethnic identity than children and young adults of parents more highly acculturated to the host culture, the latter being more inclined to adopt the culture of the host country and less likely to inform their children of their ethnic heritage. The strength of a child's and young adult's ethnic identity is developed and strengthened through parental influence from parents who have maintained close ties to their ethnic roots. Moreover, children and young adults who have friendships with peers from their own ethnic background have also been shown to have positive feelings towards their ethnic identity (Hui, Laroche and Kim, 1998; Phinney, 1992; Phinney, 1990; Xu et al., 2004).

Individuals are more likely to perceive their ethnic identity differently once they ". . . adopt the cultural traits of the host culture during the acculturation process" (Hui, Laroche and Kim, 1998, p. 872). By understanding how acculturation may change the way individuals perceive their ethnicity and ethnic identity, marketers can make an informed decision to *aggregate* ethnic groups where there are significant similarities in consumption pattern or *segment* ethnic groups where there are significant differences in consumption pattern (Pires and Stanton, 2000).

Acculturation and Consumer Behaviour

According to Quester, Karunaratna and Chong (2001, p. 8), ". . . *a consumer's degree of acculturation to a host culture may be a[n] . . . important predictor of purchase behaviour*". Leo, Bennett and Hartel (2005) found that the host culture may influence the consumer behaviour of individuals via acculturation. This view is reinforced by Kwok and Uncles (2005, p. 170) who maintain that consumer behaviour is influenced by ". . . cultural differences at national and ethnic-group levels . . ." As shown in some studies, individuals who did not identify with their ethnic heritage often displayed similar consumer behaviour patterns to those from the host culture (Kara and Kara, 1996) whilst other studies revealed there were marked differences in the consumption behaviour of ethnic minorities (e.g. Hispanics) and individuals from the host culture (e.g. Anglo-Saxon-Celtics) towards product attributes (O'Guinn and Faber, 1985).

Although an individual (or a group) maintains aspects of their ethnic origin, with time and increased exposure to a different culture the individual (or group) undergoes some alteration to their consumption behaviour (Palumbo and Teich, 2004; Chattalas and Harper, 2007). Over time, the acculturation of an ethnic consumer will impact on their ". . . *consumption and buying patterns*" (Khairullah and Khairullah, 1999; Rajagopalan and Heitmeyer, 2005, p. 85). A study on the food consumption behaviour of Hispanics living in Belgium found the process of acculturation on one's dietary behaviour and attitude a slow process of change (Verbeke and López, 2005).

Acculturation ". . . *affects a variety of marketing behaviors including consumption and buying patterns . . .*" (Dublish, 2001, p. 24). A study on the consumption behaviour of Chinese-Australians found that acculturation affected ". . . *the decision-making processes . . .*" (Quester, Karunaratna and Chong, 2001, p. 8) with differences in acculturation resulting in different purchase behaviour patterns. Ogden, Ogden and Schau, 2004, p. 4) describe this process of acculturation as consumer acculturation—a socialization process that ". . . *is specific to the consumption process . . . in which an immigrant consumer learns the behaviors, attitudes and values of a culture that are different from their culture of origin*". Through the process of socialization between immigrants and the host culture, the mutual influence between both will likely cause changes in consumption behaviour for both immigrants and the host (Luna and Gupta, 2001), thus highlighting the importance of the role played by acculturation on an individual's consumption behaviour.

A study into the differences in acculturation levels of Chinese-Australians and its influence on their decision-making process was carried out by Quester, Karunaratna and Chong (2001). The study sample of Chinese-Australian consumers was categorized into high acculturated, medium acculturated and low acculturated (to the host culture). Using Kara and Kara's classification (1996), high acculturated consumers were defined as those consumers who demonstrated greater adoption of the attitudes and values of the Australian culture (Quester, Karunaratna and Chong, 2001, p. 8). Conversely, low acculturated consumers were defined as consumers who maintained the values, beliefs and behaviour of their ethnic origin. The authors argued that the ethnic group an individual self-identifies with determines the degree of commitment and influence exerted by that ethnic group, resulting in differences in consumer patterns and decision-making. Similarly, another study of Chinese-Americans and Filipino-Americans found ". . . *significant differences between high and*

low acculturation groups" and the influence that acculturation has on
". . . *the shopping behaviour of ethnic minority groups*" (Ownbey and
Horridge, 1997).

By understanding how the process of psychological and socio-cultural
acculturation affects an individual, we learn how consumer acculturation may influence an individual's consumer behaviour (Berry, 1997).
Peñaloza (1994) links ethnic identity, acculturation and consumer behaviour by segmenting consumers into three consumer acculturation groups
(earlier identified as acculturation indicators):

1. Consumers who assimilate into the mainstream culture (Berry and
   Sam's *Assimilation*) by adopting the norms of the host society. This
   is also known as *culture shedding* (Berry, 1997);
2. Consumers who maintain their heritage culture yet do not adopt the
   mainstream culture (Berry and Sam's *Separation*). These consumers
   may develop *culture conflict* (Berry, 1997); and,
3. Consumers who adopt elements of mainstream culture but also
   retain their heritage culture (Berry and Sam's *Integration*). This
   involves *culture learning* (Berry, 1997).

Hui, Laroche and Kim (1998) sought to explain the relationship between
acculturation and consumer behaviour through a typology of consumption based on two ethnicity indicators of a person's ethnic origin, indicative of their likely consumption preferences; and actual media usage,
indicative of their consumed media and information preferences (refer to
Table 3.4).

The five alternative acculturation strategies bear similarities to prior
literature:

1. Cultural incorporation involve ethnic minorities adopting the ". . .
   consumption or lifestyle patterns . . . of the host group" while retaining their cultural customs (Mendoza, 1989; Hui, Laroche and Kim,
   1998, p. 874). This is akin to Berry and Sam's *integration* strategy.

Table 3.4 Typology of Consumption Based on Two Ethnicity Indicators

Product or Lifestyle Consumption a Function of		Yes	No
Ethnic origin (a reflective ethnicity indicator)	Yes	Cultural incorporation	Cultural shift OR cultural transmutation
Media usage (a formative ethnicity indicator)	No	Cultural resistance	Non-cultural

Adapted from Mendoza (1989) cited in Hui, Laroche and Kim (1998, p. 874).

2. Cultural transmutation involves ethnic minorities avowing their cultural heritage but also adopting mainstream culture, resulting in "... *a unique subcultural entity*" (Mendoza, 1989; Hui, Laroche and Kim, 1998, p. 875).

3. Cultural shift is the process of assimilation whereby ethnic minorities modify their "... *consumption behavior and lifestyle* ..." to mirror the behaviour and lifestyle of the host culture (Mendoza, 1989; Hui, Laroche and Kim, 1998, p. 874).

4. Cultural resistance is the process whereby ethnic minorities maintain their ethnic customs while refusing to acquire the customs of the host group. Consumer behaviour in this instance is "... *a function of ethnic origin* ..." as there are no changes to consumer behaviour regardless of increased contact with mainstream culture (Mendoza, 1989; Hui, Laroche and Kim, 1998, p. 874). This is akin to Berry and Sam's *separation* strategy.

5. Consumer behaviour is considered non-ethnic or non-cultural when "... *there is no difference in ... consumption* ..." (Mendoza, 1989; Hui, Laroche and Kim, 1998, p. 875).

Some aspects of consumer behaviour exhibited by ethnic minorities are so "... *ingrained in the minority culture* ..." (Hui, Laroche and Kim, 1998, p. 873) that they are not as easily changed. Culture-specific activities such as attending ethnic festivals are unlikely to be as amenable to acculturation as cultural-irrelevant activities that are highly utilitarian or functional in their intent (Lee and Tse, 1994). Research findings (Hui, Laroche and Kim, 1998) support this assertion that there are: (1) certain cultural-specific consumption behaviours where there is very little difference between acculturated ethnic groups versus un-acculturated ethnic groups; and (2) non-cultural consumption behaviours where there is little to no difference between ethnic minority groups and the host group.

Acculturation and Ethnic Group Dynamics

The process of acculturation suggests the possibility that in a multicultural society new arrivals can form their ethnic identity in the context of exposure and interaction to different ethnic groups, eventually identifying with one particular ethnic group. The strength of ethnic identity of new and existing group members changes over time due to the forces influencing acculturation, indicating a particular process of acculturation. Consideration of where alternative paths lead provides guidance to marketers in their assessment of the potential closeness between some groups, with that assessment leading to the consideration of pan ethnic groups, a focus of Chapter 4.

The Acculturation Process in a Culturally Diverse Country

Figure 3.1 below provides a diagrammatic approach to understanding the acculturation alternatives: Assume two possible home or source countries (A' and B'), one host country (C) and two minority ethnic groups (A and B), residing in the host country. (A) is the expatriate group of (A'). (B) is the expatriate group of (B').

Focusing on migrants from A', depending on their strength of ethnic identity, the new arrivals may acculturate towards the dominant host culture (C) (assimilate), effectively merging into the host culture. They may acculturate to their home country minority ethnic group whilst seeking to minimize interaction with the host group, represented by the light area A (separation). Alternatively, some may seek to learn and adapt to the host culture while retaining their ethnic identity and group links, effectively bi-cultural, shown by the area AC (an integration strategy). Marginalization, the process rejecting both cultures, is not shown.

Migrants from B' have similar options. Also possible is that if migrants from A' and B' have close cultural proximity the acculturation path may lead to either A or B or an emerging AB group. The broken lines reflect the possibility that the sets of values in each area change over time, towards (cross-acculturation) or apart from each other. Each area represents a potentially unique and homogeneous segment.

A range of acculturation paths and possible outcomes may result from the settlement of new arrivals in an advanced, culturally diverse country. Depending on personal and environmental circumstances a new arrival

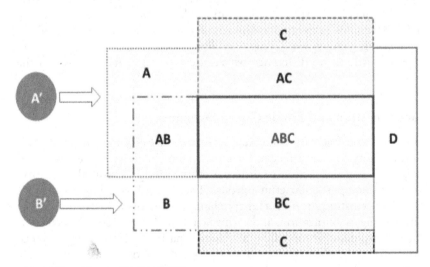

Adapted from Pires and Stanton (2015)

Figure 3.1 The Acculturation Process in a Culturally Diverse Country

will acculturate into one of a variety of different ethnic groups or to the dominant host culture. It follows that descriptors such as country of origin, birthplace or nationality are likely to be poor measures of the size of an ethnic group and poor indicators of its potential for segmentation

A minority ethnic group may maintain its identity because new arrivals perceive greater value from acculturating to an ethnic group that is closer to their culture of origin than to the dominant host culture. Arguably, adjusting to a culture in close proximity to one's own can reduce stress (Mendenhall and Oddou, 1985) arising from psychological uncertainty engendered by a new learning situation (Black, Mendenhall and Oddou, 1991). Learning is facilitated if an experienced person can guide a neophyte in the new environment (Mendenhall and Oddou, 1985), but such a relationship is more likely if there is cultural proximity. Thus, acculturating towards an ethnic group closer to their own culture of origin can provide the new arrival with a network of communications and a frame of reference for behaviour within the host country that fosters a relationship with the group.

The identification of similarities and differences between ethnic groups within a culturally diverse nation, and how these change over time, is important in making a segmentation decision in the context of ethnic marketing. The three-dimensional framework developed in this chapter illustrates how group boundaries can be defined, some of the dynamics that may cause changing ethnic boundaries over time as well as the interrelationship between ethnicity and the acculturation process in culturally diverse countries.

An evaluation of the ethnic marketing relevance of ethnic groups requires an analysis that is dynamic and involves assessment of ethnic identity and ethnic intensity, variables themselves influenced by acculturation. The rationale for the framework is that ethnic identity is socially constructed and shaped through interactions. The manner in which that ethnic identity evolves, and the importance or strength of that identity to an individual, will be reflected in the ethnic group.

Summary

Ethnic marketing strategies are predicated on a strong understanding of the values, attitudes and behaviours of each ethnic group, especially in terms of distinguishing their significant commonalities and differences. The social construction of ethnic groups and the dynamics of changes that ensues through group interactions were the focus of this chapter.

The chapter outlined different viewpoints and definitional differences in explaining acculturation, necessitating selection of a preferred approach based on acculturation as a social construction process. Groups and individuals may seek to choose acculturation strategies that may accentuate their differences and isolation from other groups over time, to strategies that eventually lead to the loss of group identity and marketing relevance. Examination of these strategies reveals a complex interaction between groups, as well as between the group and the interactions of those identifying with that group.

Corroborating the conclusion in Chapter 2, an ethnic group will consist of individuals with varying strengths of ethnic identity as well as having varying strengths of ties to other group members and those external to this ethnic group. Groups that retain a strong and salient identity over time are likely to offer more opportunities for ethnic entrepreneurship such that, as discussed in Chapters 6 and 7, Groups can convert into incubators for ethnic minority businesses, positively influencing ethnic networks as well as the acculturation process of individuals and groups.

The forces that help to shape alternative acculturation strategies needed to be examined in order to understand the choice by either an individual or group towards a particular acculturation path. Complicating our understanding of any particular group will be the need to understand that inter-generational differences will exist within any group in terms of their interaction within the group and perhaps their strength of ethnic identity. Differences in acculturation strategies at both group and individual level will give rise to differences in information and consumption preferences that also need to be understood. In short, an understanding of the acculturation process is important to understanding ethnic group dynamics and the case for aggregating ethnic groups for marketing purposes, discussed in Chapter 4.

References

ACM—Alto Comissariado para as Migrações, I. P. (2015). Strategic plan for migration (2015–2020). *Republica Portuguesa*. Accessed 4/8/2018 at www.acm.gov.pt/documents/10181/222357/PEM_ACM_final.pdf

Appiah, O. (2004). Effects of ethnic identification on web browsers' attitudes toward and navigational patterns on race-targeted sites. *Communications Research*, June, 31(3), 312–337.

Aronowitz, M. (1992). Adjustment of immigrant children as a function of parental attitudes to change. *International Migration Review*, 26, 86–110.

Becker, J. and Tausch, N. (2014). When group memberships are negative: The concept, measurement, and behavioral implications of psychological disidentification. *Self and Identity*, 13(3), 294–321.

Berry, J. (1997). Immigration, acculturation, and adaptation. *Applied Psychology: An International Review*, 46(1), 5–68.

Berry, J. (1989). Imposed etics-emics-derived etics: The operationalization of a compelling idea. *International Journal of Psychology*, 24, 721–735.

Berry, J. (1980). Acculturation as varieties of adaptation. In A. M. Padilla (ed.), *Acculturation: Theory, Models, and Some New Findings*. Boulder: Westview, pp. 9–25.

Berry, J., Phinney, J., Sam, D. and Vedder, P. (2006). Immigrant youth: Acculturation, identity and adaptation. *Applied Psychology: An International Review*, 55(3), 303–332.

Berry, J. and Sam, D. (1997). Acculturation and Adaptation. *Handbook of Cross: Cultural Psychology*, 3, 291–326.

Black, J., Mendenhall, M. and Oddou, G. (1991). Toward a comprehensive model of international adjustment: An integration of multiple theoretical perspectives. *Academy of Management Review*, 14(2), 291–317.

Chae, M. and Foley, P. (2010). Relationship of ethnic identity, acculturation, and psychological well-being among Chinese, Japanese, and Korean Americans. *Journal of Counseling & Development*, 88(Fall), 466–476.

Chattalas, M. and Harper, H. (2007). Navigating a hybrid cultural identity: Hispanic teenagers' fashion consumption influences. *Journal of Consumer Marketing*, 24(6), 351–357.

Chung, E. and Fischer, E. (1999a). Embeddedness: Socialising the "social" construction of ethnicity. *International Journal of Sociology and Social Policy*, 19(12), 34–55.

Chung, E. and Fischer, E. (1999b). It's who you know: Intracultural differences in ethnic product consumption. *Journal of Consumer Marketing*, 16(5), 482–501.

Costa, J. and Bamossy, G. (1995). *Marketing in a multicultural world: Ethnicity, nationalism, and cultural identity*. Thousand Oaks, CA: Sage Publications.

Costigan, C., Su, T. and Hua, J. (2009). Ethnic identity among Chinese Canadian youth: A review of the Canadian literature. *Canadian Psychology*, November, 50(4), 261–272.

Delener, N. and Neelankavil, J. (1990). Informational sources and media usage. *Journal of Advertising Research*, 30(3), 45–52.

Deshpandé, R., Hoyer, W. and Donthu, N. (1986). The intensity of ethnic affiliation: A study of the sociology of hispanic consumption. *Journal of Consumer Research*, 13(2), 214–220.

Dohrenwend, B. and Smith, R. (1962). Toward a theory of acculturation. *Southwestern Journal of Anthropology*, 18(1), 30–39.

Dublish, S. (2001). Advertising to ethnic subcultures: A study with bilingual Korean-Americans. *Asia Pacific Journal of Marketing and Logistics*, 22–44.

Faulkner, K. (1998). "Can Asians as Asians belong here?" Cited in Dublish, S. (1998), "Advertising to ethnic subcultures: A study with bilingual Korean-Americans". *Asia Pacific Journal of Marketing and Logistics*, 22–44.

Garcia, J. (1982). Ethnicity and chicanos: Measurement of ethnic identification, identity, and consciousness. *Hispanic Journal of Behavioral Sciences*, 4(3), 295–314.

Gordon, M. (1964). *Assimilation in American life*. Oxford: Oxford University Press.

Hui, M., Laroche, M. and Kim, C. (1998). A typology of consumption based on ethnic origin and media usage. *European Journal of Marketing*, 32(9/10), 868–883.

Huijnk, W., Verkuyten, M. and Coenders, M. (2013). Family relations and the attitude towards ethnic minorities as close kin by marriage. *Ethnic and Racial Studies*, 36(11), 1890–1909.

Jamal, A. and Chapman, M. (2000). Acculturation and inter-ethnic consumer perceptions: Can you feel what we feel. *Journal of Marketing Management*, 16, 365–391.

Jimenez, F., Hadjimarcou, J., Barua, M. and Michie, D. (2013). A cross-national and cross-generational study of consumer acculturation to advertising appeals. *International Marketing Review*, 30(5), 418–439.

Kara, A. and Kara, N. (1996). Ethnicity and consumer choice: A study of hispanic decision processes across different acculturation levels. *Journal of Applied Business Research*, Spring, 12(2), 22–34.

Keefe, S. and Padilla, A. (1987). "*Chicano ethnicity*" cited in Laroche, Kim & Tomiuk 1999, "Italian ethnic identity and its relative impact on the consumption of convenience and traditional foods". *British Food Journal*, 101(3), 201–228.

Khairullah, D. and Khairullah, Z. (1999). Behavioural acculturation and demographic characteristics of Asian-Indian immigrants in the United States of America. *International Journal of Sociology and Social Policy*, 19(1/2), 57–80.

Kim, C., Laroche, M. and Joy, A. (1990). An empirical study of the effects on consumption patterns in a bi-cultural environment. *Advances in Consumer Research*, 17, 839–846.

Kim, Y.-K. and Kang, J. (2001). The effects of ethnicity and product on purchase decision making. *Journal of Advertising Research*, March–April, 39–48.

Kizgin, H. (2016). Integration, assimilation or separation? The implications for marketers of the Turkish Muslim consumers in the Netherlands. *Journal of Islamic Marketing*, 7(2), 187–221.

Kwok, S. and Uncles, M. (2005). Sales promotion effectiveness: The impact of consumer differences at an ethnic-group level. *Journal of Product & Brand Management*, 14(3), 170–186.

Laroche, M., Kim, C. and Hui, M. (1997b). A comparative investigation of dimensional structures of acculturation for Italian Canadians and Greek Canadians. *The Journal of Social Psychology*, 137(3), 317–331.

Laroche, M., Kim, C. and Hui, M. (1997c). The effects of ethnicity factors on consumer deal interests: An empirical study of French-English-Canadians. *Journal of Marketing Theory and Practice*, 5(1), 100–111.

Laroche, M., Kim, C. and Tomiuk, M. (1998). Italian ethnic identity and its relative impact on the consumption of convenience and traditional foods. *British Food Journal*, 101(2), 201–228.

Laroche, M., Pons, F. and Richard, M. (2009). The role of language in ethnic identity measurement: A multitrait-multimethod approach to construct validation. *The Ournal of Social Psychology*, 149(4), 513–539.

Lee, C. and Devos, G. (1981). *Koreans in Japan: Ethnic Conflict and Accommodation*. Berkeley, CA USA: University of California Press.

Lee, W. and Tse, D. (1994). Becoming Canadian: Understanding how Hong Kong immigrants change their consumption. *Pacific Affairs*, 70–95.

Leo, C., Bennett, R. and Hartel, C. (2005). Cross-cultural differences in consumer decision-making styles. *Cross Cultural Management*, 12(3), 32–62.

Lumpkin, J. (1985). Shopping orientation segmentation of the elderly consumer. *Journal of the Academy of Marketing Science*, 13(1–2), 271–289.

Lumpkin, J. and Greenberg, B. (1982). Apparel-shopping patterns of the elderly consumer. *Journal of Retailing*, 58(4), 68–89.

Luna, D. and Gupta, S. (2001). An integrative framework for cross-cultural consumer behavior. *International Marketing Review*, 18(1), 45–69.

Martin, Jr., C. (1976). A transgenerational comparison: The elderly fashion consumer. *Advances in Consumer Research*, 3(1).

McCall, G. (2003). The me and the not-me. In *Advances in Identity Theory and Research*. Boston, MA: Springer, pp. 11–25.

Mendenhall, M. and Oddou, G. (1985). The dimensions of expatriate acculturation: A review. *Academy of Management Review*, 10(1), 39–47.

Mendoza, R. (1989). An empirical scale to measure type and degree of acculturation in Mexican-American adolescents and adults. *Journal of Cross-Cultural Psychology*, 24(4), 372–385.

Miller, C. (1993). Researcher says US is more of a bowl than a pot. *Marketing News*, 27(10), 6.

Montero, D. (1981). The Japanese Americans: Changing patterns of assimilation over three generations. *American Sociological Review*, 829–839.

Myers, H. and Lumbers, M. (2008). Understanding older shoppers: A phenomenological investigation. *Journal of Consumer Marketing*, 25(5), 294–301.

Nwankwo, S. and Lindridge, A. (1998). Marketing to ethnic minorities in Britain. *Journal of Marketing Practice*, 4(7), 200–216.

Ogden, D., Ogden, J. and Schau, H. (2004). Exploring the impact of culture and acculturation on consumer purchase decisions: Toward a microcultural perspective. *Academy of Marketing Science Review*, 8(3), 1–22.

O'Guinn, T. and Faber, R. (1985). New perspectives on acculturation: The relationship of general and role specific acculturation with hispanics' consumer attitudes. *Advances in Consumer Research*, 12, 113–117.

Ownbey, S. and Horridge, P. (1997). Acculturation levels and shopping orientations of Asian-American consumers. *Psychology & Marketing*, 14(1), 1–18.

Ozcaglar-Toulouse, N., Beji-Becheur, A., Fosse-Gomez, M.-H., Herbert, M. and Zouaghi, S. (2009). Ethnicity in the study of the consumer: An overview. *Recherche Et Applications En Marketing*, 24(4), 57–75.

Palumbo, F. and Teich, I. (2004). Market segmentation based on level of acculturation. *Marketing Intelligence & Planning*, 22(4), 472–484.

Peñaloza, L. (2006). *Handbook of qualitative research methods in marketing.* Cheltenham, UK: Edward Elgar Publishing Limited.

Peñaloza, L. (1994). Atravesando fronteras/border crossings: A critical ethnographic exploration of the consumer acculturation of Mexican immigrants. *Journal of Consumer Research*, 21(1), 32–54.

Phinney, J. (1992). The multigroup ethnic identity measure: A new scale for use with diverse groups. *Journal of Adolescent Research*, 7(2), 156–176.

Phinney, J. (1990). Ethnic identity in adolescents and adults: Review of research. *Psychological Bulletin*, 108(3), 499–514.

Pingol, L. and Miyazaki, A. (2005). Information source usage and purchase satisfactions for product-focused print media. *Journal of Advertising Research*, 45(1), 132–139.

Pires, G. and Stanton, P. (2000). Ethnicity and acculturation in a culturally diverse country: Identifying ethnic markets. *Journal of Multilingual and Multicultural Development*, 21(1), 42–57.

Quester, P., Karunaratna, A. and Chong, I. (2001). Australian Chinese consumers: Does acculturation affect consumer decision making? *Journal of International Consumer Marketing*, 13(3), 7–28.

Rajagopalan, R. and Heitmeyer, J. (2005). Ethnicity and consumer choice: A study of consumer levels of involvement in Indian ethnic apparel and contemporary American clothing. *Journal of Fashion Marketing and Management*, 9(1), 83–105.

Sam, D. and Berry, J. (1995). Acculturative stress among young immigrants in Norway. *Scandinavian Journal of Psychology*, 36(1), 10–24.

Schiffman, L., Bednall, D., O'cass, A., Paladino, A., Ward, S. and Kanuk, L. (2009). *Consumer Behaviour.* Frenchs Forest: Pearson Education Australia.

Seock, Y.-K. and Bailey, L. (2009). Fashion promotions in the hispanic market. *International Journal of Retail & Distribution Management*, 37(2), 161–181.

Solomon, M. (1996). *Consumer behavior: Buying, having, and being*. NJ: Prentice-Hall International, Inc.

Statistics Canada (2003). *Ethnic Diversity Survey, Portrait of A Multicultural Society*. Ottawa, Ontario: Statistics Canada.

Valencia, H. (1985). Developing an index to measure "hispanicness". *Advances in Consumer Research*, 12(1).

Verbeke, W. and López, P. (2005). Ethnic food attitudes and behaviour among Belgians and Hispanics living in Belgium. *British Food Journal*, 107(11), 823–840.

Wiley, S. (2013). Rejection-identification among Latino immigrants in the United States. *International Journal of Intercultural Relations*, 37(3), 375–384.

Xu, J., Shim, S., Lotz, S. and Almeida, D. (2004). Ethnic identity, socialization factors, and culture-specific consumption behavior. *Psychology & Marketing*, 21(2), 93–112.

Yeh, C. and Huang, K. (1996). The collectivistic nature of ethnic identity development among Asian-American college students. *Adolescence*, 31(123), 645.

Yinger, J. (1976). Ethnicity in complex societies. *The Uses of Controversy in Sociology*, 197–216.

4 Rationale for Ethnic Marketing Focus on Aggregates of Minority Ethnic Groups

Group size is often used by marketers as the major indicator of the importance that can be afforded to ethnic groups. This chapter discusses the reasons and potential shortcomings for seeking to increase group size through the aggregation of two or more minority ethnic groups, seemingly conferring the properties of ethnicity discussed in earlier chapters to a panethnic group.

Panethnic groups are most commonly understood as the aggregation of nationally defined ethnic groups using selected aspects of assumed commonality, such as some broad elements of culture; geographic origin and/ or language. In the American context this aggregative practice leads to a variety of panethnic groups, including the Native-American, African-American, Hispanic, Latino and Asian-American (Lopez and Espiritu, 1990; Okamoto, 2006; Okamoto and Mora, 2014). Emphasis is placed on the implications arising from a focus on building a critical mass based on criteria other than ethnicity criteria, such as social distance (Forman and Murguia, 2013; Kim and White, 2010), with the aim of providing more guidance when this may or may not be warranted.

From the discussion of the different approaches to marketing to ethnic groups noted in Chapter 1, as well as in our own definition, ethnic marketing applies the principles of segmentation, targeting and positioning. Given our discussion of different viewpoints concerning critical conceptual foundations, specifically ethnicity, ethnic identity, ethnic groups and the process of acculturation, the dilemma for ethnic marketers is to identify groups of persons with common ethnicity that fulfil the requirements of a strong and viable market segment, distinct from other ethnic groups. Pressures of acculturation in a multicultural environment over time can and do clearly impact on group size and on the ethnic identity of its members, adding to the natural heterogeneity (in gender, age, income, skills, parenthood, religion) that characterizes minority ethnic groups. Given this dynamism, a pressing question to ask is what are the boundaries of an ethnic group that indicate segment size and the qualities of this segment?

This chapter first briefly revisits earlier discussion in the literature (e.g. Pires and Stanton, 2015) about the criteria often used to assess whether to target a particular segment when using an *a priori* approach (Wind, 1978), selecting the variable of interest—in this case ethnicity—and classifying consumers by their ethnicity. While Smith (1956, p. 8) more than 60 years ago lauded the rise of market segmentation as asserting the pre-eminence of consumers, even then this praise was tempered by the caution that there was a cost limit to which such diversity could be carried. This constraint is particularly relevant to the identification of ethnic market segments in terms of ascertaining both the minimum critical size as well as the possibility of a maximum. The common basis is identifying the circumstances when groups can be predictably and systematically combined into segments for the purposes of an ethnic marketing strategy.

Subsequent sections in this chapter discuss the concept and growth of panethnicity and consider its impact on ethnic marketing in terms of pan-ethnicity's focus on aggregates of ethnic groups. The value of aggregation needs to be assessed against the criteria for effective segmentation. This need constrains the unqualified use of panethnic groups, but the circumstances, advantages and disadvantages of when to use panethnic groups requires careful evaluation.

General Requirements for Effective Market Segmentation

In responding to a targeted marketing mix, each market segment needs to be homogeneous in itself (that is, all customers in the group must respond in the same way, but not necessarily at the same time), as well as heterogeneous relative to all other market segments (that is, customers outside the designated segment will not respond in the same way). Effective market segmentation, however, is likely to be business specific, since different businesses can be expected to command different capabilities and competencies. Hence, it requires verifying that the proposed segments exist and are useful for marketing purposes, as well as testing the various segments for consistency with the business' own objectives and resources, prior to target market selection. Overall, to be effective, any assessment of a proposed segmentation needs to examine the requirements or preconditions for establishing segment viability; these are often referred to as criteria against which a potential segment should be assessed; similarly, they can be used to help order the attractiveness of segments although they have an inherent subjectivity.

The list and terminology for these criteria has tended to vary between writers. Wind (1978) raised nine general questions that should be addressed when seeking to identify market segments which included assessing the segment's stability, homogeneity and segmentability. Thomas (1980) argued that any proposed segmentation should be assessed against four criteria: measurability—members of the segment needing to be identifiable; accessibility—the segment was capable of being targeted and thus served; stability—the behaviour of the proposed segment needed to be predictable over time; and the segment needed to be substantial—that is, to be sufficiently profitable to repay the effort. Additional criteria addressing the internal constraints governing selection of target segments have since been added.

Table 4.1 lists the different criteria specified by different writers, accounting for different terminology, even in cases of conceptual similarity.

The external criteria seeks to assess segment characteristics that are external to or independent of the business. These include testing for identifiability, differentiability, measurability, accessibility or reachability, responsiveness or uniqueness and stability.

While substantiality has also been classified as an external criterion, it sits across the external/internal divide because substantiality or profitability is dependent on firm objectives (Stanton and Pires, 1999). Since each segment offers a targeting opportunity and because not all segments represent equally attractive opportunities for a business, it is important for businesses to evaluate the market value—substantiality—of different segments, in order to decide which segments to target. Clearly, it is not only a matter of assessing segment size, or some other indicator such as profitability. Target market selection requires evaluating the various segments for consistency with the firm's own objectives and resources, as well as each segment contribution relative to other segments.

Assessing the conditions to be met by business for effective segmentation (the internal environment) includes consideration of preliminary requirements such as environmental dynamism (related to general market instability over time) and complexity (related to the degree of heterogeneity and the dispersion of business activities, as potential barriers to delivering a variety of value propositions). Once specific segments are identified, businesses need to test for segment actionability (receptivity or viability), for targeting sustainability, and for environmental munificence, the ability of the targeting opportunity to support sustained growth as required by the business.

Segment actionability is a key consideration because a business must be able to develop feasible value propositions that effectively and efficiently satisfy segment needs, preferences and evaluation criteria (Pires, Stanton and Stanton, 2011). A further challenge when facing a variety of segments is that the value proposition that might be offered, should mass marketing be viable, needs to be adapted or customized so that it is perceived by each specific segment as the superior value proposition, independent of business geographical dispersion.

The above criteria can be used to evaluate any proposal to build a market segment, including those based on ethnicity. In the specific case of targeting of ethnic groups varying considerably in size, substantiality

Table 4.1 Criteria for Effective Market Segmentation for Marketing Purposes

External Environment	
Identifiability	Ability to distinguish the characteristics that make the segment distinct, so it can be profiled and measured (Frank, Massy and Wind, 1972; Thomas, 1980; Porter, 1986; Sun, 2009).
Differentiability/ Segmentability	Segment is conceptually distinguishable—expected to respond differently to other segments (Wind, 1978; Liu, Ram and Lusch, 2005).
Measurability	Measurable segment size/purchasing power (Thomas, 1980; Kotler, Bowen and Makens, 1997; Hassan, Craft and Kortam, 2003; Corbett, 2008)
Accessibility/ Reachability	Business must be able to reach/access and serve the consumers making up the segment (Frank, Massy and Wind, 1972; Wind, 1978; Kotler, 1997; Hassan, Craft and Kortam, 2003; Sun, 2009).
Responsiveness/ Uniqueness	The segment responds uniquely to marketing effort directed to it. (Frank, Massy and Wind, 1972; Thomas, 1980; Baker, 1996; Sun, 2009).
Stability	The segment's consumer behaviour must be predictable over time (Frank, Massy and Wind, 1972; Thomas, 1980; Hassan, Craft and Kortam, 2003).
Substantiality/ Size/Profitability	Segment size and purchasing power must be large/profitable enough to justify the targeting effort (Frank, Massy and Wind, 1972; Wind and Douglas, 1972; Thomas, 1980; Sun, 2009; van Hattum and Hoijtink, 2010).
Internal Environment	
Actionability/ Receptivity/ Viability	Effective programs can be formulated for attracting and serving the segment. Business must develop feasible, effective and efficient value propositions that satisfy segment preferences, needs and evaluation criteria. (Frank, Massy and Wind, 1972; Wind, 1978; Thomas, 1980; Donthu and Cherian, 1994; Kotler, Bowen and Makens, 1997).
Sustainability	For sustainable competitive advantage, customized value propositions need to be consistent with the business' mission and based on capabilities and/or competencies that are unique to the business and available over time (Hassan, Craft and Kortam, 2003; Calandro and Flynn, 2005).
Environmental Dynamism, Complexity and Munificence	Dynamism refers to market instability over time; complexity refers to the heterogeneity and dispersion of business' activities (e.g. geographical dispersion) and their influence on effective targeted marketing. Munificence considers the extent to which the targeting opportunity can support sustained growth (McArthur and Nystrom, 1991; Starbuck, 1976).

Note: Liu, Ram and Lusch (2005) explain that descriptive methods are optimized for segment identifiability while predictive methods are optimized for segment responsiveness. Most existing segmentation methods cannot effectively address both identifiability and responsiveness goals of market segmentation due to their focus on only one aspect of a multi-objective problem. Huh and Singh (2007) interpret "differentiability" as different segment responses to different marketing mix elements and programs (213).

becomes an important justification for the aggregation of ethnic groups with apparent commonalities. But the argument is that marketers may soundly create larger market segments combining both large and small minority ethnic groups if they follow and meet these criteria.

There is growing evidence that small ethnic groups are themselves melding into larger, and different socially constructed ethnic groups, the process of panethnicity creation discussed below, but whether this process is sufficiently advanced with some groups to provide sufficient commonalities to be treated as a market segment, and on what basis panethnic groups are targeted based on ethnicity are empirical questions. The case for the panethnic approach is pursued in the subsequent sections, recognizing that aggregation of groups should meet all internal and external criteria.

Panethnicity

Marketing to aggregates of ethnic groups linked perhaps by some key common cultural or structural commonalities, in some way encapsulated in notions such as social distance (Kim and White, 2010), has long been common practice in the USA and Canada (Kim, 2005). However, panethnicity is not always seen as an exclusive American phenomenon, and might need to be looked at in a wider historical and international context, from the role of colonial powers in categorizing native populations to the current of modern nation-states with many diverse ethnic groups and strong immigration programs seeking to create a panethnic national identity (Okamoto and Mora, 2014). This would include the cases of Australian Aboriginals or, indeed, other groups in Australia that appear to be recognized by their religion (Muslim) or geographical area of provenance (Asian), rather than for their uniqueness in terms of country of origin, for example.

Panethnicity can be seen as an emerging global phenomenon, with "European" being seen as such a group (Okamoto and Mora, 2014). More strictly, however, the globalized perspective of panethnicity for marketing purposes might be a perspective more embraced by analysts in the USA and Canada (Ocampo, 2014). In the UK, for example, a country that has long devoted attention to ethnicity and ethnic groups, panethnicity has been discussed as something that might happen in the future, based on current trends (Muttarak, 2014). In fact, the practice is conspicuous by its apparent omission in many other countries with culturally diverse populations, where marketing strategies, if targeting ethnic groups, are often focussed on groups that are more nationally based.

This section examines the rationale for aggregating small ethnic groups for marketing purposes, given the criteria previously specified for effective segmentation. First we draw on the pan ethnic research literature to find any rationale that can support the aggregation approach being used for marketing purposes. Assessment in terms of effective segmentation then follows.

What Is Panethnicity?

The term panethnicity is widely used by sociologists to describe a process increasingly observed and researched in the USA since the 1980's, where primarily national or sometimes tribal based ethnic groups cooperate in developing *"bridging organizations and solidarities among subgroups of ethnic collectivities that are often seen as homogeneous by outsiders"* (Lopez and Espiritu, 1990, p. 198). Okamoto and Mora (2014) provide a timely review of the literature.

In terms of ethnic boundaries, Okamoto and Mora see panethnicity as a socio-economic and political process that can lead to a new "categorical boundary" that consolidates ethnic, tribal, national or religious groups. They note that such a process is marked by inherent tensions between subgroups and the metagroup, but that "the maintenance of subgroup identities is necessary for the success and longevity of broader-based panethnic groupings" (p. 221). Why this is the case is not clear. Whether pan ethnic groupings can be used for marketing purposes depends on the characteristics determining such groupings and whether the process of panethnicity supplants or reduces the marketing relevance of the sub-groups.

As noted above, panethnicity has a long history in the USA, often resulting from the actions of colonial powers in their undifferentiated treatment of native tribes or the enslavement of populations from diverse populations, leading to the forging of a common identity amongst such groups.

Cornell (1990) was one of the earliest researchers seeking to explain the process of panethnic group formation. He notes that Africans forcibly brought to what is now the United States came from different ethnic groups, whilst Native Americans were also very distinct nations; yet, over time, both constructed a conscious group identity through ongoing interaction primarily with the super-ordinate group of European-Americans. Differences in the trajectories of group formation, or acculturation paths, by each group arising from differences in economic and political pressures were observed. But the commonalities have led other researchers (Lopez and Espiritu, 1990; Okamoto, 2003, 2006; Masuoka, 2006) to further examine the determinants of panethnic group formation in the United States, covering such diverse groups as Latinos, Asian-Americans, Indo-Americans and Native Americans. Table 4.2 identified four studies of panethnic group development, all in the USA context.

The various studies addressing the factors causing the growth of a panethnic group consciousness and identity have raised similar variables and processes at work but with considerable differences found between groups in the importance of particular variables and the development of a panethnic identity. Excepting Masuoka (2006), who focusses on consciousness at the individual level, the other studies seek to explain the growth of a collective group consciousness.

Lopez and Espiritu (1990) conclude that structural influences rather than cultural commonalities tend to drive the growth of panethncity, a

Table 4.2 Studies of Panethnic Group Development

Study	Panethnic Group Focus	Paper Focus	Explanatory Variables
Cornell (1990)	African Americans; Native Americans	Emergence of group consciousness	Economic (resource competition); Political; Conceptual (bases for identification)
Lopez and Espiritu (1990)	Asian-Americans, Latinos, Native-Americans, Indo-Americans	Emerging Group consciousness: Competing theories	Cultural (language and religion); Structural (Class, Race, Generation, Geographical dispersion)
Okamoto (2006)	Asian-Americans	Emerging Group consciousness: theory	Political (multiple variables capturing political opportunities and resources); Labour segregation (cultural division of labour).
Masuoka (2006)	Latinos, Asian-Americans	Factors influencing emerging individual panethnic consciousness	Socio-economic status; Immigration (recency); Racial discrimination.

view largely supported by other studies. Political variables in many cases shaped the structures of economic opportunities that different national groups faced as well as creating panethnic categories that provided opportunities for panethnic organization.

The various American studies point to considerable differences between groups in the conditions and variables at work in creating a panethnic consciousness. The land reservation system and various (US) Federal laws appear to have led to a slower urbanization of Native Americans, linking to the slower growth of their panethnic identity (Lopez and Espiritu, 1990). None of the studies conclude that panethnic consciousness is particularly strong, although it is growing differentially between groups.

As noted by Okamoto and Mora (2014), the panethnic identity has not replaced and is unlikely to replace the subgroup ethnic identities. However, the growth of panethnicity is, arguably, a dynamic process that takes place over time, such that strong identity can eventually arise, suggesting that panethnic groups can have or develop marketing relevance, depending on the strength of that identity. Accordingly, the following factors are identified as influencing the growth of panethnicity:

(a) Historical ascription by others that assign people to a racial category based on their morphology or phenotypical commonalities with no recognition of differences in tribe, ethnicity, national origin, immigration history, and culture. The growth of an African-American group identity or Indigenous Australian identity can, in part, be attributed to such a process.

(b) Governments can be a leader in such ascription with their administrative arms creating administrative and census categories to carry out, in some countries, segregationist policies or in others, socio-economic programs designed to channel assistance to broadly based disadvantaged cultural groups.

(c) Smaller ethnic groups may deliberately seek to coalesce to be a larger and stronger force in seeking to attract the resources of the state, reinforcing both (a) and (b) above.

(d) Government departments charged with providing demographic information on either ethnic, cultural, or racial lines may use classification systems that result in aggregation of smaller groups using similarity criteria. The smaller groups remain statistically invisible by themselves (Simon, 2008; Pires, Stanton and Cheek, 2003; Ghaill, 2000; Naber, 2000). Only those groups considered to be of "significant" numbers may be reported at a particular disaggregation level. For the development of social policies, a higher order aggregation may be used, again creating a classification commonality for resource allocation that can itself foster a pan ethnic group.

(e) Panethnic political/social organizations can emerge from (d), reinforcing state categorization processes through their network activities, especially if these organizations become the gatekeepers for dispensing state resources.

(f) The growth in global digital media and its relatively low-cost of distribution both encourages fragmentation of audiences as well as uniting audiences across borders. Given that many of the world's major languages, such as Spanish, transcend one ethnic group, panethnic identity can be created through programming aimed at a panethnic rather than a narrower audience.

(g) The settlement patterns of ethnic groups in regions and cities is often determined by economic forces, often followed by social and network attraction to similar others. Thus, in particular Western Sydney local government areas there is a preponderance of residents hailing from the Indian subcontinent, and in others from the Middle East. The coalescing of broad cultural or language groups in particular localities can shape the ways that groups interact, which subsequently give rise to panethnic forms.

As these forces are currently at work (Okamoto and Mora, 2014), the circumstances when panethnic groups can supplant targeting of smaller disaggregates, if at all, needs consideration.

Marketing Reasons for Aggregating Ethnic Groups

The use by marketers of panethnic groups, however determined, rests on a number of possible drivers: these include perceptions of inadequate group size, cost concerns, a marketing focus on similarities rather than differences, concerns with group instability, concerns of social retaliation, and assessments of sufficient behavioural homogeneity.

Table 4.3 provides a summary of the various explanations advanced in the literature to justify focusing on aggregates of ethnic groups for marketing purposes; that is, for pursuing a panethnic targeting approach.

Table 4.3 Reasons for Adopting a Panethnic Targeting Approach

Size	While cultural and ethnic groups with significant numbers in a country may be separately identified as of particular interest to policy makers and service providers, those deemed insignificant may be included in a residual category where the heterogeneity of this residual category means a particular small group's needs may not be met. Aggregation of small groups based on similarity criteria may be a second-best approach, rather than losing any visibility; e.g. focussing on commonalities (such as language similarity) may lead to aggregation with other groups for targeting purposes.
Cost	Targeting of narrowly defined groups raises the likelihood of higher marketing costs (Cui and Choudhury, 1998). While this may be the case, targeting ethnic consumers through their group of affiliation reduces costs because one value proposition may suffice, provided it relies on the right attributes. Cost assessment may be better considered relative to expected results of the marketing investment. This ties with misconceptions about group substantiality.
Stability	Ethnic groups are dynamic entities, depending on environmental factors. Economic conditions in the home and host countries can influence migration flows causing group instability (Svendsen, 1997). Because marketing programs take time to achieve results, group instability may increase perceived risk in targeting individual ethnic groups. Aggregation increases perceived substantiality through larger numbers and cushions the impact of group instability.
Similarities outweigh differences	Any differences between consumer groups on ethnicity grounds may be outweighed by the assessment of similarities sufficiently important to override perceived differences. This view is not clearly articulated in the marketing literature, beyond allegedly bearing a link to the development of personas and critical mass.
Social retaliation	Minority ethnic groups continue to be singled out on racial issues from time to time. As marketing to ethnic groups is likely to be conspicuous to the mainstream population, there is a risk of negative response or retaliation.
Behavioural homogeneity	The commonality of one or a few markers of ethnicity, such as language and religion, may be sufficient for the purposes of a specific marketing campaign to achieve a particular behavioural response but insufficient to achieve other goals where a stronger sense of ethnic identity may be required.

The table offers various reasons, none mutually exclusive, for marketers to pursue aggregation. Each reason noted in the table is also explained.

The primary rationale for adopting a panethnic approach is that marketing to individual ethnic groups within culturally diverse countries (treating each as a segmentable market separate from the macro market) may be potentially appealing if a group's ethnic identity is sufficiently strong, but it raises the likelihood of higher marketing costs and possible alienation of other groups (Cui and Choudhury, 1998). Ormerod (2006) posits that pragmatism engenders a focus on the practical significance of a proposition; that it supports an empirical or evidence-based approach.

Pragmatism responds to social contexts and associated uncertainty and change, providing a justification for the aggregation of groups, particularly when the members of different groups share demographic, socioeconomic and lifestyle characteristics. Notwithstanding, the growth of panethnic networks and activities provides a pragmatic basis for aggregation but not necessarily for all marketing purposes.

Homophily and Ethnic Group Formation

The basic question of whether and when to aggregate minority ethnic groups to create a larger segment is conceptually challenging. Ethnic marketing has its roots in the homogeneity of consumer groups defined by a common ethnicity—that is, by the condition that consumers belong to a particular ethnic group that is unique relative to other groups, and that consumers in the group behave similarly in response to marketing stimuli directed to the group. Most importantly, the greatest value of ethnic marketing is that this behaviour is likely to have high predictability. This is because there are group mechanisms that not only sustain the groups' continued existence in the host country but also regulate how affiliated consumers consistently behave socially and as consumers. Panethnicity involves smaller groups coalescing because of emerging commonalities of interest in the host country, suggesting there will be relevance for some, but not necessarily all, marketing purposes.

Segment substantiality explains why very few consumers in isolation are ever likely to be targeted for marketing purposes. For any given firm, substantiality is a contingent dimension that may depend on a variety of factors, including the firm's objectives, strategic planning, competitive environment and stage of the life cycle (Stanton and Pires, 1999). In any case, market segmentation is likely to involve some notional level of critical mass that, in consumer markets, is unlikely to be met by any one individual. Indeed, the general case is that an individual becomes important for marketing only when associated with other similar individuals, creating an identifiable, measurable, stable and actionable group that is homogeneous within itself and heterogeneous in relation to other groups.

This same reasoning may be applied when the targeting of ethnic minority consumers is concerned.

In Chapter 2 we saw how individual ethnic consumers are the foreground for ethnic group formation, being key figures in the process of generating ethnic group identity. For businesses considering ethnic marketing objectives, individual ethnic consumers are only collectively important as members of the ethnic group with which they identify. Individual ethnic group members, however, will need to exhibit sufficient conformity in line with other group members for this collective importance to hold. It is this requirement that ensures that the ethnic group is internally homogeneous in consumption behaviour, and that marketers can predict that behaviour.

The predictability of the group's consumer behaviour can be explained by the concept of homophily. Similarity in attributes such as "like attracts like" also known as "homophily" strengthens the ties between group members thereby increasing the level of influence that the group has over the behaviour and decision-making behaviour of its' members (Brown and Reingen, 1987; Centola et al., 2007; McAdam and Paulsen, 1993).

Homophily helps form the social network and also to adapt according to the social influence of the actors (members) where dissimilar ties are dropped in favour of ties with more similarities between the members (Centola et al., 2007). The homophily principle constrains the individual to the community to which they belong or identify and thus with whom they choose to interact (Kinket and Verkuyten, 1997).

Homophily increases as more like members of the social network increase, resulting in the group being further differentiated from other groups (Centola et al., 2007; Knoke, 1990; Duncan, Haller and Portes, 1968). The implication is that social networks change in their dynamics as members adapt to other cultural influences or assimilate to the host culture. As their attitudes and behaviours change, the landscape of the social network changes because members will cut old ties with people who no longer share similar values, beliefs or attitudes or make new friendships with those who do. Shared similarities will strengthen the bond of group members whilst creating differences between the group from other dissimilar groups (Bourdieu, 1986). This is because the structure of homophily reinforces what Centola et al. (2007) refer to as group "cultural consensus".

There are three types of homophily that contribute to group formation:

1. Value-based homophily—people sharing the same belief system (Lazarsfeld and Merton, 1954; Centola et al., 2007);
2. Culture-based homophily also known as status homophily—people sharing the same cultural background (Lazarsfeld and Merton, 1954; Centola et al., 2007); and

3. Induced homophily—where people become more alike over time (Lazarsfeld and Merton, 1954; Centola et al., 2007; McPherson and Smith-Lovin, 1987; Mcpherson, Smith-Lovin and Cook, 2001).

Ethnic groups tend to be more valued based, with several different groups often linked by common cultural traits, such as language or religion. Panethnic groups reflect an induced homophily between groups that have some degree of linked values and culture homophily, caused by close and ongoing interactions arising from the forces previously discussed as giving rise to panethnicity.

Homophily has the effect of limiting an individual's scope, restricting their access to information, the behaviour and attitudes they develop and the people they socialize with within the network, thus reinforcing the shared similarities Holzhauer, Krebs and Ernst, 2013). Individuals find comfort when engaging with others from the same ethnic background (Fischer, 1977; Lazarsfeld and Merton,1954; Marsden, 1987, 1988; Shrum, Cheek and Hunter, 1988). This is supported in a study by Jones and Estell (2010) that found members with strong intra-group ties and social status were likely to remain in the group and keep their social capital, whilst members with loose intra-group ties were likely to leave.

New arrivals tend to have very strong ethnic homophilous friendships which may decrease over time but may still remain preponderant, even after a decade of settlement (Silbereisen and Schmitt-Rodermund, 2000). Whilst friendship homophily is significant in new arrivals and remains significant even if declining with longer settlement, the reductions in homophily friendships that occur in the new arrival groups over time (Titzmann and Silbereisen, 2009) suggest the growth of panethnicity is fairly slow.

Individuals who identify strongly with their ethnic groups seek friendships or relationships with others from within their ethnic community. Although these same relationships and friendships are not as widely available in comparison to the dominant host group, ethnic minorities still display more homophily within their social networks (Mollica, Gray and Trevino, 2003). Inter-group studies on ethnic social networks suggest considerable differences between ethnic groups in the degree of ethnic friendship homophily (Titzmann, Michel and Silbereisen, 2010, Titzmann and Silbereisen, 2009; Titzmann, Silbereisen and Mesch, 2012). Findings that the intra-ethnic friendship networks of Hispanics in the USA range in the low 50 percent and for Asian between 38 percent and 42 percent, compared with African-Americans at a high 71–77 percent (Harris and Cavanagh, 2008; Titzmann, Silbereisen and Mesch, 2012) encourage a panethnic marketing approach to these two aggregates.

In short, ethnic homophily explains why newly arrived, inexperienced ethnic minority consumers are likely to source consumption information from more experienced similar-others (fellow ethnic minority consumers who are perceived to be knowledgeable about the marketplace), rather than from mainstream consumers. This may be particularly so in relation to services and service providers. Information and recommendation (verbal or behavioural) from similar-others may be used by newly arrived, inexperienced ethnic minority consumers to select their first providers in the new market, as well as to establish criteria for assessing service quality and provider credibility.

Similar-others trust, and are more trusted, compared to dissimilar others (Dwyer, Schurr and Oh, 1987). This is because similar-others may have experienced the same consumption situation whilst subject to similar handicaps. As a result, faced with the need to manage the transition between complex cultural codes, the new arrival may perceive similar-others as more sympathetic towards the handicaps and more likely to have experienced similar needs and preferences, as well as to have achieved successful consumption solutions based on similar evaluative criteria.

Because information from similar-others is more credible, minority ethnic group members exchange information and experiences with other consumers affiliated with the same minority group, and group consumer behaviour is a reference for that of the members. Ultimately, a recommendation from similar-others is likely to be adopted because it is perceived to be more credible and reduces perceived risk. Adoption results in positive or negative experiences which feedback to the group reinforcing or weakening group preference, including when suppliers to the ethnic community are concerned. The consistent way of how new arrivals manage the transition from one country to another, and the role played by ethnic entrepreneurship in that transition, perpetuates the minority ethnic group as a separate cultural entity, and explains its relevance for marketing purposes.

Homophily and the Choice of Suppliers to the Ethnic Community

Reflecting the position generally taken in the ethnic marketing literature, the questions of when and how to target ethnic minority groups has so far focused on an essentially demand side ethnic marketing perspective, dominated by the discussion of consumption behaviour issues involving ethnic minority consumers and minority ethnic groups for a business vantage point. The business doing the targeting is given a somewhat mute role, predicated on an assumption that the considerations apply to any business, including mainstream businesses targeting across cultures. This overlooks the fact that the targeting of ethnic communities is more often than not enacted by suppliers who are both ethnic minority consumers and entrepreneurs affiliated with minority ethnic groups.

The interdependency between ethnic entrepreneurs, ethnic minority businesses, ethnic minority consumers and minority ethnic groups is argued to play a crucial role in community resilience, justified by an intimate sharing of ethnic-sensitive understandings and actions. While ethnic sensitivity does not necessarily exclude panethnic environments, the considerations above involving homophily point to the need to take suppliers to minority ethnic groups into careful account. Ethnic entrepreneurship, ethnic minority businesses and ethnic marketing take central attention in subsequent chapters of this text.

Nevertheless, given the earlier discussed support for the marketing relevance of approaches focused on panethnic groups, it is justified to explore formal guidelines for the aggregation of several minority ethnic groups for particular marketing purposes.

An EMIC Approach to Creating Panethnic Segments

The complexity involved in seeking to assess and select market opportunities and to operationalize marketing strategy for international markets makes it critical to identify changes that may be required beyond what may be working successfully within a particular domestic context (Usunier and Lee, 2005). Cultural and ethnic differences are a prominent source of this complexity (de Mooij, 2004) influencing segment identification and selection, and the development of marketing tactical activities to reach them.

In cross-cultural consumer marketing, differences and similarities in consumer behaviour are assessed primarily relative to differences between national cultures (Berry, 1980), often acknowledging that cultural groups do not neatly coincide with the nation-state (Douglas and Craig, 2006). This has led to the debated distinction between etic and emic approaches, the former with its emphasis on finding common cultural criteria along which cultural groups can be arrayed and if sufficiently similar, combined; and the latter focusing on a specific culture, hence emphasizing uniqueness and differences relative to other national cultures.

At a country level, the norm is to understand consumers under the homogenizing umbrella of the prevailing national culture (the mainstream). But following this approach in a culturally diverse country can potentially oversimplify the marketing research problem of identifying consumer segments by ignoring similarities and differences between ethnic groups, as well as the eventual gains in growth of some minority ethnic consumer groups versus the mainstream. This is a phenomenon that has recently been heralded in the USA, where some minority ethnic consumer groups became recognized as the new majority (Armstrong, 2013) or the majority minority (Cui and Choudhury, 2002). Recognizing the pervasive role of culture and ethnic differences in the consumer behaviour process, a preferable way forward may be to adopt a linked emic framework.

The cross-cultural marketing research literature calls for the adoption of emic approaches within countries and of etic approaches across countries. "Etic" and "emic" are derived from the suffixes of the words phonetic and phonemic by Pike (1954). Etics is characterized by cross-cultural validity, looking for universal or culture-free theories and concepts (Luna and Gupta, 2001). Emic is characterized by specificity to one culture (country) at a time (Harris, 1976), such that "the emic approach should be followed for the study of consumer behaviour in different countries" (de Mooij, 2004, p. 95). The quest to identify similarities that enable combining ethnic groups to achieve greater segment substance (and to be able to generalize ethnicity research findings across ethnic groups) favours an etic research framework.

An etic framework uses common variables to describe and compare different ethnic groups, facing significant difficulties in establishing conceptual and functional equivalence (Malhotra, Agarwal and Peterson, 1996). Hence, theories and constructs developed in the context of one ethnic group are sometimes assumed to be applicable universally, a "pseudoetic" (Douglas and Craig, 2006) or "imposed-etic" (Berry, 1990) approach. Given such difficulties, Usunier and Lee (2005) posit that the emic approach is more reliable and provides data with greater internal validity than the etic approach (p. 182).

Berry (1990) suggests a three-stage sequence whereby imposed-etic constructs are filtered using emic insights about the other ethnic group, resulting in derived-etic constructs that can subsequently be tested. More recently, Douglas and Craig (2006) sought to reduce the potential bias embodied in pseudo-etic approaches. They propose a framework consisting of "adapted-etic" and "linked-emic" models as alternative approaches for assessing differences and similarities across ethnic groups. Arguably, such approaches can facilitate segmentation strategies aimed at enlarging segment size whist ensuring the homogeneity that may be necessary for effective targeting strategies.

Assuming that there are useful panethnic observations that enable valid generalizations, the adapted-etic research framework begins from a base ethnic perspective, adapting the framework developed to other contexts. The linked-emic framework seeks to modify the strict uniqueness assumption underlying an emic framework. While commencing from the context of a particular ethnic group, this framework identifies a process for seeking common elements across different contexts that *may* lead to a meaningful aggregate. In moving towards this goal, information inherent to each ethnic group context is involved in an approach that can result in the recognition of outcomes ranging from identification of elements and constructs that appear to be common across ethnic groups, through to recognition that certain constructs are unique to a given context.

Using an adapted etic framework tempers the search for universal constructs and their application, but the focus is still on similarities rather than differences (Douglas and Craig, 2006). In seeking to increase segment size while retaining homogeneity, this approach may have considerable appeal, but at the expense of ignoring what is emic and perhaps still important to an ethnic cultural group in a particular context.

In contrast, the linked emic framework, while emphasizing differences, seeks to build generalizations where possible but only through a process of interpreting findings from each local context. Where there are many and perhaps relatively small such contexts, this approach may not suit practitioners because of its potential cost implications. On the other hand, it is more likely to avoid the pitfalls of ethnocentrism and pseudo-etic bias, recognized as common violations of basic cross-cultural research paradigms (Sekaran, 1983), and may appeal to the local community being researched (Pires, Stanton and Cheek, 2003).

When Ethnic Groups Can Be Aggregated

The need to apply either an adapted etic or linked emic framework to ethnic marketing is rarely considered, although the existence of heterogeneity within countries has been recognized (Sabbagh, 2005; Usunier and Lee, 2005; Laroche et al., 2003). As abundantly noted, the norm is to focus on aggregates of ethnic groups, using cross-national indicators such as language as the base for segmentation, a practice that applies universals consistent with the etic approach and implicitly rejecting the emic approach. Applying an etic approach grounded on assumed national characteristics is a pseudo-etic approach although a linked emic approach may be justified.

The issue that persists is to determine when ethnic groups can be aggregated. For example, can Vietnamese, Cambodian and Laotian communities within Australia be aggregated given the relatively small size of the latter two groups, their common shared colonial history and some cultural commonalities? Emic research that seeks to understand subnational cultural differences, particularly a group's core values (Smolicz, Secombe and Hudson, 2001), may be a desirable requirement prior to applying etic approaches.

No less than internationally, there is a need to identify and determine whether an ethnic group is worthwhile targeting within a country; whether multiple targets groups are feasible or whether groups can be combined. A linked emic approach to the process of building aggregates appears well suited. This will prevent, for example, *ad hoc* combining of ethnic groups based on common language. While aggregation may provide marketing economies in reaching the larger group, it may be at the expense of group homogeneity and therefore possible overall effectiveness of the strategy. A linked emic approach focusses on the factors leading to the creation of panethnic groups, earlier discussed.

Ultimately, the benefit of a linked emic approach is its rejection of what has been an unquestioned pseudo-etic approach within culturally diverse economies. Under a linked emic approach and consistent with the framework offered in the next section, each group's values are established, enabling the search for common links to proceed. Because of the small size of some groups and the problem that they may appear invisible to marketers, a linked emic approach can give increased substance to combined small groups (panethnic groups) with linked emic similarities.

A Framework for Assessing Panethnic Segments

The use of ethnicity for market segmentation requires ethnic-group boundaries to be determined before any consideration about their marketing value can be made. Consequently, any failure to correctly ascertain the differences and overlaps among groups means that market segmentation based on ethnicity may be carried too far or not far enough.

The Framework

Chapter 3 (Figure 3.1) discussed how acculturation may lead an ethnic group either towards increased commonalities with another minority ethnic group, or towards the host group, or away from other groups towards separation. The frame of reference that guides a minority ethnic group is likely to reflect the shared values of the group's affiliates as an aggregate. The cultural values and norms endorsed at the aggregate level of the ethnic group may not match exactly the individual values and norms of group members, but the overlap is likely to be extensive.

Individually, the better the match with any group's values and attitudes the more likely the individual's acculturation to that group. Hence, individual minority consumers can be expected to have variable degrees of association (to be more or less acculturated) with different ethnic groups. This also implies that ethnic groups are not closed entities, allowing for varying degrees of interpenetration, at least between those ethnic groups with individual minority consumers whose homophily is weakened over time through the panethnic forces previously discussed.

Group strength reflects the intensity of collective shared values and each ethnic group may be expected to differ significantly from other groups, although some ethnic groups are more different than others. Figure 4.1 depicts three minority ethnic groups and one dominant ethnic group, or mainstream.

Each of the smaller ethnic groups has a distinct identity with different languages, very different cultures but commonalities shared through a colonial past and ongoing interactions caused through their geographical proximity. The intensities of the values of each separate ethnic group are shown as mostly distinct from those of other groups although the area of overlap is variable in each case. For example, the overlap between group "A" and group "B" is much larger than that between group "A" and group "C", and so is the overlap with the host ethnic group. We seek to use this figure to illustrate the differences in overlap,

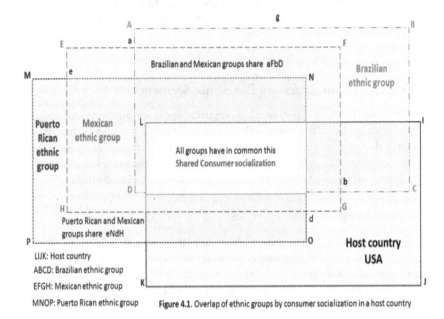

Figure 4.1. Overlap of ethnic groups by consumer socialization in a host country

Figure 4.1 Overlap of Ethnic Groups by Consumer Socialization in a Host
       Country

and aggregation possibilities that may occur between different ethnic
groups over time.

The figure shows four overlapping rectangles of equal size, each rect-
angle representing a particular ethnic group residing within the United
States. Rather than reflecting some demographic or other measure of
group size, each area represents the set of the same consumption situations and service-products facing each group, hence taking emic considerations into account. The overlaps reflect commonalities between
groups.

Unlike the Brazilians and the Whites, the Mexicans and the Puerto
Ricans share some form of the Spanish language. From social learning
theory, it is easier and possibly also more pleasurable for Puerto Rican
and Mexican consumers to inter-acculturate, coming to share a given
set of similar characteristics in their consumer socialization. The consumer socialization overlap between the Puerto Rican and the Mexican
ethnic group is substantial, suggesting that in many situations and for
certain service-products, consumption behaviour is likely to be very
similar, in which cases aggregation for segmentation purposes is a logical outcome.

The figure also shows that the Brazilian ethnic group is somewhere
in between the Mexican and the mainstream ethnic groups. Similarity

in consumption behaviour is lower in many situations and for certain service-products (relative to each of the Mexican and mainstream groups and differs across those groups), such that aggregation of the Brazilian ethnic group with either the Mexican or the mainstream is more problematic and more complex. Simply put, similarity between the two dyads does not apply for the same consumption situations and for the same service-products.

The "melting pot" argument is that all four groups will converge to one over time. The unidirectional assimilation model prescribes that the Brazilian (a Latino country), the Mexican, and Puerto Rican (both of which are Hispanic countries) groups will eventually overlap. The overlapping area is given by "L", "I", "J" and "K". But the Hispanic group is in fact an aggregate of countries with some degree of unique consumer socialization, and an alternative to the mainstream. Our prior discussion of panethnicity suggests that groups such as the Mexicans and Puerto Ricans will see increasing overlaps, enabling their aggregation for more marketing purposes.

A post-assimilationist perspective of acculturation, consistent with the bi-cultural philosophy (or eventually a more universal multicultural/ multi-identity perspective applied to ethnic consumers) would see all four groups gravitating towards each other, but not coinciding with any one group, determining a shared area of consumer socialization that may enlarge over time.

Overall, the greater the overlap in consumption socialization between ethnic groups, the lower the risk associated with aggregation of these groups. The same ethnicity-based marketing mix is likely to achieve very similar responses from consumers in the Hispanic aggregate (the Mexican and the Puerto Rican). Notwithstanding, the figure also shows 13 distinct areas, including the four areas of uniqueness for each group, eight areas involving some degree of overlap between some of the groups, and the shared consumer socialization area for the USA, with complete overlap for all four groups. This multiplicity of areas reflects a need for differentiated marketing mixes, highlighting the need for ethnicity-based segmentation, whilst supporting selective aggregation of ethnic groups with similar consumption socialization patterns.

Summary

Migrant groups and their descendants may seek to retain their perceived ethnic identity in a host country but the effluxion of time and interaction between different groups can give rise to forces that change the boundaries of such groups, some perhaps losing their separate identity, but not necessarily to the mainstream. From a marketing perspective, when the boundaries between different ethnic groups become sufficiently blurred there may be a case for considering aggregation.

This chapter has discussed the foundations for creating robust market segments and then examined the forces leading to the growth of panethnicity, to see if there is evidence supporting the aggregation of some ethnic groups to create larger but still robust segments based on ethnic group network strengths. Panethnic groups already exist arising from various political and socio-economic forces, and casual observation suggests that it may be acceptable to use such aggregates for some specific purposes. The question is "what purposes?" and "which groups?"

The key issue to consider is that, as noted earlier, some ethnic groups have more in common than others, for example, Brazilians and Portuguese groups in Australia. Hence, the greater the coincidence of values between ethnic groups—alias the narrower the social distance between the groups—the lower the risk associated with ethnic group aggregation. From a different perspective, the greater the social distance between the host ethnic group and other ethnic groups the greater the need for ethnic segmentation. This supports the view that, at least for discrete marketing purposes (like achieving critical mass and economies of scale), it may prove advantageous for marketers to aggregate some ethnic groups.

The final thought for the generality of marketers considering ethnic marketing must be that, to serve ethnic consumers, marketers must become familiar with their specific behaviours, attitudes, habits and preferences. As noted by Kaufman (1991),

> when researching ethnic groups it is important to determine if ethnic subgroups from different foreign markets can be aggregated for the purposes of analysis. . . . Subcultural groups have been found to demonstrate similar product preferences; as a result, retailers serve several ethnic groups in one enterprise.
>
> (pp. 44–45)

Clearly, reliance on a single ethnic identification indicator to determine consumer ethnicity—the condition of belonging to a particular ethnic group—is a questionable segmentation practice (Hui et al., 1990). Hence, it is questionable whether ethnic group aggregations based on single demographic indicators, can provide reliable consumer groups with predictable behaviour that marketers can use. Accordingly, there is a shift in marketing thought toward the use of multiple indicators, concentrating on cultural characteristics such as language, religion, family structures or community traditions and behaviour (Jupp, 1991; Hui et al., 1990). Ultimately, pragmatism must be used with some discretion and the consequences clearly understood.

The focus of discussion in this chapter (and in Chapter 3) has been placed on how ethnic minority groups and individuals acculturate and the consequences of this process, including for the identification of groups (sometimes panethnic groups) large enough to justify targeting.

The reference to "large enough" is understood to mean "with enough substance" to warrant the expectation of a positive outcome for the businesses doing the targeting. One major influencer of this substance is ethnic loyalty, discussed in the next chapter.

References

Armstrong, M. (2013). Minorities: The new majority. *Armstrong Economics*, June. Accessed 5/8/2018 at www.armstrongeconomics.com/uncategorized/minorities-the-new-majority/

Baker, M. (1996). *Marketing*, 6th ed. London: Macmillan.

Berry, J. (1990). Imposed etics, emics, derived etics: Their conceptual and operational status in cross-cultural psychology. In T. Headland, K. Pike and M. Harris (eds.), *Emics and Etics: The Insider/Outsider Debate*. Newbury Park, CA: Sage Publications, pp. 28–47.

Berry, J. (1980). Introduction to methodology. In H. Triandis and J. Berry (eds.), *Handbook of Cross-Cultural Psychology*, Vol. 2. Boston: Allyn & Bacon, pp. 1–28.

Bourdieu, P. (ed.) (1986). The forms of capital. In J. G. Richardson (ed.), *Handbook of Theory and Research for the Sociology of Education*. New York, USA: Greenwood Press.

Brown, J. and Reingen, P. (1987). Social ties and word-of-mouth referral behavior. *Journal of Consumer Research*, 14(3), 350–362.

Calandro, Jr., J. and Flynn, R. (2005). Premium growth, underwriting return and segment analysis. *Measuring Business Excellence*, 9(4), 27–36.

Centola, D., Gonzalez-Avella, J., Eguiluz, V. and Miguel, M. (2007). Homophily, cultural drift, and the co-evolution of cultural groups. *Journal of Conflict Resolution*, 51, 905–929.

Corbett, S. (2008). Can the cepl Phone help end global poverty? *New York Times Magazine*, April 13. Accessed 19/5/2018 www.nytimes.com/2008/04/13/magazine/13anthropology-t.html?pagewanted=all&_r=0

Cornell, S. (1990). Land, labour and group formation: Blacks and Indians in the United States. *Ethnic and Racial Studies*, 13, 368–388.

Cui, G. and Choudhury, P. (2002). Marketplace diversity and cost-effective marketing strategies. *Journal of Consumer Marketing*, 19(1), 54–73.

Cui, G. and Choudhury, P. (1998). Effective strategies for ethnic segmentation and marketing. *Proceedings* (Eds. J. Chebat and A. Oumlil), Multicultural Marketing Conference, September, Montreal, Canada, pp. 354–361.

De Mooij, M. (2004). *Consumer Behavior and Culture*. Thousand Oaks, CA: Sage Publications.

Donthu, N. and Cherian, J. (1994). Impact of strength of ethnic identification on Hispanic shopping behaviour. *Journal of Retailing*, 70(4), 383–393.

Douglas, S. and Craig, S. (2006). On improving the conceptual foundations of international marketing research. *Journal of International Marketing*, 14(4), 1–22.

Duncan, O., Haller, A. and Portes, A. (1968). Peer influences on aspirations: A reinterpretation. *American Journal of Sociology*, 74(2), 119–137.

Dwyer, F., Schurr, P. and Oh, S. (1987). Developing buyer-seller relationships. *Journal of Marketing*, 51(2), 11–27.

Fischer, C. (1977). *Networks and Places: Social Relations in the Urban Setting*. New York: Free Press.

Forman, T. and Murguia, E. (2013). Shades of whiteness: The Mexican American experience in relation to Anglos and Blacks. In *White Out*. Abingdon, UK: Routledge, pp. 69–85.

Frank, R., Massy, W. and Wind, Y. (1972). *Market Segmentation*. Englewood Cliffs: Prentice Hall.

Ghaill, M. (2000). The Irish in Britain: The invisibility of ethnicity and anti-Irish racism. *Journal of Ethnic and Migration Studies*, 26(1), 137–147.

Harris, K. and Cavanagh, S. (2008). Indicators of the peer environment in adolescence. *Key Indicators of Child and Youth Well-Being: Completing the Picture*, 259–278.

Harris, M. (1976). History and significance of the emic/etic distinction. *Annual Review of Anthropology*, 5, 329–350.

Hassan, S., Craft, S. and Kortam, W. (2003). Understanding the new bases for global market segmentation. *Journal of Consumer Marketing*, 20(5), 446–462.

Holzhauer, S., Krebs, F. and Ernst, A. (2013). Considering baseline homophily when generating spatial social networks for agent-based modelling. *Computational and Mathematical Organization Theory*, 19(2), 128–150.

Huh, C. and Singh, A. (2007). Families travelling with a disabled member: Analyzing the potential of an emerging niche market segment. *Tourism and Hospitality Research*, 7(3/4), 212–229.

Hui, M., Joy, A., Kim, M. and Laroche, M. (1990). Differences in lifestyles among four major subcultures in a bi-cultural environment. *Proceedings of the Third Symposium on Cross-Cultural Consumer and Business Studies*, October, pp. 139–150.

Jones, M. and Estell, D. (2010). When elementary students change peer groups: Intragroup centrality, intergroup centrality, and self-perceptions of popularity. *Merrill-Palmer Quarterly*, April, 56(2), 164–188.

Jupp, J. (1991). One among many. In Goodman, et al. (eds.), *Multicultural Australia: The Challenges of Change*. University of Melbourne.

Kaufman, C. (1991). Coupon use in ethnic markets: Implications from a retail perspective. *Journal of Consumer Marketing*, Winter, 8(1), 41–51.

Kim, A. (2005). Panethnicity and ethnic resources in residential integration: A comparative study of two host societies. *Canadian Studies in Population*, 32(1), 1–28.

Kim, A. and White, M. (2010). Panethnicity, ethnic diversity, and residential segregation. *American Journal of Sociology*, 115(5), 1558–1596.

Kinket, B. and Verkuyten, M. (1997). Levels of ethnic self-identification and social context. *Social Psychology Quarterly*, 338–354.

Knoke, D. (1990). *Political Networks: The Structural Perspective*. New York: Cambridge University Press.

Kotler, P., Bowen, J. and Makens, J. (1997). *Marketing Management: Analysis, Planning, Implementation, and Control*. Englewood Cliffs, NJ: Prentice-Hall.

Laroche, M., Papadopoulos, N., Heslop, L. and Bergeron, J. (2003). Effects of subcultural differences on country and product evaluations. *Journal of Consumer Behaviour*, 2(3), 232–248.

Lazarsfeld, P. and Merton, R. (1954). Friendship as a social process: A substantive and methodological analysis. *Freedom and Control in Modern Society*, 18(1), 18–66.

Liu, Y., Ram, S. and Lusch, R. (2005). A unified market segmentation method for generating pareto optimal solution sets. *Proceedings, 15th Workshop On Information Technologies and Systems*, pp. 219–224.

Lopez, D. and Espiritu, Y. (1990). Panethnicity in the United States: A theoretical framework. *Ethnicity and Racial Studies*, 13, 198–224.

Luna, D. and Gupta, S. (2001). An integrative framework for cross-cultural consumer behaviour. *International Marketing Review*, 18(1), 45–69.

Malhotra, N., Agarwal, J. and Peterson, M. (1996). Methodological issues in cross-cultural marketing research: A state-of-the-art review. *International Marketing Review*, 13(5), 7–43.

Marsden, P. (1987). Core discussion networks of Americans. *American Sociological Review*, 52, 122–131.

Marsden, P. (1988). Homogeneity in confiding relations. *Social Networks*, 10, 57–76.

Masuoka, N. (2006). Together they become one: Examining the predictors of panethnic group consciousness among Asian Americans and Latinos. *Social Science Quarterly*, 87(5), 994–1011.

McAdam, D. and Paulsen, R. (1993). Specifying the relationship between social ties and activism. *American Journal of Sociology*, 99(3), 640–667.

Mcarthur, A. and Nystrom, P. (1991). Environmental dynamism, complexity, and munificence as moderators of strategy-performance relationships. *Journal of Business Research*, 23, 349–361.

McPherson, J. and Smith-Lovin, L. (1987). Homophily in voluntary organizations: Status distance and the composition of face-to-face groups. *American Sociological Review*, 370–379.

Mcpherson, M., Smith-Lovin, L. and Cook, J. (2001). Birds of a feather: Homophily in social networks. *Annual Review of Sociology*, 27, 417–444.

Mollica, K., Gray, B. and Trevino, L. (2003). Racial homophily and its persistence in newcomers' social networks. *Organization Science*, 14(March/April), 123–136.

Muttarak, R. (2014). Generation, ethnic and religious diversity in friendship choice: Exploring interethnic close ties in Britain. *Ethnic and Racial Studies*, 37(1), 71–98.

Naber, N. (2000). Ambiguous insiders: An investigation of Arab American invisibility. *Ethnic and Racial Studies*, 23(1), 37–61.

Ocampo, A. (2014). Are second-generation Filipinos "becoming" Asian American or Latino? Historical colonialism, culture and panethnicity. *Ethnic and Racial Studies*, 37(3), 425–445.

Okamoto, D. (2006). Institutional panethnicity: Boundary formation in Asian-American organizing. *Social Forces*, 85, 1–25.

Okamoto, D. (2003). Toward a theory of panethnicity: Explaining Asian American collective action. *American Sociological Review*, 68, 811–842.

Okamoto, D. and Mora, G. (2014). Panethnicity. *Annual Review of Sociology*, 40, 219–239.

Ormerod, R. (2006). The history and ideas of pragmatism. *Journal of the Operational Research Society*, 57, 892–909.

Pike, K. (1954). *Language in Relation to a Unified Theory of the Structure of Human Behaviour*. Glendale, CA: Summer Institute of Linguistics.

Pires, G., Stanton, J. and Cheek, B. (2003). Identifying and reaching an ethnic market: Methodological issues. *Qualitative Market Research: An International Journal*, 6(2), 224–235.

Pires, G. and Stanton, P. (2015). *Ethnic Marketing: Culturally Sensitive Theory and Practice*. Abingdon, UK: Routledge.

Pires, G., Stanton, P. and Stanton, J. (2011). Revisiting the substantiality criterion: From ethnic marketing to market segmentation. *Journal of Business Research*, 64, 988–996.

Porter, M. (1986). Competition in global industries: A conceptual framework. In M. Porter (ed.), *Competition in Global Industries*. Boston, MA: Harvard Business School Press.

Sabbagh, C. (2005). An integrative etic-emic approach to portraying the halutziut system of social equity: Comparing Israeli Jew and Israeli Arab perceptions of justice. *Journal of Cross-Cultural Psychology*, 36, 147–166.

Sekaran, U. (1983). Methodological and theoretical issues and advancements in cross-cultural research. *Journal of International Business Studies*, 14, 61–73.

Shrum, W., Cheek, J. and Hunter, S. (1988). Friendship in school: Gender and racial homophily. *Sociology of Education*, 61, 227–239.

Silbereisen, R. and Schmitt-Rodermund, E. (2000). Adolescent immigrants' well-being: The case of ethnic German immigrants in Germany. *International Journal of Group Tensions*, 29, 79–100.

Simon, P. (2008). The choice of ignorance: The debate on ethnic and racial statistics in France. *French Politics, Culture & Society*, 26(1), 7–31.

Smith, W. (1956). Product differentiation and market segmentation as alternative marketing strategies. *Journal of Marketing*, 21(1), 3–8.

Smolicz, J., Secombe, M. and Hudson, D. (2001). Family collectivism and minority languages as core values of culture among ethnic groups in Australia. *Journal of Multilingual and Multicultural Development*, 2, 152–172.

Stanton, J. and Pires, G. (1999). The substantiality test: Meaning and application in market segmentation. *Journal of Segmentation in Marketing*, 3(2), 105–115.

Starbuck, W. (1976). Organizations and their environments. In M. D. Dunnette (ed.), *Handbook of Industrial and Organizational Psychology*. Chicago: Rand Mcnally.

Sun, S. (2009). An analysis on the conditions and methods of market segmentation. *International Journal of Business and Management*, 4(2), 63–70.

Svendsen, A. (1997). Building relationships with microcommunities. *Marketing News*, June 9, 13.

Thomas, M. (1980). Market segmentation. *Quarterly Review of Marketing*, 6(1), 27.

Titzmann, P., Michel, A. and Silbereisen, R. (2010). Inter-ethnic contact and socio-cultural adaptation of immigrant adolescents in Israel and Germany. *ISSBD Bulletin*, 58(3), 13–17.

Titzmann, P. and Silbereisen, R. (2009). Friendship homophily among ethnic German immigrants: A longitudinal comparison between recent and more experienced immigrant adolescents. *Journal of Family Psychology*, 23(3), 301.

Titzmann, P., Silbereisen, R. and Mesch, G. (2012). Change in friendship homophily: A German Israeli comparison of adolescent immigrants. *Journal of Cross-Cultural Psychology*, 43(3), 410–428.

Usunier, J. and Lee, J. (2005). *Marketing across Cultures*. Edinburgh Gate, England: Prentice Hall.

van Hattum, P. and Hoijtink, H. (2010). Reducing the optimal to a useful number of clusters for model-based clustering. *Journal of Targeting, Measurement and Analysis for Marketing*, 18(2), 139–154.

Wind, Y. (1978). Issues and advances in segmentation research. *Journal of Marketing Research*, 15(August), 317–337.

Wind, Y. and Douglas, S. (1972). International market segmentation. *European Journal of Marketing*, 5(1), 17–25.

5 Perspectives on Ethnic Loyalty

Dating back at least to the 1960s, the discussion of the differences of allegiance involving immigrants and the mainstream populations within a country highlighted a sentiment whereby ethnicity (tribalism) was seen as undermining the prime objective of nationalist movements (Wallerstein, 1960). The examination of loyalty in the ethnic marketing context, hereafter "ethnic loyalty", has received lesser but still significant attention to date (e.g. Padilla, 1980; de Snyder, 1987; Podoshen, 2006, 2008; Rosenbaum and Montoya, 2007), competing poorly with theories examining acculturation to the mainstream (e.g. Graves, 1967; Ogden, Ogden and Schau, 2004; Cleveland and Laroche, 2007; Cleveland et al., 2009; Luedicke, 2011; Alvarez, Dickson and Hunter, 2014; Jamal and Shukor, 2014; Segev et al., 2014; Croucher and Kramer, 2017). Greater focus has been placed on how ethnic minority groups and individuals acculturate and the consequences of this process, as discussed in two Chapters 3 and 4.

One reason for the lesser apparent attention given to ethnic loyalty in the marketing literature may be the distinct ways it can be interpreted, but mostly adopting an identity between national and ethnic loyalty to the country of provenance (Tajfel, 1970; Touwen-Bouwsma, 1996), expressed by de Snyder (1987) as "loyalty toward the mother culture". Without necessarily competing with allegiance to either the country of provenance or to the host country, which may occur simultaneously at different levels, we conceptualize ethnic loyalty in this text in a much narrower sense, as,

> *ethnic minority individuals' allegiance (wanting to be part of, or to affiliate) to a minority ethnic group within a host country.*

Consistent with this conceptualization, continued loyalty explains that minority ethnic groups have long existed within the territories of many countries. Indeed, ethnic loyalty is argued to survive at least four generations (Keefe and Padilla, 1987; Arbona, Flores and Novy, 1995). "Why" and "how" ethnic loyalty survives remains unclear and is probably best explained in context. There may be many reasons for ethnic loyalty to persist over time, many of which are discussed directly and indirectly in this text.

Reflecting an individual's perception and preference (hence, attributes and feelings) for one "culture or ethnic group" as expressed by Keefe and Padilla (1987), in practice ethnic loyalty refers to an individual's preference for a minority ethnic group rather than another (Padilla, 1980), a preference that exerts significant influence over that individual's consumption decisions (Donthu and Cherian, 1992; Chung and Fischer, 1999), including brand loyalty (Deshpande, Hoyer and Donthu, 1986) and arguably by extension, to ethnic minority businesses. Hence, congruent with Oliver's (1999) account of loyalty as

(a) deeply-held commitment to re-buy or re-patronize a preferred product/service consistently in the future, thereby, causing repetitive same brand set purchasing, despite situational influences and marketing efforts having the potential to cause switching behavior

(p. 34)

Ethnic minority consumers' loyalty to a minority ethnic group may be an important aspect to consider by businesses considering targeting that group—even in situations involving numerically small groups—since a willingness to repeat purchase can increase market-attractiveness far more than suggested by the numbers in the group (Pires, Stanton and Stanton, 2011).

The focus of this chapter is to discuss ethnic loyalty as a major factor to be taken into account in examining ethnic marketing, as well as providing the grounding for the discussion of ethnic marketing in general and, in particular, for the justification of the deployment of ethnic-sensitive tactics that are focused on developing loyalty advantages, discussed in later chapters of this text. Drawing on Oliver (1999)'s four-step loyalty development process, the discussion first focusses on loyalty drivers— accounting for loyalty development stages, loyalty dimensions and cultural affinity, followed by the consideration of switching drivers.

Interactions Between Ethnic Consumers, Groups and Businesses

From a perspective of ethnic minority consumers affiliated with a minority ethnic group, and in addition to self-interest from economic advantages related to socialization gains, emphasis may also be on ethnic loyalty encompassing altruistic feelings towards ethnically similar members of their group, invoking faith, ethnic purity or personal loyalty (Bowles and Giontis, 2004).

Some of these ethnic minority consumers are simultaneously self-employed ethnic entrepreneurs, possibly managing businesses seeking to serve the co-ethnic group. For this reason these businesses, hereafter designated as ethnic minority businesses, are recognized by the entrepreneur, consumers, suppliers, group gatekeepers and business support institutions in the host country as businesses affiliated with the group.[1] The expectation is that ethnic minority businesses may be naturally better positioned than other businesses for engaging with co-ethnic groups, and may gain from accessing a loyal network of repeat consumers, hence overcoming the eventual perspectives of restricted gains from trade related to relatively small group size.

Compared to businesses without recognized, tied ethnic attributes, ethnic minority businesses may take advantage of easier access to a potentially loyal market made out of repeat consumers. In either case, consumers' loyalty to the business will help it overcome the eventual perspectives of restricted gains from trade noted above, provided the business develops capabilities and competencies for deploying an ethnic-sensitive positioning strategy and tactics, cognizant that this is a process requiring investment likely to only be recovered/compensated *ex post* and over time, as discussed at length in later chapters.

Given the required investment in capabilities and competencies, a business decision of whether to target ethnic minority consumers with loyalty generation-oriented marketing strategies involves discerning clearly what are the benefits that accrue to consumers and to the business. In addition given that minority ethnic groups are intrinsically heterogeneous (Lindridge, 2015; Berry and Sam, 1997), businesses must decide who should be targeted?

Dealing With Intra-Group Heterogeneity

From a supplier's perspective, the decision of whether to invest in a relationship with ethnic minority consumers, namely those in the ethnic entrepreneur's group of affiliation, will depend on whether the lifetime value promised by the group's loyalty, as per the supplier's estimates, converts into a substantial value opportunity for the supplier that justifies the investment in developing and delivering ethnic-sensitive terms of exchange.

Reference to promised lifetime value reflects the challenge in determining future returns. Even using yield management or the market-attractiveness/competitive-position matrix (Walker et al., 2003), the share of consumers' wallets (all consumers, not only ethnic minority consumers) that a supplier will be able to gain over the years is necessarily volatile. Individual ethnic minority consumers may return to the home country or, at least, relocate geographically outside the supplier's practical reach, losing their situational ethnicity characteristics (Wilkinson, 2002; Stayman and Deshpandé, 1989; Okamura, 1981).

Nevertheless the challenge may be lessened by realizing that much less volatile than individual consumers' behaviour is the minority ethnic group's behaviour. Group substantiality may increase or decrease over time, but these groups are inherently stable within multicultural countries, as richly documented in the marketing literature (Jamal, Peñaloza and Laroche, 2015; Pires and Stanton, 2015) and reflected on stable ethnic loyalty even beyond four generations (Arbona, Flores and Novy, 1995). Hence, minority ethnic groups have the potential to appeal to suppliers endowed with suitable capabilities and competencies, many of which may be ethnic minority businesses.

Congruent with contemporary considerations of relationship marketing economics (Reichheld and Teal, 2001), certain economic considerations may be justified when assessing a minority ethnic group as a targeting opportunity. Examination of the opportunity presented to the supplier from targeting the group needs to take into account the return from the opportunity (or ethnic sensitivity payoff) vis a vis the normal (base) profit required by the business, and the potential investment and returns from allocating the targeting effort to alternative segments (Pires and Stanton, 1999), including the mainstream. Investment in ethnic-sensitive terms of exchange refers to the adaptation costs of the terms of exchange. Beyond normal profits gained from an initial investment in ethnic-sensitive terms of exchange that facilitate entering into a relationship, retention of the relationship may yield revenue growth and additional profits for at least four reasons, namely:

1. Increasing consumer-supplier interdependence may increase consumption of a larger product range by consumers more knowledgeable about the supplier, and by the minority ethnic group in general;
2. The increase in the number of consumers entering into a relationship with the supplier may leverage ethnic-sensitive investments, decreasing marginal costs over time;
3. Referral income may increase because the preferred supplier will continue to be recommended by a minority ethnic group to other (new and existing) group affiliates; and,
4. Subject to reflecting additional value creation, premium pricing may be possible.

A supplier's decision about whether to invest in the design and implementation of relational strategies towards minority ethnic groups must depend on their practicality and affordability (does the supplier have the required capabilities and competencies?) and on the immediate and long-term effects on the supplier's profitability and competitive position. Is there a significant payoff?

The size of the investment can be expected to depend on the strength of the ethnic characteristics of the minority group; that is, on how distinct the group is relative to other minority ethnic groups and to the mainstream. The stronger the ethnic characteristics of the consumer group relative to other groups, the higher the investment cost, the less contested the competitive environment, and the greater the payoff from ethnic sensitivity is likely to be.

In addition to the extent of distinctiveness relative to other ethnic groups and to the mainstream, ethnic-sensitive investment can be expected to depend on a minority ethnic group's heterogeneity. Considering the variety of acculturation outcomes possible (Berry and Sam, 1997), not all new arrivals will necessarily consolidate a relationship with a minority ethnic group and/or with its preferred suppliers to the same extent, if at all; determining how much ethnic-sensitive investment is required at the level of the individual consumer is a complex process, and probably an unrewarding task, since the target is the minority ethnic group, not the consumer. This is not to say that individual consumers' satisfaction with the preferred supplier doesn't matter. Poor supplier performance as experienced by a consumer can create switching pressures that may contaminate the whole minority ethnic group, through negative feedback.

The conclusion is that, while achieving sustainable competitive advantage is a desired objective for most suppliers, including those active in ethnic marketing, the process will require the use of effective segmentation, targeting and positioning analysis combined with specific supplier skills (including cultural awareness, sensitivity and responsiveness) that can be used to build consumer loyalty. Ultimately, ethnic marketing success depends on maintaining a minority ethnic group's loyalty.

The discussion of loyalty drivers in the next section shows that a minority ethnic group's loyalty to a preferred supplier will not be strong and enduring unless actions to that effect are undertaken by the supplier.

Loyalty Drivers

The viability of targeting an ethnic market segment can be improved if a supplier takes active steps to secure a high retention of the consumers in the segment. High retention can result from at least five possible drivers:

1. Establishing a nurtured relationship with consumers;
2. Imposing high switching costs (exit barriers), such that the consumer is retained even when satisfaction is low;
3. Targeting segments served by few competitors, reducing the choice of suppliers available to consumers (although a lack of competitive activity may be just a temporary condition);
4. Targeting segments characterized by consumer indifference or inertia; and
5. Strong ethnic loyalty.

Each driver offers different threats and opportunities for suppliers, justifying the need to understand what causes consumers to maintain a value relationship based on trust and commitment to specific suppliers (the loyalty drivers), as well the motives that might cause these consumers to switch suppliers (the switching drivers). Both types of drivers need to be considered in the retention strategies available to businesses targeting ethnic consumers, also bearing in mind that repeat purchase by the same consumer from the same supplier does not imply that the consumer is loyal, rather it may be due to inertia or indifference (Lee and Neale, 2012; Wu, 2011) or to ethnic loyalty. So, once the right segments are selected for targeting, how does the supplier develop consumer loyalty?

Developing Loyalty

Consumer loyalty is often cited in the marketing literature as an important determinant of long-term growth and profit margins (Reichheld, 2003; Doyle, 2000). Although there are differences regarding its definition, forms and determinants (Curasi and Kennedy, 2002; Ewing, 2000), consumer loyalty is often defined as *"a deeply held commitment to rebuy or repatronize a preferred product/service consistently in the future, thereby causing repetitive same brand or same brand-set purchasing, despite situational influences and marketing efforts having the potential to cause switching behavior"* (Oliver, 1999, p. 34).

In that definition, loyalty is both a socio-emotional attitude and a behavioural outcome—the act of consuming. This concept of loyalty does not presume consumer satisfaction, an outcome of consumption that results in pleasurable fulfilment. Loyalty, the psychological meaning of what drives the consumer to return to the same supplier, extends beyond attaining a satisfying experience, although satisfaction can be an obvious building block of loyalty. This understanding is also conveyed by Reichheld (2003) who refers to consumer loyalty as the willingness of a consumer to make an investment or personal sacrifice in order to strengthen a relationship. This may mean *"sticking with a supplier who treats him well and gives him good value in the long term even if the supplier does not offer the best price in a particular transaction"* (p. 3).

Oliver (1999) looks at loyalty as a 4-step development process that provides insight into how preferred suppliers must satisfy the minority ethnic group's needs and preferences in order to hold ethnic minority consumers' loyalty. Table 5.1 shows the type of loyalty that develops at each step as the outcome of a dynamic process that suppliers can influence in a positive way, ranging from the relatively superficial to a very strong positive affect accompanied by action.

A minority ethnic group's loyalty to a preferred supplier and affiliated consumers' loyalty to the group are the key factors:

1. *Cognitive Loyalty* is based primarily on belief rather than personal experience. Cognition may arise from information about the brand or supplier, and credence is given to that information. For recently

Table 5.1 Steps in Loyalty Development

Step	Loyalty Type	Based on	Requires	Reason for Switching	Switching Potential
1	Cognitive	Belief	Cumulative satisfaction	Counterargument and competitive blandishments	Strong
2	Affective	Satisfaction	Liking the supplier	Lack of commitment	Strong
3	Conative	• Increasing commitment • Cumulative satisfaction	Intention to repurchase	Intentions can be diverted	Weak but likely
4	Action or Ultimate	Build-up of resistance to switching motivations	• Immunity to competitors' claims; • Group preference	Lack of social relationship	Unlikely

arrived ethnic minority consumers, this information may well come from stakeholders in the minority ethnic group's ethnic network. If transactions do not require significant involvement and there is an abundance of suppliers, individual consumers' loyalty may remain shallow and undeveloped: counterargument and competitive blandishments may cause switching because there is little affect or emotional ties developed, depending mostly on ethnic loyalty concerns.

A preferred supplier may be retained solely based on a desire to comply with the minority ethnic group's recommendation, congruent with in-group behaviour reciprocity (Yamagishi, 2003). A decision to switch may be interpreted as negative feedback to the minority ethnic group. Recognizing early consumers and meeting minority ethnic group expectations is essential to move the relationship quickly into the next loyalty stage.

2. *Affective Loyalty* requires processing of satisfaction with the experience, implying confirmation of the expectations borrowed from the minority ethnic group. Evolving from the previous stage, a consumer's liking for the supplier grows based on cumulative satisfying usage occasions. There is both cognition and affect, but switching is a strong possibility if commitment is low. Ethnic minority consumers may remain accessible to competitors' offers, although retention is more likely as ethnic loyalty is strengthened with consumer satisfaction.

3. *Conative Loyalty* reflects a deepening commitment to a supplier, with previous satisfying experiences motivating repurchase intention. Since conative loyalty is essentially an intention that can be diverted,

switching is still possible. But it is highly unlikely in the case of ethnic minority consumers, who may resist even listening to competitor suppliers. This suggests that the distance between conative and action loyalty, the highest level of loyalty, may be very small where preferred suppliers to a minority ethnic group are concerned.

4. *Action Loyalty* is where motivated intention is carried through into a preparedness to act. It encompasses both readiness to act and the desire or preparedness to overcome obstacles that could prevent the intention becoming an action. This means that consumers are willing to resist situational influences and marketing efforts that might otherwise have caused switching. It may lead to future inertial rebuying because situational influences do not dissuade the action.

It is apparent that loyalty to a preferred supplier can be undermined in all four steps, including action loyalty, since it requires consumers' immunity to competitors' claims and induced dissatisfaction creation that might entice them to try another brand or supplier. But achieving this state of immunity, or *Ultimate Loyalty* as Oliver (1999) calls it, requires the building of a social relationship between consumers and the supplier. Businesses that become preferred suppliers to a minority ethnic group are in a strong position to win ultimate loyalty and a strong sustainable competitive advantage based on incumbency, providing a strong incentive for businesses to engage in relationships with ethnic minority consumers and minority ethnic groups.

Table 5.2 brings out the social role of consumption and loyalty that is missing from individually focused concepts of loyalty, using a simple matrix based on consumers' determination to stay with a brand or supplier, and the degree of social support that may assist in that endeavor.

Individual fortitude refers to a consumer's strength of will in resisting incentives to switch by competing businesses. Fortitude is high when a consumer exhibits action loyalty, because inertia extends to competitors' offers. Community or social support recognizes the social role of consumption and the importance of social approval. The minority ethnic group can provide varying impetus for consumer loyalty, passively or pro-actively.

Table 5.2 Loyalty Dimensions

Individual fortitude	Community/Social Support	
	Low	High
Low	Product superiority	Village envelopment
High	Determined self-isolation	Immersed self-identity

Source: Oliver (1999).

Both dimensions are examined; for simplicity, in terms of being either high or low. Low individual fortitude and low community/social support may correspond to a situation where only cognitive loyalty is generated. In contrast, an individual may have a high fortitude towards a particular brand, although community social support is relatively low. While this cell (determined self-isolation) reflects individual resistance to overtures from competing brands, this is likely to be difficult without the support of the individual's community.

The two cells on the far right in Table 5.2, corresponding to a situation of high community social support, suggest that strong ethnic network support is a key element in building ultimate loyalty. Consider an ethnic minority consumer newly arrived in a host country and needing to find suppliers for a variety of service-products. Individual fortitude will necessarily be low. By joining a minority ethnic group's consumer network, social support and guidance in supplier selection can largely come from the group. New arrivals' preferences for particular suppliers will tend to be shaped by stakeholders in their ethnic network, a situation of "village envelopment", in which "*the primary motivation to become loyal on the part of each consumer is to be one with the group and the primary motivation of the group overseers is to please their constituency*" (Oliver, 1999). The minority ethnic group includes the consumer in their social and economic network, offering protection from outside influences when individual fortitude is relatively low. The extreme case of this social environment, with its recommendation of preferred suppliers and of what to consume, is that the consumables sought by group members are not the purchased service-product, but the associated social relationships or camaraderie, strengthening ethnic loyalty.

Immersed self-identity, involving high individual fortitude for a brand/supplier combined with a minority ethnic group's social support, provides a case where there is both individual and social integration with the brand/supplier, such that the consumable becomes a part of the consumer's self and social identity. Belonging to a religious sect or cult is used by Oliver (1999) to illustrate this outcome. Finally, in the case of action loyalty, suppliers are able to tap into the social side of consumption, building a stronger loyalty based on minority ethnic groups' recommendations and on the importance of the group for the ethnic minority consumer, alias ethnic loyalty.

A question that remains is: can ethnic networks develop ultimate loyalty towards suppliers of all types of service-products? Clearly, low purchase frequency may simply reflect a lesser need for a service-product, rather than a loyalty deficit (Reichheld, 2003). Supported by a minority ethnic group's strong endorsement of a supplier, ultimate loyalty still requires service-product superiority, and ethnically loyal consumers who are committed to consume from, and to support, the supplier.

If the question is taken from the minority ethnic group's perspective, perennial endorsing of a preferred supplier depends only partially on individual members' loyalty and not necessarily on product type. If the question is taken from the perspective of consumer loyalty, it is unclear if ultimate loyalty is likely for all suppliers and for all types of service-products and terms of exchange.

If examined from a service logic perspective, the deployment of relational ethnic marketing strategies can be justified for all service-products regardless of the dominance of their tangible element, because consumers ultimately consume at terms of exchange developed jointly by their minority ethnic group and by the suppliers. Notwithstanding, if a goods logic perspective is chosen, the potential for loyalty creation may vary with service-product tangibility (Shostack, 1977; Rathmell, 1966). In general, service-products high in experience and credence qualities are likely to prove the most amenable to the stronger forms of loyalty creation although even search service-products can engender cognitive loyalty.

Cultural Affinity/Shared Ethnicity and Switching Costs

Building a strong loyalty by suppliers requires ethnic sensitivity in addressing minority ethnic group's needs and preferences, as well as evaluative criteria before, during and after consumption. There are many cultural variables likely to distinguish minority ethnic groups from the mainstream, so only general comments are made here. Some relate to oral pleasure (Usunier, 1998). Many are communication based and require ethnic-sensitive communication strategies and tactics recognizing these cultural differences. By addressing these differences, a cultural affinity or shared ethnicity based village envelopment that bonds the minority ethnic group and the individual affiliated consumers to a business can be constructed.

Cultural affinity or shared ethnicity can constitute an effective barrier to switching. Consider that a multicultural or multi-ethnic society is based on a collection of different minority ethnic groups alongside a majority "national" group (Yinger, 1976). This gives rise to many forms of cross-cultural interaction difficulties because the influence of a culture creates a complex mix made out of a residue of behaviours, ideas and beliefs with which people are comfortable and which they consider "proper" or the right way (Brislin, 1981), although this mix may sometimes appear overly personal or time inefficient to others.

The resulting cross-cultural interaction difficulties often ensue from communications complexity. Particularly important is the degree of reliance on non-verbal cues (Weiss and Stripp, 1998) that influence the capacity of a person from a different cultural background to appraise information provided by alternative suppliers framed in a different cultural context. This is why, in the context of a relationship with a supplier, communication complexity also creates barriers to switching. More search and other procedural costs, as well as relational costs, may be incurred by an inexperienced ethnic minority consumer compared with an experienced mainstream/ethnic minority consumer of the same service-product.

In addition to cultural affinity or shared ethnicity related barriers to switching, many retention reasons are not loyalty based, rather relating to one-time switching costs, monetary or otherwise (Kiser, 2002; Jones, Mothersbaugh and Beatty, 2000; Jones and Sasser, 1995) that consumers using a particular supplier perceive as likely to be incurred in switching to another supplier, and that will not be incurred if they retain the current supplier (Porter, 1980). Table 5.3 below shows eight types of switching costs identified by Burnham, Frels and Mahajan (2003), with types 1–6 being fully applicable to ethnic minority consumers.

Table 5.3 Perceived Costs in Switching Suppliers

Type of Perceived Risk	Higher Order Type	Costs Caused By
1 Economic	Procedural	Perceived risk of poor performance, often an accompanying financial risk and the inconvenience of changing ways of operating
2 Evaluation	Procedural	The time and effort costs incurred in searching, collecting and evaluating suppliers' information
3 Learning	Procedural	Acquiring new skills and knowledge needed to use the new supplier. Adaptation to a new system or rules is a part of the socialization associated with switching to a new supplier
4 Monetary	Financial	One-time financial outlays, such as a deposit be required to initiate service provision
5 Personal relationship	Relational	Breaking bond/ties with people with whom the consumer has interacted. Includes employees and other patrons who may provide a social attraction in using that provider (drawing on Oliver's (1999) village envelopment concept)
6 Brand relationship	Relational	Affective losses arising from the breaking of a bond with the brand or a supplier
7 Set-up	Procedural	Establishment costs of moving to a new supplier, such as installation and configuration of a software program
8 Benefit	Financial	Loss of economic benefits in switching to a new supplier (e.g. loss of loyalty points or discounts for cumulative purchases)

Socialization cost is a type of switching cost only partially catered for in the above classification, relating to the combination of performance losses (loosely accounted in economic risk) when partaking in service-encounters with some of the other costs. Importantly, these are costs that may accrue to both consumers and suppliers in a relationship, even if to different extents.

The concept of the "family doctor" is a good illustration. Following Pires and Stanton (2005), friendly doctors may also be perceived as being skilled. In addition to not querying the quality of this provider of a credence-based professional service activity, there are perceived switching costs associated with the doctor's knowledge of the person's past medical history. Conversely, there are time and efficiency benefits to the doctor from knowing the patient's medical history, personal traits, and professional communication requirements. Using the same doctor makes it easier for both stakeholders to participate in service-encounters and reduces the time required to benefit from the service performance. Switching doctors could conceivably result in a time intensive and painful process for the patient, while the relationship benefits would be lost, if not the past medical history, for both. Similar consideration would apply to lawyers, solicitors, accountants, bank managers, tax consultants, and many other professional or technical service activities.

Table 5.3 also provides information about higher order types for grouping switching costs, namely: procedural (economic risk, evaluation, learning and set-up costs); financial (benefit loss and monetary loss); and relational (personal relationship loss and brand relationship loss costs). Having to choose their first supplier in the host country, inexperienced ethnic minority consumers are naturally challenged by low socialization and by many types of procedural switching costs, justifying their reliance on recommended suppliers preferred by the minority ethnic group.

Long-term loyalty to those preferred suppliers may or may not ensue, but creating procedural and financial costs is not the way for a supplier to win these consumers' loyalty. Switching cost creation in the form of per-ceived *relational costs* must be the thrust of loyalty building. These costs are likely to have particular relevance for consumers with supplier loyalty built on the village envelopment or immersed self-identity (Oliver, 1999).

Stronger forms of loyalty (and higher relational switching costs) may be available for suppliers providing experience and credence service-products (Colgate and Hedge, 2001). Simultaneity and co-production invite integration of consumer resources with those of a preferred sup-plier (and more so in the case of preferred suppliers) to co-develop mutu-ally agreeable terms-of-exchange (Grönroos and Ravald, 2011) in an ethnic-sensitive manner, potentially raising switching costs higher.

Attraction to particular brands/suppliers of experience and credence service-products may be based on elements of cultural affinity that ease the acculturation process. Staying with a supplier because of communi-cation ease and pleasure arising from the provision of service-products using ones' own language, because of familiarity and perhaps identi-fication with employees, or because of socialization and oral pleasure provided by widespread use by similar-others, as well as good service performance, all suggest that ethnic minority consumers may incur a loss of identity and a breaking of bonds that causes psychological and/or emotional discomfort in switching providers (Burnham, Frels and Mahajan, 2003). Conversely, developing these bonds with a minority ethnic group provides the basis for Oliver's (1999) loyalty dimensions discussed earlier.

Switch Motivations

Essentially situational, the motives that encourage ethnic minority con-sumers to switch providers may be voluntary (a decision by the consumer), involuntary (the supplier ceases activity) or structural (the consumer no longer needs the service activity, as in the case of childcare). Voluntary motives may be direct, if they are triggered by perceived supplier misbe-haviour (such as poor service, or failure to remain competitive on price), or indirect, if they are not related to the quality of the immediate interac-tions that consumers maintains with the supplier.

Indirect motives may ensue from switching preferences for one sup-plier to another by the minority ethnic group, for example due to nega-tive feedback by peer consumers affiliated with that group. It may also result from a consumer's acculturation path and changes in situational ethnicity, with consumers possibly becoming aware of additional suppli-ers, some of whom may be more conveniently located (closeness to the locality of residence or workplace) or be more accessible (after hours, weekends, online). These motives, however, can be often moderated by ethnic loyalty and village envelopment (Pires, 2000).

Consumers who switch may not be dissatisfied with their provider, while those that do not may not be wholly satisfied. Other factors, such as better deals from competitors or a desire for a change (Fournier and Yao, 1997) can also play a role. Retention may fail because critical incidents are not addressed. Pricing, inconvenience, core service failure, service encounter failure, employee response to service failure, attraction by competitors and ethical problems were reasons why consumers switched providers, found in a study by Keaveney (1995).

Consumers may have limited use of ethnic resources for daily living necessities. Some will acculturate, or even assimilate to the mainstream ethnic group, although there is some suggestion that the ethnicity bond may not be easily lost, even after four generations (Arbona, Flores and Novy, 1995). Ethnic loyalty may deepen the meaning of dependence in the group (Swerdlow, 1998).

While the relative importance of the various motives may vary with service-product class, the combination of growing market knowledge and pursuit of convenience is inherent to the supplier selection process, moderating the influence of service-product class. As repeatedly shown by past research (Podoshen, 2006; Pires, 2000), inexperienced consumers rely on word-of-mouth by similar-others or on ethnic resources to reduce perceived risk in making decisions with limited information. These consumers are then subject to acculturation drivers and, importantly, to possible situational ethnicity changes. They may relocate their homes or change jobs, and may need to adjust consumption patterns to the new day-to-day reality. Since convenience, with its many facets, is an element inextricably intertwined with assessments of perceived value, switching decisions may follow.

Summary

This chapter presented theory elaborating on the importance of the interactions between ethnic minority consumers and suppliers to a minority ethnic group, as a factor in the generation of consumers' ethnic loyalty. The decision to target was addressed based on the importance of ethnic characteristics to ethnic-sensitive investment and its expected payoff; that is, ethnic-sensitive strategies that are focused on developing loyalty advantages need to be justified.

The discussion identified stages in loyalty development and loyalty dimensions, followed by an examination of why ethnic minority consumers may switch suppliers.

The chapters that follow deepen our understanding of the role played by ethnic minority businesses in ethnic marketing theory and practice.

Note

1. Examples of institutions and programs providing support to minority-owned businesses in the UK and in the USA are abundant (see for example www. nibusinessinfo.co.uk/content/support-black-asian-and-minority-ethnic-start-ups for the UK, with a focus on black, Asian and minority start-ups. An example in the USA is the Greater Boston Chamber of Commerce and their Pacesetters program (https://bostonchamber.com/programs-events/pace-setters), modelled after the Minority Business Accelerator program offered by the Cincinnati Regional Chamber which is attracting general attention in the USA (Cieslewicz, 2018; www.cincinnatichamber.com/the-inclusive-chamber/minority-business-accelerator).

References

Alvarez, C., Dickson, P. and Hunter, G. (2014). The four faces of the Hispanic consumer: An acculturation-based segmentation. *Journal of Business Research*, 67(2), 108–115.

Arbona, C., Flores, C. and Novy, D. (1995). Cultural awareness and ethnic loyalty: Dimensions of cultural variability among Mexican American College students. *Journal of Counselling and Development: JCD*, 73(6), 610–614.

Berry, J. and Sam, D. (1997). Acculturation and adaptation. In J. Berry, Y. Poortinga and J. Pandey (eds.), *Handbook of Cross-Cultural Psychology*, Vol. 3, 2nd ed. Boston: Allyn and Bacon, pp. 291–326.

Bowles, S. and Giontis, H. (2004). Persistent parochialism: Trust and exclusion in ethnic networks. *Journal of Economic Behavior & Organization*, 55, 1–23.

Brislin, R. (1981). *Cross-Cultural Encounters*. New York: Pergamon Press.

Burnham, T., Frels, J. and Mahajan, V. (2003). Consumer switching costs: A typology, antecedents and consequences. *Journal of the Academy of Marketing Science*, 31(Spring), 109–126.

Chung, E. and Fischer, E. (1999). It's who you know: Intracultural differences in ethnic product consumption. *Journal of Consumer Marketing*, 16(5), 482–501.

Cieslewicz, B. (2018). Cincinnati Minority Business Accelerator gets national attention. *Cincinnati Business Courier*, January 20. Accessed 15/6 at www. bizjournals.com/cincinnati/news/2018/01/19/cincinnati-minority-business-accelerator-gets.html

Cleveland, M. and Laroche, M. (2007). Acculturation to the global consumer culture: Scale development and research paradigm. *Journal of Business Research*, 60(3), 249–259.

Cleveland, M., Laroche, M., Pons, F. and Kastoun, R. (2009). Acculturation and consumption: Textures of cultural adaptation. *International Journal of Intercultural Relations*, 33(3), 196–212.

Colgate, M. and Hedge, R. (2001). An investigation into the switching process in retail banking services. *International Journal of Bank Marketing*, 19, 201–212.

Croucher, S. and Kramer, E. (2017). Cultural fusion theory: An alternative to acculturation. *Journal of International and Intercultural Communication*, 10(2), 97–114.

Curasi, C. and Kennedy, K. (2002). From prisoners to apostles: A typology of repeat buyers and loyal consumers in service businesses. *Journal of Services Marketing*, 16, 322–341.

Deshpande, R., Hoyer, W. and Donthu, N. (1986). The intensity of ethnic affiliation: A study of the sociology of Hispanic consumption. *Journal of Consumer Research*, 14–220.

De Snyder, V. (1987). The role of ethnic loyalty among Mexican immigrant women. *Hispanic Journal of Behavioural Sciences*, 9(3), 287–298.

Donthu, N. and Cherian, J. (1992). Hispanic coupon usage: The impact of strong and weak ethnic identification. *Psychology & Marketing*, 9(6), 501–510.

Doyle, P. (2000). *Value-Based Marketing*. Brisbane: John Wiley.

Ewing, M. (2000). Brand and retailer loyalty: Past behavior and future intentions. *Journal of Product and Brand Management*, 9, 120–127.

Fournier, S. and Yao, L. (1997). Reviving brand loyalty: A reconceptualization within the framework of consumer-brand relationships. *International Journal of Research in Marketing*, 14, 451–472.

Graves, T. (1967). Psychological acculturation in a tri-ethnic community. *Southwestern Journal of Anthropology*, 23(4), 337–350.

Grönroos, C. and Ravald, A. (2011). Service as business logic: Implications for value creation and marketing. *Journal of Service Management*, 22(1), 5–22.

Jamal, A., Peñaloza, L. and Laroche, M. (eds.) (2015). *The Routledge Companion to Ethnic Marketing*. Abingdon, UK: Routledge.

Jamal, A. and Shukor, A. (2014). Antecedents and outcomes of interpersonal influences and the role of acculturation: The case of young British-Muslims. *Journal of Business Research*, 67(3), 237–245.

Jones, M., Mothersbaugh, D. and Beatty, S. (2000). Switching barriers and repurchase intentions in services. *Journal of Retailing*, 76, 259–269.

Jones, T. and Sasser, E. (1995). Why satisfied consumers defect. *Harvard Business Review*, 73(November–December), 88–99.

Keaveney, S. (1995). Consumer switching behavior in service industries: An exploratory study. *Journal of Marketing*, 59(April), 71–92.

Keefe, S. and Padilla, A. (1987). *Chicano Ethnicity*. Albuquerque: University of New Mexico.

Kiser, E. (2002). Predicting household switching behavior and switching costs at depository institutions. *Review of Industrial Organization*, 20, 349–365.

Lee, R. and Neale, L. (2012). Interactions and consequences of inertia and switching costs. *Journal of Services Marketing*, 26(5), 365–374.

Lindridge, A. (2015). Is It Really Feasible? In *The Routledge Companion to Ethnic Marketing*. London: Routledge.

Luedicke, M. (2011). Consumer acculturation theory: (Crossing) conceptual boundaries. *Consumption Markets & Culture*, 14(3), 223–244.

Ogden, D., Ogden, J. and Schau, H. (2004). Exploring the impact of culture and acculturation on consumer purchase decisions: Toward a microcultural perspective. *Academy of Marketing Science Review*, 2004, 1.

Okamura, J. (1981). Situational ethnicity. *Ethnic and Racial Studies*, 4(4), 452–465.

Oliver, R. (1999). Whence consumer loyalty. *Journal of Marketing*, 63, 33–44.

Padilla, A. (1980). The role of cultural awareness and ethnic loyalty in acculturation. *Acculturation: Theory, Models, and Some New Findings*, 47, 84.

Pires, G. (2000). *The Selection of Service Providers by Ethnic Minority Consumers in a Culturally Diverse Society*. Unpublished Doctoral Thesis, University of Newcastle.

Pires, G. and Stanton, J. (2015). *Ethnic Marketing: Culturally Sensitive Theory and Practice*. Abingdon, UK: Routledge.

Pires, G. and Stanton, J. (2005). *Ethnic Marketing, Accepting the Challenge of Cultural Diversity*. London: Thomson Learning.

Pires, G. and Stanton, J. (1999). The substantiality test: Meaning and application in market segmentation. *Journal of Segmentation in Marketing*, 3(2), 105–115.

Pires, G, Stanton, J. and Stanton, P. (2011). Revisiting the substantiality criterion: From ethnic marketing to market segmentation. *Journal of Business Research*, 64(9), 988–996.

Podoshen, J. (2008). The African American consumer revisited: Brand loyalty, word-of-mouth and the effects of the black experience. *Journal of Consumer Marketing*, 25(4), 211–222.

Podoshen, J. (2006). Word of mouth, brand loyalty, acculturation and the American Jewish consumer. *Journal of Consumer Marketing*, 23(5), 266–282.

Porter, M. (1980). *Competitive Strategy*. New York: Free Press.

Rathmell, J. (1966). What is meant by services? *Journal of Marketing*, 30, 32–36.

Reichheld, F. (2003). The one number you need to grow. *Harvard Business Review*, December.

Reichheld, F. and Teal, T. (2001). *The Loyalty Effect: The Hidden Force Behind Growth, Profits, and Lasting Value*. Harvard Business Press.

Rosenbaum, M. and Montoya, D. (2007). Am I welcome here? Exploring how ethnic consumers assess their place identity. *Journal of Business Research*, 60(3), 206–214.

Segev, S., Ruvio, A., Shoham, A. and Velan, D. (2014). Acculturation and consumer loyalty among immigrants: A cross-national study. *European Journal of Marketing*, 48(9/10), 1579–1599.

Shostack, L. (1977). Breaking free from product marketing. *Journal of Marketing*, 41(April), 73–80.

Stayman, D. and Deshpandé, R. (1989). Situational ethnicity and consumer behavior. *Journal of Consumer Research*, 16(3), 361–371.

Swerdlow, J. (1998). Chinatown. *National Geographic*, August, 60–77.

Tajfel, H. (1970). Aspects of national and ethnic loyalty. *Social Science Information*, 9(3), 119–144.

Touwen-Bouwsma, E. (1996). Japanese minority policy: The Eurasians on Java and the dilemma of ethnic loyalty. *Bijdragen tot de taal-, land-en volkenkunde/ Journal of the Humanities and Social Sciences of Southeast Asia*, 152(4), 553–572.

Usunier, J. (1998). Oral pleasure and expatriate satisfaction: An empirical approach. *International Business Review*, 7(1), 89–110.

Walker, O., Boyd, Jr., H., Mullins, J. and Larréché, J. (2003). *Marketing Strategy: A Decision-Focused Approach*. New York: McGraw-Hill.

Wallerstein, I. (1960). Ethnicity and national integration in West Africa. *Cahiers d'études africaines*, 1(Cahier 3), 29–139.

Weiss, S. and Stripp, W. (1998). Negotiating with foreign business persons. In S. Niemeier, C. Campbell and R. Driven (eds.), *The Cultural Context in Business Communication*. Amsterdam: John Benjamin's Publishing Company.

Wilkinson, K. (2002). Collective situational ethnicity and Latino subgroups' struggle for influence in US Spanish-language television. *Communication Quarterly*, 50(3–4), 422–443.

Wu, L. (2011). Satisfaction, inertia, and consumer loyalty in the varying levels of the zone of tolerance and alternative attractiveness. *Journal of Services Marketing*, 25(5), 310–322.

Yamagishi, T. (2003). The group heuristic: A psychological mechanism that creates a self-sustaining system of generalized exchanges. *Proceedings of the Santa Fe Institute Workshop on the Coevolution of Institutions and Behavior*.

Yinger, J. (1976). Ethnicity in complex societies. In A. Lewis, et al. (eds.), *The Uses of Controversy in Sociology*. New York: Free Press.

6 Articulating Ethnic Marketing With Ethnic Entrepreneurship

The cultural diversity of many countries, both developed (e.g. Australia, Canada, the UK and the USA) and emerging (e.g. Bulgaria, China and India), is recognized in the scholarly literature. This diversity is a by-product of international immigration flows over time, leading to the formation and continued existence of minority ethnic groups within these countries national boundaries (Blagoev and Minkov, 2017; Jamal, Peñaloza and Laroche, 2015; Kumar and Marinova, 2017; Pires and Stanton, 2015).

Significantly, independent of variations in the intensity of migration flows or changes in the relative contributions by source countries, there is no indication that this diversity may reduce in the foreseeable future. In the case of the US, for example, estimates point to an increase in the size and buying power of the aggregate segment of the population identified by their ethnicity, forecasted to grow over the period from 2014 to 2019 at above 30 percent for the Latinos and Asian consumer groups, hence markedly faster when compared to a growth rate estimated at 21.3 percent for the mainstream population (Statista, 2018). This gain in the relative importance of the ethnicity identified aggregate segment of the US population is at the root of allusions to the new consumer majority (Maxwell, 2014; Burgos and Mobolade, 2011),

The discussion of cultural diversity issues from an essentially demand side ethnic marketing perspective has dominated discussion in the previous chapters of this text. Attention has centred on consumption behaviour issues involving two main stakeholders: ethnic minority consumers and minority ethnic groups.

One notable outcome of the discussion is the realization that consumption behaviour by these ethnic market stakeholders is heavily influenced by their embedding in the macro contexts of their countries of settlement prevailing at the time—arguably dominated by official policy approaches to culturally diversity—by the meso contexts of institutions such as those that assist with/regulate ethical and fair consumption, and by the micro-context related to stakeholder' eventual embedding in co-ethnic communities, in the mainstream, or somewhere in-between. With lesser prominence in the discussion, the other notable outcome of the discussion is the somewhat mute role afforded to suppliers to ethnic communities, many of which are both ethnic minority consumers and entrepreneurs affiliated to minority ethnic groups.

Indeed, the consumption of many goods and services, including ethnic-specific products delivered in culturally sensitive ways, is often assured by a large number of ethnic minority businesses (Pires and Stanton, 2015). In the UK alone, in 2012 almost 300,000 ethnic minority businesses, comprising around 6 percent of the small firm population, and contributing about £3 billion in gross value added (GVA) to the economy was estimated (Carter et al., 2015; BIS, 2013). There is no indication that the number of ethnic minority businesses may be abating.

Recognizing the relative lack of attention afforded to suppliers of goods and services to ethnic minority consumers and to minority ethnic groups, this chapter marks the transition in the text into a more holistically supported analysis of market-related cultural diversity issues, via the introduction of substantial management literature, particularly the extensive literature dealing with ethnic entrepreneurship and ethnic minority business.

The objectives going forward are:

1. To highlight the importance of accounting for the supply side, because of the potentially key role played by suppliers, many of which may consist of ethnic minority businesses, in the cohesiveness, independence and resilience of established minority ethnic groups and in their interplay with co-ethnic consumers;
2. To justify the need for research to embrace a more holistic analytical approach that accounts for demand and supply perspectives. This approach entails the articulation of ethnic marketing with ethnic entrepreneurship.

From Immigrant to Ethnic Minority Consumer

All new arrivals who purport to settle into a host country and to stay for at least 12 months can be deemed to meet the conditions required for being recognized as immigrants (Sasse and Thielemann, 2005). Some international entrepreneurship literature refers to immigrant individuals as first generation settlers embodying characteristics that they have acquired in other contexts, hence distinguishable from co-ethnic individuals who are born in the host country (Achidi and Priem, 2011). An alternative approach is to define immigrants as persons who have been born abroad, irrespective of nationality and of whether they are seen as ethnic minorities in the host country. So defined, immigrants also include their offspring such that: "ethnic entrepreneurs are either immigrants in a host country", or their "children/grandchildren" (Smallbone, 2005, p. 2).

Sidestepping eventual terminological complexities of the generational distinction, our approach endorses the conceptualization that migrants settle into host countries where they often become recognized by their ethnicity, becoming ethnic minority consumers, for contrast with the larger mainstream population—the majority.

Upon arrival and settlement, migrants are naturally exposed to processes of socialization and acculturation that can be expected to be dynamic and diachronic, with variable acculturation paths and outcomes over time (Berry, 2008, 2005; Ward, 2008; Rudmin, 2003; Peñaloza, 1989). The implication from this conceptualization is that how, where and why migrants settle early upon arrival may be influential in their acculturation path (Gibson, 2001; Berry and Sam, 1997; Berry, 1990) and needs to be understood.

Settlement in specific areas can be determined by a variety of circumstantial reasons. In Australia, for example, the area of settlement may be dictated by official emigration programs such as the Australian Migration Program (DHA, 2018), the skilled migration employment program (Birrell, 2018) or the Humanitarian *Settlement Program* (DSS, 2018), which basically pre-determines where a newcomer is going to locate. But in many other circumstances, as in the case of the family reunion program, ethnic minority consumers either tend to settle within or in the proximity of areas largely populated by individuals from the same home country (hence, co-ethnic, reflecting the same ethnic origin), or in the vicinity of settlers originating in different home countries but similar in their minority status within the host country (hence, similar-others, reflecting distinct ethnic origins), to which they may choose to affiliate (Roth et al., 2012; Takyi and Boate, 2006; Dustmann and Preston, 2001; Rishbeth, 2001; Li, 1998).

Beyond recognized feelings of birth-related attachment and belonging (Du, 2017; Kaplan, 1997), a major justification for highlighting these early locations of settlement and affiliation choices on arrival is that making the right settlement decisions may help reduce the communication and socialization challenges that characterize day-to-day living in a new country, with its own distinct way of understanding and doing things. Indeed, cultural ambiguity problems may combine with the new arrival's natural lack of market knowledge and eventual poor proficiency in the host country's language, to heighten cultural shock symptoms, ranging from oral pleasure issues (Usunier, 1998), to consumption challenges and to challenges related to their ability to earn a living by competing for and gaining effective access to mainstream employment opportunities.

Assistance by the co-ethnic community or by similar-others in settling into the host country has the potential to reduce communication and socialization deficits, both in accessing mainstream employment opportunities whenever possible, and by facilitating access to the services and support provided by that ethnic community's social and business networks. For example, access as users/consumers to any ethnic-sensitive services provided by the ethnic business network to ethnic community members is likely to simply depend on a recognized affiliation of the member to that community.

More complex, but often feasible as abundantly documented in the literature (see Chapter 7), may be to address difficulties of earning a living by engaging in self-employment and starting-up and developing an ethnic minority business within the community space, eventually joining the community's ethnic business network as a supplier to that community.

From Ethnic Minority Consumer to Ethnic Entrepreneur

Self-employment is an important issue to consider because the vast specialist literature acknowledges that a substantial number of ethnic minority consumers, particularly in the case of newly arrived immigrants, are unable to secure stable and rewarding employment within the mainstream economy. This explains that newly arrived ethnic minority individuals, often with their families, seek to address their earning a living problem upon settlement by either

- Seeking to take advantage of employment opportunities available within the business networks of their minority ethnic group of affiliation (Nee and Sanders, 2001; Nee, Sanders and Sernau, 1994); or by
- Engaging in ethnic entrepreneurship and creating their own ethnic minority business, focusing on the unmet needs and demands of their minority ethnic group of affiliation.

Hence, the ethnic community may provide co-ethnic individuals with shelter, camaraderie, consuming satisfaction and income earning opportunities. For those individuals who decide to engage in business, as a rule the ethnic community may provide the market, comprising suppliers, business support services and customers.

A particularly expressive exception to the rule refers to recent instances when highly educated, newly arrived settlers may be able to secure suitable employment within the mainstream or, indeed, to engage in professional business activities, such as healthcare, equally targeting the mainstream and ethnic-identified populations. Jones, Mascarenhas-Keyes and Ram (2012) report the case of the Indian community in the UK as an example of "ethnic entrepreneurial transition", with the growing convergence of Indian self-employment with white-owned businesses, a trend first noted in 2003, reflecting an increasing presence of Indian individuals in the professions and diversification into new and emerging sectors.

Whether prompted by an inability to secure suitable employment, motivated by independence aspirations or for other reasons, ethnic minority individuals may opt for self-employment, engaging in entrepreneurship activity (hence becoming recognized as ethnic entrepreneurs), which implies the recognition of a business opportunity, and the subsequent start-up and development of an ethnic minority business.

This chapter provides a first insight into the argument developed in the following chapters that the contribution made by new ethnic minority businesses in joining ethnic business networks over time strengthens those networks and expands the service provided to the ethnic community, reducing socialization complexities. This increases the value perceived by co-ethnic consumers and entrepreneurs in their affiliation to the group, which naturally increases the resilience over time of minority ethnic communities within the territories of democratic multicultural societies. This abundantly justifies the need to understand how ethnic marketing perspectives interact and combine with perspectives of ethnic entrepreneurship.

Socialization and Entrepreneurship

The resilience of minority ethnic groups has instigated substantial discussion in the literature (Costigan et al., 2010; Riccio, 2001), often by reference to the group's contribution to its affiliates' socialization and acculturation to life in the host country. The group contributes by facilitating its affiliates' access to ethnic group resources, including access to ethnic social and business networks, effectively reducing culture shock effects (Usunier, 1998; Oberg, 1960). One by-product from the improved socialization process is the potential fostering of ethnic entrepreneurship, often reflected in business opportunities that give way to the development and start-up of ethnic minority businesses.

A salient feature of early business efforts by ethnic minority individuals is, arguably, their dependence on the minority ethnic group of their affiliation for support, either by friends, relatives and similar-others and/or by a large network of ethnic community institutions, including religious associations, political bodies, gatekeeper personalities and co-ethnic businesses. Reliability in this dependence on strong community support based on co-ethnicity might justify the development of small ethnic minority businesses with some degree of independence from the host community (Wilson and Portes, 1980). Hence, the minority ethnic group of affiliation acts as a de-facto gatekeeper between the group's supply chain and consumption demand (the group's operative ethnic resources), and prospective co-ethnic entrepreneurs, to whom it implicitly recognizes a status of supplier to the group (Ulaga and Eggert, 2006), that may culminate with the addition of the entrepreneur's ethnic minority business to those ethnic resources.

Either in a business-to-consumer or business-to-business context, user engagement involves interaction with their group of affiliation via the suppliers of goods and services in the ethnic business network, whether public (such as Council services and TV broadcasting) or private. Private suppliers of community resources include community stakeholders such as social and sporting clubs, providers of childcare services, community cultural interest groups, agents of banks from the home countries, travel agents, community newspapers and radio stations, and many other business activities provided by trades and professional individuals.

Clearly, the importance/significance of business networks associated with a minority ethnic community depends on how engaged the affiliated ethnic consumers and businesses are as users, with the operative ethnic resources afforded by the group. A requirement is effective recognition of, and preference for, ethnic minority businesses amidst all the competing suppliers available to the ethnic community.

Recognition of Ethnic Minority Business by Ethnic Communities

The recognition of an ethnic minority business as having the characteristics to be a potentially good supplier to a given minority ethnic group can be, first and foremost, an informal outcome from the simple recognition by the group of the ethnic entrepreneur's identity as a valued group affiliate. In cases where intra-group communications are predominantly in the primordial language, those communications can convert into competitive advantage for an ethnic minority business. But there is no reason to expect that the advantage will be sustainable, or that it warrants either a necessary or a sufficient condition for any other status or preference to be given, either overtly or implied, to that ethnic minority business by the group.

The process transforming ethnic minority businesses into preferred suppliers to the minority ethnic group of reference is elaborated in Chapter 9 of this text, dealing with the articulation of preferred suppliers with ethnic networks. Pre-empting that discussion, it is recognized that a large number of attributes or characteristics are required for businesses to be promoted by minority ethnic groups and its affiliated consumers to a position that confers a preferential status as suppliers. These attributes or characteristics include supplier *reliability* in the provision of the right product at the right price (involving financial terms, quality assurance and service performance), appropriate *responsiveness* to customers' concerns and perceived risk, including demonstrated awareness of, *sensitivity* to, and *agility* in reacting to changes in either general consumer needs or changes specific to the minority ethnic group, as well as *flexibility* in the use of existing capabilities to adapt to changed circumstances, and *low barriers* whether cultural or communicational in serving the relevant ethnic minority consumers (Larson and Kulchitsky, 2000; Verma and Pullman, 1998; Min, 1994).

Reflecting on those attributes indicates that value proposition attributes or characteristics, such as product-related advantage and price, might have lost some of their importance as differentiators of suppliers to minority ethnic groups over time, perhaps due to technologic development, greater availability to all business and convergence across markets. Along this line of reasoning, Ulaga and Eggert (2006) report that product quality, delivery performance, and economics have become only moderate supplier differentiators, price being the weakest, with service support and personal interaction benefits exhibiting a much stronger potential as core supplier differentiators. Notwithstanding, while the importance of delivery performance is supported across the board, there is recent research highlighting the offering of competitive prices as the second most important ethnic-related attribute after delivery performance (Huang, Oppewal and Mavondo, 2013). This an area clearly requiring further research.

Consideration of the identified shift in most valued attributes and characteristics invites the suggestion that minority ethnic groups adopt a benefits-based focus in assessing supplier performance, with greater importance being given to the relational benefits ensuing from the establishment of relationships with suppliers, compared with the previous focus on transactional approaches. While the establishment of relationships with mainstream or other suppliers independent of shared ethnicity cannot be ruled out, co-ethnic minority businesses may be able to position themselves so as to be in good stead with co-ethnic consumers and, possibly, with established preferred suppliers to the ethnic community.

The underlining implication from the change from a transactional to a relational perspective is that being the best of all suppliers of a particular service-product may ensure recognition of the supplier by the group, but this may not be sufficient to generate preference—being a good supplier of long-term relational benefits and being recognized as such by the ethnic community of interest is imperative to being a preferred supplier. The postulate from here is a clear support for the argument developed in this text that relational ethnic marketing strategies and tactics deployed by ethnic minority businesses need to focus on the minority group over the longer term, as compared with possibly transactional, short-term tactics focused on individual ethnic minority consumers.

It is apparent that the supplier differentiators identified above neither create a position of privilege for ethnic minority businesses, nor necessarily bar access by any other type of business—whether mainstream, multinational or global—without shared ethnicity connotations, to a privileged supplier position relative to an ethnic group. Hence, the suggestion is that shared ethnicity may not be either important or determinant for that statute to be achieved by a supplier. This is a suggestion that can gain further support when we recognize that the specialist literature often deals with aggregates of minority ethnic groups as if they were groups determined based on one shared ethnicity. In this case the question is, which ethnicity should an ethnic minority business hold for shared ethnicity to occur when dealing with aggregates of minority ethnic groups?

The importance of shared ethnicity for minority ethnic groups and ethnic minority businesses is a topical area in need of systematic marketing intelligence because the management literature devoted to entrepreneurship offers theoretical and practical insights into ethnic minority business start-up, development, growth and demise that unambiguously link ethnic entrepreneurs (and often their family members) to their minority ethnic group of affiliation and to its networks. The objective is to provide clarity on the role played by shared ethnicity in the process of transforming suppliers to an ethnic group into preferred suppliers to that group. This clarity can be expected to be critical to considerations of the similarities and differences in the marketing strategies and tactical activities deployed by co-ethnic and other businesses targeting a minority ethnic group.

From Ethnic Marketing to Marketing by Ethnic Minority Businesses

Ethnic marketing has been defined as "differentiated marketing towards an ethnic group" (Cui, 1998, p. 88), comprising all marketing efforts and instruments used to target specific ethnic groups within a society and to satisfy their particular needs (All Business, 2014). Drawing on the definition of marketing offered by the American Marketing Association (AMA), Pires and Stanton (2015) expressed ethnic marketing as "the activity, set of institutions, and processes for creating, communicating, delivering and exchanging offerings that have value for ethnic-identified customers, clients, partners and communities, and for society at large" (pp. 8–9).

Except for the narrow focus on ethnic groups, the deployment of ethnic marketing does not place *a priori* restrictions on either which group or set of groups is targeted, or on the nature of the business doing the targeting. It is therefore totally plausible for a mainstream business to aim at serving any number of market segments, some of which may be minority ethnic groups determined by their ethnicity.

The challenge when reflecting on the deployment of ethnic marketing strategies from the vantage point of any generic business is that effective targeting by the business needs to develop and implement ethnic-sensitive strategies that respond to the characteristics, demands and needs of the group being targeted, often in the group's native language. As noted by Pires and Stanton (2015), this requires:

- Knowledge of the group's special needs, preferences and evaluative criteria, based on carefully developed community profiles;
- Knowledge of the context of the minority ethnic group;
- Awareness of the cultural nuances that make the group distinct from other groups;
- Deployment of ethnic-sensitive tactics—this may involve ethnic-embedded service-products, service-encounters and communications, possibly in the group's language.

It is apparent that, at least theoretically, ethnic marketing deployed by ethnic minority businesses targeting their own group of affiliation should be "naturally" ethnic-sensitive, hence likely to face less challenges and to hold a competitive advantage over other types of businesses, given "natural" socialization and proficiency in the ethnic group language, with service often delivered by co-ethnic employees (Baumann and Setogawa, 2015; Rosenbaum and Montoya, 2007; Ram et al., 2000; Lyer and Shapiro, 1999). The expectation, henceforth, is that strategies and associated tactical activities will likely vary across ethnic minority businesses and other businesses without ethnicity connotations.

The chapters that follow adopt a more holistic analytical approach that brings together demand and supply perspectives. The main objectives going forward are:

1. To highlight the importance of the supply side, because of the potentially key role played by suppliers, many of which may consist of ethnic minority businesses, in the cohesiveness, independence and resilience of established minority ethnic groups and in their interplay with co-ethnic consumers;
2. To understand how the minority ethnic group contributes opportunities for ethnic minority businesses to develop;
3. To explain how the articulation of ethnic minority businesses with minority ethnic groups can develop into a preferred supplier status grounded on the establishment of long-term relationships between the parties, and extensive to social and business networks associated with the minority ethnic group; and
4. To examine the implications for ethnic marketing strategy and tactics.

Chapter 7 establishes the basic knowledge required to examine the relationship and interdependence of ethnic entrepreneurs, ethnic minority businesses and minority ethnic groups. Drawing from relevant ethnography/cultural, entrepreneurship/economics and sociology literatures, the chapter seeks to understand the inner-workings of ethnic entrepreneurship, exploring the close link between minority ethnic groups and ethnic minority businesses during these businesses' creation and consolidation phases. An important output of the discussion is to explain that the entrepreneur's minority ethnic group of affiliation is the business incubator that supports enterprise consolidation, the principal market and the natural habitat for ethnic minority businesses, whereas a lack of access to the minority ethnic group is likely to justify declining sales and loss of business.

Maintaining a strong focus on the examination of how crucial is the role played by minority ethnic groups for the development of ethnic entrepreneurship—from a natural incubator to being a facilitator in entrepreneurs' access to ethnic resources and the fundamental target market offered by the minority ethnic group, Chapter 8 discusses the role played by minority ethnic groups in the break out strategies that are likely to underpin an ethnic minority business growth potential, that is, after the ethnic minority business is formally created and its operations are consolidated as a young business targeting their initial co-ethnic market.

Rather than examining the business strategies deployed by ethnic minority businesses in exploiting the growth opportunities eventually provided by the entrepreneurs' minority ethnic group, perhaps involving improved performance as reflected on revenue or on cost minimization through operational efficiency, the main focus is on business growth through expansion to alternative markets, distinct from the minority ethnic group of affiliation, whether minority, mainstream, international, transnational or even global.

Chapter 9 discusses how ethnic minority consumers contribute to ethnic minority business growth, involving these businesses' interaction with their minority ethnic group of affiliation, and that group's demand and supply networks. Emphasis is given to ethnic minority businesses as potential preferred suppliers to the relevant minority ethnic group, seeking to highlight the distinct attributes required for their successful performance in two distinct markets, one made up of co-ethnic consumers, and the other involving relationships with businesses in the ethnic network. One objective is to examine how a minority ethnic group offers opportunities for ethnic minority businesses to develop by accessing the group's resources, eventually promoting and nurturing them as preferred suppliers to the group.

Chapter 10 discusses the strategies and tactics involving ethnic minority businesses and their targeting markets. The discussion distinguishes business objectives and strategies from the marketing activities that make up the tactical approaches they undertake to meet business and marketing objectives. Departing from recent discussions of the ethnic marketing mix forwarded by Jamal, Peñaloza and Laroche (2015) and Pires and Stanton (2015), the various factors in the mix are revisited from an ethnic minority business perspective. Chapters 11, 12 and 13 turn to tactical activities deployed by ethnic minority businesses, namely place, process, physical evidence, product, price, promotion, personalization and people, within the constraints of ethical behaviour.

References

Achidi, H. and Priem, R. (2011). Immigrant entrepreneurs, the ethnic enclave strategy, and venture performance. *Journal of Management*, 37(3), 790–818.

All Business (2014). *Ethnic Marketing*. Accessed 8/6/2018 at www.allbusiness.com/barrons_dictionary/dictionary-ethnic-marketing-4966319-1.html

Baumann, C. and Setogawa, S. (2015). Asian ethnicity in the West: Preference for Chinese, Indian and Korean service staff. *Asian Ethnicity*, 16(3), 380–398.

Berry, J. (2008). Globalisation and acculturation. *International Journal of Intercultural Relations*, 32(4), 328–336.

Berry, J. (2005). Acculturation: Living successfully in two cultures. *International Journal of Intercultural Relations*, 29(6), 697–712.

Berry, J. (1990). Understanding individuals moving between cultures. *Applied Cross-Cultural Psychology*, 14(1), 232.

Berry, J. and Sam, D. (1997). Acculturation and adaptation. *Handbook of Cross-Cultural Psychology*, 3(2), 291–326.

Birrell, B. (2018). *Australia's* skilled migration program: Scarce skills not required the Australian Population Research Institute. *Research Report*, March 13. http://tapri.org.au/

BIS (2013). *Small Business Survey 2012: Estimates for Women-Led, Minority Ethnic Group (MEG) Led and Social Enterprises in the UK*. London: Department for Business, Innovation & Skills.

Blagoev, V. and Minkov, M. (2017). Marketing in Bulgaria: A small emerging economy and multicultural markets. *Research Handbook of Marketing in Emerging Economies*, 265.

Burgos, D. and Mobolade, O. (2011). *Marketing to the New Majority: Strategies for a Diverse World*. St. Martin's Press, McMillan.

Carter, S., Mwaura, S., Ram, M., Trehan, K. and Jones, T. (2015). Barriers to ethnic minority and women's enterprise: Existing evidence, policy tensions and unsettled questions. *International Small Business Journal*, 33(1), 49–69.

Costigan, C., Koryzma, C., Hua, J. and Chance, L. (2010). Ethnic identity, achievement, and psychological adjustment: Examining risk and resilience among youth from immigrant Chinese families in Canada. *Cultural Diversity and Ethnic Minority Psychology*, 16(2), 264.

Cui, G. (1998). Ethical issues in ethnic segmentation and target marketing. *Proceedings of the 1998 Multicultural Marketing Conference*. Springer, Cham, pp. 87–91.

DHA (2018). *Fact Sheet: Australia's Migration Programme, Department of Home Affairs*. Accessed 1/6/2018 at www.homeaffairs.gov.au/about/corporate/information/fact-sheets/01backgd

DSS—Debarment of Social Services (2018). *Humanitarian Settlement Program*. Accessed 8/6/2018 at www.dss.gov.au/settlement-services/programs-policy/settlement-services/humanitarian-settlement-program

Du, H. (2017). Place attachment and belonging among educated young migrants and returnees: The case of Chaohu, China. *Population, Space and Place*, 23(1).

Dustmann, C. and Preston, I. (2001). Attitudes to ethnic minorities, ethnic context and location decisions. *The Economic Journal*, 111(470), 353–373.

Gibson, M. (2001). Immigrant adaptation and patterns of acculturation. *Human Development*, 44(1), 19–23.

Huang, Y., Oppewal, H. and Mavondo, F. (2013). The influence of ethnic attributes on ethnic consumer choice of service outlet. *European Journal of Marketing*, 47(5/6), 877–898.

Jamal, A., Peñaloza, L. and Laroche, M. (eds.) (2015). *The Routledge Companion to Ethnic Marketing*. Abingdon, UK: Routledge.

Jones, T., Mascarenhas-Keyes, S. and Ram, M. (2012). The ethnic entrepreneurial transition: Recent trends in British Indian self-employment. *Journal of Ethnic and Migration Studies*, 38(1), 93–109.

Kaplan, D. (1997). The creation of an ethnic economy: Indochinese business expansion in Saint Paul. *Economic Geography*, 73(2), 214–233.

Kumar, S. and Marinova, S. (2017). Value branding in emerging markets as a social dimension in the Indian context. In *Research Handbook of Marketing in Emerging Economies*. Edward Elgar Publishing, Incorporated.

Larson, P. and Kulchitsky, J. (2000). The use and impact of communication media in purchasing and supply management. *Journal of Supply Chain Management*, 36(2), 29–39.

Li, W. (1998). Anatomy of a new ethnic settlement: The Chinese ethnoburb in Los Angeles. *Urban Studies*, 35(3), 479–501.

Lyer, G. and Shapiro, J. (1999). Ethnic entrepreneurial and marketing systems: Implications for the global economy. *Journal of International Marketing*, 7(4), 83–110.

Maxwell, L. (2014). US school enrollment hits majority-minority milestone. *The Education Digest*, 80(4), 27.

Min, H. (1994). International supplier selection: A multi-attribute utility approach. *International Journal of Physical Distribution & Logistics Management*, 24(5), 24–33.

Nee, V. and Sanders, J. (2001). Understanding the diversity of immigrant incorporation: A forms-of-capital model. *Ethnic and Racial Studies*, 24(3), 386–411.

Nee, V., Sanders, J. and Sernau, S. (1994). Job transitions in an immigrant metropolis: Ethnic boundaries and the mixed economy. *American Sociological Review*, 849–872.

Oberg, K. (1960). Cultural shock: Adjustment to new cultural environments. *Practical Anthropology*, 7(4), 177–182.

Peñaloza, L. (1989). Immigrant consumer acculturation. *ACR North American Advances*. http://acrwebsite.org/volumes/6890/volumes/v16/NA-16

Pires, G. and Stanton, J. (2015). *Ethnic Marketing: Culturally Sensitive Theory and Practice*. Abingdon, UK: Routledge.

Ram, M., Sanghera, B., Abbas, T., Barlow, G. and Jones, T. (2000). Ethnic minority business in comparative perspective: The case of the independent restaurant sector. *Journal of Ethnic and Migration Studies*, 26(3), 495–510.

Riccio, B. (2001). From "ethnic group" to "transnational community"? Senegalese migrants' ambivalent experiences and multiple trajectories. *Journal of Ethnic and Migration Studies*, 27(4), 583–599.

Rishbeth, C. (2001). Ethnic minority groups and the design of public open space: An inclusive landscape? *Landscape Research*, 26(4), 351–366.

Rosenbaum, M. and Montoya, D. (2007). Am I welcome here? Exploring how ethnic consumers assess their place identity. *Journal of Business Research*, 60, 206–214.

Roth, W., Seidel, M., Ma, D. and Lo, E. (2012). In and out of the ethnic economy: A longitudinal analysis of ethnic networks and pathways to economic success across immigrant categories. *International Migration Review*, 46(2), 310–361.

Rudmin, F. (2003). Critical history of the acculturation psychology of assimilation, separation, integration, and marginalization. *Review of General Psychology*, 7(1), 3.

Sasse, G. and Thielemann, E. (2005). A research agenda for the study of migrants and minorities in Europe. *JCMS: Journal of Common Market Studies*, 43(4), 655–671.

Smallbone, D. (2005). *Entrepreneurship by Ethnic Minorities: Institutions*. Background Paper. Brussels: OECD.

Statista (2018). *Growth in Buying Power of Consumers in the United States between 2014 and 2019, by Ethnic Group*. www.statista.com/statistics/452102/us-consumer-buying-power-change-by-ethnicity/

Takyi, B. and Boate, K. (2006). Location and settlement patterns of African immigrants in the US: Demographic and spatial context. In *The New African Diaspora in North America: Trends, Community Building, and Adaptation.* Lanham, MD: Lexington Books, pp. 50–67.

Ulaga, W. and Eggert, A. (2006). Value-based differentiation in business relationships: Gaining and sustaining key supplier status. *Journal of Marketing*, 70(1), 119–136.

Usunier, J. (1998). Oral pleasure and expatriate satisfaction: An empirical approach. *International Business Review*, 7(1), 89–110.

Verma, R. and Pullman, M. (1998). An analysis of the supplier selection process. *Omega*, 26(6), 739–750.

Ward, C. (2008). Thinking outside the Berry boxes: New perspectives on identity, acculturation and intercultural relations. *International Journal of Intercultural Relations*, 32(2), 105–114.

Wilson, K. and Portes, A. (1980). Immigrant enclaves: An analysis of the labor market experiences of cubans in Miami. *American Journal of Sociology*, 86(2), 295–319.

7 Understanding Ethnic Entrepreneurship

Suppliers of goods and services to ethnic minorities may not come from the same minority ethnic group that binds the consumers they serve. For example, there is clear evidence that many ethnic minority consumers use a variety of mainstream suppliers to satisfy some of their needs and wants, particularly when the goods procured are service-products with search attributes. These are amenable to consumer's choice, perusal/trial and consumption without a need for extensive interaction with the supplier (Zeithaml, 1981). Hence, while ethnic minority consumers may select ethnic minority businesses as suppliers when demanding ethnic-specific service-products not available in mainstream outlets, the same consumers may well consume non-ethnic specific products available from mainstream establishments such as supermarkets, pharmacies and service stations, as well as use public transport, fast-food outlets, fish-markets, taxis and many other services offered by suppliers to the mainstream.

The relative growth of ethnic minorities above mainstream rates and their increasing purchase power within multicultural societies such as the USA, UK and Australia, justifies their targeting by a variety of minority and mainstream suppliers. In the USA, the growing Hispanic and Asian populations have driven demand in the ethnic supermarkets industry, which is composed of ethnocentric food retailers that sell culturally diverse food for consumption at home, and which together make up a significant share of industry sales (Ibisworld, 2017; Zitelli, 2017). In the UK, Tesco decided to cater for the estimated 600,000 Poles, with Polish food becoming the fastest-growing ethnic food in the chain (The Guardian, 2007). In Australia, supermarkets, such as Woolworths, have long responded to ethnic diversity, adding ethnic-specific product lines (such as Chinese, halal and Kosher), in an attempt to persuade ethnic minorities to buy those products from them, together with many other non-ethnic products in their weekly shopping cart (Meryment, 2011).

Notwithstanding the relative attention given to the consumption needs of minority ethnic groups by mainstream suppliers such as supermarkets, those groups' consumption of ethnic-specific service-products delivered in culturally sensitive ways is commonly reported as being assured by ethnic minority businesses with affiliation to the minority ethnic group. As reported by Carter et al. (2015) for the UK alone, around 2012 there were almost 300,000 ethnic minority businesses comprising at least 6 percent of the small firm population, and contributing about £3 billion in gross value added (BIS, 2013), and about £40 billion to the economy overall (Jones and Ram, 2012, p. 947).[1]

Overall, ethnic minority businesses make a significant contribution to a nation's well-being, by promoting innovation, engendering competition, creating employment and creating economic wealth and spending power (London Research Centre, 1999, cited in Altinay and Altinay, 2006). As well, they play an important role in the social adaptation and integration of newly arrived migrants in local economies and communities (Jones et al., 2012; Zhou, 2004), contributing to the revival of declining sectors and places (McEwan, Pollard and Henry, 2005) and to the resilience of minority ethnic groups (Pires and Stanton, 2015). From a functional perspective, ethnic minority businesses are alleged to contribute to the overall economy by providing low-priced and better-valued goods and services, fuelling entrepreneurial ambition and offering training and knowledge resources (Jamal, 2005).

Drawing from relevant ethnography/cultural (Peet and Hartwick, 2015; Mohanty, 2005), entrepreneurship/economics (Langlois, 2007; Harper, 2003) and sociology (Landstrom, 1999; Reynolds, 1991) literatures, this chapter seeks to understand the inner-workings of ethnic entrepreneurship, exploring the close link between minority ethnic groups and ethnic minority businesses during the latter's creation and consolidation phases.

An important objective of the chapter is to explain that the entrepreneur's minority ethnic group of affiliation is the business incubator that supports enterprise consolidation, the principal market and the natural habitat for ethnic minority businesses, whereas a lack of access to the minority ethnic group is likely to justify declining sales and loss of business (Komakech and Jackson, 2016). Conversely, focus on the cultural side of minority ethnic groups suggests that entrepreneurship has more of an influence on the development of a minority ethnic group's economic stability than through the process of assimilation (Greene and Butler, 1996; Butler, 1991).

Conceptualizing Ethnic Entrepreneurship

Far from characterized by a single and unambiguous definition, "entrepreneurship" has a wide range of meanings (Dana, 2006), hence it is hard to define. A common starting point is to think of entrepreneurship as a noun referring to what an entrepreneur does, described broadly as people who create and grow enterprises (Thornton, Ribeiro-Soriano and Urbano, 2011).[2] More rigorous, even if still somewhat subjective given the inherent measurement challenges, is the definition of entrepreneurship as the willingness to start, develop and manage a new business (or enterprise), in order to gain profit by taking several risks in the corporate world (http://entrepreneurhandbook.co.uk/entrepreneurship/; Baron and Shane, 2008), Arguably, this is done by combining resources in novel ways so as to create something of value (Bird, 1989), thus generating superior returns that result in the creation of wealth (quick MBA, 2007).

The focus on wealth and value creation through innovation and creative destruction (Schumpeter, 1942) is traceable to Schumpeter's emphasis on opportunity-seeking behaviour focused on new products, new production methods, new markets and new business forms (Schumpeter, 1951, 2000). But this focus is, perhaps, the major cause of variation in the conceptualization of entrepreneurship, because Schumpeter's definition is more amenable to large enterprises; those with substantial wealth and innovation investment capabilities, producing substantial returns in a relatively short time. This is less applicable to entrepreneurship related to small business, characterized (as is often the case of ethnic entrepreneurs and their businesses) by often focusing on generating an income stream that replaces employment income, with limited innovation and relatively high risk.

Following Masurel, Nijkamp and Vindigni's (2004, p. 77) research, successful entrepreneurs combine motivational determinants (embodied in personal traits such as family culture, own skills and business experience, commitment and forward-looking attitude) with contextual factors such as resources determined by new market possibilities, regulatory systems and technological change. But entrepreneurship can also be seen as the entrepreneurs' discovery and pursuit of a business opportunity without regard to the resources they currently control, with a clear vision and confidence on the success of the enterprise, guided by strategy, planning and organization, but also with the flexibility to change course as necessary, and with the will to rebound from setbacks (Hupalo, 2007; Reiss and Cruikshank, 2000).

Mostly perceived as entrepreneurship in a small business context, several studies commissioned in the European Union and in the UK define ethnic minority businesses as businesses that are either wholly or at least 50 percent owned by people of ethnic minority origin who are from a different cultural and linguistic background to those businesses that are managed predominantly by "white", European, English speaking people (European Commission, 2008; Ram, 2006).[3] But that definition is advanced for the specific purpose of those studies and overall agreement on the identification of ethnic minority businesses is lacking. For example, Carter et al. (2015) recommend caution in using the term to describe enterprises owned and managed by ethnic minorities, "*since many EMBs themselves eschew the ethnic label* (such that) *ethnicity should not be taken as the defining characteristic of EMBs"* (p. 51). Nevertheless, Carter et al. (2015) succumb to the convenience of identifying ethnic minority businesses as those businesses whose owners/operators are categorized by their distinct ethnicity/culture/religion relative to the indigenous population (Masurel, Nijkamp and Vindigni, 2004; Phizacklea and Ram, 1996), independently of whether they are immigrants or descendants of immigrants, such that they self-ascribe themselves (and are seen by others as belonging) to a specific minority ethnic group with a common origin and culture (Yinger, 1985). This is also the conceptualization endorsed in this text.

In the context of ethnic entrepreneurship, an important aspect to understand is whether ethnic entrepreneurs are immigrants or descendants of immigrants. Businesses run by individuals residing in a country for many years may still be considered as ethnic minority businesses, depending on the entrepreneur's level of ethnic involvement in the minority ethnic group they serve and/or products they transact. *Ethnic involvement* refers to the personal and professional linkages among members and institutions within the identified boundaries of a minority ethnic group. Chaganti and Greene (2002) surveyed ethnic entrepreneurs of Hispanic, Asian, Middle Eastern and South Asian origin. The study found that more involved entrepreneurs had smaller personal resources, significantly less industry experience and more years of foreign work experience. Their ethnic minority businesses were younger and sole proprietorship service firms.

Ethnic entrepreneurship is identified as involving

> a set of connections and regular patterns of interaction among people sharing common national background or migrant experiences.
> (Waldinger. Aldrich and Ward, 1990, p. 3)

It has been argued to refer to mostly small or medium sized business activities, involving the entrepreneur's family (Lo and Teixeira, 2015; Ram and Smallbone, 2002), commenced by foreign migrants with the main aim of covering the socio-economic needs of immigrants of various ethnic or socio-cultural groups (Van Delft, Gorter and Nijkamp, 2000; Waldinger, 1999). Other ethnic-identified groupings include the *ethnic economy*, the *ethnic ownership economy*, and the *ethnic control economy* (Light and Gold, 2000).[4]

Nevertheless, most studies on ethnic entrepreneurship focus on the entrepreneur's own minority ethnic group (Volery, 2007), involving a set of connections and regular patterns of interaction among people sharing a common national background or migration experiences (Waldinger, Aldrich and Ward, 1990), such that the characteristics of a minority ethnic group can be said to reflect its affiliates' entrepreneurial behaviour.

Drivers and Impediments in the Creation of Ethnic Minority Business

Similar to individuals in the mainstream, there may be many reasons for ethnic minority individuals to start a business. However, the latter may venture into business for reasons related to their ethnic minority status as a means of overcoming real or perceived disadvantages in the new country of settlement, perhaps seeking to improve their socio-economic position in their own community and to fulfil upward mobility ambitions through entrepreneurship, since entrepreneurship is perceived to lie at the heart of economic empowerment for affiliates of minority ethnic groups (Lagendijk et al., 2011; Clark and Drinkwater, 2010).

Table 7.1 summarizes four theories attempting to explain the rationale for ethnic minority business creation and consolidation (Greene and Butler, 1996), and how it links to a minority ethnic group's consumption and employment creation, namely: enclave theory, middleman theory, disadvantage theory and cultural theory. Each of these theories can explain the business entry decision of a single ethnic entrepreneur and perhaps of small groups with comparable immigration history and entrepreneurial activity (Volery, 2007).

The Ethnic Enclave Theory

The ethnic enclave theory (Portes, 1987) reflects the normal human desire to remain within one's comfort zone, and the reluctance to move precipitously outside that zone. Combined with a possible lack of locally accepted diplomas of qualifications (Lagendijk et al., 2011), cultural shock felt both by the newly arrived migrant and by the mainstream's fear of a hypothetical threat to their economic status (for example by accepting lower wages) can also affect an ethnic minoritie's ability to secure employment, and even constrain establishing their residence outside the ethnic enclave through restrictive housing covenants (Rudolph Jr., 2015). Cultural shock may, therefore, create incentives for self-employment, and residence within the comfort of the minority ethnic group of affiliation, generating better returns than if the economy at large were served (Wilson and Portes, 1980).

The (structuralist) ethnic enclave theory recognizes the opportunity for ethnic entrepreneurs to serve their minority ethnic group's particular needs, such as ethnic speciality grocery stores (McEvoy and Hafeez, 2007, cited in Jones-Evans, Thompson and Kwong, 2011) including their preference for ethnic-sensitive strategies (Pires and Stanton, 2015), while facing little competition from mainstream businesses (Iyer and Shapiro, 1999). It differs from a co-ethnic market model in that it is more diversified and connected beyond the local co-ethnic economy (Portes and Bach, 1985).

Table 7.1 Theories of Ethnic Minority Business Creation and Links to Minority Ethnic Groups

Enclave theory (structuralist approach)	A voluntary ethnic enclave is a geographic area with high ethnic concentration within a host country, characteristic cultural identity and economic activity, providing fertile ground for EMBs to develop (Zhou and Cho, 2010). With their apex in the nineteenth century, the evidence is that self-segregation ethnic enclaves (contrasting with involuntary segregated enclaves or ghettoes) continue to exist today, even in multicultural countries such as Australia, UK and the USA— with some MEGs choosing to live in their own enclaves so as to feel at home, as they don't feel welcome elsewhere (Veiszadeh, 2011). Chinatowns, Little Italies and Germantowns are common enclaves sustained by EMBs, many of which cater to their MEGs' specific tastes and needs, while also providing jobs for its affiliates. Allegedly EMBs discriminately favour co-ethnics over outsiders. Hence, ethnic enclaves often provide EMBs with economically secure footings from which to venture into the broader society (Rudolph Jr., 2015). This theory has been discredited, in terms of its explanation power (Portes and Shafer, 2007).
Middleman theory (culturalist approach)	Self-employment is a survival strategy in the host society. Minority ethnic groups (MEG; e.g. Jews and Chinese) may be frowned upon (face discrimination) by the mainstream, facing limited access to employment opportunities, or blocked mobility (Lo, Teixeira and Truelove, 2002). Given MEG substantiality (Pires, Stanton and Stanton, 2011), solidarity among its members (Greene and Butler, 1996), an EMB typically starts when an entrepreneur focus is on co-ethnic consumers, satisfying their specific ethnic needs (Greene and Owen, 2004; Cherry, 1990; Bonacich, 1973). The EMB may assume an intermediate position between the minority ethnic group and the mainstream, typically engaging in activities such as labour contracting, brokerage, travel agencies, clothing shops, tearooms, fast-food stands and specialized grocery shops. The *pseudo-middleman minority* case refers to geographically dispersed EMBs servicing an out-group clientele.
Disadvantage theory (structuralist approach)	Focus is on newly arrived immigrants' disadvantages which explain their behaviour (Fregetto, 2004). A lack of human capital such as language skills, education and experience, poor mobility, discrimination and a lack of market knowledge are disadvantages that can prevent newly arrived immigrants' from obtaining payed employment, leaving self-employment as the only choice (Levie, 2007). Entrepreneurship is simply the fallback from unemployment.
Culturalist or collectivist theory	Emphasizing self-help institutions, minority ethnic groups are equipped with culturally determined features such as dedication to hard work, frugality, group membership, risk aversion, collectivism, solidarity and loyalty and orientation towards self-employment (Masurel, Nijkamp and Vindigni, 2004; Lovell-Troy, 1980). These features can facilitate and encourage entrepreneurial behaviour and support the ethnic self-employed (Fregetto, 2004; Butler, 1991). Cultural aspects are particularly popular for explaining the propensity of Chinese people to become self-employed in the catering sector (Leung, 2002), although the influence of other critical aspects, such as employment alternatives, immigration policies, market conditions and availability of capital also merit consideration.

Extracted from the literature discussed in this chapter. EMB: Ethnic minority business; MEG: Minority ethnic group.

An example of the complexity of ethnic enclave theory is provided by Fenwick's (2012) observation of Sino-Vietnamese businesses in Toronto's Chinatown (Canada): diverse networks cut across Chinese, Vietnamese and Hong Kong suppliers with customers and employers constrained as well as facilitated by the competitive culture of the Chinatown enclave (Phan and Luk, 2007).

Ethnic enclaves can create entrepreneurial opportunities in particular urban neighbourhoods, providing a local market and access to relatively inexpensive labour. The theory suggests that ethnic entrepreneurship involves a complex system of co-ethnic social networks within a self-sustained geographical area (Zhou, 2004). While excessive reliance on family or co-ethnic labour can be detrimental to a business (Casson et al., 2006; Evald, Klyver and Svendsen, 2006; Barrett, Jones and McEvoy, 1996), ethnic minority businesses are not restricted to the enclave itself. Thus, population size and concentrations are not necessary conditions for ethnic enclaves to develop.

The literature proposes that the enclave theory has been discredited in terms of its explanation power (Portes and Shafer, 2007), a sentiment that is somewhat supported by claims that Chinatowns are dying, in Sydney, Australia and elsewhere. From a focal point of newly arrived Chinese immigrants, who tended to congregate together and to start businesses, it is now claimed that later better-educated generations have become professionals able to access mainstream white collar employment, being unwilling to continue with the family business (Jones and Ram, 2012) and, as in the case of Indians in Britain, justifying an entrepreneurial transition to a decline in self-employment (Jones, Mascarenhas-Keyes and Ram, 2012).

Generational change and changes in immigrants' country of origin explain that, consistent with ethnic succession theory, Chinese shops in Chinatown are being replaced by entrepreneurs with different ethnicities (Krase, 2006). Ethnic succession theory states that a minority ethnic group may settle in a neighbourhood or urban area until achieving economic viability to move onto more attractive areas (White, 1984). When that group moves to the new area, a new minority ethnic group might settle in the freshly vacant area. This pattern will repeat over time, creating a succession of minority ethnic groups as occupants. Ethnic succession is a common recurrence in the history of most major United States cities, particularly in New York City where this process has taken place since the nineteenth century (Stark, 2007, p. 551),

For example, in Sydney's Chinatown, once a close-knit community with all ethnic minority business owners belonging to one of eight clans from the Guang Dong province, there are now new ethnic minority businesses, suggesting that Thai Town or Korea Town may be more appropriate designations (Mudditt, 2017). Nevertheless, it may be argued that while upward mobility, generational change and bilateral acculturation between a minority ethnic group and the mainstream may facilitate dilution of an ethnic enclave into the mainstream, the phenomena can also be interpreted as the displacement of one ethnic enclave by another,

The Middleman Minority Model

Contrasting with the ethnic enclave theory, the middleman minority model (Greene and Owen, 2004; Bonacich, 1973) is advanced in the literature as the primary economic explanation for ethnic entrepreneurship (Volery, 2007).

One view of the theory is that it presumes that aspiring minority entrepreneurs facing mainstream hostility reflected in socio-economic exclusion (including in accessing employment opportunities) respond by distancing themselves from the mainstream, if they see themselves as permanent residents, becoming initially dependent on the substantiality of their minority ethnic group for support. This dependency develops into strong bonds of mutual solidarity and enforceable trust (Chaganti and Greene, 2002; Bonacich and Modell, 1980), helping to generate social capital through which resources of all types are circulated through the minority ethnic group (Butler and Greene, 1997). Rather than focused on remittances to their home country (possibly using up potential start-up capital), family reunion serves as a push factor to engage in business when employment is not readily available, as illustrated by the cases of the multicultural city of Thessaloniki, Greece (Piperopoulos and Ikonomu, 2007), the Chinese-Canadian community in Canada (Lin and Tao, 2012) and Italian immigrants in New York (Butler and Greene, 1997; Waldinger, McEvoy and Aldrich, 1990).

A distinct view omits the eventuality of socio-economic exclusion "to focus on ethnic minority businesses as providers of services either to the general population or to less entrepreneurial minorities", illustrated by speciality restaurants and discount stores, drawing on their "specialist ethnic skills or networks to generate income from the general public" (Jones-Evans, Thompson and Kwong, 2011, p. 222). As argued by Aldrich and Waldinger (1990), ethnic minority businesses associated with minority ethnic groups such as the "Koreans in the US, East Indians in Britain, and Moroccans in France [. . .] principally depend on transactions with out-group members" (p. 121).

The middleman minority holds distinctive social and cultural characteristics that promote solidary communities and a preference for family and co-ethnic labour, along with other characteristics (O'Brien and Fugita, 1982). However, while a large proportion of ethnic minority businesses rely on family and co-ethnic labour (Kitching, Smallbone and Athaide, 2009; Smallbone, Bertotti and Ekanem, 2005), other ethnic minority businesses employ non-co-ethnic staff, as illustrated by common and recurring observations in many service small businesses in Australia, in the UK, and in major cities of the USA and Canada, particularly in restaurants and similar businesses.

The Disadvantage Theory

The (structuralist) disadvantage theory (Light and Gold, 2000) essentially proposes that self-employment/ethnic minority business creation results from newly arrived immigrants' inability to get paid employment, due to limited language skills, education and experience, poor mobility, lack of market knowledge, discrimination, de-industrialization and racism (Ram and Jones, 2006).

The theory suggests that ethnic entrepreneurs are pushed into self-employment when they give up on securing employment, although they can also be "pulled" into self-employment by cohesive family strategies, attracted by expected rewards and autonomy (Verheul et al., 2010; Dawson, Henley and Latreille, 2009; Ram and Jones, 2008; Borooah and Hart, 1999). As noted by Lazaridis and Koumandraki (2003), self-employment can be perceived as "an opportunity to avoid oppressive constraints" (:9), because those successful in getting employment

> are not really getting paid that much. As noted by an ethnic entrepreneur, "I have got friends that work and what they make in a month I can make in three days".
>
> (p. 10)[5]

The Cultural Theory

Finally, the cultural or collectivist theory (Lovell-Troy, 1980) attributes ethnic entrepreneurship to specific cultural/ethnic embedded characteristics—such as reliance on family-based networks, frugal lifestyle, low risk aversion, solidarity and appetence for hard work—rather than to the opportunity structures, which are often obscure (Oliveira, 2007). Contrasting with the case of Asian and African/Caribbean ethnic minority businesses in the UK which were found not to be culturally predetermined (Ram and Jones, 1998), the theory proposes that individuals' cultural traits may explain that, in addition to disadvantage symptoms, some minority ethnic groups have greater natural propensity to engage in entrepreneurial activity leading to ethnic minority business creation, seemingly immune to normal economic laws. Nevertheless this immunity has been questioned, at least in the case of ethnic minority businesses related to Asian minority ethnic groups in the UK, who need to conform to the rules of a possibly hostile, larger political economy and to the external structure of markets and regulatory regimes (Jones and Ram, 2012).

While aspiring ethnic entrepreneurs may seek to replace employment related income with gains from entrepreneurial activity, this intent may be made difficult by limited access to business opportunities, resources and support, particularly when a strong ethnic economy is lacking (Lo and Teixeira, 2015). A possibility would be to focus on the mainstream market, but ethnic entrepreneurs often face barriers in reaching the mainstream market, as well as in accessing government support, mainstream funding sources and actual funding (see for example Davidson, Fielden and Omar, 2010).

Underfunding is identified as the largest obstacle faced by ethnic entrepreneurs, at least in the case of Asian and African-Caribbean groups in the UK (Ram and Jones, 1998), Arguably, many aspiring ethnic entrepreneurs may not be able to meet the requirements imposed by most credit providers—which are conscious of information asymmetry issues related to small businesses such as ethnic minority businesses (OECD, 2006, 2015)—including for example a good credit history, the demonstration of an ability to payback borrowed funds, sufficient equity, some form of collateral and, not the least, a business plan and experience in running a business (see www.business.vic.gov.au/money-profit-and-accounting/raising-funds-for-your-business/small-business-and-commercial-loans, accessed 30/11/2017).

Aspiring ethnic entrepreneurs may experience limited access to official sources of information and to business opportunities. In the USA, for example, minority-owned businesses typically see fewer contracting opportunities and, in the rare cases where they can secure venture capital, the amount is relatively small. The only federal agency dedicated to the creation, growth and expansion of minority-owned businesses is the Minority Business Development Agency (www.mbda.gov), which offers guidance on matters such as loans, grants and certifications.

While ethnic entrepreneurship is first and foremost conditioned by prevailing government regulations and guidelines and by the context of the market environment in the space where ethnic entrepreneurs seek to operate, it is often their minority ethnic group of affiliation and the entrepreneur's own informal social network (family, friends and business contacts at home and in the host country) that provides the opportunities that justify the creation of ethnic minority businesses. Indeed, it is noted that early information about business and employment opportunities and accommodation is often passed on from established migrants to aspiring migrants at home (Phizacklea and Ram, 1996), involving a migration network linking aspiring and former migrants with a common origin and destination (Butler and Greene, 1997). The entrepreneur's own informal social network includes the social structures through which members of a minority ethnic group relate to each other and that determine how they are used, as well as access to invaluable ethnic resources, as illustrated by the case of Korean minority entrepreneurs in Chicago (see Kim and Hurh, 1985).

An entrepreneur's social network is defined as the

> sets of interpersonal ties that link migrants, former migrants, and non-migrants in origin and destination areas through the bonds of kinship, friendship, and shared community origin.
>
> (Massey, 1988, p. 384)

The social network is a central source of "social capital" and can play an important role not only in the creation of ethnic minority businesses but also in the decision to migrate to a new country in the first place (Volery, 2007; Birley, 1985). Given the limited access to business opportunities noted above, the social network can deliver crucial resources for the creation of the ethnic enterprise, such as capital and loyal employees, easing the self-employment decision by reducing economic risks.

Notwithstanding, ownership of an ethnic minority business and its ability to consolidate operations over time is understood to depend somewhat on the level of intra-minority ethnic group competition for jobs and businesses. Opportunities may arise in a limited range of industries when the competition is high while very intensive competition may exclude the more lucrative activities, either by squeezing ethnic minority businesses into interstitial lines or pushing them out of business altogether (Storey, 2000). Accordingly, rather than generating their own demand through innovation and targeting the wider market, ethnic entrepreneurs might first recognize unmet demand within their minority ethnic group, perhaps for specific ethnic goods and services which they can fulfil given their knowledge of tastes and buying preferences (Volery, 2007). Hence, their focus might be more on replication/reproduction of products, processes, or business type, than on innovation and risk. This provides some explanation of why most ethnic minority businesses might be found in the retail and services sectors.

Finally, in contrast with the focus on successful and innovative ethnic minority business operations, capable of securing first and foremost an income stream for ethnic entrepreneurs and their families—a main reason for ethnic minority business creation—some literature refers to attenuated social risks due to understanding by peers in the event of failure, the ease of regaining relatively low standard jobs previously held, and a low risk of social exclusion, although no empirical evidence is provided.

Table 7.2 provides a summary of the drivers (push and pull) and impediments to ethnic minority business creation.

Following Shapero and Sokol (1982), entrepreneurial events are shaped by groupings of social variables (e.g. minority ethnic groups) and by the social and cultural environment. They are denoted by initiative-taking, resources consolidation, management, relative autonomy, and risk-taking. Many push drivers involve negative displacement factors such as job-related changes (e.g. being sacked, excluded, demoted or transferred), cultural shock, racism, hostility and discrimination; internal

Table 7.2 Drivers and Impediments in Ethnic Minority Business Creation

Drivers		Impediments
Push	*Pull*	
• Ethnic minority status and cultural shock	• Desire to improve socio-economic position	• Limited access to official sources of information
• Mainstream hostility, racism and/or discrimination	• Fulfilment of upward mobility ambitions	• Limited access to business opportunities
• Exclusion from lucrative activities (well paid jobs)	• Attraction of rewards and autonomy	• Few contracting opportunities
• Restricted opportunities for career advancement	• Accumulate family wealth	• Age
• Lack of blue collar jobs	• Desire for autonomy	• Gender
• High uncertainty about employment prospects	• Desire for economic and financial independence	• High level intra-minority ethnic group competition for business opportunities
• Limited opportunities to find work	• Family Business tradition	• Conditioning by prevailing government regulations and guidelines
• Identified opportunities serving the minority ethnic group of affiliation and/or other minority ethnic groups	• Generate employment opportunities for family members	• Lack of own capital and other business resources
• Access to informal social network (family, friends and business contacts)	• Specific embedded entrepreneurial characteristics	• Fear of business failure
• Limited mainstream language skills and education	• Permanent settlement	• Lack of sufficient funding
• Low risk aversion		• No business experience
• Appetence for hard work		• Conditioning by business environment
• Frugal lifestyle		• Sojourning
• Poor mobility		• Focus on remittances to the home country
• Co-ethnic group's solidarity		• Mistrust of government initiatives
• Family reunion		
• Ability to draw on resources from the host and home countries		

displacements are caused by attitude shifts such as age, life stage, landmarks or midlife crises. Positive pulls include perceptions of desirability, financial reward, personal values, family, peers and work experience together with perceptions of feasibility. Impediments include mistrust of government initiatives (Vickers, Lyon and North, 2009).

Ethnic Minority Business' Creation and Consolidation

A starting point to systematically understand the issues inherent to ethnic minority business creation and consolidation is through the framework offered by Waldinger, Aldrich and Ward (1990). It consists of three interacting components, namely existing mainstream opportunity structures (i.e. the market environment), existing characteristics of the minority ethnic group (ethnic resources or minority ethnic groups' social capital) and the ethnic management strategies required for aspiring ethnic entrepreneurs to address any challenges in ethnic minority business creation and consolidation, given those structures and characteristics (see also Romero and Valdez, 2016; Valdez, 2011). Figure 7.1 is an adaptation of that framework.

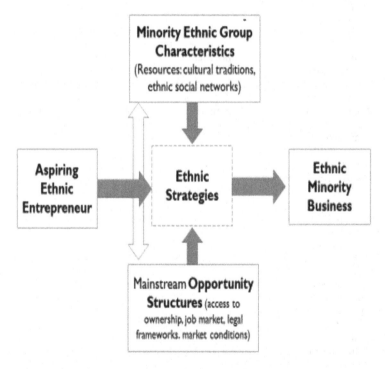

Adapted from Pütz (2003) and Waldinger, Aldrich, and Ward (1990).

Figure 7.1 The Interactive Model of Ethnic Minority Business Creation and Consolidation

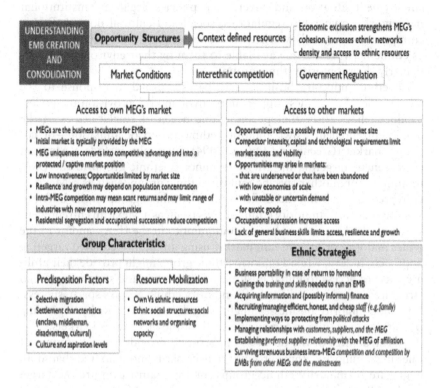

Figure 7.2 A Framework to Understand Ethnic Minority Business Creation and Consolidation

Adapting a comprehensive approach, this framework is known as the ethnic market niche or interactive (or interactionist) model, but it also integrates the structuralist and culturalist perspectives. Following the typology with three phases applied by Klyver and Foley (2012), in the discovery phase, aspiring entrepreneurs look for start-up opportunities to pursue in market niches created by the interaction between opportunities in society and the characteristics of the immigrant group, relying on information from accessible and creditable sources. Once an opportunity perceived as feasible is found, the projected enterprise moves to the start-up phase, followed by the young business phase of consolidation. Drawing on the relevant literature organized around the framework, Figure 7.2 presents a depiction of the various aspects of the interactive model that need to be understood.

Business Opportunity Structures

Business opportunity structures open to potential ethnic minority businesses are shaped by the minority and mainstream environments/contexts (Aldrich and Waldinger, 1990). These include market conditions, employment situation and government policies (legal and institutional frameworks, ownership regulations, social and cultural norms). Ethnic entrepreneurs can only work with the resources (social structures, such as ethnic networks) made available to them by their environments, particularly their minority ethnic group.

An ethnic minority business may be established in response to the recognition of a business opportunity involving the provision of service-products that satisfy the specific ethnic needs of similar-others in the ethnic entrepreneur's own minority ethnic group of affiliation—or co-ethnic market (Greene and Owen, 2004). Examples include a Mexican entrepreneur targeting the Mexican minority ethnic group in the USA, to affiliates of another specific minority ethnic group (such as a Mexican entrepreneur targeting the Chilean minority ethnic group in the USA), to some aggregate of minority ethnic groups (such as a Mexican entrepreneur targeting the Hispanic or Latino communities in the USA), and/or to the wider majority or mainstream market using an undifferentiated targeting approach. Indeed, while a minority ethnic group might provide their affiliates ease of access to initial business opportunities and supporting social structures only within the specific minority ethnic group's space, successful ethnic minority businesses might consolidate and grow by expanding operations over time, reaching one or all of the other three markets.

The structures of the business opportunity provided in the context of one single minority ethnic groups are necessarily more limited than if an aggregate of minority ethnic groups, or the mainstream are the target market. But ethnic minority businesses might benefit from a protected market and access to ethnic resources in the first case, in contrast with potentially highly aggressive competition in wider markets in the second case, where access to opportunities is likely to be controlled by non-co-ethnic stakeholders.

Reflecting on this "protected market hypothesis" (Light, 1972, cited in Aldrich and Waldinger, 1990), it affords a number of potential advantages and disadvantages to ethnic minority businesses and to other businesses considering entering that market. Advantages include:

- If minority ethnic groups have needs and preferences that are best served by those who are sensitive to those same ethnic-related needs rather than by mainstream competitors, then affiliated ethnic minority businesses may devise and implement customized and even personalized ethnic-sensitive strategies to best serve similar-others' needs and wants, offering superior value propositions to gain competitive advantage. This advantage might result from

  1. Invisibility of the minority ethnic group to unaffiliated businesses (related with group size);
  2. The recognition by the ethnic entrepreneur, and ultimately by the minority ethnic group, of shared needs and wants within the

minority ethnic group related to a deficit in socialization capabilities that may be invisible to outsiders;

3. The cost likely to be incurred by outsider businesses in acquiring/
    developing the specific ethnic-sensitive knowledge that might be
    needed for competing in a minority ethnic groups' market; and

4. The time cost involved in acquiring the specific ethnic-sensitive
    knowledge and in developing and deploying appropriate ethnic-
    sensitive strategies; This is a particularly important issue given
    the short time period (the window of opportunity) usually char-
    acterizing the nature of business opportunities. (Baron, 2006).

•   If the constituency of a minority ethnic group is mostly concentrated
    in a geographical area, this is likely to allow ethnic minority busi-
    nesses easy and low-cost access to the minority ethnic groups' stake-
    holders, including access to the network of preferred suppliers, while
    providing favourable conditions for the ethnic minority businesses
    to join that network. This concentration also facilitates access to
    workers affiliated with the minority ethnic group, strengthening the
    group's perception of the ethnic minority business as a proprietary
    asset, an effective ethnic resource;

•   Ethnic minority businesses successful in serving one minority ethnic
    group may gain access to other minority ethnic groups' markets and
    even be able to expand to the mainstream market. Opportunities for
    expansion may arise in markets that are underserved or have been
    abandoned, perhaps due to low economies of scale and/or unstable
    or uncertain demand, both of which preclude effective within-group
    supply. Consistent with the middleman minority theory Grey, Rodrí-
    guez and Conrad (2004) exemplify with the opening of a grocery
    store in an urban area where large grocery chains choose not to have
    a presence. Opportunities may also be explained by service-product
    type, such as the provision of exotic (from the mainstream perspec-
    tive) service-products, of service-products from the minority ethnic
    group's country of origin, or of service-products characterized by
    credence attributes that may be embodied in the provider;

•   Successful expansion might depend on competitive intensity and on
    capital and technological requirements. Hence, the expanding ethnic
    minority businesses may be able to diversify their business activity,
    depending on the type of service-products they offer and on the con-
    text of the particular market.

In terms of disadvantages,

•   Ethnic minority businesses' growth potential may be impaired if the
    minority ethnic group is unable to generate enough buying power (or
    critical mass). In this case the group may not be substantial enough
    to sustain a dedicated ethnic minority business (van Delft, Gorter

and Nijkamp, 2000), or the impairment may be due to high levels of competitive activity;

- In a further demonstration of the importance of context, minority ethnic groups experiencing high unemployment may result in high levels of entrepreneurial self-employment activity, combining lower buying power with an increase in competition, ultimately risking the viability of the ethnic minority business and the ethnic entrepreneur's subsistence.

An important point to make is the reciprocity effect accruing to ethnic minority businesses and to the minority ethnic group. The example of the Cuban minority ethnic group in Miami, Florida, offered by Levine (1985, cited in Aldrich and Waldinger, 1990 and summarized below) abundantly demonstrates how minority ethnic groups and stakeholders in their ethnic network may benefit from ethnic minority businesses' success.

> The early Cuban refugees converged on a depressed area in Miami, where housing costs were low and low-rent vacant space was available. Growth in the refugee population and a lack of employment opportunities saw the proliferation of self-employment and ethnic minority businesses dedicated to serving an expanded customer base. Ease of access to a low-cost labour force via informal (ethnic) networks enabled Cuban entrepreneurs to branch out into other industries, such as garments and construction, where they secured a non-ethnic clientele. These "export industries" served as a base for further expansion of the ethnic economy, generating a surplus that trickled down to ethnic minority businesses serving the local, specialized needs of the vibrant Cuban minority ethnic group. As a result, the Cuban group has turned Miami into a center for investments from Latin America as well as an entrepôt for trade with that area, and Cuban entrepreneurs have been able to move into more sophisticated and higher profit fields.

It is apparent that the business opportunities offered to the Cuban community were clearly shaped by context. The community arose originally from the convergence of refugees into a particular area due to attractive housing prices and available low-rent spaces. Congruent with the structuralist approach, most employment opportunities were characterized by occupational succession conditions (Rosenfeld and Tienda, 1999). Those community members with a low realistic chance of becoming employed, due to lacking the necessary competencies or to a lack of suitable employment opportunities, were pushed into ethnic entrepreneurship as a last resort. Other community members were pulled to self-employment, possibly motivated by higher rewards expectations and by the benefits of being one's own boss, against working for others (Borooah and Hart, 1999).

Much of the way the community responded to context had to do with the characteristics of the Cuban ethnic group. The suggestion here is that group characteristics also play a role in the process leading to the creation and consolidation of ethnic minority businesses. The importance of group characteristics is the focal point for discussion in the next section.

Group Characteristics

Following Hirschman (1982), the socio-economic achievements of a minority ethnic group are, at least partly, a function of its members' human capital and of the minority ethnic groups' socio-cultural orientation-motives and ambitions derived from group membership, which combine to form the cultural characteristics that ultimately define the group. In the spirit of the culturalist approach, these characteristics explain why particular minority ethnic groups are disproportionately concentrated in ethnic minority businesses (Portes, 1987), reflecting the predisposing factors—the skills/goals that individuals and minority ethnic groups bring to an opportunity—and accounting for how ethnic minority businesses acquire the resources that support them (Masurel, Nijkamp and Vindigni, 2004; Pütz, 2003). This acknowledges that while labour and capital are basic resources for every business, the underlying environment, personal characteristics and family related ties also have a role to play in ethnic minority businesses' operations (Zimmer and Aldrich, 1987). Indeed, combining the culturalist and structuralist approaches may afford a better understanding of ethnic entrepreneurship drivers (Volery, 2007). The various elements of the predisposition factors leading to the creation of ethnic minority businesses and resource acquisition behaviour are compiled in Table 7.3.

Resource acquisition theory recognizes that ethnic minority businesses are no different from other businesses insofar as skills and resources are required for success, which explains why business failure is a recurring outcome for many ethnic minority businesses (Greene and Butler, 1996). However, where ethnic social structures are concerned, there is clear distinction relative to the mainstream.

Newly arrived migrants may take advantage of employment opportunities offered by ethnic minority businesses owned by entrepreneurs affiliated with the same minority ethnic group, arguably gaining automatic access to contacts, opportunities to learn on the job and role models. This supports a higher likelihood of subsequent advancement into ethnic minority business ownership for those employees than for similar-others working for mainstream businesses. Similarly, entrepreneurs' ability to turn to family as a source for funding, mentoring and even for a formal and informal workforce can make the difference vis-a-vis other types of businesses (Danes et al., 2008; Noon, 2007; Olson et al., 2003) although these sources are by no means exclusive to ethnic minority businesses.

Table 7.3 Predisposition Factors for Ethnic Minority Business Creation and Resource Acquisition

Predisposing Factors	
Selective migration	Refers to the human capital immigrants bring to the host society (such as previous business experience, language deficiency and low education). Buying and selling experience is as important for immigrants entering self-employment, as capital, connections and specific business skills.
Settlement characteristics	Influence business development trajectories. Minority ethnic groups' size and residential concentration may be most important. Focus is on the minority ethnic group due to residential clustering and dominated by retail and service EMBs catering to a co-ethnic clientele; Four distinct theories (ethnic enclave, middleman, disadvantage and cultural) support the close link between minority ethnic groups and EMBs (see Table 7.1). But overlapping patterns are likely.
Culture and aspiration levels	Some minority ethnic groups have high rates of entrepreneurship which persist over several generations. But structural factors (e.g. Government regulations, socio-political policies, and discriminatory behaviour) may limit the groups' capacity to preserve and pass on "traditional" ethnic customs and values (Steinberg, 1981).

Resource Acquisition	
Own vs ethnic resources	Own resources are private property in the means of production and distribution, human capital, money to invest and bourgeois values, attitudes, knowledge and skills transmitted intergenerationally (Light, 1984). Ethnic resources refer to all the minority ethnic group's assets that are available to ethnic entrepreneurs, such as cultural endowments, reactive solidarity and sojourning orientation. Differences in ethnic resources explain different rates of self-employment between equally disadvantaged groups (Waldinger, Aldrich and Ward, 1990).
Ethnic social structures: social networks and organizing capacity	Refer to networks of variable relational complexity (affinity and friendship) between ethnic minority consumers making up the minority ethnic group, and how these relate to job opportunities, housing and formal ethnic institutions). For example, information about permits, laws and management practices is typically obtained through the entrepreneurs' informal personal networks. Information about business opportunities within the minority ethnic group, specific group assets such as rotating credit associations (Gugerty, 2007; Geertz, 1962) and reliable preferred suppliers to the group are mostly sourced from the group as a quasi-formal network (Greene and Butler, 1996). The role played by family can also be vital as a support mechanism for EMBs creation and consolidation, despite mixed evidence in the literature.

EMB: Ethnic minority business

Ethnic entrepreneurs often support ethnic institutions for business reasons, as a sense of in-group loyalty and solidarity, as a way of reciprocating support by those institutions, and as a two-way supporting reaction to hostility by other groups, whether other minority ethnic groups or the mainstream. These social structures, including ethnic networks, can help ethnic minority businesses access a favourable supply chain and acquire needed resources.

The third factor in the framework exploring the creation and development of ethnic minority businesses is discussed in the next section, focusing on ethnic strategies emerging from the interaction of business opportunities and a minority ethnic group's characteristics.

Ethnic Strategies and the Typical Ethnic Minority Business

In the interactive model the focus of ethnic strategies is to provide solutions for particular problems (e.g. gathering of information, customers and suppliers, capital, training and skills, human resources, political attacks and competition) that might occur during the interaction between the mainstream opportunity structures (determined by context as earlier explained) and the minority ethnic group's specific characteristics, namely its social networks and cultural traditions.

An ethnic entrepreneur's personal characteristics may explain a focus on ease of business portability, should the entrepreneur decide to return to the home country in the future (Volery, 2007). However, more generally, ethnic business strategies emerge from the interaction of opportunities and group characteristics, as minority ethnic groups possibly facing a large range of challenges adapt to their environments, building on their own characteristics and favouring a relatively low degree of service-product innovativeness, often focusing on replication of what is already being done in other markets but with operational efficiency gains (Iyer and Shapiro, 1999). These opportunities often arise in low value added sectors with high failure rates (Blackburn and Smallbone, 2014).

"Typical" ethnic minority businesses are described by the European Commission (2008) as micro businesses with low capital requirements, no or few employees and low skill requirements. Mostly owned and managed by male ethnic entrepreneurs, ethnic minority businesses often operate in markets with low entry barriers. Their limited knowledge of marketing differentiation techniques make them vulnerable to price competition in markedly competitive environments, which explains labour intensive production, long working hours and low wages, as well as lower turnover and lower profit than typical mainstream businesses.

Ethnic minority businesses are likely to face many challenges prompted by a lack of business skills in all its dimensions. These range from opportunity assessment and access to capital, human capital limitations (involving language skills, education and experience), poor mobility, discrimination outside their minority ethnic group and a lack of market knowledge. Ethnic minority businesses, particularly in the early days of operation, are also likely to confront intra-minority ethnic group competition by other co-ethnic businesses, competition by ethnic minority businesses associated with other minority ethnic groups and even by mainstream businesses, as well as problems related to on the job management training and skills acquisition, and reliance on family and co-ethnic labour.

In order to stay ahead and remain competitive, ethnic entrepreneurs arguably need protection from government officials, as well as from rival owners outside their ethnic community. Government is, allegedly, dealt with by ethnic entrepreneurs in much the same way that non-ethnic owners always have: bribery, paying penalties, searching for loopholes and organizing protests. Indeed, as noted by Rath and Kloosterman (2002), survival may justify ethnic entrepreneurs' temptation to apply informal practices with respect to taxes, labour regulations, minimum wages and employing children and immigrant workers without documents. Ultimately, as argued by Aldrich and Waldinger (1990), the above challenges and the intense competition generated in the niches occupied by ethnic minority businesses are often dealt with through self-exploitation: by expanding the business through moving forward in the chain of production, by opening other shops, by founding and supporting ethnic trading associations and even by cementing alliances to other families through marriage (Sway, 1988).

From the perspective of ethnic marketing, the key focus of ethnic strategies is on customers and clients because building a loyal following and a reliable supply chain can offset the high level of uncertainty potentially facing ethnic minority businesses. As discussed elsewhere in Chapter 9 of this text, it can be advantageous for these businesses to be perceived by their minority ethnic group and by other like suppliers as a preferred supplier to the minority ethnic group. This often requires the design and implementation of a continuum of ethnic-sensitive marketing strategies, from transactional to relational, as well as substantial business acumen in managing those strategies. This is not easily accomplished because, as noted by Jones and McEvoy (1986), immigrants often become aware of the advantages their own minority ethnic group of affiliation might offer to them only after arriving in the new environment:

> Whether one is English, Albanian or Mongolian, the very act of transferring to a new society with alien customs and incomprehensible language is in itself likely to heighten awareness of one's own cultural and national identity.
>
> (p. 199)

Hence, the entrepreneur's affiliation to a particular minority ethnic group might be a first step, but it does not guarantee an appropriate understanding of which strategies are ethnic sensitive. Moreover, the range of service-products provided by ethnic minority businesses to co-ethnic consumers are often highly intangible, implying the extra challenges usually surrounding the provisions of services. An audit and review of ethnic marketing strategies deployed by ethnic minority businesses is provided in Chapters 11–13. Can ethnicity and disadvantage turn search/experience goods into credence goods?

In summary, the interactionist approach is grounded in a perspective of the world. The creation and performance of ethnic minority businesses is largely a function of the ethnic entrepreneur's diligence/agency given their social embedding within the solidarity of co-ethnic social capital networks (Portes and Sensenbrenner, 1993; Light, 1972). Depending on access to family and friends' loans and labour at cheap rates can provide minority ethnic groups with a decisive competitive advantage, providing a compelling argument for migrants to use self-employment as a means to earn a living, rising above any events of exclusion, whether due to ethnic based discrimination or for other reasons.

The interactive model is subject to criticism in the relevant literature for its methodology (Light and Rosenstein, 1995). It presumes that ethnic entrepreneurs behave unlike mainstream entrepreneurs (Kloosterman and Rath, 2003), have a focus on the supply side of entrepreneurship, neglect intra-ethnic diversity and disregard the impact of the mainstream (e.g. banking) on ethnic entrepreneurial activities (Light and Gold, 2000), basically ignoring the context where entrepreneurialism takes place (Pang and Rath, 2006).

Volery (2007) sought to enhance the interactive model. Taking for granted that the immigrant is an entrepreneur that affiliates with a minority ethnic group (hence s/he is an ethnic entrepreneur), the model recognizes that the entrepreneur is constrained by the three relevant areas of the interactive model (minority ethnic group's resources, opportunity structure, and ethnic strategies) but includes a fourth area of influence related to the entrepreneur's location characteristics (metropolitan characteristics is the term used by Volery).

The model identifies an entrepreneurship dimension that applies equally to all entrepreneurs (ethnic and mainstream) comprising four interdependent aspects drawn from Schaper and Volery (2004). The four aspects are (1) the entrepreneur's psychological characteristics (e.g. need for achievement and risk taking), (2) access to restricted information and knowledge, (3) creative processing of the information allowing the recognition and exploitation of opportunities, and (4) the ability to apply cognitive heuristics to solve problems in the entrepreneurial process of recognizing, evaluating and exploiting business opportunities.

The model also considers an "ethnic dimension" which refers to the extent of "the cultural differences between host and home country", the discrimination the entrepreneur is subjected to, the progression of the social integration of the concerning ethnic group, the experience gained in the new environment, age and gender, and the education level of the entrepreneur, such that for "highly educated and very well integrated individuals, the influence of the ethnic dimension can shrink to a level where it is no longer relevant" (p. 37).

The enhanced model recognizes that there is a set of characteristics that apply to all entrepreneurs, albeit how they apply can be expected to differ from individual to individual. Even people with the same nationality or from the same ethnic group have differences which affect the way they recognize and pursue opportunities. Ultimately, relevance to ethnic entrepreneurs depends on their differences to the mainstream, and their advantage is likely to derive from their extensive use of "social networks because these are a central source of 'social capital'" (p. 37).

Overall, it is apparent that ethnic entrepreneurs are likely to be inextricably intertwined with their minority ethnic group, which plays a wide role in ethnic minority business viability. Indeed, beyond providing these businesses with a stable and substantial market, minority ethnic groups can be seen as natural incubators for ethnic minority businesses, as discussed in the next section.

Ethnic Groups as Natural Incubators for Ethnic Businesses

There is marked latitude in the conceptualization of business incubators, from a mere offering of management training or affordable office space to helping entrepreneurs in the discovery and start-up phases of their business (www.rdacc.org.au/incubator, accessed 4/10/2017), to much more elaborate facilities established to nurture and consolidate young small businesses during their early months or years. Business incubators usually provide affordable essential space, shared offices and support services, such as hands-on management training, marketing support and even access to some form of financing (www.businessdictionary.com/definition/business-incubator.html, accessed 4/10/2017). Expressed in another way, business incubation refers to a unique and highly flexible combination of business development processes, infrastructure and people designed to nurture new and small businesses by helping them to survive and grow through the difficult and vulnerable early stages of development (Allen and McCluskey, 1990).

Where ethnic minority businesses are concerned, an observation that recurs in the literature is that, particularly in the UK, the availability and effectiveness of support services for ethnic minority businesses is problematic. Additional to a lack of credible evidence of their availability (Ram and Jones, 2008), what services are available may need marked improvement, given the alleged persistence of anti-immigrant sentiment (Jones et al., 2012).

These support services might focus on the clarification of business objectives, of business and marketing strategies and in the fomenting of networking opportunities (Ram and Jones, 1998). However, there is some evidence that ethnic entrepreneurs can access some of these support services within their minority ethnic group of affiliation.

Drawing on anthropology and sociology research, all four theories underlining ethnic minority businesses' creation and their relationship with minority ethnic groups (see Table 7.1) focus on the creation and consolidation of new ventures within minority ethnic groups, providing insights of how ethnic minority businesses are created, nurtured and sustained—as in formal business incubators and using many of the same tools (Greene and Butler, 1996) -, hence further justifying the natural incubator qualifier advanced in this text.

Conclusion

The discussion in this chapter is premised on the assumption that the ethnic entrepreneurship decision may be both prompted and conditioned by the minority status of the aspiring entrepreneurs, converting into access to a smaller set of opportunities (the opportunity structure) than that facing mainstream aspiring entrepreneurs.

The chapter discussed theoretical frameworks that provide guidance to the discussion of the motivations prompting ethnic entrepreneurs to create ethnic minority businesses, potentially related to exclusionary practices reducing access to mainstream opportunities of employment to minority individuals. It is apparent that the single most important inference from the discussion of the various theoretical perspectives surrounding ethnic minority business creation and consolidation is the focal role played by the ethnic entrepreneur's minority ethnic group of affiliation as a natural incubator. That is, not only do minority ethnic groups add to newly arrived affiliates' informal social networks, and assist with their process of socialization to the new environment, but these groups may also generate employment, business entrepreneurship opportunities and support for the exploitation of those opportunities.

Business opportunities arise when minority ethnic groups have the potential to offer a critical mass of potential ethnic minority consumers with shared ethnicity and unmet demands and preferences, underpinning viable market niches. Business support encompasses a minority ethnic group's preference for affiliated suppliers and access to ethnic networks, as well as opportunities offered within a minority ethnic group's environment for networking between like entrepreneurs, as in the case of socialization opportunities offered by social clubs serving the Portuguese community in Sydney, Australia. Therefore, it can be conceived that ethnic minority businesses are created to take advantage of such business opportunities offered by these markets, targeting the needs and wants of the membership of the minority ethnic group, while creating demand for co-ethnic labour that understands the cultural nuances of the group. That demand may be met by entrepreneurs' family members, or by a minority ethnic group's affiliates.

But, the role of the minority ethnic group goes even further, given the noted dependency of most ethnic minority businesses, at least during their early stages, on the custom of the minority ethnic group's affiliates. The minority ethnic group's ethnic networks can help ethnic minority businesses access a favourable supply chain and cheap employees, and in acquiring needed resources (such as information and financing capital), as well as providing the consumers for ethnic minority businesses' goods and services.

On the negative side, ethnic minority business dependency on a niche market such as a minority ethnic group can create vulnerability to competition by other ethnic minority businesses given potentially low access barriers, as well as limited opportunities for business expansion, which might explain higher rates of business failure amongst ethnic minority businesses relative to mainstream small businesses (Ortiz-Walters, Gavino and Williams, 2015; Clydesdale, 2008; Masurel, Nijkamp and Vindigni, 2004; Aldrich and Waldinger, 1990), as well as their limited growth potential.

The next chapter examines the conditions for ethnic minority businesses to transform consolidation into growth, or for their demise.

Notes

1. There is a lack of statistical data regarding ethnic entrepreneurship. A major source of data for entrepreneurship is the Global Entrepreneurship Monitor, with yearly reports being produced since 1999. Mostly congruent with previous reports, the 2016 report provides data for 64 world economies, tracking rates of entrepreneurship across multiple phases of entrepreneurship activity, assessing the characteristics, motivations and ambitions of entrepreneurs and exploring the societal attitudes towards entrepreneurship. However, there is no identifiable data or discussion considering ethnic minority businesses. Indeed, ethnicity is not examined as a personal attribute of an entrepreneur (GEM, 2017).
2. Entrepreneurs have been variably defined. Carland et al. (2007) differentiate entrepreneurs from small business owners, and Bjørnskov and Foss (2010) refer to individuals who exercise their ability and willingness to perceive new economic opportunities and to introduce their specific ways of seizing these opportunities into the market in the face of uncertainty (Knight, 1921; Wennekers and Thurik, 1999, pp. 46–47).
3. Following the recommendations of the European Commission (2008), there is no unique and clear definition of EMB. While earlier studies focussed on businesses operating mainly on closed economies, limited to certain immigrant communities and highlighted the role of ethnic resources in the definition of immigrants' entrepreneurial strategies, later research argued that group characteristics should be considered in relation to their interaction with a

surrounding opportunity structure, including the market conditions. Accordingly, entrepreneurship related to what customers want to buy and what EMBs can provide. Ultimately the lack of a universal definition of ethnic minority business must compromise, or at least challenge, research findings based on the examination of distinct phenomena.

4. Following Bonacich and Modell (1980), Light and Gold (2000) define *ethnic economy* as 'any ethnic or immigrant's self-employed group, its employers, their co-ethnic employees, and their unpaid family workers' (3), whereas the *ethnic ownership economy* consists of SMEs owned by ethnic/immigrant entrepreneurs and their co-ethnic helpers and workers. Distributed among industries and neighbourhoods, it differs from the *ethnic enclave economy* in the spatial clustering of ethnic minority businesses, clustered around a territorial core and requiring economic interdependency and co-ethnic workers.

   Completely independent is the *ethnic control economy* , made out of mainstream industries, occupations and organization in which co-ethnic employees (not owners) exert significant economic power resulting from numerical clustering or preponderance, organization and/or government mandates. Arguably, the ethnic-controlled economy facilitates access to more and better jobs in the mainstream economy, reduce unemployment and improve working conditions (adapted from Volery, 2007, p. 31).

5. Research indicates that employment stability, access to public services and standard of living increases with the length of stay in the host country. Noussia (2003) identifies a settling process with three stages: (1) immigrants, mostly male, live collectively in poor conditions, (2) each immigrant establishes an individual household unit with family members and (3) those earning enough rent from houses outside of poor neighbourhoods and become increasingly incorporated with the local population (:207).

References

Aldrich, H. and Waldinger, R. (1990). Ethnicity and entrepreneurship. *Annual Review of Sociology*, 16, 111–135.

Allen, D. and McCluskey, R. (1990). Structure, policy, services and performance in the business incubator industry. *Entrepreneurship Theory and Practice*, 14(Winter), 61–77.

Altinay, L. and Altinay, E. (2006). Determinants of ethnic minority entrepreneurial growth in the catering sector. *The Service Industries Journal*, 26(2), 2013–2021.

Baron, A. (2006). Opportunity recognition as pattern recognition: How entrepreneurs "connect the dots" to identify new business opportunities. *Academy of Management Perspectives*, 20(1), 104–119.

Baron, R. and Shane, S. (2008). *Entrepreneurship: A Process Perspective*, 2nd ed. Mason, OH: Thomson/South-Western.

Barrett, G., Jones, T. and McEvoy, D. (1996). Ethnic minority business: Theoretical discourse in Britain and North America. *Urban Studies*, 4–5, 783–809.

Bird, B. (1989). *Entrepreneurial Behavior*. Glenview, III; Scott, Foresman.

Birley, S. (1985). The role of networks in the entrepreneurial process. *Journal of Business Venturing*, 1(Winter), 107–117.

BIS (2013). *Small Business Survey 2012: Estimates for Women-Led, Minority Ethnic Group (MEG) Led and Social Enterprises in the UK*. London: Department for Business, Innovation & Skills.

Bjørnskov, C. and Foss, N. (2010). Economic freedom and entrepreneurial activity: Some cross-country evidence. In *Entrepreneurship and Culture*. Berlin, Heidelberg: Springer, pp. 201–225.

Blackburn, R. and Smallbone, D. (2014). Sustaining self-employment for disadvantaged entrepreneurs. *Background paper for the OECD Centre for Entrepreneurship, SMEs and Local Development*.

Bonacich, E. (1973). A theory of middleman minorities. *American Sociology Review*, 38, 583–594.

Bonacich, E. and Modell, J. (1980). *The Economic Basis of Ethnic Solidarity: Small Business in the Japanese-American Community*. Berkeley, CA: University of California Press.

Borooah, V. and Hart, M. (1999). Factors affecting self-employment among Indian and Black Caribbean men in Britain. *Small Business Economics*, 13(2), 111–129.

Butler, J. (1991). *Entrepreneurship and Self-Help among Black Americans*. Albany, NY: State University of New York Press.

Butler, J. and Greene, P. (1997). Ethnic entrepreneurship: The continuous rebirth of American enterprise. In D. L. Sexton and R. W Smilor (eds.), *Entrepreneurship 2000*. Chicago, IL: Upstart Publishing Co., pp. 267–289.

Carland, J., Hoy, F., Boulton, W. and Carland, J. (2007). Differentiating entrepreneurs from small business owners: A conceptualization. In *Entrepreneurship*. Berlin, Heidelberg: Springer, pp. 73–81.

Carter, S., Mwaura, S., Ram, M., Trehan, K. and Jones, T. (2015). Barriers to ethnic minority and women's enterprise: Existing evidence, policy tensions and unsettled questions. *International Small Business Journal*, 33(1), 49–69.

Casson, M., Yeung, B., Basu, A. and Wadeson, N. (eds.). (2006). *The Oxford Handbook of Entrepreneurship*. New York, NY: Oxford University Press.

Chaganti, R. and Greene, P. (2002). Who are ethnic entrepreneurs? A study of entrepreneurship; ethnic involvement and business characteristics. *Journal of Small Business Management*, 40(2), 126–143.

Cherry, R. (1990). American Jewry and Bonacich's middleman minority theory. *Review of Radical Political Economics*, 22(2–3), 158–173.

Clark, K. and Drinkwater, S. (2010). Recent trends in minority ethnic entrepreneurship in Britain. *International Small Business Journal*, 28, 136–146.

Clydesdale, G. (2008). Business immigrants and the entrepreneurial nexus. *Journal of International Entrepreneurship*, 6(3), 123–142.

Dana, L. (2006). *Handbook of Research on International Entrepreneurship*. Cheltenham: Edward Edgar.

Danes, S., Lee, J., Stafford, K. and Heck, R. (2008). The effects of ethnicity, families and culture on entrepreneurial experience: An extension of sustainable family business theory. *Journal of Developmental Entrepreneurship*, 13(3), 229–268.

Davidson, M., Fielden, S. and Omar, A. (2010). Black, Asian and minority ethnic female business owners: Discrimination and social support. *International Journal of Entrepreneurial Behavior & Research*, 16(1), 58–80.

Dawson, C., Henley, A. and Latreille, P. (2009). Why do individuals choose self-employment? *IZA Discussion Paper No. 3974*, January. Available at http://ftp.iza.org/dp3974.pdf

European Commission (2008). Supporting Entrepreneurial Diversity in Europe-Ethnic Minority Entrepreneurship/ Migrant Entrepreneurship: Conclusions and Recommendations of the European Commission's Network "Ethnic Minority Businesses", Enterprise and Industry Directorate-General. Available at ec.europa.eu/DocsRoom/documents/2365/attachments/1/translations/en/. . ./pdf

Evald, M., Klyver, K. and Svendsen, S. (2006). The changing importance of the strength of ties throughout the entrepreneurial process. *Journal of Enterprising Culture*, 14(1), 1–26.

Fenwick, T. (2012). Negotiating networks of self-employed work strategies of minority ethnic contractors. *Urban Studies*, 49(3), 595–612.

Fregetto, E. (2004). Immigrant and ethnic entrepreneurship: A U.S. perspective. In H. P. Welsch (ed.), *Entrepreneurship: The Way Ahead*. New York: Routledge, pp. 253–268.

Geertz, C. (1962). The rotating credit association: A "middle rung" in development. *Economic Development and Cultural Change*, 10(April), 241–263.

GEM, Global Entrepreneurship Monitor (2017). Global report 2016/17. Accessed 29/11/2017 at www.gemconsortium.org/

Greene, P. and Butler, J. (1996). The minority community as a natural business incubator. *Journal of Business Research*, 36, 51–58.

Greene, P. and Owen, M. (2004). Race and ethnicity. In W. B. Gartner, K. G. Shaver, N. M. Carter and P. D. Reynolds (eds.), *Handbook of Entrepreneurial Dynamics: The Process of Business Creation*. Thousand Oaks, CA: Sage Publications, pp. 26–38.

Grey, M., Rodríguez, N. and Conrad, A. (2004). *Immigrant and Refugee Small Business Development in Iowa: A Research Report with Recommendations*. Cedar Falls, IA: New Iowans Program, University of Northern Iowa.

The Guardian (2007). Going global. Accessed 2/10/2017 at www.theguardian.com/business/2007/may/16/supermarkets.food

Gugerty, M. (2007). You can't save alone: Commitment in rotating savings and credit associations in Kenya. *Economic Development and Cultural Change*, 55(2), 251–282.

Harper, D. A. (2003). *Foundations of Entrepreneurship and Economic Development* (Vol. 11). New York: Routledge.

Hirschman, C. (1982). Immigrants and minorities: Old questions for new directions in research. *International Migration Review*, 16, 474–490.

Hupalo, P. (2007). Thinking like an entrepreneur. [Online]. Accessed 25/9/2017 at www.thinkinglike.com/AboutUs.html

Ibisworld (2017). Ethnic supermarkets: Market research report, industry-trends, January. Accessed on 2/10/2017 at www.ibisworld.com/industry-trends/specialized-market-research-reports/consumer-goods-services/food-beverage-stores/ethnic-supermarkets.html

Iyer, G. and Shapiro, J. (1999). Ethnic entrepreneurial and marketing systems: Implications for the global economy. *Journal of International Marketing*, 7(4), 83–110.

Jamal, A. (2005). Playing to win: An explorative study of marketing strategies of small ethnic retail entrepreneurs in the UK. *Journal of Retailing and Consumer Services*, 12(1), 1–13.

Jones, T., Mascarenhas-Keyes, S. and Ram, M. (2012). The ethnic entrepreneurial transition: Recent trends in British Indian self-employment. *Journal of Ethnic and Migration Studies*, 38, 93–109.

Jones, T. and McEvoy, D. (1986). Ethnic enterprise: The popular image. In J. Curran, J. Stanworth and D. Watkins (eds.), *The Survival of the Small Firm*, Vol. 1. Gower: Aldershot, pp. 197–219.

Jones, T. and Ram, M. (2012). Revisiting . . . ethnic-minority businesses in the United Kingdom: A review of research and policy developments. *Environment and Planning C: Government and Policy*, 30, 944–950.

Jones, T., Ram, M., Edwards, P., Kisilinchev, A. and Muchenje, L. (2012). New migrant enterprise: Novelty or historical continuity? *Urban Studies*, 49, 3159–3176.

Jones-Evans, D., Thompson, P. and Kwong, C. (2011). Entrepreneurship amongst minority language speakers: The case of Wales. *Regional Studies*, 45(2), 219–238.

Kim, K. and Hurh, W. (1985). Ethnic resources utilization of Korean immigrant entrepreneurs in the Chicago minority area. *The International Migration Review*, 19(1), 82–111.

Kitching, J., Smallbone, D. and Athaide, R. (2009). Ethnic diasporas and business competitiveness: Minority-owned enterprises in London. *Journal of Ethnic and Migration Studies*, 35(4), 689–705.

Kloosterman, R. and Rath, J. (2003). *Immigrant entrepreneurs: Venturing abroad in the age of globalization*. Oxford/New York: Berg/University of New York Press.

Klyver, K. and Foley, D. (2012). Networking and culture in entrepreneurship. *Entrepreneurship & Regional Development*, 24(7–8), 561–588.

Knight, F. (1921). *Risk, Uncertainity, and Profit*. Boston, MA: Hart, Schaffner & Marx.

Komakech, M. and Jackson, S. (2016). A study of the role of small ethnic retail grocery stores in urban renewal in a social housing: Project, Toronto, Canada. *Journal of Urban Health: Bulletin of the New York Academy of Medicine*, 93(3), 414–424.

Krase, J. (2006). Seeing ethnic succession in little Italy: Change despite resistance. *Modern Italy*, 11(1), 79–95.

Lagendijk, A., Pijpers, R., Ent, G., Hendrikx, R., van Lanen, B. and Maussart, L. (2011). Multiple worlds in a single street: Ethnic entrepreneurship and the construction of a global sense of place. *Space and Polity*, 15(2), 163–181.

Landstrom, H. (1999). The roots of entrepreneurship research: New England. *Journal of Entrepreneurship*, 2(2), 9–20.

Langlois, R. (2007). *The Dynamics of Industrial Capitalism Schumpeter, Chandler, and the New Economy*. London: Routledge.

Lazaridis, G. and Koumandraki, M. (2003). Survival ethnic entrepreneurs in Greece: A mosaic of informal and formal business activities. *Sociological Research Online*, 8(2), 1–12.

Leung, S. (2002). Career counseling in Hong Kong: Meeting the social challenges. *The Career Development Quarterly*, 50(3), 237–245.

Levie, J. (2007). Immigration, in-migration, ethnicity and entrepreneurship in the United Kingdom. *Small Business Economics*, 28(2–3), 143–169.

Levine, B. (1985). The capital of Latin America. *Wilson Q*, 9, 47–69.

Light, I. (1984). Immigrant and ethnic enterprise in North America. *Ethnic and Racial Studies*, 7(2), 195–216.

Light, I. (1972). *Ethnic enterprise in America*. Berkeley University, California Press.

Light, I. and Gold, S. (2000). *Ethnic Economies*. San Diego: Academic Press.

Light, I. and Rosenstein, C. (1995). Expanding the interaction theory of entrepreneurship. In A. Portes (ed.), *The Economic Sociology of Immigration: Essays on Networks, Ethnicity, and Entrepreneurship*. New York: Russell Sage Foundation, pp. 166–212.

Lin, X. and Tao, S. (2012). Transnational entrepreneurs: Characteristics, drivers, and success factors. *Journal of International Entrepreneurship*, 10(1), 50–69.

Lo, L. and Teixeira, C. (2015). Immigrants doing business in a mid-sized Canadian city: Challenges, opportunities, and local strategies in Kelowna, British Columbia. *Growth and Change*, 46(4), 631–653.

Lo, L., Teixeira, C. and Truelove, M. (2002). *Cultural Resources, Ethnic Strategies, and Immigrant Entrepreneurship: A Comparative Study of Five Immigrant Groups in the Toronto CMA*. Toronto: CERIS- Joint Centre of Excellence for Research on Immigration and Settlement.

London Research Centre (1999). 1998 Round Ethnic Group Projections P1/M96. London Research Centre.

Lovell-Troy, L. (1980). Clan structure and economic activity: The case of Greeks in small business enterprise. In S. Cummings (ed.), *Self-Help in Urban America: Patterns of Minority Economic Development*. Port Washington, NY: Kennikat Press, pp. 58–85.

Masurel, E., Nijkamp, P. and Vindigni, G. (2004). Breeding places for ethnic entrepreneurs: A comparative marketing approach. *Entrepreneurship & Regional Development*, 16, 77–86.

Massey, Douglas S. (1988). Economic development and international migration in comparative perspective. *Population and Development Review*, 14, 383–413.

MBDA. Minority Business Development Agency. Accessed on 26/9/2017 at www.mbda.gov

McEvoy, D. and Hafeez, K. (2007). Dispersal and diversity in ethnic minority enterprise in England and Wales. *1st International Colloquium on Ethnic Entrepreneurship and Management*, Bradford, UK, March.

McEwan, C., Pollard, J. and Henry, N. (2005). The "global" in the city economy: Multicultural economic development in Birmingham. *International Journal of Urban and Regional Research*, 29, 916–933.

Meryment, E. (2011). More choice than ever before on our supermarket shelves. *The Sunday Telegraph*, June 19. Accessed 2/10/2017 at www.dailytelegraph.com.au/more-choice-than-ever-before-on-our-supermarket-shelves/news-story/2b4084113e77faeec6e3da7d64f9275c

Mohanty, S. (2005). *Fundamentals of Entrepreneurship*. New Delhi: PHI Learning.

Mudditt, J. (2017). Chinatowns are dying: Why the Chinese centres of Australian cities are disappearing. *News.com.au*, August 6.

Noon, M. (2007). The fatal flaws of diversity and the business case for ethnic minorities. *Work, Employment and Society*, 21(4), 773–784.

Noussia, A. (2003). Heritage recycled: Migration and tourism as factors in the heritage of vernacular settlements. *International Journal of Heritage Studies*, 9(3), 197–213.

O'Brien, D. and Fugita, S. (1982). Middle-man minority concept: Its explanatory value in the case of the Japanese in California agriculture. *Pacific Sociology Review*, 25, 185–204.

OECD (2015). New approaches to SME and entrepreneurship financing: Broadening the range of instruments. OECD Publishing. Accessed on 26/9/2017 at www.oecd.org/cfe/smes/New-Approaches-SME-full-report.pdf

OECD (2006). The SME financing gap: Theory and evidence, Vol. 1. OECD Publishing.

Oliveira, C. (2007). Understanding the diversity of immigrant entrepreneurial strategies. In L.-P. Dana (ed.), *Handbook of Research on Ethnic Minority Entrepreneurship: A Co-evolutionary View on Resource Management*. Cheltenham: Edward Elgar, pp. 61–82.

Olson, P., Zuiker, V., Danes, S., Stafford, K., Heck, R. and Duncan, K. (2003). The impact of the family and the business on family business sustainability. *Journal of Business Venturing*, 18(5), 639–666.

Ortiz-Walters, R., Gavino, M. and Williams, D. (2015). Social networks of latino and latina entrepreneurs and their impact on venture performance. *Academy of Entrepreneurship Journal*, 21(1), 58.

Pang, C. and Rath, J. (2006). The force of regulation in the land of the free: The persistence of Chinatown, Washington DC as an ethnic commercial enclave. *Workshop on Migrations between East and West: Normalizing the Periphery*. Research School for Southeast Asian Studies, Xiamen University, China.

Peet, R. and Hartwick, E. (2015). *Theories of development: Contentions, arguments, alternatives*, Guilford Publications.

Phan, M. and Luk, C. (2007). "I don't say I have a business in Chinatown": Chinese subethnic relations in Toronto's Chinatown West. *Ethnic and Racial Studies*, 31, 294–326.

Phizacklea, A. and Ram, M. (1996). Being your own boss: Ethnic minority entrepreneurs in comparative perspective. *Work, Employment & Society*, 10(2), 319–339.

Piperopoulos, P. and Ikonomu, T. (2007). Entrepreneurship in ethnic groups: The case of the multicultural city of Thessaloniki, Greece. *International Journal of Business and Globalisation*, 1(2), 272–292.

Pires, G. and Stanton, J. (2015). *Ethnic marketing: Culturally sensitive theory and practice*. Abingdon, UK: Routledge.

Pires, G., Stanton, J. and Stanton, P. (2011). Revisiting the substantiality criterion: From ethnic marketing to market segmentation. *Journal of Business Research*, 64(9), 988–996.

Portes, A. (1987). The social origins of the Cuban enclave economy of Miami. *Sociological Perspectives*, 30, 340–372.

Portes, A. and Bach, R. (1985). *Latin Journey*. Berkeley: University of California Press.

Portes, A. and Sensenbrenner, J. (1993). Embeddedness and immigration: Notes on the social determinants of economic action. *American Journal of Sociology*, 98(6), 1320–1350.

Portes, A. and Shafer, S. (2007). Revisiting the enclave hypothesis: Miami twenty-five years later. In M. Ruef and M. Lounsbury (ed.), *The Sociology of Entrepreneurship* (Research in the Sociology of Organizations, Vol. 25). Emerald Group Publishing Limited, pp. 157–190.

Pütz, R. (2003). Culture and entrepreneurship: Remarks on transculturality as practice. *Tijdschrift voor Economische en Sociale Geografie*, 94(5), 554–563.

Quick MBA (2007). Entrepreneurship. *Internet Center for Management and Business Administration Inc.* [Online]. Accessed 25/9/2017 at www.quickmba.com/entre/

Ram, M. (2006). Ethnic minority businesses in the uk: An overview-Council of Europe. Available at www.coe.int/t/dg3/socialpolicies/socialcohesiondev/source/. . ./2006ram_en.doc

Ram, M. and Jones, T. (2008). Ethnic-minority businesses in the UK: A review of research and policy developments. *Environment and Planning C: Government and Policy*, 26, 352–374.

Ram, M. and Jones, T. (2006). Ethnic minority businesses in the West Midlands: A review. *Report to Advantage West Midlands, Centre for Research into Ethnic Minority Enterprise (CREME)*, De Montfort University, Leicester.

Ram, M. and Jones, T. (1998). *Ethnic Minorities in Business.* Small Business Research Trust Report. Milton Keynes, UK: Small Business Research Trust.

Ram, M. and Smallbone, D. (2002). Ethnic minority business support in the era of the small business service. *Environment and Planning 'C': Government and Policy*, 20(2), 235–249.

Rath, J. and Kloosterman, R. (2002). Working on the fringes: Immigrant businesses, economic integration and informal practices. Accessed 26/9/2017 online at http://users.fmg.uva.nl/jrath/downloads/@rath%20NUTEK.pdf

Reiss, B. and Cruikshank, J. (2000). *Low-Risk, High-Reward: Starting and Growing Your Small Business with Minimal Risk.* New York: The Free Press.

Reynolds, P. (1991). Sociology and entrepreneurship: Concepts and contributions. *Entrepreneurship, Theory and Practice*, 16(2), 47–67.

Romero, M. and Valdez, Z. (2016). Introduction to the special issue: Intersectionality and entrepreneurship. *Ethnic and Racial Studies*, 39(9), 1553–1565.

Rosenfeld, M. and Tienda, M. (1999). Mexican immigration, occupational niches, and labor-market competition: Evidence from Los Angeles, Chicago, and Atlanta, 1970 to 1990. In F. D. Bean and S. Bell-Rose (eds.), *Immigration and Opportunity: Race, Ethnicity, and Employment in the United States.* Russell Sage Foundation.

Rudolph Jr., J. (2015). Ethnic enclaves. *immigrationtounitedstates.org.* Accessed 1/10/2017 at http://immigrationtounitedstates.org/484-ethnic-enclaves.html

Schaper, M. and Volery, T. (2004). *Entrepreneurship and Small Business: A Pacific Rim Perspective.* Milton: John Wiley & Sons Australia.

Schumpeter, J. (2000). *Entrepreneurship as innovation: The social science view*, pp. 51–75. Available at SSRN: https://ssrn.com/abstract=1512266.

Schumpeter, J. (1951). *Essays: On Entrepreneurs, Innovations, Business Cycles, and the Evolution of Capitalism.* Transaction Publishers.

Schumpeter, J. (1942). Creative destruction. *Capitalism, Socialism and Democracy.* London: Routledge, 825, 82–83.

Shapero, A. and Sokol, L. (1982). The social dimensions of entrepreneurship. *Encyclopaedia of Entrepreneurship*, 72–90. Accessed at SSRN: https://ssrn.com/abstract=1497759

Smallbone, D., Bertotti, M. and Ekanem, I. (2005). Diversification in ethnic minority business: The case of Asians in London's creative industries. *Journal of Small Business and Enterprise Development*, 12(1), 41–56.

Stark, R. (2007). *Sociology*, 10th ed. Thompson Wadsworth.

Steinberg, S. (1981). *The Ethnic Myth: Race, Ethnicity, and Class in America.* New York: Atheneum.

Storey, D. (ed.). (2000). *Small Business: Critical Perspectives on Business and Management*, Vol. 2. London: Taylor & Francis.

Sway, M. (1988). *Familiar Strangers: Gipsy Life in America.* Urbana, IL: University of Illinois Press.

Thornton, P., Ribeiro-Soriano, D. and Urbano, D. (2011). Socio-cultural factors and entrepreneurial activity: An overview. *International Small Business Journal*, 29(2), 105–118.

Valdez, Z. (2011). *The New Entrepreneurs: How Race, Class, and Gender Shape American Enterprise.* Stanford, CA: Stanford University Press.

Van Delft, H., Gorter, C. and Nijkamp, P. (2000). In search of ethnic entrepreneurship opportunities in the city: A comparative policy study. *Environment and Planning C: Government and Policy*, 18, 429–451.

Veiszadeh, M. (2011). Is Sydney a city of enclaves? *The Sydney Morning Herald*, November 12. Accessed 1/10/2017 at www.smh.com.au/federal-politics/the-question/is-sydney-a-city-of-enclaves-20111111-1nb68.html

Verheul, I., Thurik, R., Hessels, J. and van der Zwan, P. (2010). Factors influencing the entrepreneurial engagement of opportunity and necessity entrepreneurs. *EIM Research Report H201011.* Available at http://ondernemerschap.panteia.nl/pdf-ez/h201011.pdf

Vickers, I., Lyon, F. and North, D. (2009). Removing barriers to enterprise through targeted support for disadvantaged groups. *Paper presented at ISBE Conference*, November.

Volery, T. (2007). Ethnic entrepreneurship: A theoretical framework. In *Handbook of Research on Ethnic Minority Entrepreneurship: A Co-Evolutionary View on Resource Management.* Cheltenham: Edward Elgar, pp. 30–41.

Waldinger, R. (1999). *Still the Promised City?: African-Americans and New Immigrants in Post-Industrial New York.* Cambridge, MA: Harvard University Press.

Waldinger, R., Aldrich, H. and Ward, R. (1990). Opportunities, group characteristics and strategies. In R. Waldinger, H. Aldrich and R. Ward (eds.), *Ethnic Entrepreneurs: Immigrant Business in Industrial Societies.* London: Sage, pp. 13–48.

Waldinger, R., McEvoy, D. and Aldrich, H. (1990). Spatial dimension of opportunity structures. In R. Waldinger, H. Aldrich and R. Ward (eds.), *Ethnic Entrepreneurs: Immigrant Business in Industrial Societies.* London: Sage, pp. 106–130.

Wennekers, S. and Thurik, R. (1999). Linking entrepreneurship and economic growth. *Small Business Economics*, 13, 27–55.

White, M. (1984). Racial and ethnic succession in four cities. *Urban Affairs Review*, 20(2), 165–183.

Wilson, K. and Portes, A. (1980). Immigrant enclaves: An analysis of the labour market experience of Cubans in Miami. *American Journal of Sociology*, 86, 295–319.

Yinger, J. (1985). Ethnicity. *Annual Review of Sociology*, 11, 151–180.

Zeithaml, V. (1981). How consumer evaluation processes differ between goods and services. In J. A. Donnelly and W. R. George (eds.), *Marketing of Services*. Chicago: AMA, pp. 186–190.

Zhou, M. (2004). Revisiting ethnic entrepreneurship: Convergences, controversies, and conceptual advancements. *International Migration Review*, 38, 1040–1074.

Zhou, M. and Cho, M. (2010). Noneconomic effects of ethnic entrepreneurship: A focused look at the Chinese and Korean enclave economies in Los Angeles. *Thunderbird International Business Review*, 52, 83–96.

Zimmer, C. and Aldrich, H. (1987). Resource mobilization through ethnic networks: Kinship and friendship ties of shopkeepers in England. *Sociological Perspectives*, 30(4), 422–445.

Zitelli, J. (2017). Ethnic markets may be the next trend in retail. *The Food Institute Blog*, January 19. Accessed on 2/10/207 at https://foodinstitute.com/blog/ethnic-markets-may-be-next-trend

8 Ethnic Minority Business Growth, Demise and Failure

There are a large number of drivers pushing/pulling ethnic minority individuals into entrepreneurship as well as a variety of impediments that may need to be taken into account by these individuals in deciding on whether to become ethnic entrepreneurs. Accordingly, the previous chapter has argued that aspiring ethnic entrepreneurs can face considerable challenges in discovering feasible business opportunities, as well as hurdles in starting-up and consolidating young ethnic minority businesses. Much of the challenges depend not only on the constraints integral to mainstream opportunity structures, but also on the characteristics and resources of the aspiring entrepreneur's minority ethnic group of affiliation, and on the ethnic strategies that emerge from the interaction of opportunities with the group's characteristics (Boissevain et al., 1990), all of which are embedded within evolving historical conditions (Aldrich and Waldinger, 1990).

Maintaining a strong focus on the examination of how crucial is the role played by minority ethnic groups for the development of ethnic entrepreneurship—from a natural incubator to being a facilitator in entrepreneurs' access to ethnic resources and the fundamental target market offered by the minority ethnic group—this chapter discusses the role played by minority ethnic groups in the break out strategies that are likely to underpin an ethnic minority business growth potential, that is, after the business is formally created and its operations are consolidated as a young business targeting their initial co-ethnic market.

More precisely, rather than examining business strategies exploiting the growth opportunities eventually provided by the entrepreneur's minority ethnic group, perhaps involving improved performance as reflected on revenue or on cost minimization through operational efficiency, the main focus is on ethnic minority business growth through expansion to alternative markets that are distinct from the minority ethnic group of affiliation, whether minority, mainstream, international, transnational or even global.

There is agreement in the ethnic entrepreneurship literature that ethnic minority business creation, consolidation and growth or demise cannot be usually explained by any one particular characteristic or perspective. Hence, the literature sought to develop models and theories integrating the relevant theories exposed in the previous chapter, so as to provide holistic perspectives on ethnic minority businesses' behaviour. Summarized in Table 8.1, these models and theories are used here as a stepping

Table 8.1 Ethnic Minority Business Creation Theory and Relationship With Minority Ethnic Groups

Interactive model	Complex interaction between opportunity structures and minority ethnic group's resources, but omits exposure of ethnic entrepreneurship to the political-institutional environment. Examines the structure of economic opportunities and constraints produced by market forces. But cannot explain international variations in ethnic entrepreneurship performance
Social embeddedness theory	Ethnic entrepreneurs prefer to engage in business with co-ethnics and all economic behaviour is embedded in networks and communities of interpersonal relationships. Embeddedness in a minority ethnic group may facilitate/constrain action, reducing transactional costs and possibly gaining access to economic resources that may explain consolidation into a young EMB and its eventual growth. The approach requires understanding entrepreneurial behaviour and outcomes resulting from the interaction between social and economic opportunity structures faced by immigrants on arrival, the attributes characterizing different minority ethnic groups and the ethnic strategies EMBs may/may not use in forging ahead.
	Social embeddedness can constrain entrepreneurship depending on the extent of embedding and how committed entrepreneurs are to their ethnic group, affecting their ability to draw on social and economic resources, influencing the shape of the EMB. But the theory is deemed unrealistic for considering an unregulated and undifferentiated economy. EMBs should be seen as embedded both in their minority ethnic group's social environment and in the environment that determines their group.
Mixed embeddedness theory	Enhances the interactive model by taking the SMEs' economic environment and combining it with the legal environment to influence SMEs' creation and growth. Although laws and regulations help shape EMBs' general commercial environment, providing guidance and certainty, they can also pose intractable obstacles that may deter EMBs' creation and consolidation. Hence, the legal and regulatory environment can be expected to influence the uptake of opportunities in the discovery phase.
	Since all SMEs, including EMBs, are subject to the same legal and regulatory environment, the theory is not able to deal with broad variation in inter-ethnic entrepreneurial concentration among minority ethnic groups.

(Continued)

Table 8.1 Continued

Enhanced mixed embeddedness theory	Aims to enhance the interactive mode. Acknowledges the relevance of the entrepreneur's location. The model identifies four interdependent aspects that apply equally to ethnic and mainstream entrepreneurs, comprising: 1. Entrepreneur's psychological characteristics, 2. Access to restricted information and knowledge, 3. Creative information processing allowing opportunity recognition and exploitation, and 4. The ability to apply cognitive heuristics to solve problems related to recognizing, evaluating and exploiting business opportunities. Also includes an "ethnic dimension", given by the extent of "the cultural differences between host and home country, the discrimination the entrepreneur is subjected to, social integration of the minority ethnic group, the experience gained in the new environment, age and gender, and the education level of the entrepreneur".

EMB: Ethnic minority business; MEG: Minority ethnic group

Extracted from the literature discussed in this chapter.

stone for broader looking models and theories, namely the interactive model, the social embeddedness theory and the mixed embeddedness theory, deemed more appropriate to assist in explaining the ethnic minority business's growth process.

The interactive model is first discussed, followed by a discussion of the social embeddedness theory, both of which highlight ethnic minority business reliance on the entrepreneur's minority ethnic group of affiliation. Focus then shifts to the mixed embeddedness theory, which recognizes that ethnic entrepreneurs and their minority ethnic groups are enveloped in the wider environment determined by government regulation of markets. Discussion of these theories provides the foundation for examining ethnic minority business growth and demise.

Interactive Model

Developed by Waldinger, Aldrich and Ward (1990) applying a multi-dimensional approach, the interactive model explains the essential inter-acting factors in ongoing ethnic minority business operations. It explains that ethnic minority business strategies are steered by both the opportunity structure of the given economic environment (i.e. market conditions and access to business ownership) and the minority ethnic group's characteristics (which depend on an entrepreneur's predisposing traits and ability to mobilize resources). Noting the opacity of the opportunity structures (Oliveira, 2007), these are divided into the market conditions (ethnic products vs product for the mainstream) and the entrepreneur's ability to achieve business ownership (in terms of market shortage, competition and legislation about business ownership).

The opportunity structure of the economic environment interacts with the entrepreneur's group characteristics, encompassing the entrepreneur's predisposition traits—such as motivations for self-employment (Lo, Teixeira and Truelove, 2002), entrepreneurial background prior to arrival in the host country and reasons for migrating and aspiration levels—and the entrepreneur's ability to mobilize resources due to cultural ties, proximity to the minority ethnic group and access to a strong social ethnic network.

Social Embeddedness Theory

Granovetter (1985, 1992) posits that all economic behaviour is embedded, submerged and absorbed in networks and communities of interpersonal relationships and that economic action is affected by the actor's dyadic relationships and by the structure of the overall network of relations, such that economic goals are accompanied by non-economic ones related to social context (Sarasvathy and Venkataraman, 2011). This section argues that imperatives of in-group behaviour reciprocity between an ethnic minority business and the minority ethnic group of affiliation illustrate the dual goals (Yamagishi, 2003).

McKeever, Anderson and Jack (2014) offer useful commentary on social embeddedness in entrepreneurship research. Identified broadly as the nature, depth and extent of an individual's ties into an environment, community or society, and indicating a direct link to entrepreneurship (Anderson and Miller, 2003), embeddedness recognizes the opportunity to form a deeper understanding of how membership of social groups, such as minority ethnic groups, may facilitate or constrain agency (Waldinger, 1995; Portes and Sensenbrenner, 1993). But entrepreneurs need to negotiate a complex and dynamic process to benefit from their social embedding (Rath, 2010).

In the context of ethnic entrepreneurship, individual ethnic entrepreneurs partake in ethnically specific economic networks that help start and develop their business (Rath, 2006). Accordingly, the social embeddedness thesis (Polanyi, 1946; Phizacklea and Ram, 1996) proposes that ethnic entrepreneurs prefer to engage in business with others they know and trust through kinship ties, social networks and/or membership of a close-knit minority ethnic group. This preference is justified because entrepreneurs do not function in a social vacuum, rather they are entrenched in social networks characterized by trust, expectations and enforceable norms (Portes, 1995) that can be used to assist in meeting their economic objectives (Rath and Kloosterman, 2000), reducing transactional costs and possibly gaining access to valuable economic resources (Rothbart, 1993). Hence, independently of the factors that led to an ethnic minority business creation/start-up, its embedding in the minority ethnic group's network sustains and explains its consolidation into a young business and, eventually, its growth.

Congruent with the interactive model, the social embeddedness approach requires understanding entrepreneurial behaviour and outcomes resulting from the interaction between the social and economic opportunity structures immigrants face on arrival in the new country, the attributes characterizing different minority ethnic groups, and the ethnic strategies ethnic minority businesses may or may not use in forging ahead (Light and Rosenstein, 1995; Waldinger, Aldrich and Ward, 1990).

Embeddedness can contribute to performance and growth based on the nature of the linkage to the local context, meaning privileged access to the benefits present in the structure (Lechner and Dowling, 2003), potentially leading to the achievement by the ethnic minority business of a preferred (and possibly protected) supplier status to their minority ethnic group. But access to the benefits comes at a cost, and embeddedness can also act as a constraint or even a retardant to entrepreneurship (Gedajlovic et al., 2013).

The extent to which entrepreneurs are socially embedded and how they are embedded, will affect their ability to draw on social and economic resources (Jack, 2005), impacting upon the nature of the entrepreneurial process and influencing the shape of business. Hence, social embeddedness depends on ethnic entrepreneurs' commitment (Jamal, 2005), such that involvement in their minority ethnic group of affiliation—given by the number and diversity of the entrepreneurs' personal linkages to that minority ethnic group—is a better indicator of ethnicity than mere demographic identification (Menzies et al., 2007; Chaganti and Greene, 2002).

Social embeddedness theory has been questioned on the grounds that it is unrealistic because it considers an unregulated and undifferentiated economy, which is not the case in real life (Rath, 2006). Arguably, ethnic minority businesses do not operate entirely on their own terms, and their ability to deploy their minority ethnic group's social capital is subject to regulatory regimes (Ram and Jones, 2008). Ethnic entrepreneurs and their ethnic minority businesses are subject to own personal, distinctive informal social networks and to their minority ethnic group's ethnic networks—comprising consumers, other ethnic minority businesses and institutions with a parochial cultural affinity, characterized by cooperation among its members, in contrast with simple interactional avoidance towards dissimilar others (Serino, Giovagnoli and Làdavas, 2009).

In the same way that ethnic networks have boundaries that determine access to the resources they enable, ranging from open access to impermeable to outsiders (Wimmer, 2008; Mummendey et al., 1999), the very creation of an ethnic minority business is often if not always subject to regulation by Government. The literature notes that while some ethnic minority businesses might partake in illegal operations related to black and grey markets—such as engaging in the employment of illegal immigrants (Jones, Ram and Edwards, 2006) and flouting official regulations (Jones and Ram, 2012; Ram, Jones and Edwards, 2007)—and to participation in shadow and underground economies working outside the formal/legal structures regulated by government (Ojo, Nwankwo and Gbadamosi, 2013), the norm is for mainstream regulations to apply to, and be equally respected by, mainstream businesses and ethnic minority businesses. The suggestions are that ethnic minority businesses should be seen as embedded both in their minority ethnic group's social environment, as well as in the environment that determines their minority ethnic group.

One Model Doesn't Fit All

The umbilical link between ethnic entrepreneurship and the minority ethnic group of affiliation of the ethnic entrepreneur is a recurring point of discussion in the ethnic entrepreneurship literature, as discussed in the previous chapter. This view stands because ethnic entrepreneurship is seen to ensue from the exclusion and discrimination to which newly arrived immigrants are subject to in securing attractive employment opportunities in the host country, a predicament that might be compensated or at least attenuated by the advantages emanating by affiliation with a substantial minority ethnic group. This is sometimes the case, of course, but exclusion and discrimination are neither exclusive to the motivations to engage in self-employment, nor unique to newly arrived immigrants in a host country or, indeed, to migrants.

> Older people, African-Americans, and Hispanics remain disproportionately among the long-term unemployed; from 2007 to 2009, so did workers from specific industries such as sales and management, according to recent research from the Labor Statistics Bureau. Even a college degree was not enough, at the height of the recession, to stave off long-term unemployment. What a terrifying wake-up call to anyone who thought that higher education would protect them from an economic mishap
>
> (Cook, 2015)

Many countries, including Australia, Germany, Slovakia, UK and US, have created appeals—such as the New Enterprize Incentive Scheme (2017) program in Australia—targeting those with long-term unemployment prospects to overcome their predicament by engaging in self-employment (Bryson and White, 1996; Páleník, 2011; Huffingpost, 2013; Cook, 2015).

Clearly, not every ethnic entrepreneur is a product of actual or perceived inability to make a living by working for others, including co-ethnic employers in the new country. Self-employment may be an aspiration as a pathway to financial independence and enhanced social status, as well as the outcome of an expansionary strategy by an existing business in the country of provenance or elsewhere. Self-employment may also occur simultaneously with employment, perhaps as a supplementary source of income, or to take advantage of an unexpected business opportunity with an attractive payoff.

Immigrants arrive in a host country for many disparate reasons and assume different status, such as economic immigrants, a status commonly applicable to skilled workers and business people. Self-employment is the usual objective of the latter, although the businesses they create might be larger, better connected and better resourced than the typical ethnic minority business.

Overall, both the interactive and social embeddedness models ignore gender issues and, most important in the present context, they largely ignore host society influences on ethnic entrepreneurial activities (Light and Bhachu, 1993), namely the banking system and the complexity of the regulatory and policy framework (Oliveira, 2007). It was this that prompted the development of the mixed embeddedness model (Kloosterman and Rath, 2003), attempting to take the political regime into greater consideration, and breaking down the opportunity structure of ethnic strategies into three different categories: vacancy chain, post-industrial low skilled sector and post-industrial high skilled sector.

Mixed Embeddedness Theory

Interactive model perspectives of ethnic entrepreneurship are almost solely determined by the entrepreneurs and their ethnic minority business social embeddedness within the socio-economic environment surrounding a possibly protected co-ethnic market offered by their minority ethnic group. (Light, 1972). One explanation for this, drawn from the case of Chinese business immigrants in Vancouver in the 1980s, refers to the structural constraints and blocked mobility in the non-ethnic/open market, relegating ethnic entrepreneurs to the ethnic/closed market (Wong and Ng, 1998). An alternative, perhaps more comprehensive view is that, independent of their dependence on a minority ethnic group's environment, ethnic entrepreneurs and their ethnic minority businesses are also embedded in an external business environment context (Kloosterman, van der Leun and Rath, 1999), notably comprising government regulated competitive markets open to business in general, hence targeting both minority and mainstream consumers.

While government regulation can be repressive and constraining as well as enabling, it usually applies to *all* businesses in a given jurisdiction. Business ownership by foreigners is not usually illegal, but it may be subject to special requirements and restrictions in the case of ethnic minority businesses, for example in terms of the products that can be imported and distributed, such as ethnic foodstuffs. That stringency may vary markedly across countries, and between regions within a country (Razin, 2002), ultimately reflected in the specific location of ethnic networks (Razin and Light, 1998). These are major and important aspects to consider in understanding ethnic minority business performance during the phases of opportunity discovery, start-up and consolidation into young ethnic minority businesses. Different opportunities may be more or less accessible to ethnic entrepreneurs due to the need to meet regulations or to benefit from special concessions (Rath, 2006; Engelen, 2001), rather than for reasons of exclusion (Hindle and Moroz, 2010).

Departing from the social embeddedness perspective (Portes and Sensenbrenner, 1993), Kloosterman (2010) refers to ethnic minority businesses as part of a larger political economy of the country of settlement to whose rules they must conform, such that their capacity to mobilize and deploy their minority ethnic group's social capital must also be assessed in relation to the external structure of relevant markets and regulatory regimes. Consistent with the mixed embeddedness thesis, ethnic entrepreneurs need to be cognizant of their ethnic minority business's potential exposure to a variety of environmental contexts, including the impact that laws, public institutions, and general regulatory practices might have on their entrepreneurship activity (Kloosterman and Rath, 2003).

The multi-level, mixed embeddedness thesis, therefore, recognizes the significant effects that government regulations and disparate socio-economic factors may have in the process of discovery of business opportunities by ethnic entrepreneurs, leading to ethnic minority business start-up. Sensitive to the spectrum of contexts in which ethnic minority businesses operate, capturing the opportunities and constraints stemming from local institutional and market conditions, the mixed embeddedness thesis entails two major levels in the embedding of ethnic entrepreneurs:

1. Embedding in the environment of their co-ethnic minority group, recognizing and abiding by that group's own ethos, gaining access both to social and ethnic networks, as well as to family and friends' loans and labour, possibly at sub-market rates, which might convert into a decisive competitive advantage for the entrepreneur (Portes and Sensenbrenner, 1993). Availing themselves of the competitive advantage may be sufficient as a compelling argument for newly arrived migrants to affiliate themselves to a specific minority ethnic group and to resort to using self-employment as a means to rise above discrimination and exclusion by mainstream institutions, as well as overcoming ongoing multi-level structural disadvantages (Sepulveda, Syrett and Lyon, 2011),

2. Embedding in the environment determined by the structures of the mainstream economy and small business regulations common to all businesses in general, noting that these structures are themselves

embedded in the opportunities afforded by the minority ethnic group (Lagendijk et al., 2011).

These two major levels of embedding support the view that the mixed embeddedness approach should contextualize immigrant entrepreneurial behaviour as moulded by the dynamic interaction among micro-level socio-cultural forces, meso-level economic-structural conditions and the macro-level political-institutional setting of the immigrant receiving society, all embedded within their larger geographical setting (Lo and Teixeira, 2015). As noted by Ortiz-Walters, Gavino and Williams (2015), the ethnic entrepreneur's network size might be restricted by the nature of the outer-group membership and that this is a result of the mixed embedding because social relations are related to institutional agents, social hierarchies and the old boy's networks, which "often systematically exclude the out-group represented by members who are diverse in race, ethnicity, religion, class, and gender" (p. 73),

Identified as the sine qua non of the mixed embeddedness model, the melding together of ethnic entrepreneur's *economic* and social relationships within the general environment of the host country allows for a better framework for understanding ethnic entrepreneurship and ethnic minority businesses. But the usefulness of the model depends on three assumptions related to the accessibility, substantiality and actionability of the opportunities being examined. Adapted from Volery (2007, p. 35):

1. Opportunities must not be blocked by too high barriers of entry or government regulations;
2. An opportunity must be recognized through the eyes of a potential entrepreneur as one that can attract a positive and sufficient payoff; and
3. An entrepreneur must be able to seize an opportunity in a tangible way.

While it is unwarranted to understand the interactive (social embedding) model as a one-size-fits-all or even the lone model to explain all the possible antecedents of the decision to consider, embark into, consolidate, promote growth and/or discontinue entrepreneurial activity in the host country, it may be argued that the model provides the "as the rule" position with areas of objection, such as multi-level embedding, becoming the exception position. Clearly, context matters:

- Not all immigrants are perceived or perceive themselves as affiliated to an ethnic minority;
- Not all immigrants are equally challenged (if at all) by the mainstream culture and by its way of doing things;
- Immigrants' socialization in the host country can be expected to evolve with time (see the discussion of Sydney's Chinatown in the previous chapter);

- Not all immigrants emanate from countries represented by substantial minority ethnic groups in the host country, even if they settle in large metropolitan areas usually attractive to minority ethnic groups. Invisibility may indicate smaller end less powerful ethnic networks;
- Even if immigrants and their minority ethnic group of affiliation settle in large metropolitan areas, such as London, New York, Sydney or Toronto, different urban milieus in those areas can be expected to have characteristics either favourable or unfavourable to entrepreneurship prospects. What might matter is the milieu, not the city, because "the size of communities, varying widely from one milieu to another, has an impact on the self-employment rates" (Volery, 2007, p. 37; Razin and Langlois, 1996);
- There are many types of immigrants identified in the literature, including entrepreneurial and economic immigrants; in the case of these types of immigrants, most decisions leading to the creation of an enterprise may be taken before arrival in the host country;
- Not all immigrants settle in large metropolitan areas where a non-mainstream solution may be possible; existing theories have not been tested for cases where settlement is in non-immigrant cities or in small and medium cities, where ethnic networks may not be available;
- Sojourners are immigrants whose settlement is only temporary, and that status is known from the outset (www.thefreedictionary.com/sojourner). They are unlikely to behave like committed immigrants (Siu, 1952, p. 34).

Lo and Teixeira (2015) found that ethnic minority businesses in Kelowna (Canada) are less socially embedded than those in large cities given "the absence of institutionally complete communities or strong ethnic economies" (p. 631), allegedly because of less specific support by municipal governments (this is allegedly in line with the mixed embeddedness approach to immigrant entrepreneurship (Kloosterman and Rath, 2001), and because of a lack of a supporting minority ethnic group.

Bernard (2008) and Lo and Li (2011) found that immigrants settling in small cities generally experienced a higher degree of economic integration in the mainstream than their counterparts in large metropolitan centres (Lo and Teixeira, 2015), but evidence from the case of refugees in NSW offers contradictory evidence, with the resettlement of refugees from regional settlements into major cities (Virtue, 2017).

Mixed Embeddedness: The Norm and a Potential Barrier to Growth

The conclusion from the discussion of the social and mixed embeddedness approaches above is that these approaches are not mutually exclusive and, in practice, they offer few departures from the interactive model, depending on the importance afforded to Government regulation. The assumption is that ethnic entrepreneurs benefit from the support of their own social network and social capital, and are subject to the two major levels of embedding earlier discussed. One, as discussed, is the ethnic minority business' social embedding in the environment of the ethnic-entrepreneur's co-ethnic group, with its own ethos and with access to proprietary social and ethnic networks; the other refers to the minority ethnic group's embedding in the unavoidable legal environmental structures of their country of settlement, including the laws, incentives, public institutions and general regulatory practices.

Figure 8.1 is a representation of the different environmental constraints that ethnic minority business must face in assessing the structure of business opportunities discovered in the country of settlement involving the targeting of the minority ethnic group of affiliation, some other minority ethnic group or the mainstream. The figure shows an ethnic entrepreneur's exposure to different environmental constraints in the host country, depending on which target market is selected. Ethnic entrepreneurs and their ethnic minority businesses are exposed to legal environment compliance, and dependent on support from the informal social network, both of which need to be taken into account to successfully negotiate the different environmental constraints pegged to different target markets and their environments, individually identified by the boxes on the right-hand side. Which environments need to be taken into account depends on, as well as determines, the opportunities considered by the entrepreneur in the discovery phase. Hence, the focus of the typical ethnic minority business on serving the entrepreneur's minority ethnic group implies that the business is geared or engineered to

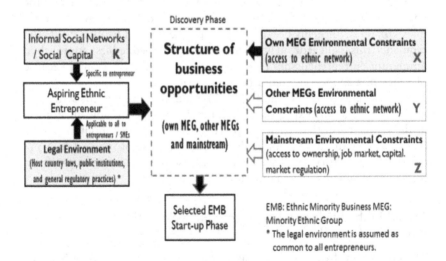

Figure 8.1 Exposure to Environmental Constraints in the Host Country, Ethnic Minority Business

comply with, and take advantage of, two distinct environments.[1] One is the entrepreneur's informal social network. The other is the minority ethnic group's environment, including its social and ethnic networks and affiliates.

It is apparent that any decision to undertake self-employment comes with the question "doing what"? The answer might emerge from discussions and shared experiences with similar co-ethnic others in a process that can help shape the nature and intensity of the ethnic entrepreneur's motivation, as well as serve as early testing. But, of course, the structure of opportunities that underpin the discovery phase is necessarily challenging for aspiring ethnic entrepreneurs, including the selection and early testing of a perceived opportunity (Dodd and Keles, 2014).

Beyond the inherent difficulty in assessing the promise of a positive payoff, well informed aspiring ethnic entrepreneurs will need to decide on whether they have what it takes to take advantage of the discovered opportunities. In contrast with potential payoff, the feasibility of the various opportunities that are discovered can be assessed by attempting to match own capabilities (e.g. capital, availability of appropriate staff, availability of products) and competencies (e.g. language proficiency, sector knowledge, business skills) to the capabilities and competencies required to take advantage of each of those opportunities. Given the commonalities usually offered by co-ethnic markets, the likelihood of a good match between the attributes valued by the target market and those of the ethnic entrepreneurs and their ethnic minority businesses can be expected. Hence, ethnic entrepreneurs supported by their informal social networks would choose to target their own minority ethnic group of affiliation and, naturally, would be able to do so by deploying ethnic-sensitive strategies (Pires and Stanton, 2015).

Importantly, using the same rationale, any opportunities involving the targeting of other MEGs or the Mainstream would involve many more demands on the capabilities and competencies required from ethnic minority businesses. Targeting other minority ethnic groups or the mainstream will require adjustment by the ethnic entrepreneur to the different ethos of those markets, justifying the need to develop skills in ethic sensitivity to the new markets, indispensable to the provision of effective differentiated value propositions. Competing in other minority ethnic groups' markets means that the ethnic minority business' own minority ethnic group's ethnic networks may not be very effective at the time that the ethnic entrepreneur will be facing ethnic minority businesses aligned to the targeted group which may be supported by that group's ethnic networks.

Overall, the set of skills required from ethnic entrepreneurs will also be different and more extensive than if focused on their own minority ethnic group as the target market. The effectiveness of informal social networks may also decrease, and access to the support networks of the other minority ethnic groups or of the mainstream may be difficult to assess *a priori*, which questions the ability to compete with ethnic minority businesses aligned to those minority ethnic groups or the mainstream, possibly deterring the adoption of those opportunities. Deterrence would result because ethnic entrepreneurs would recognize the need for the skills and competencies they lacked, ultimately barring their ability to develop appropriate value propositions for those markets, hence to compete effectively. The question is whether all the above noted challenges also get in the way of ethnic minority business growth. Is the dependence by an ethnic minority business on the minority ethnic group of affiliation a barrier to its continued growth?

Considering Growth Capabilities and the Role of the Co-Ethnic Minority Group

The co-ethnic market is commonly characterized by low barriers to entry, intense competition, low margins, and low liquidity, therefore not designed for significant levels of growth (Butler and Greene, 1997). Yet the proclivity of ethnic minority business is to rely on their minority ethnic group's market for initial business success, perhaps grounded on a protected market position. The common justification for this is that the minority ethnic group's tastes may give preference to co-ethnic minority businesses, which can discourage competition by dissimilar others (Aldrich and Waldinger, 1990).

As noted in the previous chapter, in serving their minority ethnic group's market successful ethnic minority businesses may gain access to markets related to other groups, and even be able to expand to the mainstream market. Opportunities for expansion may arise in markets that are underserved or have been abandoned, perhaps due to low economies of scale and/or unstable or uncertain demand, both of which preclude effective supply by co-ethnic minority businesses. Successful expansion might depend on competitive intensity, on capital and technological requirements and on the ability to adapt relevant social networks to each different market of expansion.

Expansion opportunities may be related to the type of service-products that are offered in different markets, such as the provision of exotic (from the mainstream perspective) goods. For example, ethnic minority businesses of various provenances offering all sorts of relaxation massages have become a recurring feature in shopping malls in many Australian cities. This shows that ethnic minority businesses may be able to expand their offers to a variety of markets, although this might depend on the nature of the business activity, on the type of service-products they offer and on the context of the particular market. A focus on co-ethnic products was found to have a positive effect on ethnic minority business growth, reinforcing the view that idiosyncratic resources should not be overlooked as drivers of ethnic entrepreneurship (Dodd and Keles, 2014).

Table 8.2 consists of a list of possible types of markets that an ethnic minority business might target for growth. The table basically differentiates between the minority ethnic group of affiliation and minority

Table 8.2 Ethnic Minority Business Selection of Growth Markets

---

Minority Ethnic Group of Affiliation (Equi-Provenance)

Type A: At one location (e.g. the Portuguese MEG in Sydney, Australia).

Type B: Expansion to different locations (e.g. the Portuguese MEG in Sydney and in Melbourne, Australia). The community at different locations is served by different networks and, often, different businesses).

Type C: Expansion to different locations in different countries (e.g. a Portuguese EMB targeting the Portuguese diaspora in Australia, Canada, UK).

Jones and Ram (2012) note that EMBs can tap into much larger social capital and markets by becoming transnational enterprises (Honig, Drori and Carmichael, 2010), exploiting links to home country and diaspora. They also advise caution because transnationalism is a conceptual subset of globalism and faces scepticism (Judt, 2010, p. 193),

Minority ethnic group with distinct provenance

Consistent with the middleman philosophy, young EMBs may consolidate and start to grow by engaging in trade with entrepreneurs from other minority ethnic groups.

Type D: Expansion to different minority ethnic groups at one location (e.g. the Chinese group in Sydney, Australia).

Type E: Expansion to different minority ethnic groups at different locations in the same country (e.g. Italian and Greek in different Australian cities);

Type F: Expansion to different diaspora at different locations in different countries (e.g. Italian and Greek in Australia and NZ).

Other markets

Type G: Expansion to the mainstream market—EMBs may gain acceptance in the mainstream market once they reach a critical mass in targeting their minority ethnic group and gain positive visibility. If the EMB gains acceptance within the mainstream population, it may be viable to expand into the high-volume trade with the mainstream population.

Type H: Expansion to the home country (reverse transnationalism)— Transnational ethnic minority business are embedded in both home and host country, and this enables the perception and enactment of opportunities across borders, although "bifocality" is required to identify and deploy various capitals effectively across both contexts (Patel and Conklin, 2009). Reasoning is also applicable to Type C ethnic minority businesses.

Type I: Expansion by way of internationalization, multinationalization or globalization.

Type J: Expansion through e-commerce.

EMB: Ethnic minority business; MEG: Minority ethnic group

ethnic groups with distinct provenance (for both cases, the table considers markets at one location, at different locations in the same country and at many locations in many countries). Types G–J refer to other markets, including the mainstream and the home country, by way of internationalization, multinationalization and/or globalization, as well as via e-commerce. Using the previous discussed rationale, it is clear that different types of ethnic minority businesses (by selected market) will be embedded in contrasting environments, each requiring an adapted set of capabilities and competencies, and facing heightened and possibly unique sets of challenges.

Bonacich (1973) proposed that ethnic minority businesses (Type A) can only prosper if they breakout from local co-ethnic market limitations, suggesting transformation into Type B by expansion to different locations (regional or national) where their minority ethnic group is present, or even Type G by targeting prosperous mainstream markets (Jones-Evans, Thompson and Kwong, 2011; McEvoy and Hafeez, 2007). The need to breakout from the co-ethnic group has been advocated by Basu (2010), Altinay (2008), Nwankwo (2005) and many other analysts.

Transnationalism is not an uncommon practice for ethnic minority businesses, slotting as Type C. Such is the case, for example, of Chinese entrepreneurs in Vancouver, Canada, who circulate themselves and their resources between Canada and Asia in the operation of their businesses (Wong and Ng, 1998). Other examples include a variety of ethnic minority businesses affiliated with the Portuguese minority ethnic group in Sydney and "a handful of highly successful firms", whose profitability is not due to their break out from the low value business ghetto, . . . but to their successful transfer of substantial capital assets from previous business in Afghanistan, Iraq and Poland (Edwards et al., 2016, cited in Ram, Jones and Villares-Varela, 2017, p. 9).

In the case of ethnic minority businesses Type D and Type E, furthering their reach beyond the frontiers of their own minority ethnic group involves breaking into more challenging markets because of the management and social processes that are needed (Ram and Jones, 1998), exposure to unfamiliar environments, diminished support from co-ethnic minority group's networks and a general need for innovation. While starting-up an ethnic minority business requires a move from discovery, selection and planning of opportunities with co-ethnic significant others, growth requires new ideas, new resources, new networks (Dodd and Keles, 2014) and, eventually, new service-products. That is, the strengths that justify successful performance in the co-ethnic market can become the weaknesses when attempting to break out from that market (Masurel et al., 2002).

Ethnic minority businesses Type I relate to cases where exploitation of the co-ethnic market may serve as an export platform from which these businesses may expand and grow. The extract from Aldrich and Waldinger (1990) is an excellent example of the process by focusing on the Cuban community in Miami, Florida:

> One case in point is the experience of Cuban refugees in Miami, Florida (Portes, 1987). The early refugees converged on a depressed area in the central city, where housing costs were low and low-rent

vacant space was available. As the refugee population grew, and the customer base expanded, retail businesses proliferated (Mohl, 1985). The availability of a near-by, low-cost labour force, linked together through informal networks, enabled Cuban entrepreneurs to branch out into other industries, such as garments and construction, where they secured a non-ethnic clientele. Once in place, these "export industries" served as a base for additional expansion of the ethnic economy: the export industries generated a surplus that trickled down to merchants serving the local, specialized needs of the Cuban communities. The export industries also enabled ethnic entrepreneurs to diversify, by moving backward or forward into related industries. The vibrant Cuban ethnic economy has turned Miami into a center for investments from Latin America as well as an entrepôt for trade with that area, and Cuban entrepreneurs have been able to move into more sophisticated and higher profit fields.

(Levine, 1985)

In broader terms, opportunities for ethnic minority businesses type I are related to interactions of social capital with international opportunity development. While these opportunities may arise in ad hoc ways, there is evidence that "ethnic ties, in opposite to non-ethnic ties, are observed to influence internationalisation" (Prashantham, Dhanaraj and Kumar, 2015; Tian et al., 2018, p. 3). This is of particular relevance because social capital and emerging opportunity creation are not usually linked in the specialist literature, Zaefarian, Eng and Tasavori (2016) being a recent exception, albeit in a family business context.

Finally, in relation to ethnic minority businesses Type J, there is evidence that these businesses are late adopters of information and communications technology (ICT), although the prognosis is positive about closing the gap with earlier users of ICT (Dodd and Keles, 2014; Beckinsale, Ram and Theodorakopoulos, 2011).

Figure 8.2 presents a summary of the various aspects influencing ethnic minority businesses' growth that need to be understood.

The figure identifies five classes of influencers, each of which is supported by a table that summarizes the major issues of relevance, recognizing that an ethnic minority business' growth is a function of the ethnic entrepreneur's characteristics, of the business characteristics, of the informal networks, characteristics of the minority ethnic group and human relations (HR). The five classes of influencers are:

- Entrepreneurs characteristics—discussed in Table 8.3;
- Ethnic minority business characteristics—discussed in Table 8.4;
- Informal networks—discussed in Table 8.5;
- Minority ethnic group's characteristics—discussed in Table 8.6; and
- HR strategy—discussed in Table 8.7.

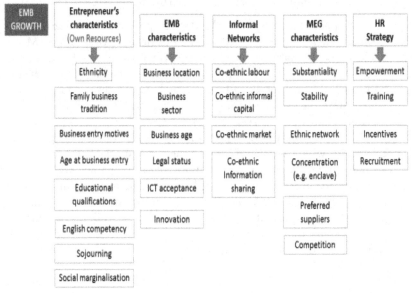

Business Growth (y) = f (Entrepreneur's own resources; EMB characteristics; Networks; MEG characteristics; HR Strategy)

Figure 8.2 Influencers on Ethnic Minority Business Growth

Business growth (y) = f(Entrepreneur's personal resources; the firm characteristics; networks; human resource strategy)

Table 8.3 Entrepreneurs' Characteristics That Foment Growth (Own Resources)

Entrepreneur's Characteristics (Own Resources)

Ethnicity

Some minority ethnic groups are more entrepreneurial than others. Minority groups with strong ethnicity ties and informal networks can gain competitive advantage and growth capabilities (Waldinger, Aldrich and Ward, 1990; Werbner, 1990).

- UK: East African Asian entrepreneurs do better than Indians and Pakistanis (Metcalf, Modood and Virdee, 1996);
- US: Korean entrepreneurs do better than European, Chinese and other Asian entrepreneurs (Zhou, 1992; Light, 1984; Kim, 1981)
- Canada: Macedonian entrepreneurs less successful than other ethnic groups (Herman, 1979).

Business entry motives

Positive motivations stimulate growth, which is hindered by negative motivations, such as forced self-employment to avoid being unemployed (Reitz, 1980); social marginalization (Altinay and Altinay, 2006), unemployment, discrimination and redundancy (Basu, 2004; Basu and Altinay, 2002; Rafiq, 1992; Ram, 1992).

Family business tradition

Growth is stimulated by a strong tradition of enterprise and self-employment, work experience and parental training (Dodd and Keles, 2014; Basu and Goswami, 1999; Duchesneau and Gartner, 1990).

Table 8.3 Continued

Entrepreneur's Characteristics (Own Resources)

Age at business entry (inconclusive)

- *Early start* leads to growth because younger entrepreneurs have fewer family responsibilities and commitments; they may sacrifice a little comfort to survive at least 1 year without salary (Kalleberg and Leicht, 1991);
- *Older start* explains lesser energy and comes with family commitments;
- *Middle age start* is better (Barkham et al., 1996; Storey, 1994).

Educational qualification

More education leads to growth (Basu and Goswami, 1999; Casson, 1991; Roper, 1998), provided this combines with English fluency (Altinay and Altinay, 2006).

English competency

Has significant impact on socio-economic integration, productivity and success in the labour market (Dustmann et al., 2003; Heath, 2001). Lack of fluency explains high unemployment (Light, 1984). English fluency helps integration into the mainstream (Dhaliwal, 2008), attracting customers by communicating with them and helping them access biz resources like advice and start-up bank loans.

Sojourning orientation

To make more money fast, self-employed sojourners work hard, long hours, willing to suffer short-term deprivation to hasten the long-term objective of returning to their country of origin (Bonacich, 1973), as in the case of the Filipino in Hong Kong. This makes it important to understand who the immigrant is (Cornelius, 1986).

Social marginalization

Influences the business entry decision and market selection (Anthias and Cederberg, 2009; Essers and Benschop, 2009; Masurel et al., 2002; Basu and Goswami, 1999).

Table 8.4 Ethnic Minority Business Characteristics That Influence Growth

Characteristics of the Ethnic Minority Business
Not Culturally Predetermined (Ram and Jones, 1998)

Business location

Ethnic minority businesses at different locations have different opportunities. Important in explaining the growth of firms in general (Almus and Nerlinger, 1999; Storey, 1994).

Business sector

Some sectors offer different opportunities and EMBs arguably look for those with low barriers to entry, low margins, and low liquidity (Butler and Greene, 1997).

Business age

Younger firms grow faster than older ones (Davidson et al., 2002; Wijewardena and Tibbits, 1999).

Business legal status

Limited liability EMBs are more willing to take risks and more likely to grow, whereas sole proprietors are less inclined to take risks because their personal wealth is not protected from excessive losses (Almus and Nerlinger, 1999; Storey, 1994).

Table 8.5 Characteristics of Informal Networks for Growth

Characteristics of EMBs' Informal Networks for Growth

Informal networks involve capital raising, labour recruitment, co-ethnic customers/ suppliers/ products identification and information gathering (Basu, 1998).

To be competitive and grow EMBs rely heavily on their informal social networks, namely co-ethnic customers and suppliers and information and advice from their families and co-ethnics.

Co-ethnic capital (it is usually difficult to gather this information)
Importance depends on the extent of informal capital and of ethnic products in the product mix. Positive interaction between ethnic resources in the form of cheap finance from extended family, and business growth (Basu and Goswami, 1999; Ward, 1983).

Co-ethnic labour
Using family and co-ethnic staff may lead to competitive advantage and growth potential due to lower recruitment and payroll costs. Co-ethnic labour may work for less if they have an illegal status and/or are unable to secure other employment.

Learning on the job may reduce training costs.

Recruitment of co-ethnic staff can be justified if they know the ethnic products being supplied, and are able to inform customers about these products.
This helps with service differentiation. But research also found an inverse relationship between growth and proportion of co-ethnic or family employees (Basu, 1998; Ram and Jones, 1998; Jones, McEvoy and Barrett, 1994). Competitive advantage is unlikely to derive from the exploitation of unskilled co-ethnic labour ready to work for less, or from practices of nepotism in recruitment and selection (Dhaliwal, 2008).

Co-ethnic market (customers and suppliers)
EMBs rely heavily on selling ethnic products to co-ethnic markets particularly early in the start-up, as it is easier to exchange in a language familiar to all (Werbner, 1990).

But some argue that heavy reliance on co-ethnic customers and failure to attract mainstream ones constrains growth (Basu, 1998; Smallbone et al., 1999; Waldinger, 1990). Growth needs a "breakout" into the mainstream market (Ethnic Minority Business Initiative, 1991).

Wang and Altinay (2012) found a positive effect of co-ethnic products and a negative effect of co-ethnic suppliers of utilities and facilities.

Co-ethnic sharing of information
Information about markets is very important for growth, and those businesses that maintain strong ties and informal networks have advantages compared to their counterparts (Bonacich, 1973). Combines with the minority ethnic group's ethnic networks to provide early-warning systems for new opportunities and threats (de Koning, 1999).

Table 8.6 Minority Ethnic Groups' Characteristics Influencing Growth

---

Substantiality

Reflected in consumption, minority ethnic group's substantiality indicates that the segment chosen as the target market must be large enough to be profitable (a requirement for effective segmentation), and it is also an indication of marketing potential (Pires, Stanton and Stanton, 2011). Substantial groups provide the fuel for co-ethnic EMBs' growth.

Stability

A minority ethnic group's ethno-cultural characteristics must remain *without* significant change (Barth, 1969). This must be able to sustain co-ethnic EMBs in their start-up, consolidation and growth stages. Stability reflects on trust and commitment, reducing the EMBs' perceived risk of innovation and growth

Ethnic network

These open up opportunities by facilitating access to collective resources (Jack et al., 2010) and fostering business relationships. It can lead to the generation of innovation and adds to the EMB's clout when these are young and small, promoting their growth (Jack, 2005).

Concentration

If a minority ethnic group is concentrated in a location (as in an enclave), this implies a logical concentration of EMBS in that same location, with easy access to their co-ethnic target market. This may also mean less exposure to mainstream and other expansion opportunities, increasing dependence on the minority ethnic groups for growth.

Preferred suppliers

EMBs face competition from other co-ethnic EMBs. In the USA, many mainstream businesses also target ethnic minority communities adding to competition for EMBs (Jamal, 2005; Burton, 2000). Being a preferred supplier to a minority ethnic group can be important to EMBs due to loyalty behaviour by co-ethnic consumers, reflected in repurchasing activity, and ultimate competitive advantage (Kabiraj and Shanmugan, 2011; Hingley, 2005), such that "becoming the preferred supplier is the goal" (Deshpande, 2002, p. 228).

Competition

EMBs operate in competitive environments, possibly facing intra-minority ethnic group opposition by co-ethnic minority businesses, by EMBs affiliated to other groups and by mainstream suppliers (Chaganti and Greene, 2002; Phizacklea and Ram, 1996). EMB's growth mode depends on the type of activity/product being delivered, because more markets also attract more competition (also see above for "preferred suppliers" increasing dependence on the minority ethnic groups for growth.

EMB: Ethnic minority business

Table 8.7 Ethnic Minority Businesses' HR Strategies for Growth

EMBs' HR Strategies for Growth

Empowerment of employees
Empowerment provides employees with a sense of autonomy, authority and control, motivating employees to serve the EMB as well as they are able to, with additional commitment and effort providing better service to customers. More satisfied customers will yield more sales and more profit powering further growth via increased perceived value. Research indicates that power should be delegated to non-family members for faster growth (Basu and Goswami, 1999; Casson, 1991). The conclusion is that employee empowerment increases commitment and efficiency, supporting growth (Waldinger, Aldrich and Ward, 1990).

Training
Training develops skills and changes attitudes, having a positive influence on growth (Basu and Goswami, 1999). Effectively trained employees contribute to increased sales, effective team building, improved quality standards and a stronger new organizational culture (Daniels, 2003).

Incentives
EMBs can increase productivity and attractiveness (hence facilitating growth strategies) to existing and potential employees. Increasing job satisfaction via job enrichment, recognition, internal pay equity and the use of skilled manager.

Recruitment
Informal sources such as employee referrals may yield better performance and a more stable workforce than formal recruiting sources (Kirnan, Farley and Geisinger, 1989). Ethnic entrepreneurship research is geared towards the recruitment of family labour and co-ethnic groups via informal sources. But such channels might encourage nepotism in selection and promotion decisions and leads to a growth problem (Bates, 1994). This raises a need for a formal recruitment approach. Staff cultural diversity can increase ability to compete (Smallbone, Bertotti and Ekanem, 2005), particularly in expanding to other minority ethnic groups' markets.

Even a superficial examination of the six tables provides overwhelming evidence of the complexity surrounding practical understanding of the challenges faced by ethnic entrepreneurs aiming at growing their ethnic minority businesses. Notwithstanding, reflection on the relevant issues needs to go further by recognizing that ethnic entrepreneurs are individuals who are subject to processes of acculturation and possible cultural shock upon arriving in the host country, before usually settling into some state of socialization equilibrium. Since the ethnic entrepreneur is often an ethnic minority business, and these businesses usually retain their small size (Butler and Greene, 1997), it is justified to argue that ethnic minority businesses are also subject to an acculturation process. This argument is further developed in the next section.

Ethnic Minority Business and the Acculturation Process

While an ethnic minority business may be initially created to explore an opportunity provided by unmet needs and wants within an ethnic entrepreneur's minority ethnic group of affiliation, its successful performance may enhance not only the entrepreneur's business acumen but also the ethnic minority business's ability to take advantage of opportunities on offer within other minority ethnic groups' markets, starting with those sharing the most ethnic-sensitive characteristics and co-locating or locating in relatively close proximity to the minority ethnic group of affiliation. This might be the case particularly where aspects of a minority ethnic group's culture—such as language, race and language—are somewhat similar to those of other minority groups, but key factors might also be the ongoing shared handicap of market segregation/exclusion and the shared feeling of poor socialization relative to the mainstream.

If several minority ethnic groups share the same suburb, their affiliates can be expected to become acquainted, at least visually, sharing adjoining properties, streets and government services. In Australia, residents are expected to make their garbage bins available for collection by Council on particular days and will suffer together the consequences of blackouts, noise and other phenomena that can get people to start talking to each other, perhaps striking friendships over time, an eventuality that is only likely to augment when their children share the same public school, sports activities, and other similar group activities. It is also likely that co-locating minority ethnic groups share a variety of businesses as users, such as local restaurants, pharmacies, pool supplies stores, as well as the local supermarket.

Razin and Light (1998) provided evidence of spatial variations for a same minority ethnic group, and variations between different groups in the same economic milieu. The local influence depends not only on the local economy structure, but also on the characteristics of the local ethnic community, such as the specific location of ethnic networks. A further attribute is discrimination through the absorbing environment but also through the local community. Opportunities should therefore be analysed on a national, regional and local level (Boissevain et al., 1990; Volery, 2007, p. 35).

In the process of discovering and taking advantage of opportunities on offer within other minority ethnic groups' markets, the ethnic minority business might also gain access to other minority groups' ethnic resources, widening its ethnic network to become multi-ethnic, and perhaps achieving a preferred supplier status to more than its minority ethnic groups of affiliation.

By the same token, market diversification may also provide the opportunity for ethnic minority business to widen their cultural sensitivity skills in serving a variety of minority ethnic groups, as well as the mainstream, in a process that may culminate in the loss/exchange of the ethnic minority connotation for that of a mainstream supplier. Clearly, there are many mainstream businesses managed by minority entrepreneurs, although those businesses might not meet the common definitional requirements of an ethnic minority business.

Whether the status of preferred supplier to one or more minority ethnic groups may be kept over time depends on the ethnic minority business' intent and ability to maintain and even enhance its bridges to those minority ethnic groups, while also establishing bridges of access to the markets of expansion. This is also the reason why a minority ethnic group's ethnic network may include mainstream businesses in their set of preferred suppliers. Other mainstream businesses include grocery stores, pharmacies, restaurants, childcare services, travel agents and many other activities (Pires, 2001). As forwarded by Ram, Jones and Villares-Varela (2017), ethnic minority business research has overlooked high' value activities such as professional services (Vallejo and Canizales, 2016). Breakout strategies from the ethnic economy include the study of ethnic firms in Italy, which are likely to become more culturally hybrid over time, reducing their dependence on ethnicity, opening up to mainstream markets and assimilating to Italian companies (Arrighetti, Bolzani and Lasgni, 2014).

The question is whether ethnic minority business acculturation follows the personal acculturation pattern followed by ethnic entrepreneurs on arrival in the new country. That is, if an ethnic entrepreneur becomes highly socialized to the mainstream and expands operations into the mainstream market, what happens to the ethnic minority business? This is a relevant question because "ethnic . . . communities have specific needs which only co-ethnics are capable of satisfying" (Waldinger, Aldrich and Ward, 1990; Volery, 2007, p. 34). Will ethnic minority businesses lose their ethnic connotation?

Ram, Jones and Villares-Varela (2017) highlights some of these aspects by pointing out how the field of migrant entrepreneurship has overlooked research on entrepreneurs in high value activities, such as professional services (Vallejo and Canizales, 2016), and the ways in which class positions are vital to understand the strategies of Latino entrepreneurs in the USA. Accounting for context in breakout strategies from the ethnic economy is a theme explored by Arrighetti, Bolzani and Lasgni (2014) in their study of migrant firms in Italy; they conclude that firms are likely to become more multicultural (or culturally hybrid) over time, moving beyond the over-reliance on ethnic markets and opening up to mainstream markets and assimilating to Italian companies. While these elaborations on the future are exciting and appealing, evidence is still lacking.

Growth and Demise

The environment confronting ethnic entrepreneurs and their ethnic minority businesses is fraught with difficulty since self-employment may be due to exclusion from job opportunities, justifying a proliferation of small ethnic minority businesses, intense competition and, allegedly, a high failure rate (Ekanem and Wyer, 2007; Aldrich and Waldinger,

1990). Needing to become an inexperienced and possibly unprepared entrepreneur as a means to escape market exclusion is quite distinct from wanting and being prepared to engage in business. Notwithstanding, even in the case of better prepared aspiring ethnic entrepreneurs, as reported by Clydesdale (2008), their proposed ethnic minority businesses either did not materialize or ended in failure. There are also accounts of ethnic minority businesses affiliated with the Latino community who have historically achieved extensive business start-up growth, even above that of mainstream entrepreneurs, although their record is considered poor in terms of business failure and demise (Ortiz-Walters, Gavino and Williams, 2015).

The difficulty in developing strong insights into ethnic minority business growth is inextricably linked to a lack of clarity about how to measure performance. Ethnic minority business performance is difficult to assess separate from criteria applicable to business in general, by means of indicators such as volume of sales, revenue and profitability. But even when these indicators are available, their real meaning and trustworthiness is questioned given numerous reports of underpayment for extremely long hours worked by co-ethnic employees and, particularly, family employees.

Furthermore, there is more to performance than tangible indicators. It may be argued that assuring family employment or enhancing one's social status may be important key performance indicators, if those are the entrepreneur's/ethnic minority business' key business objectives. Gathering data on those indicators is difficult and often requires longitudinal research designs. Unfortunately there are few longitudinal studies of ethnic businesses (Benavides-Velasco, Quintana-García and Guzmán-Parra, 2013; Stewart, 2003).

Even if the challenges of identifying performance indicators are set aside, monitoring ethnic minority business growth is challenging due to a lack of clarity on when ethnic minority businesses lose their "ethnicity" connotation. Following Vandor and Franke (2016), Dietrich Mateschitz, Elon Musk and Sergey Brin share their history as migrants and their success as entrepreneurs who started ethnic minority businesses in host countries. Today they are recognized for their association as founders or co-founders of other businesses, respectively of Red Bull, Tesla and Google. Few would recognize these enterprises as ethnic minority businesses. Hence it is appropriate to ask when ethnic entrepreneurs lose their ethnic label.

Manifestations of growth experienced by ethnic minority businesses have been associated with cultural and social factors (Waldinger, Aldrich and Ward, 1990), some of which relate to the employment of family and co-ethnics, contrasting with suggestions that some of those factors can hinder ethnic minority business growth due to reluctance to delegate responsibilities to non-family employees, as in the case of South Asian ethnic minority businesses in Great Britain (Basu and Goswami, 1999). The takeaway here is that the employment of unskilled or untrained family members can be both an asset and an important handicap in securing the capabilities and competencies needed for ethnic minority businesses to pursue growth opportunities.

A further eventuality to consider in explaining the declining growth experience of an ethnic minority business is the cessation of the objectives that led to the creation of the ethnic minority business in the first place. Ability, need and opportunity were identified as major business start-up determinants in Sweden. That need-related issues appear more important than ability and opportunity supports Davidsson's (1991) argument that needs satiation is a major reason why small firms such as ethnic minority businesses stop growing, or altogether cease their activity.

Overall, there are no clear, general guidelines that can be put forward with confidence involving ethnic minority business growth, except for growth derived from the delivery of more efficient, value-creating marketing activities to the minority ethnic group. Increases in group size and in the wealth of its affiliates can sponsor ethnic minority business growth, provided the enterprise develops the appropriate set of capabilities and competencies grounded on a reciprocally beneficial relationship with the group's ethnic networks. In contrast, there is evidence that ethnic minority business lack of access to their minority ethnic groups, or their group's loss of substantiality, is likely to explain declining sales, ethnic minority business demise and even loss of the business altogether (Komakech and Jackson, 2016).

Intertwined with the attempt to discern threats and opportunities in the growth efforts of ethnic minority businesses, and perhaps weighing even more in its outlook, is the need for change within the business in response to dynamic ethnic markets. Better-educated ethnic entrepreneurs can be expected to be more apt in negotiating expansion into more demanding higher quality markets but, as noted in the previous chapter, educational progress also explains a growing switch from self-employment to professional and white collar employment, as is the case of Indian and Chinese entrepreneurs in the UK (Jones, Mascarenhas-Keyes and Ram, 2012) or, indeed, the case of Chinatown in Sydney. While it may not be reasonable to assess cases such as these as ethnic business failure, they are cases of demise.

Conclusion

The discussion of the importance of minority ethnic groups for the discovery, start-up and consolidation of ethnic minority businesses in the previous chapter highlighted the crucial role of access by these businesses to a minority ethnic group's ethnic networks. The main focus in this chapter was on ethnic minority business growth through expansion to alternative markets, distinct from the minority ethnic group of affiliation, whether minority, mainstream, international, transnational or even global.

Dependence on social and ethnic networks can be fundamental in the uptake of expansion opportunities. What this means is that the capabilities and competencies of an ethnic minority business are shaped by these networks, which can be the source of competitive advantage. Notwithstanding, the link between culture and social networks remains open to clarification (Klyver and Foley, 2012).

The major discovery in this chapter was that ethnic minority businesses are embedded in a variety of environments determined by the markets being targeted. The decision to extend operations to a different minority ethnic group's market needs to be cognizant of potential changes in the access to ethnic networks. Furthermore, because effective performance in different environments implies that the ethnic minority business must have appropriate sets of skills and competencies for each market this can be a major inhibitor to the uptake of potential expansion opportunities to the different markets. That is, the strengths that justify successful performance in the co-ethnic market can become the weaknesses when attempting to break out from that market (Masurel et al., 2002). If growth is sought by engaging in different cultural environments, the advantage can turn into a disadvantage.

Note

1. For the purpose of this analysis, the legal environment is excluded for simplicity, since it is deemed to apply equally to all entrepreneurs. An inability to meet legal requirements would preclude prospective EMBs from operating.

References

Aldrich, H. and Waldinger, R. (1990). Ethnicity and entrepreneurship. *Annual Review of Sociology*, 16, 111–135.

Almus, M. and Nerlinger, E. (1999). Growth of new technology-based firms: Which factors matter? *Small Business Economics*, 13(2), 141–154.

Altinay, L. (2008). The relationship between an entrepreneur's culture and the entrepreneurial behaviour of the firm. *Journal of Small Business and Enterprise Development*, 15(1), 111–129.

Altinay, L. and Altinay, E. (2006). Determinants of ethnic minority entrepreneurial growth in the catering sector. *The Service Industries Journal*, 26(2), 203–221.

Anderson, A. and Miller, C. (2003). Class matters: Human and social capital in the entrepreneurial process. *Journal of Socio- Economics*, 32(1), 17–26.

Anthias, F. and Cederberg, M. (2009). Using ethnic bonds in self-employment and the issue of social capital. *Journal of Ethnic and Migration Studies*, 35(6), 901–917.

Arrighetti, A., Bolzani, D. and Lasgni, A. (2014). Beyond the enclave? Break outs into mainstream markets and multicultural hybridism in ethnic firms. *Entrepreneurship and Regional Development*, 26(9–10), 753–777.

Barkham, R., Gudgin, G., Hart, M. and Hanvey, E. (1996). *The Determinants of Small Firm Growth: An Inter-Regional Study in the UK, 1986–90*. London: Jessica Kingsley Publishers.

Barth, F. (1969). *Ethnic Groups and Boundaries: The Social Organization of Culture Difference*. Waveland Press.

Basu, A. (2010). From "break out" to "breakthrough": Successful market strategies of immigrant entrepreneurs in the UK. *International Journal of Entrepreneurship*, 15, 59–81.

Basu, A. (2004). Entrepreneurial aspirations amongst family business owners: An analysis of ethnic business owners in the UK. *International Journal of Entrepreneurial Behaviour and Research*, 10(1), 12–33.

Basu, A. (1998). The role of institutional support in Asian entrepreneurial expansion in Britain. *Journal of Small Business and Enterprise Development*, 5(4), 317–326.

Basu, A. and Altinay, E. (2002). The interaction between culture and entrepreneurship in London's immigrant business. *International Small Business Journal*, 20(4), 371–394.

Basu, A. and Goswami, A. (1999). Determinants of South Asian entrepreneurial growth in Britain: A multivariate analysis. *Small Business Economics*, 13, 57–70.

Bates, T. (1994). Social resources generated by group support networks may not be beneficial to Asian-immigrant owned small businesses. *Social Forces*, 72(3), 671–689.

Beckinsale, M., Ram, M. and Theodorakopoulos, N. (2011). ICT adoption and ebusiness development: Understanding ICT adoption amongst ethnic minority businesses. *International Small Business Journal*, 29(3), 193–219.

Benavides-Velasco, C., Quintana-García, C. and Guzmán-Parra, V. (2013). Trends in family business research. *Small Business Economics*, 40(1), 41–57.

Bernard, A. (2008). Immigrants in the hinterlands. *Perspectives on Labour and Income*, 20(1), 27–36.

Boissevain, J., Blaschke, J., Grotenbreg, H., Joseph, I., Light, I., Sway, M., Waldinger, R., Ward, R. and Werbner, P. (1990). Ethnic entrepreneurs and ethnic strategies. *Immigrant Business in Industrial Societies*, 131–156.

Bonacich, E. (1973). A theory of middleman minorities. *American Sociology Review*, 38, 583–594.

Bryson, A. and White, M. (1996). *From Unemployment to Self-Employment: The Consequences of Self-Employment for the Long-Term Unemployed*. (PSI report; 820). London: Policy Studies Institute.

Burton, D. (2000). Ethnicity, identity and marketing: A critical review. *Journal of Marketing Management*, 16, 853–877.

Butler, J. and Greene (1997). Ethnic entrepreneurship: The continuous rebirth of American enterprise. In D. L. Sexton and R. W. Smilor (eds.), *Entrepreneurship 2000*. Chicago, IL: Upstart Publishing Co., 267–289.

Casson, M. (1991). *The Entrepreneur: An Economic Theory*. London: Gregg Revivals.

Chaganti, R. and Greene, P. (2002). Who are ethnic entrepreneurs? A study of entrepreneurship; ethnic involvement and business characteristics. *Journal of Small Business Management*, 40(2), 126–143.

Clydesdale, G. (2008). Business immigrants and the entrepreneurial nexus. *Journal of International Entrepreneurship*, 6(3), 123–142.

Cook, N. (2015). The long-term unemployment trap. *The Atlantic*. Accessed 9/12/2017 at www.theatlantic.com/business/archive/2015/04/the-long-term-unemployment-trap/425856/

Cornelius, W. (1986). *From Sojourners to Settlers: The Changing Profile of Mexican Migration to the United States*. Americas Program, Stanford University.

Daniels, S. (2003). Employee training: A strategic approach to better return on investment. *Journal of Business Strategy*, 24(5), 39–42.

Davidson, P., Kirchhoff, B., Hatemi-J. A. and Gustavsson, H. (2002). Empirical analysis of business growth factors using Swedish data. *Journal of Small Business Management*, 4(4), 332–eau349.

Davidsson, P. (1991). Continued entrepreneurship: Ability, need, and opportunity as determinants of small firm growth. *Journal of Business Venturing*, 6(6), 405–429.

De Koning, A. (1999). Opportunity formation as a socio-cognitive process. In P. D. Reynolds, W. D. Bygrave, S. Manigart, C. M. Mason, G. D. Meyer, H. J. Sapienza and K. G. Shaver (eds.), *Frontiers of Entrepreneurship Research*. Wellesley, MA: Babson College.

Deshpande, R. (2002). Performance companies. *International Journal of Medical Marketing*, 2(3), 225–232.

Dhaliwal, S. (2008). Business support and minority ethnic businesses in England. *Journal of Immigrant & Refugee Studies*, 6(2), 230–246.

Dodd, S. and Keles, J. (2014). Expanding the networks of disadvantaged entrepreneurs. *OECD Technical Report*. OECD Local Economic and Employment Development Programme. Accessed 14/12/2017 at http://aspheramedia.com/wp-content/uploads/2015/11/Expanding-the-networks-of-disadvantaged-entrepreneurs.pdf

Duchesneau, D. and Gartner, W. (1990). A profile of new venture success and failure in an emerging industry. *Journal of Business Venturing*, 5(5), 297–312.

Dustmann, C., Fabbri, F., Preston, I. and Wadsworth, J. (2003). Labour market performance of immigrants in the UK labour market. *Home Office Online Report*.

Edwards, P., Ram, M., Jones, T. and Doldor, S. (2016). New migrant businesses and their workers: Developing, but not transforming, the ethnic economy. *Ethnic and Racial Studies*, 39(9), 1587–1617.

Ekanem, I. and Wyer, P. (2007). A fresh start and the learning experience of ethnic minority entrepreneurs. *International Journal of Consumer Studies*, 31(2), 144–151.

Engelen, E. (2001). Breaking-in and breaking-out: A weberian approach to entrepreneurial opportunities. *Journal of Ethnic and Migration Studies*, 27(2), 203–223.

Essers, C. and Benschop, Y. (2009). Muslim businesswomen doing boundary work: The negotiation of Islam, gender and ethnicity within entrepreneurial contexts. *Human Relations*, 62, 403–424.

Ethnic Minority Business Initiative (1991). *Ethnic Minority Business Development Team: Final Report*. London: Home Office.

Gedajlovic, E., Honig, B., Moore, C., Payne, G. and Wright, M. (2013). Social capital and entrepreneurship: A schema and research agenda. *Entrepreneurship: Theory and Practice*, 37, 455–478.

Granovetter, M. (1985). Economic action and social structure: The problem of embeddedness'. *American Journal of Sociology*, 91, 481–510.

Granovetter, M. (1992). *Problems and Explanation in Economic Sociology, Networks and Organisations*. Harvard Business School Press.

Heath, A. (2001). *Ethnic Minorities in the Labour Market*. Report to the PIU. London: Cabinet Office.

Herman, H. (1979). Dishwashers and proprietors: Macedonians in Toronto's restaurant trade. In S. Wallman (ed.), *Ethnicity at Work*. London: Macmillan.

Hindle, K. and Moroz, P. (2010). Indigenous entrepreneurship as a research field: Developing a definitional framework from the emerging canon. *International Entrepreneurship and Management Journal*, 6(4), 357–385.

Hingley, M. (2005). Power to all our friends? Living with imbalance in supplier-retailer relationships. *Industrial Marketing Management*, 34(8), 848–858.

Honig, B., Drori, I. and Carmichael, B. (eds.). (2010). *Transnational and Immigrant Entrepreneurship in a Globalized World*. Toronto, ON: University of Toronto Press.

Huffington Post (2013). Accessed 9/12/2017 at www.huffingtonpost.com.au/entry/self-employment-joblessness_n_3100518

Jack, S. (2005). The role, use and activation of strong and weak network ties: A qualitative analysis. *Journal of Management Studies*, 42(6), 1233–1259.

Jack, S., Moult, S., Anderson, A. and Dodd, S. (2010). An entrepreneurial network evolving: Patterns of change. *International Small Business Journal*, 28(4), 315–337.

Jamal, A. (2005). Playing to win: An explorative study of marketing strategies of small ethnic retail entrepreneurs in the UK. *Journal of Retailing and Consumer Services*, 12(1), 1–13.

Jones, T., Mascarenhas-Keyes, S. and Ram, M. (2012). The ethnic entrepreneurial transition: Recent trends in British Indian self-employment. *Journal of Ethnic and Migration Studies*, 38(1), 93–109.

Jones, T., McEvoy, D. and Barrett, G. (1994). Labour intensive practises in the ethnic minority firm. In J. Atkinson and D. Storey (eds.), *Employment, the Small Firm and the Labour Market*. London: Routledge, pp. 172–205.

Jones, T. and Ram, M. (2012). Revisiting . . . ethnic-minority businesses in the United Kingdom: A review of research and policy developments. *Environment and Planning C: Government and Policy*, 30, 944–950.

Jones, T., Ram, M. and Edwards, P. (2006). Ethnic minority business and the employment of illegal immigrants. *Entrepreneurship and Regional Development*, 18(2), 133–150.

Jones-Evans, D., Thompson, P. and Kwong, C. (2011). Entrepreneurship amongst minority language speakers: The case of Wales. *Regional Studies*, 45(2), 219–238.

Judt, A. (2010). *Ill Fares the Land*. London: Penguin.

Kabiraj, S. and Shanmugan, J. (2011). Development of a conceptual framework for brand loyalty: A Euro-Mediterranean perspective. *Journal of Brand Management*, 18(4/5), 285–299.

Kalleberg, A. and Leicht, K. (1991). Gender and organisational performance: Determinants of small business survival and success. *The Academy of Management Journal*, 34(1), 136–161.

Kim, I. (1981). *New Urban Immigrants: The Korean Community in New York*. Princeton, NJ: Princeton University Press.

Kirnan, J., Farley, J. and Geisinger, K. (1989). The relationship between recruiting source, applicant quality and hire performance: An analysis by sex, ethnicity and age. *Personnel Psychology*, 42, 293–308.

Kloosterman, R. (2010). Matching opportunities and resources: A framework for analysing (migrant) entrepreneurship from a mixed embeddedness perspective. *Entrepreneurship and Regional Development*, 22, 25–45.

Kloosterman, R. and Rath, J. (2003). *Immigrant Entrepreneurs: Venturing Abroad in the Age of Globalization*. Oxford/New York: Berg/University of New York Press.

Kloosterman, R. and Rath, J. (2001). Immigrant entrepreneurs in advanced economies: Mixed embeddedness further explored. *Journal of ethnic and migration studies*, 27(2), 189–201.

Kloosterman, R., van der Leun, J. and Rath, J. (1999). Mixed embeddedness (in)formal economic activities and immigrant businesses in the Netherlands. *International Journal of Urban and Regional Research*, 23, 252–266.

Klyver, K. and Foley, D. (2012). Networking and culture in entrepreneurship. *Entrepreneurship & Regional Development*, 24(7–8), 561–588.

Komakech, M. and Jackson, S. (2016). A study of the role of small ethnic retail grocery stores in urban renewal in a social housing: Project, Toronto, Canada. *Journal of Urban Health: Bulletin of the New York Academy of Medicine*, 93(3), 414–424.

Lagendijk, A., Pijpers, R., Ent, G., Hendrikx, R., van Lanen, B. and Maussart, L. (2011). Multiple worlds in a single street: Ethnic entrepreneurship and the construction of a global sense of place. *Space and Polity*, 15(2), 163–181.

Lechner, C. and Dowling, M. (2003). Firm networks: External relationships as sources for the growth and competitiveness of entrepreneurial firms. *Entrepreneurship and Regional Development*, 15, 1–26.

Levine, B. (1985). The capital of Latin America. *Wilson Q*, 9, 47–69.

Light, I. (1984). Immigrant and ethnic enterprise in North America. *Ethnic and Racial Studies*, 7(2), 190–217.

Light, I. (1972). *Ethnic Enterprise in America*. Berkeley University, California Press.

Light, I. and Bhachu, P. (1993). *Immigration and Entrepreneurship: Culture, Capital and Ethnic Networks*. New Brunswick: Transaction Publishers.

Light, I. and Rosenstein, C. (1995). *Race, Ethnicity, and Entrepreneurship in Urban America*. Transaction Publishers.

Lo, L. and Li, W. (2011). Economic experiences of immigrants. *Immigrant Geographies in North American Cities*, 112–137.

Lo, L. and Teixeira, C. (2015). Immigrants doing business in a mid-sized Canadian city: Challenges, opportunities, and local strategies in Kelowna, British Columbia. *Growth and Change*, 46(4), 631–653.

Lo, L., Teixeira, C. and Truelove, M. (2002). *Cultural Resources, Ethnic Strategies, and Immigrant Entrepreneurship: A Comparative Study of Five Immigrant Groups in the Toronto CMA*. Toronto: CERIS-Joint Centre of Excellence for Research on Immigration and Settlement.

Masurel, E., Nijkamp, P., Tastan, M. and Vindigni, G. (2002). Motivations and performance conditions for ethnic entrepreneurship. *Growth and Change*, 33, 238–260.

McEvoy, D. and Hafeez, K. (2007). Regional and sub-regional variations in ethnic minority entrepreneurship in Britain. *Interdisciplinary European Conference on Entrepreneurship Research (IECER)*.

McKeever, E., Anderson, A. and Jack, S. (2014). Social embeddedness in entrepreneurship research: The importance of context and community. In *Handbook of Research on Small Business and Entrepreneurship*. London: Edward Elgar, Chapter 13, pp. 222–236.

Menzies, T., Filion, L., Brenner, G. and Elgie, S. (2007). Measuring ethnic community involvement: Development and initial testing of an index. *Journal of Small Business Management*, 45(2), 267–282.

Metcalf, H., Modood, T. and Virdee, S. (1996). *Asian Self-Employment: The Inter-action of Culture and Economics in England.* London: Policy Studies Institute.

Mohl, R. (1985). An ethnic "boiling pot": Cubans and Haitians in Miami. *The Journal of Ethnic Studies*, 13(2), 51.

Mummendey, A., Kessler, T., Klink, A. and Mielke, R. (1999). Strategies to cope with negative social identity: Predictions by social identity theory and rela-tive deprivation theory. *Journal of Personality and Social Psychology*, 76(2), 229–245.

New Enterprize Incentive Scheme - NEIS (2017) Australia Government, Business, available at https://www.business.gov.au/assistance/new-enterprise-incentive-scheme (accessed 9/11/2018).

Nwankwo, S. (2005). Characterisation of Black African entrepreneurship in the UK: A pilot study. *Journal of Small Business and Enterprise Development*, 12(1), 120–136.

Ojo, S., Nwankwo, S. and Gbadamosi, A. (2013). Ethnic entrepreneurship: The myths of informal and illegal enterprises in the UK. *Entrepreneurship & Regional Development*, 25(7–8), 587–611.

Oliveira, C. (2007). Understanding the diversity of immigrant entrepreneurial strategies. In L.-P. Dana (Ed.), *Handbook of Research on Ethnic Minority Entrepreneurship: A Co-evolutionary View on Resource Management.* Chel-tenham: Edward Elgar, pp. 61–82.

Ortiz-Walters, R., Gavino, M. C. and Williams, D. (2015). Social networks of latino and latina entrepreneurs and their impact on venture performance. *Academy of Entrepreneurship Journal*, 21(1), 58–81.

Páleník, M. (2011). Young unemployed: Help them into self-employment or wait until they have long term unemployment status? *Mutual Learning Program: Peer Country Comments Paper—Slovakia, Spain (November).*

Patel, P. and Conklin, B. (2009). The balancing act: The role of transnational habitus and social networks in balancing transnational entrepreneurial activi-ties. *Entrepreneurship Theory and Practice*, 33(5), 1045–1078.

Phizacklea, A. and Ram, M. (1996). Being your own boss: Ethnic minority entre-preneurs in comparative perspective. *Work, Employment & Society*, 10(2), 319–339.

Pires, G. (2001). *The Selection of Service Providers by Ethnic Minority Consum-ers in a Culturally Diverse Society.* Unpublished Doctoral Thesis, University of Newcastle.

Pires, G. and Stanton, J. (2015). *Ethnic Marketing: Culturally Sensitive Theory and Practice.* New York City, NY, USA: Taylor and Francis.

Pires, G., Stanton, J. and Stanton, P. (2011). Revisiting the substantiality cri-terion: From ethnic marketing to market segmentation. *Journal of Business Research*, 64(9), 988–996.

Polanyi, K. (1946). *Origins of Our Time: The Great Transformation.* London: Victor Gollancz.

Portes, A. (1995). *The Economic Sociology of Immigration; Essays on Networks, Ethnicity, and Entrepreneurship.* New York: Russell Sage Foundation.

Portes, A. (1987). The social origins of the Cuban enclave economy of Miami. *Sociological Perspectives*, 30, 340–372.

Portes, A. and Sensenbrenner, J. (1993). Embeddedness and immigration: Notes on the social determinants of economic action. *American Journal of Sociology*, 98(6), 1320–1350.

Prashantham, S., Dhanaraj, C. and Kumar, K. (2015). Ties that bind: Ethnic ties and new venture internationalisation. *Long Range Planning*, 48(5), 317–333.

Rafiq, M. (1992). Ethnicity and enterprise: A comparison of Muslim and Muslim-owned Asian businesses in Britain. *New Community*, 19(1), 43–60.

Ram, M. (1992). Coping with racism: Asian employers in the inner-city. *Work Employment and Society*, 6(4), 601–618.

Ram, M. and Jones, T. (2008). *Ethnic Minorities in Business*. Milton Keynes, Bucks: Small Business Research Trust.

Ram, M. and Jones, T. (1998). *Ethnic Minorities in Business*. Small Business Research Trust Report. Milton Keynes, UK: Small Business Research Trust.

Ram, M., Jones, T. and Edwards, P. (2007). Staying underground: Informal work, small firms and employment regulation in the UK. *Work and Occupations*, 34, 290–317.

Ram, M., Jones, T. and Villares-Varela, M. (2017). Migrant entrepreneurship: Reflections on research and practice. *International Small Business Journal*, 35(1), 3–18.

Rath, J. (2006). Entrepreneurship among migrants and returnees: Creating new opportunities. Accessed 7/10/2017 at www.un.org/esa/population/migration/turin/Symposium_Turin_files/P05_Rath.pdf

Rath, J. (2010). Ethnic entrepreneurship: Concept paper, European Foundation for the improvement of living and working conditions. Accessed 4/12/2017 at www.eurofound.europa.eu/pubdocs/2010/39/en/1/EF1039EN.pdf

Rath, J. and Kloosterman, R. (2000). Outsiders business: Research of Immigrant Entrepreneurship in the Netherlands. *International Migration Review*, 34(3), 656–680.

Razin, E. (2002). The economic context, embeddedness and immigrant entrepreneurs. *International Journal of Entrepreneurship Behaviour & Research*, 8(1/2), 162–167.

Razin, E. and Langlois, A. (1996). Metropolitan characteristics and entrepreneurship among immigrants and ethnic groups in Canada. *International Migration Review*, 30(3), 703–727.

Razin, E. and Light, I. (1998). Ethnic entrepreneurs in America's largest metropolitan areas. *Urban Affairs Review*, 33, 332–360.

Reitz, J. (1980). *The Survival of Ethnic Groups*. Toronto: McGraw Hill.

Roper, S. (1998). Entrepreneurial characteristics, strategic choice and small business performance. *Small Business Economics*, 11, 11–24.

Rothbart, R. (1993). The ethnic saloon as a form of immigrant enterprise. *International Migration Review*, 27(2), 332–358.

Sarasvathy, S. and Venkataraman, S. (2011). Entrepreneurship as method: Open questions for an entrepreneurial future. *Entrepreneurship: Theory and Practice*, 35, 113–135.

Sepulveda, L., Syrett, S. and Lyon, F. (2011). Population super-diversity and new migrant enterprise: The case of London. *Entrepreneurship and Regional Development*, 23, 469–497.

Serino, A., Giovagnoli, G. and Làdavas, E. (2009). I feel what you feel if you are similar to me. *PLoS One*, 4(3), e4930.

Siu, P. (1952). The sojourner. *American Journal of Sociology*, 58(1), 34–44.

Smallbone, D., Bertotti, M. and Ekanem, I. (2005). Diversification in ethnic minority business: The case of Asians in London's creative industries. *Journal of Small Business and Enterprise Development*, 12(1), 41–56.

Smallbone, D., Fadahunsi, A., Supri, S. and Paddison, A. (1999). The diversity of ethnic minority enterprises. *RENT XIII, London*, 25–26.

Stewart, A. (2003). Help one another, use one another: Toward an anthropology of family business. *Entrepreneurship Theory and Practice*, 27(4), 383–396.

Storey, D. (1994). *Understanding the Small Business Sector.* New York: Routledge.

Tian, Y. A., Nicholson, J. D., Eklinder-Frick, J., and Johanson, M. (2018). The interplay between social capital and international opportunities: A processual study of international "take-off" episodes in Chinese SMEs. *Industrial Marketing Management*, 70, 180–192.

Vallejo, J. and Canizales, S. (2016). Latino/a professionals as entrepreneurs: How race, class, and gender shape entrepreneurial incorporation. *Ethnic and Racial Studies*, 39(9), 1637–1656.

Vandor, P. and Franke, N. (2016). Why are immigrants more entrepreneurial? *Harvard Business Review*, October 27. Guardian 161101 pg 19 Why are immigrants more.pdf.

Virtue, R. (2017). Effectiveness of refugee re-settlement strategy in regional NSW under question. *ABC Newcastle*, posted May 16. Accessed 16/12/2017 at www.abc.net.au/news/2017-05-16/refugees-leaving-regional-nsw-cities-due-to-lack-of-housing/8527062 on 16/12/2017

Volery, T. (2007). Ethnic entrepreneurship: A theoretical framework. In *Handbook of Research on Ethnic Minority Entrepreneurship: A Co-Evolutionary View on Resource Management.* Cheltenham: Edward Elgar, pp. 30–41.

Waldinger, R. (1995). The "other side" of embeddedness: A case-study of the interplay of economy and ethnicity. *Ethnic and Racial Studies*, 18(3), 555–580.

Waldinger, R., Aldrich, H. and Ward, R. (1990). *Ethnic Entrepreneurs: Immigrant Business in Industrial Societies*, Vol. 1. London: Sage.

Wang, C. and Altinay, L. (2012). Social embeddedness, entrepreneurial orientation and firm growth in ethnic minority small businesses in the UK. *International Small Business Journal*, 30(1), 3–23.

Ward, R. (1983). Ethnic communities and ethnic businesses: An overview. *New Community*, 11, 1–9.

Werbner, P. (1990). Renewing an industrial past: British Pakistani entrepreneurship in Manchester. *Migration*, 8, 7–41.

Wijewardena, H. and Tibbits, E. (1999). Factors contributing to the growth of small manufacturing firms: Data from Australia. *Journal of Small Business Management*, 37(2), 88–96.

Wimmer, A. (2008). The making and unmaking of ethnic boundaries: A multi-level process theory. *American Journal of Sociology*, 113(4), 970–1022.

Wong, L. and Ng, M. (1998). Chinese immigrant entrepreneurs in Vancouver: A case study of ethnic business development. *Canadian Ethnic studies Journal*, 30(1), 64–87.

Yamagishi, T. (2003). The group heuristic: A psychological mechanism that creates a self-sustaining system of generalized exchanges. *Proceedings of the Santa Fe Institute Workshop on the Coevolution of Institutions and Behavior.*

Zaefarian, R., Eng, T.-Y. and Tasavori, M. (2016). An exploratory study of international opportunity identification among family firms. *International Business Review*, 25(1), 333–345.

Zhou, M. (1992). *Chinatown: The Socioeconomic Potential of an Urban Enclave.* Philadelphia, PA: Temple University Press.

9 Ethnic Networks and the Adoption of Relational Strategies

This chapter elaborates on the importance of the promotion of suppliers to a minority ethnic group to a perceived "preferred supplier" status, as a factor in the generation of affiliated ethnic minority consumers' loyalty to the supplier and to the group.

Contrasting with an implied restriction in the identification of "preferred suppliers" to routinely purchased products in business-to-business relationships (Ulaga and Eggert, 2006), preferred supplier status can be conferred to suppliers of all types of service-products in minority ethnic markets. The distinctive factor is that the de facto consumer is the minority ethnic group rather than any one individual consumer. In this way, while individuals' consumption of a service-product may be episodic, routine purchase occurs when all consumers in the group are considered.

Becoming a preferred supplier to a minority ethnic group with sufficient substantiality may be a source of advantage for suppliers over their competitors (Pires, Stanton and Stanton, 2011), which can be made more meaningful when advantage is complemented by strong, long-term loyalty of the group, even if not necessarily by all group members. As a rule, preferred suppliers to a minority ethnic group can be expected to be co-ethnic minority businesses, and to deploy reciprocal and mutually beneficial relational marketing strategies. The loyalty anchored competitive advantage is likely to be as sustainable as the group's resilience and stability.

Provided preferred suppliers are able to sustain performance effectiveness by reliably meeting the group's needs and preferences over time, the necessary conditions are created for performance to be rewarded by complementing ethnic loyalty with consumer loyalty (Sirdeshmukh, Singh and Sabol, 2002). This makes it difficult for other (non-preferred or backup) suppliers to gain even a testing of the service-product they have to offer, let alone arriving at terms of exchange.

Preferred Suppliers, Ethnic Networks and Minority Ethnic Markets

A minority ethnic market can assume many shapes depending on the analytical perspective that is taken. Here it is understood as the set of stakeholders and interactions that take place in the context of a given minority ethnic group.

Chapters 7 and 8 in this text sought to understand what causes ethnic minority businesses to emerge, and the forces, such as networks, that subsequently shape their development (Fadahunsi, Smallbone and Supri, 2000). Borrowing from that understanding, this chapter provides a networked perspective of ethnic minority markets, whereby focus is on the social and business networks operating in the realm of a given minority ethnic group, with the inherent relationships within those ethnic networks explaining how and why stakeholders' behave the way they do.

Bowles and Gintis (2004) define ethnic networks as

> sets of agents unified by similarity of one or more ascriptive characteristics (such as race, ethnic identification and religion) engaged in non-anonymous interactions, structured by high entry and exit costs, but lacking a centralized authority.
>
> (p. 2)

Conforming to the definition, a minority ethnic group may be described as an ethnic network comprising group institutions (such as social clubs, cultural centres, religious and academic associations), social structures of individuals (consumers) affiliated to the group, including its consumer network, similarly affiliated businesses and their business networks. It is also the minority ethnic market.

Ethnic networks are expected to exhibit a parochial cultural affinity characterized by cooperation, interpersonal commitment and collective action among its co-ethnic members, in contrast with exclusionary practices and interactional avoidance towards dissimilar others (Serino, Giovagnoli and Làdavas, 2009; Kim, 2007; Bowles and Gintis, 2004; Stephan et al, 1991). Focusing on relationships among social entities within ethnic networks and driven by the shared activities and affiliations of their members (Kossinets and Watts, 2006), social networks are deemed to involve interactions of a social nature between group affiliates that generate social ties (Chung and Whalen, 2006) and influence entrepreneurial activity (Batjargal, 2010; Zhao, Frese and Giardini, 2010). In contrast, business networks involve business interactions between suppliers and consumers (B2C) and between businesses (B2B) affiliated with the minority ethnic group.[1] Together with group institutions, the group's social networks and business networks make up the ethnic network.

Focused on the relational interdependence of social structures created by repeated interactions of the parties to an exchange over time (Cook et al., 2013; Dwyer, Schurr and Oh, 1987; Hallen, Johanson and Seyed-Mohamed, 1991; Portes and Sensenbrenner, 1993), the boundaries of ethnic networks determine the access to the resources that they enable, ranging from open access to impermeable to outsiders (Wimmer, 2008; Mummendey et al., 1999).

The idea that interpersonal interaction is guided by calculations of costs and rewards is central to social exchange theory (Stafford, 2008; Cropanzano and Mitchell, 2005; Emerson, 1976), helping to understand why socialization benefits and economic advantages may convert into preference for interactions within the social network over the long term (Ram, Jones and Villares-Varela, 2017). These may be complemented by a reluctance to go outside the network and bear the costs of interacting with dissimilar others.

Given the resilience of minority ethnic groups within host countries, ethnic networks have potential as a source of economic advantages for suppliers that accrue over time. It can therefore be argued that these advantages work against suppliers' concerns about restricted gains from trade and foregone economies of scale when targeting a small minority ethnic group (Pires and Stanton, 1999).

From a perspective of ethnic minority consumers affiliated with a minority ethnic group, rather than simply expressing ethnic loyalty encompassing altruistic feelings towards co-ethnic members (Bowles and Gintis, 2004), emphasis may also be on their identification with ethnic networks in terms of economic advantage and avoidance of eventual exposure to exclusionary practices in other markets. Some of these consumers may also be self-employed ethnic entrepreneurs managing ethnic minority businesses seeking to serve the co-ethnic group.

Bringing together the social embeddedness theory (Granovetter, 1985, 1992), Waldinger, Aldrich and Ward (1990) interactive model, and the mixed embeddedness theory (Kloosterman, van der Leun and Rath, 1999), the next section establishes the compelling rationale for examining minority ethnic groups by reference to their inner networks and related relational drivers.

Ethnic Networks as Relational Drivers

The presumption by suppliers that ethnic minority consumers are in a relationship with their minority ethnic group, thus favouring in-group behaviour reciprocity (Yamagishi, 2003), and that these consumers value a relationship with the suppliers preferred by their co-ethnic group, provides two starting premises for examining relational ethnic marketing drivers in the perspective of ethnic networks, namely:

1. The focus of ethnic minority business is on the minority ethnic group, operationalized by serving one consumer at a time;
2. Ethnic minority consumers reward ethnic minority businesses with loyalty, possibly complementing ethnic loyalty with consumer loyalty.

In-group behaviour reciprocity is likely to apply more strongly to ethnic minority consumers with a strong group identity, with the added premise that there may be compelling reasons why switching preferred suppliers may be undesirable for these consumers.

Amidst significant disadvantages such as language skills, education, lack of mobility and discrimination, ethnic minority consumers newly arrived in a host country may be challenged by a lack of market knowledge in satisfying their consumption requirements, which places them at an economic disadvantage and steers their behaviour (Volery, 2007; Fregetto, 2004). They may overcome the challenge by joining co-ethnic consumers (making up the consumer network) and taking advantage of the minority ethnic group of affiliation's ethnic network. In this process they may develop interdependencies with like consumers, with the minority ethnic group itself and with the set of preferred suppliers to that group, effectively adding up to the ethnic network depicted in Figure 9.1.

The minority ethnic group and its relevant consumer network are central to the informal elevation of specific suppliers to a "preferred" status, perceived as well positioned to satisfy the new arrivals' consumption needs and preferences, based on similar others' previous consumption experiences. While any business may achieve the preferred status, this may be more at the reach of ethnic minority businesses. A positive (or negative) interaction between the newly arrived consumer and the preferred supplier recommended by experienced similar-others in the consumer network

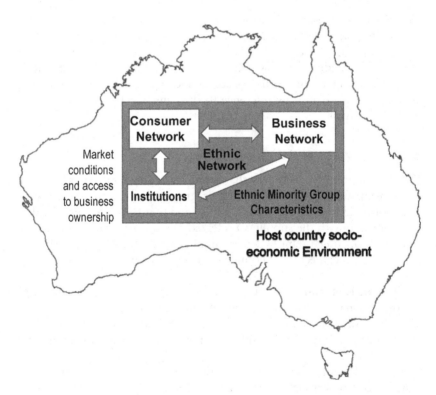

Figure 9.1 The Ethnic Network for a Minority Ethnic Group in a Host Country

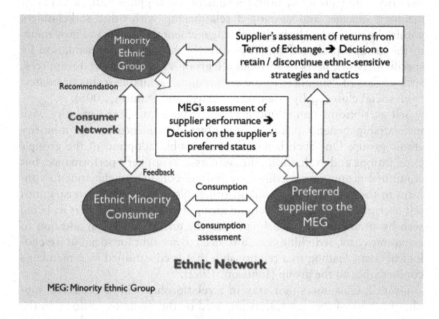

Figure 9.2 Ethnic Network Operations

results in terms of exchange seen by the supplier as contributing to its retention (or discontinuation) of ethnic-sensitive tactics towards the group affiliates. Retention can be seen as a strengthening the supplier's commitment to its relationship with the consumer network and partaking in the ethnic network. Figure 9.2 depicts ethnic network operations, including the set of decisions and interdependence between the different stakeholders in the ethnic network.

Ethnic network operations involve processes that contribute to inexperienced ethnic minority consumers' perceptions of the ethnic network as an economic asset in their consumption socialization, adding to group strength. In the case of preferred suppliers, the loyalty of the minority ethnic group is fundamental but insufficient in their targeting decision. Sufficiency requires a positive payoff from the cost-benefit analysis of the targeting opportunity offered by the minority ethnic group. Subsequently, the targeting decision also needs to account for opportunity cost (Buchanan, 1991). Positive outcomes pave the way to engage in mutually beneficial relationships between preferred suppliers, minority ethnic groups and their affiliates.

Networks Imply Relational Imperatives

Over time, repeated successful exchanges build up trust in the ethnic network recommendations and contribute to increasing commitment to the minority ethnic group by both consumers and suppliers. Ethnic network members engage, and develop a relationship with other stakeholders within the network. Through their engagement they come to know many of the group's preferred suppliers directly through recommendation by specific network peers or through the group's institutions and resources, such as lists of "suppliers to the community" available from consulates, from social clubs, or by other means (Pires and Stanton, 2005).

Self-ascription to an ethnic network is based on peer similarity with membership benefits justifying voluntary dependence on the minority ethnic group. One such benefit is the possible adoption of the group's expectations and evaluation criteria to assess supplier's performance, but continued group membership may require consumer behaviour to conform to the group's values and attitudes. Notwithstanding, conspicuous self-ascription to a minority ethnic group may be required, that is, being seen by similar-others as belonging to the group. Hence, in addition to economic costs, switching costs also need to account for social or psychological costs, leading to a relationship that is constrained by a member's conformance to the group (Johnson, 1982).

Overall, consumers may stay in a relationship with a preferred supplier because of the constraints imposed by the desire to conform to the co-ethnic group, or as a result of consumer satisfaction with the supplier, which may be due to the adoption by the supplier of group oriented, ethnic-sensitive strategies and tactics (Bendapudi and Berry, 1997) when justified (Bartikowski, Taieb and Chandon, 2016).

Initial consumer satisfaction by itself is rarely sufficient to justify the development and maintenance of a long-term relationship. Continued support for, and referral to a specific supplier by a minority ethnic group implies consistently positive experiences together with switching constraints. Hence, the combination of a minority ethnic group's uniqueness and evaluation difficulties may result in personal loyalty, as advocated by Bowles and Gintis (2004).

While achieving sustainable competitive advantage is a desired objective for most suppliers, including those active in ethnic marketing, the process will require the use of effective segmentation, targeting and positioning analysis, combined with specific supplier skills (including cultural awareness, sensitivity and responsiveness) that can be used to build consumer loyalty. Ultimately, ethnic marketing success depends on maintaining a minority ethnic group's loyalty, justifying the adoption of relational approaches by business.

Decision to Adopt a Relational Marketing Approach

Many businesses engage in transactional approaches in their targeting of consumers or consumer groups, and this may be the logical approach to adopt in situations where a business has power over the market, as in the case of monopolist businesses—the supply of utilities is a common example—or in cases of powerlessness over market demand, characteristic of perfect competition or hypercompetition situations (Gummesson, 1997). An alternative is for businesses to differentiate themselves from competitors by adopting relational strategies (Ravald and Grönroos, 1996).

From a marketing perspective, any business can consider adopting relational strategies to identify, grow, maintain and enhance profitable exchanges with a network of individual consumers, such as a minority ethnic group, effectively partaking in the group's ethnic network as a supplier, even when network membership is not a deliberate objective.

While all businesses may gain from accessing a loyal network of repeat consumers, relationship related investments are usually necessary, and likely to be recovered/compensated only *ex post* and over time. For example, targeting a minority ethnic group with ethnic-sensitive strategies may require a variety of competencies, from an ability to communicate in the group's language to the ability to behave in a way reflective of cultural awareness. Depending on their level of preparedness for intercultural exchanges, some businesses may face higher investment costs than others, both in time and in financial resources.

Given the relationship related investment involved in developing capabilities and competencies for deploying sensitive positioning strategy and tactics, the business decision of whether to target ethnic minority consumers with a loyalty-generation oriented, relational marketing approach involves discerning clearly what the benefits are that accrue to consumers and to the business, given the costs they face. In other words, the relational approach depends on the net value it generates vis-a-vis a transactional approach.

In addition, given that minority ethnic groups are intrinsically heterogeneous (Lindridge, 2015; Berry and Sam, 1997), businesses must decide who should be targeted. This is a difficult decision to make, with clear implications for the assessment of the net value that can be generated.

Because relational marketing strategies involve mutually dependent investments by all parties in the relationship (Holm, Eriksson and Johanson, 1999), the relational strategy and associated tactics must derive mutual benefit to the business, to the minority ethnic group (Shrivastava and Kale, 2003) and to the individual consumers affiliated with the group. This also has an impact on the targeting decision.

The targeting decision using a relational approach refers to consumer segments (minority ethnic groups or part thereof) identified based on ethnicity-related characteristics that influence behaviour (such as language and ethics). Hence, in addition to assessing segment substantiality, businesses need to access/develop accurate segment profiles for substantial segments and to ensure, subsequently, they possess the capabilities and competencies required to deliver to the segment the value proposition attributes revealed by the profiles through an appropriate ethnic-sensitive positioning strategy. This is a demanding process with at least six main steps, outlined in Table 9.1.

Table 9.1 Targeting Decision Process for Consumer Segments Based on Ethnicity

The Targeting Decision Process for Consumer Segments Based on Ethnicity	
Step 1	Recognize the opportunity offered by the minority ethnic group and define desired objectives.
Step 2	Apply a screening framework to assess substantiality (primary research). See Pires and Stanton (2015, Chapter 6) for a guide to this step based on external signs of substantiality.
Step 3	Develop a segment profile that reveals valued proposition attributes (primary research might be needed to distinguish the important and determinant attributes that characterize the group's consumption preferences).
Step 4	Verify that the business is able to perform in delivering the identified attributes by analyzing own resources, capabilities and competencies to ensure alignment in the provision of the identified attributes.
Step 5	Develop a suitable ethnic-sensitive positioning strategy.
Step 6	Evaluate vis objectives identified in step 1 and correct as required.

A mainstream supplier considering a minority ethnic group for targeting purposes must first establish the need for a differentiated ethnic marketing strategy towards that group. Only when the supplier discovers significant consumer behaviour differences between the mainstream, or other consumer groups, and the minority ethnic group (inter-group heterogeneity), is it justifiable to examine the minority ethnic group as a separate potential value opportunity, following effective marketing segmentation procedures (Dibb and Simkin, 2010) for achieving competitive advantage.

Determinant attributes, likely intertwined with ethnicity aspects, are crucial for competitive advantage. For example, issues of language, meaning and demeanour may be determinant aspects to consider. Since it is taken for granted in this analysis that the minority and mainstream groups behave differently in consumption, the likelihood is that some adjustment will be required to the mainstream suppliers' capabilities and competencies before ethnic-sensitive, effective and efficient value propositions/terms of exchange can be offered to the consumers affiliated with the minority ethnic group.

Given the umbilical connection between ethnic entrepreneurs, their ethnic minority businesses and the minority ethnic group of affiliation, ethnic minority businesses may be naturally better positioned for engaging with co-ethnic groups. Suppliers engaging in relationships with individual ethnic minority consumers requiring customization and who are not affiliated with a minority ethnic group are likely to be uncommon. Suppliers aim at the group's substantiality, stability and munificence, all of which are lacking in outlying consumers. Conspicuous affiliation with the minority ethnic group is the key indicator for suppliers, and the relationship with the group occurs via its affiliated consumers, one at a time.

For their part in the exchange, consumers assess their perception of the supplier's performance drawing on assessment criteria received from the minority ethnic group. After the exchange takes place, feedback is provided to the group about whether borrowed expectations were confirmed or disconfirmed. Positive feedback is consistent with consumer satisfaction and supports future recommendation of the supplier to other group affiliates, as well as building a positive attitude of the consumer towards the group.

Relationship Between Consumers and Preferred Suppliers

To the extent that supplier involvement and reliance on a minority ethnic group brings about an effective reduction in culture shock through gains in consumer socialization (Oberg, 1960), ethnic minority consumers are able to adapt better to the host country's environment. Beyond feeling more confident in their adaptation to a new life, the desire to maintain these benefits over time explains their continued reliance on, and affiliation to the minority ethnic group, generating feelings of ethnic loyalty and possible gratitude towards the group (Bridger and Wood, 2017; Palmatier et al., 2009; Soscia, 2007), to the group's network and to its recommended suppliers. Repeated positive feedback to the group about recommended suppliers after an exchange may generate stronger group preference for the supplier.

It is the consumer's acceptance of the suppliers recommended by the minority ethnic group that operationalizes the "preferred" qualifier conferred on the suppliers, eventually establishing new direct relationships (between these consumers and the suppliers) and indirectly strengthening the existing one between the consumer, the minority ethnic group and the supplier. That is, satisfaction with the interaction with preferred suppliers in the ethnic network leads to further interactions, resulting in relationship building that may lead to the justification and consolidation of the advantageous terms of exchange offered by the supplier to consumers affiliated with the minority ethnic group, strengthening the ethnic network overall.

The consumer's decision to partake in a relationship with a preferred supplier may be justified because their alternative is to search independently for suitable suppliers in a space to which they are foreign, investing time and effort while risking making the wrong selection, given their lack of market knowledge and language-related communication challenges. As noted by Bendapudi and Berry (1997), informational investments range *"from informing a hairdresser about one's personal style and preferences . . . to gathering financial records and participating in a series of in-depth discussions to educate a personal financial planner"* (p. 24). Additional to informational investments, consumers also incur sacrifices related to time, effort and money, from an economic perspective, all of which are taken into account by consumers when considering switching providers (Shaw and Pirog III, 1997).

Once a relationship is established, situational ethnicity—which accounts for the contexts in which consumption choices are made (Stayman and Deshpandé, 1989)—can contribute to the development and enhancement of the relationship. If ethnic minority consumers are only fluent in their ethnic language, consumption needs can easily convert into communication discomfort and in a reduced ability to pass on and to retrieve information during interactions outside the co-ethnic network environment. This condition is clearly demonstrated by widely used tactics in the healthcare and banking industries involving the purposeful employment of individuals from within the minority communities they wish to serve (Subeliani and Tsogas, 2005; Shanmuganthaan, Stone and Foss, 2004). More generally, this is the case, for example, of consumer-supplier interactions where the service-products being exchanged are high in interpersonal contact and in credence qualities, such that customization, responsiveness and personalization have the potential to further differentiate the preferred supplier and enhance the related terms of exchange. In situations such as these, changing suppliers can be expected to increase perceived switching costs for consumers, hence reinforcing their dependence on their preferred supplier. It is well known that higher switching costs and greater dependency fosters relationship maintenance (Ganesan, 1994).

Notwithstanding, even communication difficulties may be overcome depending on the consumption situation. In cases where service-product quality is easy to assess (as in the case of highly tangible search products such as groceries and hardware, or even in the case of some experience service-products such as fast-food) ethnic minority consumers may prefer standard offerings to ethnically adapted ones. Ultimately, these are cases with high complexity, as consumption experience may not be assessed simply in terms of service-product quality or fluency in communications. Sharing the consumption space with co-ethnic consumers and with similar-others may be the determinant attribute in the choice of a supplier.

This highlights both the need for businesses to understand consumers' needs and wants in all their facets, as well as the opportunity for non-ethnic minority businesses to successfully target minority ethnic groups. For example, for product categories such as electronics, a Tunisian minority in France was found to react negatively to ethnically adapted websites (Bartikowski, Taieb and Chandon, 2016).

The link between ethnic minority consumers and their co-ethnic group's ethnic network can be strong or weak. Arguably, it is weak in the case of groups with low rates of self-employment such as the Koreans and Mexicans in the Chicago area (Raijman and Tienda, 2003). In any case, the link is likely to support a long-term relationship with preferred suppliers to the network, provided interactional experiences are not negative; that is, suppliers' performance should continuously meet with consumers' expectations, remaining reliable and credible. Beyond situational circumstances, inexperienced ethnic minority consumers may associate with a minority ethnic group for perceived strategic utility reasons (Espiritu, 1993), and to benefit from the support of that group through lower perceived risk and faster market socialization. It is also through their identification with that group that they become important for suppliers, justifying their deployment of loyalty generating relational strategies and tactics.

Loyalty to Preferred Suppliers

As time goes by, exposure to everyday consumption situations enables consumers' to overcome their inexperience, becoming less challenged by socialization needs. It cannot be questioned, for example, that it is not uncommon for newly arrived immigrants to settle in areas without an ethnic community of significant mass. With more or less difficulty these settlers deal with their consumption difficulties (possibly in kind and in communication) and often acculturate to the dominant local population.

More common, however, is settlement into areas with more or less mature ethnic communities. Provided there is a continued allegiance to a minority co-ethnic group, when combined with ethnic loyalty satisfaction with preferred suppliers rationally excludes any incentive to search for new information, for new information sources or for new suppliers; indeed, at least theoretically, less than full satisfaction may be tolerated, since changing suppliers may be perceived as re-establishing risk, although strong dissatisfaction may incentivize negative feedback to the minority ethnic group.

The scenario just described is somewhat aligned to an economic *ceteris paribus*, consumption-as-usual view of the world (Girod, de Haan and Scholz, 2011). It should not preclude the reality that we live in a dynamic and turbulent world characterized by intense competitive activity. Hence, although ethnic minority consumers may form close relationships with preferred suppliers recommended by their co-ethnic group, and these may develop into a strong form of ethnic group—ethnic consumer—preferred supplier loyalty as per the depiction of an ethnic network in Figure 9.1, competition for these consumers may result in switching, even if not targeted as a group. Therefore, close attention is required to ethnic minority consumers' switching behaviour.

Switching Preferred Suppliers

Ethnic minority consumers may consider switching preferred suppliers for situational reasons, including:

1. Suppliers closing down or relocation, or changing ownership;
2. Consumers relocating themselves, such that current supplier retention may become inconvenient. Inconvenience is a recurring switching motivation in the literature (Keaveney, 1995). The effect of inconvenience is likely to vary with service-product type, with higher

switching rates in search service-products than in the other classes of credence and experience;

3. 'Pricing' is also a possible switching motivation, likely to be more important for service-products in the search class. "Core service failure" and "service encounter failure" were respectively the largest and second largest switching motivations in the Keaveney (1995) study.

4. For newly arrived ethnic consumers, improved market knowledge is likely to be an important switching reason for service-products in the experience and credence classes. Consumer socialization gains encompass a growing awareness of alternative suppliers, possibly indicative that the preferred supplier recommended by the minority ethnic group has failed to develop a strong relational strategy. It may also reflect acculturation away from the group over time.

5. Consumers may become disappointed with a preferred supplier if performance is below expectations such that service quality failure and dissatisfaction contribute to switching suppliers (Grace and O'Cass, 2001; Mihelis et al., 2001). In this case, the perceived net value of retaining the supplier will be reduced. Whether the consumer will switch requires comparing the new perceived value relative to the net values of available alternatives. Endorsement by the minority ethnic group, for example, may suffice to deter switching due to in-group behaviour reciprocity. But the switching decision may also inform the group's perception about the particular supplier. While one consumer's switching may not be enough to jeopardize the group's preference/recommendation for a supplier, similar feedback by other members may result in the supplier losing its status.

Dissatisfaction with the preferred provider's service is likely to be a major reason for the minority ethnic group to seek alternative providers. For the business, because of group dynamics, rather than facing a slow attrition from consumers' switching, loss of ethnic loyalty may cause a large and rapid loss of the target group altogether. Hence, having targeted and attracted the patronage of a minority ethnic group, there is also an economic imperative for the business to continually address and monitor the relationship.

This switching scenario might possibly be averted if the preferred supplier emphasizes relationship benefits. Service support and high quality personal interactions may be major retention factors, even more important than product quality or price (Ulaga and Eggert, 2006), leading to a preferred supplier's competitive advantage.

Relationships, Networks and Competitive Advantage

Competitive advantage at a point in time requires that suppliers offer their consumers value propositions/terms of exchange that are perceived by those consumers as superior to those offered by competitors. If superiority is based on attributes that competitors cannot offer, the conditions for continued competitive advantage are met. If the delivered attributes match those required by consumers, competitive advantage can be sustainable.

More formally, sustainable competitive advantage requires a business taking a distinctive position in the market that is more attractive to the target market than competitors' offers and difficult for competitors to emulate (Porter, 1996). Emulation difficulties may arise from many possible bases for distinctiveness that a business may seek to develop, including quality, innovation and special features of their service-products. Price or lowest cost are not included because it generally means offering the same as competitors, only cheaper, and this is rarely sustainable for a long period.

Minority ethnic groups are groups of consumers with distinct needs and preferences relative to other groups. To win and hold a minority ethnic group requires that a business find the differences in determinant and important service-product attributes that matter to the group's affiliates, positioning itself to attend to those differences in their value proposition. Even if ethnic minority consumers share mainstream consumers' needs, their ethnic preferences, situational ethnicity and consumer socialization deficits are likely to be distinct, perhaps unique, providing an opportunity for ethnic-sensitive suppliers to tailor their offerings focusing on that uniqueness. Since core service-products are becoming standardized (Sundbo, 2002), it may be the targeting of ethnic minority consumers' situational uniqueness that makes value propositions (or terms of exchange) superior.

The implication here is that suppliers wishing to target ethnic minority consumers must discover what attributes they should draw upon to offer distinctive value propositions. Importantly, the source of this knowledge is the relevant minority ethnic group. Group profiling may provide the necessary information about what makes the group distinctive. Using this information to develop value propositions may or may not guarantee superiority and, even in cases of superiority, the competitive advantage that ensues may not be sustainable. In principle, any supplier can develop minority ethnic group profiles and use this information to target ethnic minority consumers with ethnic-sensitive strategies, so there must be something else that prevents competitors from accessing the same opportunities available to preferred suppliers.

It is mutual benefit that helps to promote suppliers to a preferred status, for these suppliers to be recommended to affiliated ethnic consumers, and for consumer loyalty to the business to develop over time. By itself, satisfaction is not sufficient to engender loyalty. Loyalty is best considered as dynamic and varying in its possible strength. In terms of the earlier discussed four stages/phases of loyalty development proposed by Oliver (1999), beyond action loyalty, ultimate loyalty requires a socio-emotional involvement to which the minority ethnic group contributes as a social network. Successful relationship marketing requires the consumer to derive benefit from the relationship. In the case of ethnic minority consumers, the growth of village envelopment generates this benefit in many ways, ranging from the reduction of perceived risk for individual members to the social ties that are formed.

A targeting strategy that will lead to a high retention of ethnic minority consumers may also include the creation of perceived procedural and financial switching costs. However, these are elements that may well engender group dissatisfaction that undermines a loyalty strategy.

Clearly, competitive advantage is linked to the building of a strong relationship, but this requires special competencies and capabilities, especially implementing cross-cultural awareness and ethnic-sensitive practices. The networked, relational interdependence between the minority ethnic group, the individual ethnic consumer and the preferred co-ethnic supplier makes this relationship difficult to penetrate by others.

Given the central role played by ethnic identity in network operations, the findings may not apply equally to consumers not bound by ethnicity, discussed in the next section.

Implications for Consumer Groups Not Bound by Ethnicity

The findings from two contrasting studies help to identify the group conditions for a relationship to develop. The first, an American study (Berkowitz, Bao and Allaway, 2005) investigated whether there was any relationship between ethnicity and store loyalty. Hispanics were defined as the ethnic group and the particular question of interest was whether Hispanic consumers were different from non-Hispanic consumers in store loyalty. The authors conclude that the finding of no loyalty differences is not "too surprising" with the claim that their results support the contention that cultural differences between Hispanics and Anglo-Americans are "prone to possible exaggerations" (p. 20). Yet the study's findings are to be expected given its parameters: the broad coverage of Hispanics as an "ethnic group", the criterion of being Hispanic based on family name, while strength of identification was not taken into account. Further, store loyalty pertained to grocery shopping, generally a low involvement exercise, with no evidence that the single store took measures to build loyalty specifically with this group.

Separated by nearly a decade in time, Huang, Oppewal and Mavondo (2013) used a stronger conceptual and research framework to identify members of a Chinese minority ethnic group. Using self-identification by Chinese living in Australia, whether they considered themselves Chinese, and whether they had previously travelled overseas, the study examined attraction to the travel agent used and the agent they would have used if their first agent had not been available. Institutional theory was used to distinguish the role of a consumer, as an individual seeking the best outcomes in terms of competitive price, consumer service, atmosphere and accessibility; and as a member of an ethnic community, valuing actions bringing benefits to their community. In the latter context, the theory of intercultural accommodation was applied to draw attention to service providers using ethnic attributes to establish both pragmatic and social legitimacy with the minority ethnic group. Four accommodation behaviours were examined for their importance: ability to speak the ethnic language, employing ethnic staff (Murphy, 2011), being located near the ethnic community and support for the ethnic community.

While consumer service had the largest effect on attraction to the agent, it was noted that this "partly acts as an ethnic related attribute" (p. 891). Despite a smaller effect than service and price, ethnic-related attributes contributed positively to perceived attractiveness of a service outlet, supporting the conclusion that businesses should take care to properly communicate their position as an ethnic retailer or service provider. Mainstream providers seeking to become preferred providers were also recommended to consider focusing on such attributes if they wanted to make a positive impression and establish a service relationship with ethnic minority consumers.

Performance attributes in seeking a minority ethnic group's support include strong relationship elements. Perceived pragmatic legitimacy can be achieved through performance attributes that include atmosphere and consumer service. These help to establish social legitimacy through perceived sensitivity to ethnic culture. The contrasting outcomes from the two studies demonstrate the need to carefully identify a minority ethnic group and to recognize the long-term benefit of interactive relationship building. A stronger, ethnicity-based rationale beyond language alone is likely to be required, to justify a business investing in meeting the group's preferences while consumer groups that are not bound by ethnicity, tradition and difference to other groups will not be amenable to ethnic marketing.

Conclusion

From a supplier's perspective, the decision of whether to invest in a relationship with ethnic minority consumers will depend on whether the lifetime value promised by their co-ethnic group (not the individual group affiliates per se), as per the supplier's estimates, converts into a substantial value opportunity for the supplier that justifies the investment in developing and delivering ethnic-sensitive terms of exchange. Provided all conditions are met, effective supplier performance can lead to its promotion to a preferred status within the ethnic network.

Preferred suppliers may compromise their status if they become condescending about their performance and cease to meet the minority ethnic group's expectations. Their status is aligned to the perception by the group that those distinguished are the best suppliers of net value. Responsiveness and personalization, for example, may be attributes that clinch the "preferred supplier" status through consumer-oriented ethnic-sensitive strategies. But, as in most market situations, the good performance of the agreed terms of exchange in a competitive fashion cannot be compromised. Continued support and referral by the co-ethnic group is essential for sustainable competitive advantage and implies consistently positive service experiences, together with switching constraints. Hence, the combination of the uniqueness of group and the nature of the terms of exchange may result in greater loyalty by ethnic minority consumers.

The selection of new suppliers is the culmination of the switching process, unless the particular service activities are no longer required. Three points to keep in mind are:

1. There is no reason to expect that motivations for switching be in the selection criteria for new suppliers. Once ethnic minority consumers become more knowledgeable about the market, they may use different criteria for selecting new suppliers;
2. Switching does not question ethnic loyalty;
3. Economic and switching costs need to account for social or psychological costs, leading to a relationship that is constrained by a member's conformance to the minority ethnic group.

(Johnson, 1982)

This chapter relied on relevant literature to offer an explanation of how and why minority ethnic groups are important for ethnic minority consumers and for suppliers seeking to target minority ethnic groups.

If a business can become a preferred supplier to a minority ethnic group, it is likely to have a source of advantage over competitors that can be as sustainable as the resilience and stability of the group. Provided the business is able to sustain its performance as a preferred supplier, consumer loyalty may join with ethnic loyalty to make it difficult for competing businesses to gain even a testing of the service-product they have to offer. Because minority ethnic groups have certain characteristics that underpin their resilience and stability, there is a need to find an ethnicity-based rationale that justifies a business investing in meeting the group's preferences.

Chapter 10 delves into issues of marketing strategy and tactics. One aspect that is discussed is that reciprocity between ethnic minority businesses and consumers may entail the promotion of the minority ethnic group to a "preferred customer status" and group affiliated consumers to become members of the preferred customer program.

Note

1. A social network is an expression with multiple interpretations in the literature, today most commonly used in the context of computer-mediated communication (Ellison, 2007). This not the interpretation adopted in this chapter.

References

Bartikowski, B., Taieb, B. and Chandon, J. (2016). Targeting without alienating on the Internet: Ethnic minority and majority consumers. *Journal of Business Research*, 69(3), 1082–1089.

Batjargal, B. (2010). The effects of network's structural holes: Polycentric institutions, product portfolio, and new venture growth in China and Russia. *Strategic Entrepreneurship Journal*, 4(2), 146–163.

Bendapudi, N. and Berry, L. (1997). Consumers' motivations for maintaining relationships with service providers. *Journal of Retailing*, 73(1), 15–37.

Berkowitz, D., Bao, Y. and Allaway, A. (2005). Hispanic consumers, store loyalty and brand preference. *Journal of Targeting, Measurement and Analysis for Marketing*, December, 14(1), 9–24.

Berry, J. and Sam, D. (1997). Acculturation and adaptation. In J. Berry, Y. Poortinga and J. Pandey (eds.), *Handbook of Cross-Cultural Psychology*, Vol. 3, 2nd ed. Boston: Allyn & Bacon, pp. 291–326.

Bowles, S. and Gintis, H. (2004). Persistent parochialism: Trust and exclusion in ethnic networks. *Journal of Economic Behavior & Organization*, 55, 1–23.

Bridger, E. and Wood, A. (2017). Gratitude mediates consumer responses to marketing communications. *European Journal of Marketing*, 51(1), 44–64.

Buchanan, J. (1991). Opportunity cost. In *The World of Economics*. London, UK: Palgrave Macmillan, pp. 520–525.

Chung, E. and Whalen, K. (2006). The embedded entrepreneur: Recognizing the strength of ethnic social ties. *New England Journal of Entrepreneurship*, 9(1), 51–61.

Cook, K., Cheshire, C., Rice, E. and Nakagawa, S. (2013). Social exchange theory. In *Handbook of Social Psychology*. Dordrecht: Springer.

Cropanzano, R. and Mitchell, M. (2005). Social exchange theory: An interdisciplinary review. *Journal of Management*, 31(6), 874–900.

Dibb, S. and Simkin, L. (2010). Judging the quality of customer segments: Segmentation effectiveness. *Journal of Strategic Marketing*, 18(2), 113–131.

Dwyer, F., Schurr, P. and Oh, S. (1987). Developing buyer-seller relationships. *Journal of Marketing*, 51(April), 11–27.

Ellison, N. (2007). Social network sites: Definition, history, and scholarship. *Journal of Computer-Mediated Communication*, 13(1), 210–230.

Emerson, R. (1976). Social exchange theory. *Annual Review of Sociology*, 2(1), 335–362.

Espiritu, Y. (1993). *Asian American Panethnicity: Bridging Institutions and Identities*. Temple University Press.

Fadahunsi, A., Smallbone, D. and Supri, S. (2000). Networking and ethnic minority enterprise development: Insights from a North London study. *Journal of Small Business and Enterprise Development*, 7(3), 228–240.

Fregetto, E. (2004). Immigrant and ethnic entrepreneurship: A U.S. perspective. In H. P. Welsch (ed.), *Entrepreneurship: The Way Ahead*. New York: Routledge, pp. 253–268.

Ganesan, S. (1994). Determinants of long-term orientation in buyer-seller relationships. *Journal of Marketing*, 58(April), 1–19.

Girod, B., de Haan, P. and Scholz, R. (2011). Consumption-as-usual instead of ceteris paribus assumption for demand. *The International Journal of Life Cycle Assessment*, 16(1), 3–11.

Grace, D. and O'Cass, A. (2001). Attributions of service switching: A study of consumers' and providers' perceptions of child-care service delivery. *Journal of Services Marketing*, 15(4), 300–321.

Granovetter, M. (1992). Economic institutions as social constructions: A framework for analysis. *Acta sociologica*, 35(1), 3–11.

Granovetter, M. (1985). Economic action and social structure: The problem of embeddedness. *American Journal of Sociology*, 91(3), 481–510.

Gummesson, E. (1997). In search of marketing equilibrium: Relationship marketing versus hypercompetition. *Journal of Marketing Management*, 13(5), 421–430.

Hallen, L., Johanson, J. and Seyed-Mohamed, N. (1991). Interfirm adaptation in business relationships. *Journal of Marketing*, 55(April), 29–37.

Holm, D., Eriksson, K. and Johanson, J. (1999). Creating value through mutual commitment to business network relationships. *Strategic Management Journal*, 467–486.

Huang, Y., Oppewal, H. and Mavondo, F. (2013). The influence of ethnic attributes on ethnic consumer choice of service outlet. *European Journal of Marketing*, 47(5/6), 877–898.

Johnson, M. (1982). The social and cognitive features of the dissolution of commitment relationships. In S. Duck (ed.), *Personal Relationships: Dissolving Personal Relationships*. New York: Academic Press, pp. 51–73.

Keaveney, S. (1995). Consumer switching behavior in service industries: An exploratory study. *Journal of Marketing*, 59(April), 71–92.

Kim, Y. (2007). Ideology, identity, and intercultural communication: An analysis of differing academic conceptions of cultural identity. *Journal of Intercultural Communication Research*, 36(3), 237–253.

Kloosterman, R., Van Der Leun, J. and Rath, J. (1999). Mixed embeddedness: (In) formal economic activities and immigrant businesses in the Netherlands. *International Journal of Urban and Regional Research*, 23(2), 252–266.

Kossinets, G. and Watts, D. (2006). Empirical analysis of an evolving social network. *Science*, 311(5757), 88–90.

Lindridge, A. (2015). Market segmentation by ethnicity: Is it really feasible? *The Routledge Companion to Ethnic Marketing*, 235–253.

Mihelis, G., Grigoroudis, E., Siskos, Y., Politis, Y. and Malandrakis, Y. (2001). Consumer satisfaction measurement in the private bank sector. *European Journal of Operational Research*, 130, 347–360.

Mummendey, A., Kessler, T., Klink, A. and Mielke, R. (1999). Strategies to cope with negative social identity: Predictions by social identity theory and relative deprivation theory. *Journal of Personality and Social Psychology*, 76(2), 229.

Murphy, C. (2011). Latino influence emphasized at chamber breakfast. *Mclatchy—Tribune Business News, Washington*, March 3.

Oberg, K. (1960). Cultural shock: Adjustment to new cultural environments. *Practical Anthropology*, 7, 177–182.

Oliver, R. (1999). Whence consumer loyalty. *Journal of Marketing*, 63, 33–44.

Palmatier, R., Jarvis, C., Bechkoff, J. and Kardes, F. (2009). The role of customer gratitude in relationship marketing. *Journal of Marketing*, 73(5), 1–18.

Pires, G. and Stanton, J. (2015). *Ethnic Marketing: Culturally Sensitive Theory and Practice*. Abingdon, UK: Routledge.

Pires, G. and Stanton, J. (2005). *Ethnic Marketing, Accepting the Challenge of Cultural Diversity*. London: Thomson Learning.

Pires, G. and Stanton, J. (1999). The substantiality test: Meaning and application in market segmentation. *Journal of Segmentation in Marketing*, 3(2), 105–115.

Pires, G., Stanton, J. and Stanton, P. (2011). Revisiting the substantiality criterion: From ethnic marketing to market segmentation. *Journal of Business Research*, 64(9), 988–996.

Porter, M. (1996). What is strategy? *Harvard Business Review*, November–December.

Portes, A. and Sensenbrenner, J. (1993). Embeddedness and immigration: Notes on the social determinants of economic action. *American Journal of Sociology*, 98(6), 1320–1350.

Raijman, R. and Tienda, M. (2003). Ethnic foundations of economic transactions: Mexican and Korean immigrant entrepreneurs in Chicago. *Ethnic & Racial Studies*, 26(5), 783–801.

Ram, M., Jones, T. and Villares-Varela, M. (2017). Migrant entrepreneurship: Reflections on research and practice. *International Small Business Journal*, 35(1), 3–18.

Ravald, A. and Grönroos, C. (1996). The value concept and relationship marketing. *European Journal of Marketing*, 30(2), 19–30.

Serino, A., Giovagnoli, G. and Làdavas, E. (2009). I feel what you feel if you are similar to me. *PLoS One*, 4(3), e4930.

Shanmuganthaan, P., Stone, M. and Foss, B. (2004). Ethnic banking in the USA. *Journal of Financial Services Marketing*, 8(4), 388–400.

Shaw, E. and Pirog III, S. (1997). A systems model of household behavior. *Journal of Marketing Theory and Practice*, Summer, 17–29.

Shrivastava, S. and Kale, S. (2003). Philosophizing on the elusiveness of relationship marketing theory in consumer markets: A case for reassessing ontological and epistemological assumptions. *Australasian Marketing Journal*, 11(3), 61–71.

Sirdeshmukh, D., Singh, J. and Sabol, B. (2002). Consumer trust, value, and loyalty in relational exchanges. *Journal of Marketing*, 66(1), 15–37.

Soscia, I. (2007). Gratitude, delight, or guilt: The role of consumers' emotions in predicting postconsumption behaviors. *Psychology & Marketing*, 24(10), 871–894.

Stafford, L. (2008). Social exchange theories. *Engaging Theories in Interpersonal Communication: Multiple Perspectives*, 377–389.

Stayman, D. and Deshpandé, R. (1989). Situational ethnicity and consumer behavior. *Journal of Consumer Research*, 16(3), 361–371.

Stephan, W., Stephan, C., Wenzel, B. and Cornelius, J. (1991). Intergroup interaction and self-disclosure. *Journal of Applied Social Psychology*, 21(16), 1370–1378.

Subeliani, D. and Tsogas, G. (2005). Managing diversity in the Netherlands: A case study of Rabobank. *The International Journal of Human Resource Management*, 16(5), 831–851.

Sundbo, J. (2002). The service economy: Standardisation or customisation? *Service Industries Journal*, 22(4), 93–116.

Ulaga, W. and Eggert, A. (2006). Value-based differentiation in business relationships: Gaining and sustaining key supplier status. *Journal of Marketing*, 70(1), 119–136.

Volery, T. (2007). Ethnic entrepreneurship: A theoretical framework. In *Handbook of Research on Ethnic Minority Entrepreneurship: A Co-Evolutionary View on Resource Management*. Cheltenham: Edward Elgar, pp. 30–41.

Waldinger, R., Aldrich, H. and Ward, R. (1990). *Ethnic Entrepreneurs: Immigrant Business in Industrial Societies*, Vol. 1. Sage Publications, Inc.

Widmer, A. (2008). The making and unmaking of ethnic boundaries: A multilevel process theory1. *American Journal of Sociology*, 113(4), 970–1022.

Yamagishi, T. (2003). The group heuristic: A psychological mechanism that creates a self-sustaining system of generalized exchanges. *Proceedings of the Santa Fe Institute Workshop on the Coevolution of Institutions and Behavior.*

Zhao, X., Frese, M. and Giardini, A. (2010). Business owners' network size and business growth in China: The role of comprehensive social competency. *Entrepreneurship and Regional Development*, 22(7–8), 675–705.

10 Ethnic Entrepreneurship and the Marketing Mix

Theory, Practice, Strategy and the Segmentation Dilemma

The discussion of ethnic entrepreneurship and ethnic minority businesses in previous chapters identified relatively extensive research on supply and demand issues that pertain, directly or indirectly, to minority ethnic groups within culturally diverse countries. Much less attention has been given to ethnic marketing strategic practices by consideration of what businesses targeting minority ethnic groups actually do. One possible explanation is that extant research tends to concur that there is a gap between strategic discussions grounded or theoretical/logical reasoning (Pires and Stanton, 2015), and what marketing practitioners do in practice, but the importance of the gap is perceived differently while attitudes towards addressing the gap also differ.

Some analysts see the gap as a good thing, necessary to advance knowledge, fostering new and better ways to address real world challenges (Holbrook, 2008; Serrão, 1977), while others posit that it is important for strategic business behaviour to seek the reconciliation of the research and practice perspectives (Coutant, 1938) because theory must be relevant (Corley and Gioia, 2011) if, at least to some extent, pragmatic (Martin, 2004).

A common example of the gap between theory and practice occurs when the theoretical recognition of distinctive consumer behaviour related to minority ethnic groups uniqueness gives way, somehow, to the targeting of aggregates of minority ethnic groups, as if bound by homogeneous consumption behaviour. This is often recognized in research, as expressed by Lindridge's (2015) concern about the ethnic market segmentation dilemma, valid for narrowly defined groups and for group aggregates, since

> it is important to recognise that some ethnic groups are not a homogeneous group ensuring their market segmentation remains a challenge.
>
> (p. 247)

It may be that the dilemma, if unresolved, makes ethnic marketing deployment seem impracticable, as suggested below.

A View of the Gap Between Theory and Practice

In the several years of preparation for this text, the authors had the opportunity to discuss the gap between theory and practice with many marketing professors (a detailed discussion of those extensive discussions is available together with Pires and Stanton, 2015) and practitioners. While there was no strong dissent, if any, within the group of interview participants about the theoretical justification for targeting to focus on narrowly defined minority ethnic groups, there was also a strong agreement on the challenges that this involves, possibly justifying that some concessions needed to be made, namely in terms of the segmentation dilemma. The general sentiment was eloquently and succinctly voiced by Maria Charlton (of MAP Marketing, Newcastle, NSW, Australia): "It is just too difficult". The explanation rested with the need for one indicator, not two or three as usually prescribed in research, to reliably identify a homogeneous segment based on ethnicity. Given a lack of sufficient secondary information, doing primary research would make it too expensive for businesses to consider rigorous ethnic marketing targeting.

Reflecting different perspectives about the gap, the decision about how to target a minority ethnic group was identified early in Chapter 9 as requiring a demanding six step process (outlined in Table 9.1), justified by the need for extensive and rigorous information about the group and the business itself. In some contrast, Lindridge (2015) identifies seven key steps that marketing managers can undertake in ethnic marketing segmentation and targeting, shown in Table 10.1.

There are many similarities between the steps identified in Table 9.1 and those listed here. Beyond important and contrasting views about the depth and rigour of the needed information, arguably reflective of the gap, the most important distinction, we argue, lies with the need to assess own resources, capabilities and competencies to deliver on the attributes desired by the minority ethnic group, as per Table 9.1. If a business lacks own resources, capabilities and competencies, then the group is unlikely to represent a feasible opportunity at the time of the analysis. Other differences include an analysis of the current customer base and the selection of appropriate segmentation bases. Finally, it can be expected that assessment of current ethnic group behaviour and behaviour after the implementation of the targeting program should be distinct, meaning that actual payoff may not be necessarily the expected payoff, adding additional risk to assessments.

Overall, the challenging informational requirements we advocate may build an apparently insurmountable perceptual barrier to the practice of related theoretical based recommendations. Reflection on the way the various steps are addressed in the process outlined in Table 10.1 suggests some concern, further contributing to the "too difficult" syndrome. Nevertheless, we reiterate that effective targeting of a minority ethnic group

Table 10.1 Key Steps in Ethnic Market Segmentation

Key Steps Marketing Managers Can Undertake in Ethnic Market Segmentation	
Step 1 Justification for targeting	What do we wish to achieve by targeting the ethnic group?
Step 2 Understand existing customers	Look into existing customer base for customers with different ethnicities. Conduct in-depth analysis to identify which ethnic groups are buying your products, how often and how much. *Broadly similar to developing a segment profile that reveals valued proposition attributes. Table 9.1, Step 3.*
Step 3 Focus on value of ethnic groups for your business	Assess current value of existing and potential ethnic groups for your business in terms of financial value, customer potential and loyalty, using secondary research.
Step 4 Undertake some primary marketing research	The objective is to understand what the needs, wants and benefits are. *Similar to Table 9.1, Step 1.*
Step 5 Assess which segmentation approaches will work	Consider demographic, geographic, psychographic and behaviouristic variables. Consider implications from acculturation effects.
Step 6 Implement marketing activities that will appeal to ethnic market segments	Develop a marketing strategy and tactics that address segment needs, drawing upon symbolisms indicative of the ethnic group's cultural values to ensure success. *Similar to Table 9.1, Step 5.*
Step 7 Evaluate	Verify effectiveness of the targeting strategy and correct as necessary.

Adapted from Lindridge (2015, pp. 247–250)

as a business opportunity requires the collection and rigorous use of the information recommended in Table 9.1.

The gap between theory and practice refers directly to the pivotal cornerstone of ethnic marketing strategy, laying the foundations of how the ethnic market is segmented. Should a minority ethnic group be defined narrowly to, as much as possible, ensure homogeneous consumer behaviour, or should aggregates of minority ethnic groups be considered based on a need for pragmatism?

Consistent with the ethnic marketing focus offered in this text, the first tier strategy must be to attend to business objectives by targeting the minority ethnic group or its consumers, the second tier strategy. Recognizing the importance of theoretical development that is also pragmatic, a discussion of strategic ethnic marketing issues is provided. The discussion distinguishes ethnic minority business objectives and strategies from the marketing strategies and activities that make up the businesses' tactical approach to meeting the objectives. An earliest step is, therefore, to separate the business objectives that are the focus of most of the ethnic marketing literature under the strategy banner—most of which are related to ethnic minority businesses' creation and development—from the distinct ethnic marketing strategies and tactics that are deployed by businesses targeting markets determined by their ethnicity. Based on the discussion and evidence provided in previous chapters emphasizing loyalty and the importance of networks, focus in this chapter is on the development of relational marketing strategies.

Following a preliminary discussion of the distinction between strategy and tactics in general terms, attention is given mostly to ethnic minority businesses affiliated with co-ethnic groups as the prominent area for consideration of ethnic marketing strategy. This is not to say that businesses other than ethnic minority businesses, including mainstream businesses, can be excluded outright. However, it is recognized that such businesses will rarely target narrowly defined minority ethnic groups with strategies specific to those groups, focusing more on some aggregate of groups, mostly based on language or region of provenance, or on seeing the consumers in those groups undifferentiated from the dominant population, as is the case of mainstream supermarkets (e.g. Woolworths, Coles, IGA and Aldi in Australia), cinemas, entertainment parks and fast-food outlets such as McDonalds, Hungry Jacks or Pizza Hut.

Business Opportunities and Ethnic Minority Business

Ethnic minority businesses are defined as businesses whose owners/operators are categorized by their distinct ethnicity/culture/religion relative to the indigenous population (Carter et al., 2015; Masurel, Nijkamp and Vindigni, 2004; Phizacklea and Ram, 1996), independently of whether they are immigrants or descendants of immigrants, such that they self-ascribe themselves (and are seen by others as belonging) to a specific minority ethnic group with a common origin and culture (Yinger, 1985). Such a definition is silent about the business objectives, business strategies, markets selected for targeting and marketing strategies, as well as about the marketing tactics deployed by ethnic minority businesses to achieve a desired strategic positioning in a particular market. Specifically, it does not imply any particular dependence or supplier—consumer relationship with the minority ethnic group of affiliation.

Mainstream and even global companies are able to make decisions about which markets to target. These decisions include whether to target or to not target narrowly defined minority ethnic groups in a fragmented world market within one country, or to adopt a diaspora marketing approach and focus on one minority ethnic group in a variety of countries (Demangeot, Broderick and Craig, 2015; Kumar and Steenkamp, 2013).

Similarly, ethnic entrepreneurs and their ethnic minority businesses may well adopt the strategic decision to target minority ethnic groups, aggregates of minority ethnic groups, the mainstream, their home country market or any other market at all, including targeting global consumers in the global market. The first option, however, is the norm.

Clearly, this text does not support a perspective of host countries made out of a plethora of ghettoized minority ethnic groups served by affiliated ethnic minority businesses in a voluntary or involuntary state of segregation as the norm. However, such a scenario is possible in some adapted way, as illustrated by the excerpt from *The Economist* as recently as 2013, in the UK context (for the USA, Canada and Europe see, for example, Ram, Jones and Villares-Varela, 2017; Phillips, 2013; Walks and Bourne, 2006; Anas, 2004):

> Stockbridge is . . . one of Britain's most concentrated urban ethnic ghettos. . . . Fully 96% of the population of Stockbridge is of the same race: Caucasian.
>
> Ghettos are normally thought of as black or Asian: the Bangladeshi housing estates of Tower Hamlets or the intensely African neighbourhood of Peckham, both in London. But Stockbridge Village qualifies, too. It is whiter than Britain or Merseyside as a whole, as well as far more homogeneously working-class. And it has social problems to match any ethnic-minority ghetto. . . . In short . . . its isolation is partly geographical . . . but mostly cultural. Its residents are trapped in a cycle of low achievement and low earnings. . . . These days, overt discrimination is not nearly as big a problem as isolation. This is true of blacks and Asians as much as whites. . . . (B)ehaviour has changed. . . . With the odd and not too worrying exception of the Chinese, every ethnic group is becoming less segregated.

But we maintain that the discussion of ethnic entrepreneurship and ethnic minority businesses in previous chapters indicates that early ethnic market niche (Waldinger et al., 1990) and ethnic enclave theories (Portes, 1987) can help us understand that the underpinnings of these businesses' strategic decisions about target markets are likely to remain mostly situational, and closely related to the ethnic minority status of the relevant entrepreneur (Morales, 2008). Accordingly, the most common scenario for ethnic entrepreneurs when starting-up their ethnic minority businesses may be to target co-ethnic consumers that make-up their minority ethnic group.

Reliance on the minority co-ethnic group can be justified by the critical role played by ethnicity in predicting and explaining affiliated consumers' decision-making and choice processes (Podoshen, 2009; Laroche, Chung and Clarke, 1997). Co-ethnicity and sharing of the same minority ethnic group might endow ethnic entrepreneurs with a reassuring degree of confidence on their perceived market knowledge and on the success of their entrepreneurial activities, as well as in the perceived competitive advantage of their ethnic minority businesses in that particular market. Lack of access to the minority ethnic group may herald a proclivity for feelings of poor entrepreneurial performance (Komakech and Jackson, 2016), possibly entwined with perceived market inexperience and a lack of self-confidence.

In general terms, knowing the specific market being targeted, such as a minority ethnic group, may provide indicative clues on the type of marketing activities (e.g. ethnic marketing, social marketing, mass marketing, global marketing, social media marketing) that are deployed by businesses targeting that market, but contributes much less to the characterization/classification of the businesses doing the targeting. Not-withstanding, given the caution commonly raised against the targeting of minority ethnic groups based on arguments ranging from cultural and language barriers to the group's potential heterogeneity and small size, poor substantiality and lack of stability (Pires and Stanton, 2015; Pires, Stanton and Stanton, 2011; Simpson and Akinwale, 2007; Pires, 1999; Okazaki and Sue, 1995; Evans, 1989), it will not be surprising if the business specifically targeting consumers affiliated with a particular minority ethnic group is an ethnic minority business.

Congruent with the aforementioned definition, the identification of a business as an ethnic minority business is substantially linked to its owner-manager being distinguishable for her/his self-ascribed and market recognized ethnic identity, even if emanating originally from a different country of provenance than the minority ethnic group s/he affiliates with. Hence, the discussion of the development of ethnic entrepreneurship has often focused on the close link/dependency between an ethnic entrepreneur's business and their minority ethnic group as the business incubator (Komakech and Jackson, 2016), as discussed in Chapter 7, at least during the ethnic minority business creation and consolidation phases.

Ethnic marketing involves the design and deployment of strategies based on the ethnicity-related characteristics of the market (Pires and Stanton, 2015), but such deployment is neither a sufficient nor a necessary condition for a business to be classified as an ethnic minority business. Large global businesses, such as McDonald's, may choose to deploy ethnic marketing strategies involving tailored menus and advertising at certain locations favoured by a minority ethnic group (Helm, 2010), and an ethnic minority business may predominantly target outside their ethnic group of affiliation, as in the case of Cuban entrepreneurs in Miami targeting a non-ethnic clientele by branching out into industries, such as garments and construction (Levine, 1985).

However, it can be expected that the business and marketing strategies deployed by ethnic minority businesses may often emerge from the interaction of business opportunities, arising from the environmental challenges facing a minority ethnic group, with the co-ethnic characteristics shared by the ethnic entrepreneur with that group. These opportunities are likely to arise in low value added sectors with low barriers to entry, intense competition, low margins, low liquidity and high failure rates (Blackburn and Smallbone, 2014), hence not designed for significant levels of growth (Butler and Greene, 1997). But the aspect to highlight here is that, while entailing a relatively low degree of service-product innovativeness possibly focusing on replication of what is already being done in other markets by other businesses, these opportunities may afford operational efficiency gains (Iyer and Shapiro, 1999) derived from ethnic-sensitive tactical behaviour. An understanding of the context linking business objectives to marketing strategy and tactics is clearly justified.

Objectives, Strategies and Tactics

The business literature is unanimous and unambiguous in considering that business strategy must follow the establishment of goals. Business goals come first, and each objective should be at the origin of a specific strategy, or combination of strategies, to achieve the objective. A business strategy is likely to comprise a variety of functional goals and associated (second tier) strategies, such as financial, human resources, innovation, productivity, resources, social responsibility and, of course, marketing (Lim and Reid, 1992). Finally, the associated second tier strategies give way to the tactics that will be used to reach the functional goals. Distinct functional goals will command distinct strategies and distinct tactics (Vorhies and Morgan, 2003).

In the marketing context and in simple terms, a marketing strategy is the conceptualization of a plan for reaching a specific marketing related goal (e.g. to increase sales, or to achieve a specific position in a particular market or markets), while the associated tactics are determined in the marketing program, comprising the activities that are taken to execute the strategy to reach that goal (e.g. lower prices and tailored, detailed integrated marketing communications). The complicating factor is that the tactics used to execute the marketing strategy also depend on, and have implications for, other functions within the business.

For example, a strategy for increasing sales (the objective) may start with the definition of new reasons why consumers might buy more. These reasons may then be the focus of tactical integrated marketing communications, involving magazine ads, search engine marketing, TV advertising, social media, and other promotional activities, such as retail promotions. Each of these activities has timing implications and costs that must be funded by the business, and for which the other functional departments need to prepare/plan (Rust, Lemon and Zeithaml, 2004).

It is apparent that not all functions are distinguishable in every business, being more likely to exist as separate functional areas in large businesses.

However, the need to attend to the different functional imperatives does not depend on business size. Rather, the different responsibilities may become encapsulated in a certain business manager's job description, often the owner or the owner-partnership, with or without the benefit of outsourcing of critical functions, such as accounting and legal. Business managers driving job descriptions with multiple functional attributes are commonly niche and small business managers. Some of these are ethnic entrepreneurs running ethnic minority businesses.

Depending on business experience, a business plan can assist managers in the definition of objectives and associated strategies, and the overall plan can include a detailed marketing program comprising several tactics or action items. But the postulate that matters is that there are no reliable marketing tactics without a solid and clear marketing strategy that is driven by clear goals, and a corresponding inter-functional support.

If a business faces liquidity problems before its marketing tactics can be implemented, business objectives may not be met. This is a common justification for advocating the need for businesses, particularly those without multiple functional departments, to engage in business planning. The lack of a business plan is a commonly recognized explanation for business failure, particularly in the case of small businesses (Chwolka and Raith, 2012; Achidi and Priem, 2011; Cook, Campbell and Kelly, 2012; Perry, 2001; Mata and Portugal, 1994; Gaskill, Van Auken and Manning, 1993). This conclusion is also applicable to ethnic minority businesses (Beckinsale and Ram, 2006; Masurel et al., 2002), as illustrated by the case of the high business failure among African entrepreneurs in the UK, post-2008 financial crisis (Mendy and Hack-Polay, 2018).

Ethnic Minority Business Objectives, Strategies and Tactics

Whether the entrepreneur is affiliated with a minority ethnic group or the mainstream, the first experience in starting a business is commonly recognized as a big step, where the convenience and security of holding a paid job is exchanged for the opportunity of a promising but uncertain financial future. Business success is a function of a large variety of success factors. In addition to personal entrepreneurial and psychological characteristics (Sarri and Trihopoulou, 2005; Littunen, 2000; Begley and Boyd, 1987), and to personal endowments (including capabilities, competencies, risk-taking attitudes, access to initial and ongoing working capital, and family support), success is usually reliant on extensive acquisition of information about products, markets, competitors and many other environmental aspects, as well as government support. For example, for indigenous entrepreneurs in the South Pacific region, the four most critical success factors were good management, access to financing, personal qualities and satisfactory government support (Yusuf, 1995).

All the success factors noted above are recognized as fundamental to a business opportunity if it is to be properly analysed in the first place, and then to be taken advantage of. Success is also seen as dependent on a great deal of planning, a lack of which has notoriously been recognized as a major source of business failure for small businesses. Chapter 8 noted the likelihood that the potential reasons for small business success and failure also can be expected to apply to ethnic minority businesses.

The eventual decision of whether to engage in entrepreneurial activities, such as the start-up of an ethnic minority business as a means of self-employment, is often explained in the specialist literature as having more to do with the push by entrepreneurs' personal predicaments, such as labour market constraints (Jones, McEvoy and Barrett, 1992) that justify necessity entrepreneurship (Carter et al., 2013; Jones, Ram and Edwards, 2006), than with the pull of personal "cultural" attitudes and ambitions about enterprise (Basu, 1998), or to take advantage of a recognized opportunity (Williams, 2009). This explanation accommodates the questioning of many ethnic entrepreneurs' preparedness and experience for running their businesses.

The thrust of the argument is that, beyond the incentives to engage in business that are common to all entrepreneurs (e.g. income potential, pursuing a passion, following a "good" idea, seeking a new lifestyle, self-expression), an ethnic entrepreneur's decision may be simultaneously constrained and compelled by a feeling of having no choice, no other way of alleviating the circumstances that surround them in the new country and to achieve their objectives. For example, Table 10.2 identifies the motivations and objectives for ethnic minority business start-up in Greece.

Even if survival and social exclusion are set aside for extreme conditions, although not unlikely, provided the ethnic entrepreneurs have settled, or are in the process of settling, into a particular minority ethnic group of affiliation in the host country, it is conceivable that they might engage in, and rely upon, a series of tactical manoeuvres that are solely guided by the objective of selling service-products to that group of

Table 10.2 Reasons for Ethnic Minority Business Start-Up in Greece

Motivations/Objectives for Immigrants to Set Up Their Own EMB in Greece	
• As a means of survival	• To send money back to relatives in their countries of origin
• Economic self-sufficiency	
• As a social incorporation strategy, in their struggle against social exclusion	• To gain emotional satisfaction
	• For self-fulfilment
• To integrate into community life	• To serve the consumer needs of fellow newcomers
• To have control over own work situation	

Source: Lazaridis and Koumandraki (2003, p. 1)

affiliation (the business strategy) in order to achieve a steady income and to achieve a desired status within the group (1st order objectives). Clearly, these objectives can be entirely justified but strictly they are not marketing objectives per se and are silent about either marketing strategy or related tactical manoeuvres. On their own, these objectives would explain ethnic minority businesses' high failure rate (Ekanem and Wyer, 2007; Aldrich and Waldinger, 1990).

Ethnic minority businesses were characterized in Chapter 7 by their focus on generating an income stream that replaces employment income, while involving limited innovation and relatively high risk. But we argue that this characterization depends on the ethnic entrepreneur's outlook when considering their business activities. Some entrepreneurs are business migrants who settle in a new country with a business idea in hand. This business idea might have emerged from at least four different opportunities with distinct complexity, namely:

1. Opportunities related to unmet consumer needs and wants of service-products identified by family and/or friends in the host country, for example when holidaying in their home country of origin where the service-products may be readily available. This might involve opportunities of manufacturing and distribution, or distribution only of new to the market and substitute service-products with home-country brands for which the ethnic entrepreneur has representation and agency rights agreed with businesses operating in the ethnic entrepreneur's country of origin.

    For example, based in Montreal (Canada), Alivin Wines is an ethnic minority business that specializes in the import and distribution of Portuguese wines, olive oil and water (www.alivin.ca/en/). In Toronto, one of many small mixed-business store deals exclusively with Brazilian products, competing with Portuguese grocery stores, but with the exclusive distributorship for Brazilian branded products such as "Aviação" butter, Turma da Mônica comic books, chocolates (Amandita, Bis, Laka, Sonho de Valsa, Ouro Branco, and Garoto) and an extensive selection Audio CDs (www.yelp.com.au/biz/brazil-direct-import-and-export-toronto, accessed 15/4/2018). In Australia, the Portuguese tart (pastel de nata) is an example of a product manufactured and distributed by several Portuguese ethnic minority businesses in major cities, where the non-availability of the product was the major opportunity for the start-ups (Galletly, 2018; also see www.belembakery.com.au/).

2. Opportunities associated with diaspora transnational expansion strategies, such that service-products offered to a particular minority ethnic group in one country are offered to the equivalent group in another country.

    Commonly involving transnational family networks (Puig, 2015), examples include Vietnamese nail-shops in the UK (Bagwell, 2008), and the internationalization of ethnic minority businesses in Malaysia and Singapore (Mustafa and Chen, 2010). Chinese (Yeung, 2000) and or Indian family businesses (Tumbe, 2017) are examples resulting from these strategies.

3. Opportunities sponsored by government and by large corporations, such as banks, that emerge from the mass mobility of populations, with millions of people moving across the planet to take up new lives in new places. One example refers to the banking and investment services offered by a travel agent in Sydney, Australia, as a service to the Portuguese diaspora and as a means to facilitate Portuguese immigrants' remittance flows.

   Broader examples of a diaspora strategy include the building and facilitation of transnational business links, networks and partnerships, as in the case of Advance Australia, KEA New Zealand, the ScotsIn network, the Global Organisation of People of Indian Origin (GOPIO), Irishabroad.com and EuropeanIrish.com. Diaspora strategy is an explicit and systematic policy initiative, or series of policy initiatives, aimed at developing and managing relationships with a diaspora (Ancien, Boyle and Kitchin, 2009).

4. Essentially situational opportunities arising in the context of non-ethnic or open markets that may be unattractive to major suppliers (e.g. unstable, with low economies of scale, specific to the provision of ethnic goods) and markets that are underserved or have been abandoned by previous suppliers. This was noted in Chapter 7 as being consistent with the middleman minority theory, illustrated with the opening of a grocery store in an urban area where large grocery chains choose not to have a presence.

The implication is that, independently of how the opportunities came to be, the strategies and tactics to be deployed by ethnic minority businesses must depend on the context of the opportunity/ies being pursued, which may be highly variable. It is therefore important to clarify the type of business activities pursued by such businesses. To this end, a panel of experts in marketing and management issues was used to identify the various types of business activities likely to involve ethnic minority businesses.

Besides identifying seven types of business activities that may arise in the context of different types of opportunities, Table 10.3 also establishes the basic requirements for deciding whether a business is an ethnic minority business by reference both (1) to the type of business activities pursued by entrepreneurs' ascribed (by the self and by others) to a minority ethnic group or to the mainstream, and (2) to the dependence/independence on a minority ethnic group for deployment of the business activities.

Consistent with the conceptualization of an ethnic minority business forwarded in Chapter 7 of this text, the table shows that the decisive

Table 10.3 Basic Requirements for Ethnic Minority Business Identification

Business Activity	Owner /Operator	Business		Notes
	Perceived Ethnic Ascription	Depends on a MEG	Is an EMB?	
Delivery of service activity to a specific MEG	To a MEG	Yes No	Yes (*)	(*) Uncertain
	To mainstream	Yes No	No	
Delivery of service activity to the mainstream	To a MEG	Yes No	(*) No	(*) Uncertain
	To mainstream	Yes No	No	Scenario unlikely
Manufacture/ distribution/retail involving ethnic goods	To a MEG	Yes No	Yes (*)	(*) Uncertain
	To mainstream	Yes No	No	
Manufacture/ distribution/retail involving non-ethnic goods	To a MEG	Yes No	Yes (*)	(*) Uncertain
	To mainstream	Yes No	No	Scenario unlikely
Primary Producers/ Suppliers of ethnic produce	To the MEG	Yes No	Yes (*)	(*) Uncertain
	To mainstream	Yes No	No	
Import/export/ wholesaler of ethnic products	To a MEG	Yes No	Yes (*)	(*) Uncertain
	To mainstream	Yes No	No	
Mainstream franchise	To a MEG	Yes No	Yes No	Scenario unlikely
	To mainstream	Yes No	No	

MEG: Minority Ethnic Group
EMB: Ethnic Minority Business
(*) Uncertain—May involve expansion growth by an EMB and/or reliance on a MEG's supply.
Dependence on a MEG may be with respect to demand and/or supply and is a key factor.
Business size can be micro (most common), small (fairly common) or large (uncommon) and does not affect classification.
The table does not account for the extent of an EMB's actual dependency on a minority ethnic group, reducing objectivity. While a critical dependence level could be applied, this would be largely arbitrary and mostly theoretical due to a lack of information.

condition in unambiguously recognizing an ethnic minority business is whether the business activity is deployed by an owner-operator ascribed to a minority ethnic group and depends on a minority ethnic group's custom for success. All such cases are independent of the business activity that is deployed.

Also unambiguous are situations where the business activity is deployed by an owner-operator ascribed to the mainstream and does not depend on a minority ethnic group's custom for success. All such cases are equally independent of the business activity that is deployed and the relevant businesses are not ethnic minority businesses.

The table also shows that business activities deployed by owner-operators ascribed to a minority ethnic group may not depend on that group's custom for success, hence depending either on other minority ethnic groups, or their aggregate or on the mainstream. These cases are identified in the table as "uncertain" regarding the status of the business as an ethnic minority business, hence depending on context. In some cases, the business may have expanded outside the markets offered by minority ethnic groups, although the vast majority of the business characteristics remain consistent with those of ethnic minority businesses discussed in Chapter 7 (e.g. Table 7.2). Hence, provided the vast majority of challenges facing these businesses are congruent with those faced by ethnic minority businesses, it is appropriate for these businesses to maintain their ethnic minority business' status.

The Outgrowth Threshold

The cases of uncertainty identified in the table lend their support to the conceptualization of an *outgrowth threshold* that determines whether a business loses its ethnic minority connotation, depending on how dependent the business is on a minority ethnic group's demand and/or supply. When both of these are outgrown the business no longer meets the conditions to be classified as an ethnic minority business.

In practice, it is apparent that the decision about the outgrowth threshold must be context dependent (see an in-depth discussion of environmental forces that may limit ethnic minority business ability to outgrow the threshold in Chapter 14 of this text) and difficult to ascertain without primary research, justifying the relative subjectivity of the classification in Table 10.2. In some cases, ethnic entrepreneurs chose to shed their businesses' ethnic connotation as a means to overcome any real or perceived negative effects (such as prejudice, discrimination and stereotyping) due to consumer ethnocentrism (Balabanis and Diamantopoulos, 2004; Sharma, Shimp and Shin, 1994; Shimp and Sharma, 1987) when entering mainstream markets. It is well known that minority ethnic groups from distinct provenances may face different effects from ethnocentrism, including positive and negative bias. For example, there may be "haloing" biases based on whether their ethnic products are from developed or developing countries (Jiang et al., 2011; Han, Lee and Ro, 1994).

Ethnic Minority Business Customer Portfolio

The dependence of an ethnic minority business on a particular co-ethnic minority group does not imply that the business is not available to other customers, whether to other minority ethnic groups or the mainstream. Indeed, the very existence of an outgrowth threshold pre-empts that it is possible for these other customers to gain in importance over time, to a point where business' dependence on a co-ethnic group may effectively cease.

However, business independence from the co-ethnic group should not be seen as either unavoidable or time dependent. Many ethnic minority businesses, such as those serving the group with ethnic-specific service-products, are highly likely to remain co-ethnic group dependent. For other ethnic minority businesses, access to consumer segments lacking a shared ethnicity is likely to be unintended, unimportant and inconsequential to the adoption of more open business strategies. That is, demand by dissimilar others may not justify tailored strategies.

Nevertheless, there are case studies of ethnic entrepreneurs hoping to grow/expand their businesses into new markets or geographical areas. In a study of Albanian entrepreneurs in Greece involving 65 ethnic minority businesses relying on their group affiliation almost exclusively for employees and sales, 12 (19 percent) hoped to maintain their activity unchanged, and nine (14 percent) were intending to shut down. While 67 percent in the retail and manufacturing sectors aspired to grow, they faced tight margins and need for volume trade, both in terms of customer retention and acquisition. Of these, seven (10 percent) were considering diversification and 37 (57 percent) aspired to expansion into other markets (Halkias, 2017) while maintaining their ethnic minority business status due to continued dependence on the co-ethnic group. This is an important consideration because business affiliation with a minority ethnic group is necessary but insufficient for the business to maintain its ethnic minority status. Dependence on the group is required, hence the lesser importance afforded here to businesses depending on consumer segments lacking a shared ethnicity.

Why Adopt an Ethnic-Sensitive Relational Marketing Strategy?

Not all suppliers depending on their co-ethnic group become preferred suppliers to that group. Similar to small and medium enterprises in general, some ethnic minority businesses flourish, particularly those facing little competition, while others fail. While this is also a case in ethnic marketing where context matters, a justification for failure may be the implementation of ad hoc essentially transactional strategies, even more likely when lacking in ethnic sensitivity.

Clearly, co-ethnicity cannot be assumed to imply ethnic sensitivity. However, as established in previous chapters, ethnic minority businesses are naturally better positioned than other businesses to gain access to their co-ethnic group resources and networks, and to aspire at eventually achieving a position as a preferred supplier based on their performance. The complexity in this aspiration is that the loyalty of the co-ethnic group, which is what matters, is attained one consumer at a time, triggering a process of recommendation and feedback that brings the minority ethnic group, affiliated consumers and businesses together in an exclusive ethnic network (as depicted in Figures 9.1 and 9.2 in Chapter 9).

While it is entirely possible for individual consumers affiliated with the minority ethnic group to actively cease their affiliation (for example by returning to the home country or by moving outside the supplier area of reach), the likelihood is that their place in the group will be taken by co-ethnic newcomers. But even if replacement does not occur, the development of an effective ethnic network requires the existence of a consumer group of sufficient substantiality. Ultimately, it is the sustainability of the minority ethnic group that creates relational value for the supplier, a value that needs to be understood by the supplier and reciprocated to the group via the consumer, as reflected in the value proposition on offer.

The questions is: What are the skills, capabilities and competencies that ethnic minority businesses need to have so as to successfully target the co-ethnic group, via the affiliated consumers, with loyalty generating strategies? As noted in Chapter 9, the requirement is for extensive and rigorous information about the group and the business itself because relational marketing strategies involve mutually dependent investments by all parties in the relationship, hence requiring relational marketing tactics that derive mutual benefit to those parties. This benefit needs to be identified and assured.

A notable observation from the outset is that the marketing literature dealing with ethnic marketing strategy reveals a paucity of tactical activities that can be claimed as being unique to the context of minority ethnic groups. Our view is that that those activities may entail an emphasis on the "how" rather than the "what" of the adopted tactical approach. That is, while the ethnic marketing mix remains essentially unchanged (the eight 'P's remain the same), the eventual challenges faced by ethnic minority consumers provide the opportunity for tactical differentiation by the co-ethnic minority business, by means of ethnic-sensitive marketing practices embedded in a relational environment.

Figure 10.1 represents the embedding of types of tactical activities (the 8 'P's) into a relational tactical environment where business objectives are pursued by means of relational strategy (targeting the minority ethnic group, one co-ethnic consumer at a time), represented by the outer circle.

The inner circle includes eight types of tactical activities—product, promotion, place, price, physical evidence, people, process and personalization. Each type of activity is segmented between two arrows pointing outwards, indicating their contribution to the deployment of broad tactical activities that support a relational tactical positioning (the middle-circle) and, finally, combined to make up the relational strategy. The figure could also be interpreted as a top-down view of an octagonal pyramid, with the minority ethnic group at the top.

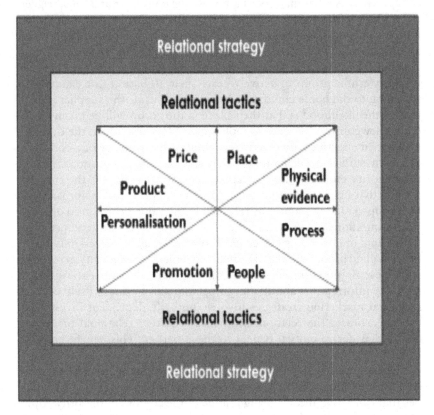

Figure 10.1 The Embedding of Tactical Activities Into a Relational Strategy

Relational Embedding of Ethnic-Sensitive Tactical Activities

The deployment of relational ethnic strategies by ethnic minority businesses depends on objectives that are set in the face of particular problems (e.g. information scarcity, need to deal with customers and suppliers, capital requirement issues, positioning versus competition) within a dynamic environment that characterizes the interaction over time between the contextual opportunity structures and the specific characteristics of the group and of the business, namely cultural traditions and ethnic network participation.

Established relationships are assets in a business' targeting decision, and the deployment of strategies to develop, establish and enhance relationships also can afford important relational benefits for consumers. But how to measure these assets and benefits remains a challenging task. In the case of businesses, Ang and Buttle (2002) identified four difficulties in calculating returns on investment from their relationships with customers related to: (1) defining the relationship boundaries, (2) defining what is considered as an investment, (3) deciding what the investment returns are and (4) setting a time frame for the assessment (see also Grönroos and Helle, 2012). A further challenge is to account for intangible factors outside the business control such as ethnic sensitivities, particularly because this is possibly what provides competitive advantage.

In the case of consumers, yields are calculated mostly based on subjective non-financial indicators that may vary from consumer to consumer and that may have an impact on consumer participation in the relationship with the supplier. Rather than consumers simply articulating their identification with ethnic networks in terms of economic advantage—such as a discounted price or prompt service—emphasis may be on ethnic loyalty encompassing altruistic feelings towards co-ethnic members in their group of affiliation—such as co-ethnic entrepreneurs and their businesses—invoking faith, ethnic purity or personal loyalty, all of which may be independent of suppliers' relational investments.

While the justification for the adoption of a relational strategy towards the minority ethnic group and affiliated consumers by an ethnic minority business has been amply justified, the complexity in the measurement of assets and benefits complicates the decision about which tactical activities should be implemented and justifies caution in their deployment, as well as careful monitoring for their success.

Given the relational imperative, ethnic minority businesses must consider tactical activities that support the deployment of a relational strategy toward the co-ethnic group (the middle-circle in Figure 10.1), but those activities should also be assessed on their merits and within good business practice principles. Ultimately, as for any other business, the purpose of the strategy and related tactics deployed by an ethnic minority business is first and foremost to meet business objectives.

Table 10.4 assembles a set of first order structural tactical activities that underpin the strategic relational imperative adopted by ethnic minority businesses towards co-ethnic consumers and, possibly, similar-others. The suggestion is that, while context is always relevant in ethnic marketing, the entries in the table are likely to have generalized application to ethnic minority businesses seeking to benefit from relational benefits.

The table is divided into four complementary sections. Primary focus is on the co-creation (with consumers and the minority ethnic group) of a derived relational value proposition. It is a derived value proposition because it is drawn from consumer and group demands. Given the relational investments that need to be made, returns are estimated in terms of lifetime value and take the group into account, rather than any particular consumer. That is, the value proposition is made stable by focusing on what is stable (the group) and reducing consumer heterogeneity. It is

Table 10.4 Relational Strategy—Tactical Activities

Relational Tactical Activities	
Value proposition	Devise a relational value proposition taking group lifetime value into account.
	Fiercely ensure value proposition upkeep and value over time—deliver on your promises.
	Ensure a stable value proposition by focusing on what is stable (the group) and reduce inter-consumers' dissonance.
	Continuously keep an eye on customer needs—evolutionary repositioning.
	Carry appropriate and consistent range of ethnic products relevant to the specific community. à Ethnic-sensitive behaviour.
	Sell branded products from country of origin. Do not push inferior products and do not incur into opportunistic price behaviour. ·
Loyalty generation	Loyalty schemes (reward cards to collect points and earn gifts).
	Use membership tactics to focus on maintenance contracts (rather than one-off interactions)—More frequent interactions keep you top of mind.
	Instil long-term loyalty through relationships building; Consider offering discounts (focus should be on value creation and maintenance).
	Offer phased-out payment terms and reward prompt-payment for membership promotions.
Interaction and communication	Make continued and consistent use of ethnic media (such as magazines, radio, newspapers, radio and television).
	Encourage and facilitate interactions with consumers by WOM.
	Develop professional relationships with all good consumers.
	Provide excellent and tireless service to all consumers.
Networking	Networking and clear customer service strategy.
	Keep links with local cultural and religious bodies e.g. community centres and mosques to demonstrate deep understanding of cultural values.

also differentiated by encompassing an appropriate and consistent range of ethnic service-products relevant to, and delivered in a manner that is appropriate for, the minority ethnic group.

The outcome from the development effort is a value proposition that must be fiercely guarded while acknowledging that the business operates in a dynamic environment and that consumers' needs and wants, as well as consumption behaviour, competition and even business objectives, change over time. Hence, businesses need mechanisms to detect the important changes in their environment and to enact any necessary updates in their proposition by adopting evolutionary repositioning strategies so as to maintain or even enhance its value over time, as well as maintaining or strengthening their competitive edge.

Overall, an ethnic minority business needs to always deliver on the promises inherent to its value proposition—for example by selling branded products from the home country—and rule out taking opportunistic advantage of consumers, for example by pushing inferior quality products or overcharging. Consumer satisfaction needs to be maintained at all times so as to avoid negative feedback to the group and to garner the group's custom and loyalty for the longer term. Loyalty generation is the focus of the second sector in Table 10.4.

Generating long-term loyalty involves building the relationship with the target market, preferably by deploying membership tactics conducive to increased value creation and increased barriers to exit. The focus of membership tactics is on frequent interactions with customers as opposed to one-off interactions. Hence, loyalty programs may be justified, enhancing value for the customer and for the business. Value for customers may accrue for example from earning gifts, benefiting from discounts and favourable terms of payment. Collecting loyalty points towards higher recognition is an important tactic for generating repeated interactions, but care needs to be taken to ensure that loyalty rewards are paid promptly and accurately. Benefits for businesses include more frequent interactions with target consumers which keep the business atop of those consumers' minds; however, care is needed to ensure a focus on value creation and maintenance. Providing professional, excellent, and tireless service to all consumers is fundamental, although development of long-term relationship investments should be only with good consumers,

In considering loyalty, it is also important to recall that relational strategies must be mutually beneficial if they are to be successful. Ethnic minority businesses need to demonstrate commitment and to generate trust, for example by:

- Delivering on promises;
- Openly recognizing and addressing exceptions; and
- Always getting customer approval before engaging in any chargeable repairs/Improvements.

More frequent interactions with consumers are also achieved by promoting effective and frequent communications. This may be achieved by making continued and consistent use of ethnic media (such as magazines, radio, newspapers, radio and television), and both encouraging and facilitating word of mouth communications with and between consumers.

Finally, effective network tactics, the fourth section in Table 10.4, can also add value for the business, for consumers and for the group by extending professional relationships to a social level, perhaps enhancing the profile of the ethnic minority business though community event sponsorship. Businesses can also exhibit shared ethnicity with consumers by keeping links with local cultural and religious bodies, such as community centres and mosques, to demonstrate deep understanding and sharing of cultural values.

Summary

By definition, ethnic minority businesses target their co-ethnic group via their co-ethnic consumers, depending on the group for their survival. Shared ethnicity, however, neither guarantees an appropriate understanding of which strategies and tactical activities are ethnic sensitive, nor does it guarantee business success. Understanding that ethnic minority businesses are just like any other business facing a somewhat protected market justifies a clear distinction between business objectives and subordinated strategies. Similarly, marketing objectives guide marketing strategies and related tactical activities.

This chapter highlighted the benefits that can accrue to all stakeholders (ethnic minority businesses, co-ethnic consumers and minority ethnic groups) from the deployment of relational strategies. While it is important to account for context, it is possible to identify tactical activities that are expected to apply to ethnic businesses seeking to adopt a relational approach to ethnic marketing. The next three chapters extend the discussion by examining tactical activities for each element of the marketing mix.

References

Achidi, H. and Priem, R. (2011). Immigrant entrepreneurs, the ethnic enclave strategy, and venture performance. *Journal of Management*, 37(3), 790–818.

Aldrich, H. and Waldinger, R. (1990). Ethnicity and entrepreneurship. *Annual Review of Sociology*, 16, 111–135.

Anas, A. (2004). Ethnic segregation and ghettos. *A Companion to Urban Economics*, 94–122.

Ancien, D., Boyle, M. and Kitchin, R. (2009). Exploring diaspora strategies: An international comparison. *Workshop Report*, June. Accessed 14/4/2018 at http://eprints.maynoothuniversity.ie/2053/1/RK_Exploring_Diaspora_Strategies_International_Comparison.pdf

Ang, L. and Buttle, F. (2002). ROI on CRM: A customer-journey approach. *Proceedings, IMP Conference*, December, Perth, Australia.

Bagwell, S. (2008). Transnational family networks and ethnic minority business development: The case of Vietnamese nail-shops in the UK. *International Journal of Entrepreneurial Behavior & Research*, 14(6), 377–394.

Balabanis, G. and Diamantopoulos, A. (2004). Domestic country bias, country-of-origin effects, and consumer ethnocentrism: A multidimensional unfolding approach. *Journal of the Academy of Marketing Science*, 32(1), 80–95.

Basu, A. (1998). An exploration of entrepreneurial activity among Asian small businesses in Britain. *Small Business Economics*, 10, 313–326.

Beckinsale, M. and Ram, M. (2006). Delivering ICT to ethnic minority businesses: An action-research approach. *Environment and Planning C: Government and Policy*, 24(6), 847–867.

Begley, T. and Boyd, D. (1987). Psychological characteristics associated with performance in entrepreneurial firms and smaller businesses. *Journal of Business Venturing*, 2(1), 79–93.

Blackburn, R. and Smallbone, D. (2014). Sustaining self-employment for disadvantaged entrepreneurs. *Background paper for the OECD Centre for Entrepreneurship*, SMEs and Local Development.

Butler, J. and Greene (1997). Ethnic entrepreneurship: The continuous rebirth of American enterprise. In D. L Sexton and R. W. Smilor (eds.), *Entrepreneurship 2000*. Chicago, IL: Upstart Publishing Co., 267–289.

Carter, S., Mwaura, S., Ram, M., Trehan, K. and Jones, T. (2015). Barriers to ethnic minority and women's enterprise: Existing evidence, policy tensions and unsettled questions. *International Small Business Journal*, 33(1), 49–69.

Carter, S., Ram, M., Trehan, K. and Jones, T. (2013). Diversity and SMEs. *Enterprise Research Center White Paper* (3), 13.

Chwolka, A. and Raith, M. (2012). The value of business planning before start-up: A decision-theoretical perspective. *Journal of Business Venturing*, 27(3), 385–399.

Cook, R., Campbell, D. and Kelly, C. (2012). Survival rates of new firms: An exploratory study. *Small Business Institute Journal*, 8(2), 35–42.

Corley, K. and Gioia, D. (2011). Building theory about theory building: What constitutes a theoretical contribution? *Academy of Management Review*, 36(1), 12–32.

Coutant, F. (1938). President's annual report. *Journal of Marketing*, 2(April), 269–271.

Demangeot, C., Broderick, A. and Craig, C. (2015). Multicultural marketplaces: New territory for international marketing and consumer research. *International Marketing Review*, 32(2), 118–140.

The Economist (2013). A new kind of ghetto. *Special Report*, November 9. Accessed 25/6/2018 at www.economist.com/special-report/2013/11/09/a-new-kind-of-ghetto

Ekanem, I. and Wyer, P. (2007). A fresh start and the learning experience of ethnic minority entrepreneurs. *International Journal of Consumer Studies*, 31(2), 144–151.

Evans, M. (1989). Immigrant entrepreneurship: Effects of ethnic market size and isolated labor pool. *American Sociological Review*, 950–962.

Galletly, J. (2018). The story behind Adelaide's first real deal Portuguese tarts. *Adelaide Now*, January 23. Accessed 21/6/2018 at www.adelaidenow.com.au/thesourcesa/the-story-behind-adelaides-first-real-deal-portuguese-tarts/news-story/79d57ea1cd4801eba1d54cd29dfe5674

Gaskill, L., Van Auken, H. and Manning, R. (1993). A factor analytic study of the perceived causes of small business failure. *Journal of Small Business Management*, 31(4), 18.

Grönroos, C. and Helle, P. (2012). Return on relationships: Conceptual understanding and measurement of mutual gains from relational business engagements. *Journal of Business & Industrial Marketing*, 27(5), 344–359.

Halkias, D. (2017). Characteristics and business profiles of immigrant owned small firms: The case of Albanian immigrant entrepreneurs in Greece. *UC San Diego Working Papers*. Accessed 29/6/2018 at https://cloudfront.escholarship.org/dist/prd/content/qt0983g0w5/qt0983g0w5.pdf

Han, C., Lee, B. and Ro, K. (1994). The choice of a survey mode in country image studies. *Journal of Business Research*, 29(2), 151–162.

Helm, B. (2010). Ethnic marketing: McDonald's is lovin' it. *Bloomberg*, July 9. Accessed 21/5/2018 at www.bloomberg.com/news/articles/2010-07-08/ethnic-marketing-mcdonalds-is-lovin-it

Holbrook, M. (2008). Compromise is so . . . compromised: Goldilocks, go home. *European Business Review*, 20(6), 570–578.

Iyer, G. and Shapiro, J. (1999). Ethnic entrepreneurial and marketing systems: Implications for the global economy. *Journal of International Marketing*, 83–110.

Jiang, C. X., Chua, R. Y., Kotabe, M. and Murray, J. Y. (2011). Effects of cultural ethnicity, firm size, and firm age on senior executives' trust in their overseas business partners: Evidence from China. *Journal of International Business Studies*, 42(9), 1150–1173.

Jones, T., McEvoy, D. and Barrett, G. (1992). *Small Business Initiative: Ethnic Minority Component*. Swindon: ESRC.

Jones, T., Ram, M. and Edwards, P. (2006). Ethnic minority business and the employment of illegal immigrants. *Entrepreneurship and Regional Development*, 18(2), 133–150.

Komakech, M. and Jackson, S. (2016). A study of the role of small ethnic retail grocery stores in urban renewal in a social housing: Project, Toronto, Canada. *Journal of Urban Health: Bulletin of the New York Academy of Medicine*, 93(3), 414–424.

Kumar, N. and Steenkamp, J. (2013). Diaspora marketing. *Harvard Business Review*, 91(10), 127.

Laroche, M., Chung, K. and Clarke, M. (1997). The effects of ethnicity factors on consumer deal interests: An empirical study of French- and English-Canadians. *Journal of Marketing Theory and Practice*, 5(1), 100–112.

Lazaridis, G. and Koumandraki, M. (2003). Survival ethnic entrepreneurs in Greece: A mosaic of informal and formal business activities. *Sociological Research Online*, 8(2), 1–12.

Levine, B. (1985). The capital of Latin America, *Wilson Q*, 9, 47–69.

Lim, J. and Reid, D. (1992). Vital cross-functional linkages with marketing. *Industrial Marketing Management*, 21(2), 159–165.

Lindridge, A. (2015). Market segmentation by ethnicity: Is it really feasible? *The Routledge Companion to Ethnic Marketing*, 235–253.

Littunen, H. (2000). Entrepreneurship and the characteristics of the entrepreneurial personality. *International Journal of Entrepreneurial Behavior & Research*, 6(6), 295–310.

Martin, A. (2004). Addressing the gap between theory and practice: IT project design. *Journal of Information Technology Theory and Application*, 6(2), 23–42.

Masurel, E., Nijkamp, P., Tastan, M. and Vindigni, G. (2002). Motivations and performance conditions for ethnic entrepreneurship. *Growth and Change*, 33(2), 238–260.

Masurel, E., Nijkamp, P. and Vindigni, G. (2004). Breeding places for ethnic entrepreneurs: A comparative marketing approach. *Entrepreneurship & Regional Development*, 16, 77–86.

Mata, J. and Portugal, P. (1994). Life duration of new firms. *Journal of Industrial Economics*, 42(3), 227–245.

Mendy, J. and Hack-Polay, D. (2018). Learning from failure: A study of failed enterprises of self-employed African migrants in the UK. *Journal of Small Business and Enterprise Development*, 25(2), 330–343.

Morales, M. (2008). The ethnic niche as an economic pathway for the dark skinned: Labor market incorporation of Latina/o workers. *Hispanic Journal of Behavioral Sciences*, 30(3), 280–298.

Mustafa, M. and Chen, S. (2010). The strength of family networks in transnational immigrant entrepreneurship. *Thunderbird International Business Review*, 52(2), 97–106.

Okazaki, S. and Sue, S. (1995). Methodological issues in assessment research with ethnic minorities. *Psychological Assessment*, 7(3), 367.

Perry, S. (2001). The relationship between written business plans and the failure of small businesses in the US. *Journal of Small Business Management*, 39(3), 201–208.

Phillips, D. (2013). Minority ethnic segregation, integration and citizenship: A European perspective. In *Linking Integration and Residential Segregation*. Abingdon, UK: Routledge, pp. 49–66.

Phizacklea, A. and Ram, M. (1996). Being your own boss: Ethnic minority entrepreneurs in comparative perspective. *Work, Employment & Society*, 10(2), 319–339.

Pires, G. (1999). Domestic cross-cultural marketing in Australia: A critique of the segmentation rationale. *Journal of Marketing Theory and Practice*, 7(4), 33–44.

Pires, G. and Stanton, J. (2015). *Ethnic Marketing: Culturally Sensitive Theory and Practice*. New York City, NY, USA: Taylor and Francis.

Pires, G., Stanton, J. and Stanton, P. (2011). Revisiting the substantiality criterion: From ethnic marketing to market segmentation. *Journal of Business Research*, 64(9), 988–996.

Podoshen, J. (2009). Distressing events and future purchase decisions: Jewish consumers and the holocaust. *Journal of Consumer Marketing*, 26(4), 263–276.

Portes, A. (1987). The social origins of the Cuban enclave economy of Miami. *Sociological Perspectives*, 30, 340–372.

Puig, N. (2015). Brokering trust: The construction of transnational family business networks, 1980–2010. *Jahrbuch für Wirtschaftsgeschichte/Economic History Yearbook*, 56(1), 21–45.

Ram, M., Jones, T. and Villares-Varela, M. (2017). Migrant entrepreneurship: Reflections on research and practice. *International Small Business Journal*, 35(1), 3–18.

Rust, R., Lemon, K. and Zeithaml, V. (2004). Return on marketing: Using customer equity to focus marketing strategy. *Journal of Marketing*, 68(1), 109–127.

Sarri, K. and Trihopoulou, A. (2005). Female entrepreneurs' personal characteristics and motivation: A review of the Greek situation. *Women in Management Review*, 20(1), 24–36.

Serrão, J. (1977). *A emigração Portuguesa*, 3rd ed. Lisbon: Livros Horizonte.

Sharma, S., Shimp, T. and Shin, J. (1994). Consumer ethnocentrism: A test of antecedents and moderators. *Journal of the Academy of Marketing Science*, 23(1), 26–37.

Shimp, T. and Sharma, S. (1987). Consumer ethnocentrism: Construction and validation of the CETSCALE. *Journal of Marketing Research*, 280–289.

Simpson, L. and Akinwale, B. (2007). Quantifying stability and change in ethnic group. *Journal of Official Statistics*, 23(2), 185.

Tumbe, C. (2017). Transnational Indian business in the twentieth century. *Business History Review*, 1–29.

Vorhies, D. and Morgan, N. (2003). A configuration theory assessment of marketing organization fit with business strategy and its relationship with marketing performance. *Journal of Marketing*, 67(1), 100–115.

Walks, R. and Bourne, L. (2006). Ghettos in Canada's cities? Racial segregation, ethnic enclaves and poverty concentration in Canadian urban areas. *The Canadian Geographer/Le Géographe Canadien*, 50(3), 273–297.

Williams, C. (2009). The motives of off-the-books entrepreneurs: Necessity-or opportunity-driven? *International Entrepreneurship and Management Journal*, 5(2), 203.

Yeung, H. (2000). Limits to the growth of family-owned business? The case of Chinese transnational corporations from Hong Kong. *Family Business Review*, 13(1), 55–70.

Yinger, J. (1985). Ethnicity. *Annual Review of Sociology*, 11, 151–180.

Yusuf, A. (1995). Critical success factors for small business: Perceptions of South Pacific entrepreneurs. *Journal of Small Business Management*, 33(2), 68.

An Alternative View of Ethnic Minority Business

Sivaram Vemuri[1]

The structure, conduct and performance of the unit of inquiry depends on the terminology used. I believe the adopted methodological framework defines the parameters and creates boundaries for any discussion.

I prefer the use of EFB (Ethnic Focused Business), EB (Ethnic Business) and EMB (Ethnic Migrant Business), especially if the focus of inquiry is on the current ethnic minority populations engaging in business of their ethnicity. I give two reasons:

1. The term minority has a connotation of being static. In reality the dynamism of population movements from one ethnic background imposes changes to the ethnic composition in a country such as Australia. For instance, the ABS data on the shift in percentage of people born to overseas parents suggests that minority businesses may not remain a minority for a long period of time.
2. The focus on the minority restricts the method of inquiry so that businesses face a ceiling that inevitably prevents them from becoming mainstream businesses. There will be boundaries imposed on the growth of the firm. If this is not intentional my preference would be similar to that of EMB.

Furthermore, the analysis will depend on what is being discussed—the formation of the firm or the engagement of the ethnic entrepreneur in an already established business.

Using the Marketing Mix and to Establish "Ethnic Authenticity"

Drawing from the extensive literature on diasporas and business, ethnic authenticity is manifested in a variety of forms. For instance, ethnic cuisine is diverse. So the notion of "sameness" and "differences" emerge at the same time as one considers the authenticity of the nature of business in the cuisine field.

In short, the contemporary focus of inquiry is shifting from considering ethnic business in isolation of the mainstream and also independent of the influences of features of country of residence (COR) and country of origin (COO). Incorporating the mainstream as well as country specific issues, what is emerging is the notion of "same thing but different". It is in this context this vignette is a brief foray into the future research agenda.

Same Thing But Different

When considering ethnicity in the COR, it is the individual's innate characteristics, pre- and post-migration experiences as well as issues related to settlements that shape an individual's perception of reality. This informs the appropriateness of the framework for examining ethnic authenticity. As a result, one needs to present a suitable framework to be able to interpret the reality and decisions made by the individual in the ethnic business.

In discussing the links between ethnicity and business, the focus of inquiry should be broad and should incorporate the eight elements of the marketing mix to establish and maintain ethnic authenticity. These elements influence the decisions made by ethnic individuals in discussing ethnic business. Therefore, researchers need to pay attention to these in their investigations.

1. Product/Service—The question to be considered is how can ethnic develop products/ services? To answer this question researchers need to investigate some of the influencing factors: quality, image, branding, features of product/service, variants of the product/service, mix, support, customer service, use occasion, availability, warranties and familiarity.
2. Promotion—How can ethnic add value to/substitute through a combination of paid, owned and earner media channel? Similarly factors that ethnic takes into consideration in making these decisions are: existing marketing communications, ability for personal promotion as well as sales promotion, PR, branding and direct marketing.
3. Price—How can the price of the established product or service be altered? Investigation that accounts for ethnic involvement includes positioning, discounts, credit, payment methods and free or value-added elements at the disposal of ethnic entrepreneur.
4. Place/Access—What new distribution options are there for customers to experience the product/service? To answer this, ethic entrepreneur focusses on the following—trade channels, sales support and number of channels as well as if these are segmented or not.
5. People—Who are "our" people? Are there skills gaps? The answer and hence the emphasis will be on characteristics of individuals in marketing activities, individuals with customer contacts, recruitment, culture/image, training and skills and remuneration.

6. Process—What are the processes that ethnic businesses employ? Is it customer focus/business-led focus? Is the business IT supported and to what extent? What are the design features of the business? And the whole research and development process underpinning the business comes under consideration.

7. Physical Evidence—How can the EB reassure its customers? This depends on sales/staff contact and experience of brand, product packaging and online presence and experience.

8. Partners—As stated earlier here I would be examining the whole question of whether EB is seeking new partners or managing existing partners or both. This depends on the structure of the firm—sole, family owned, etc.

Note

1. Dr Sivaram Vemuri is an Associate Professor of Economics at Charles Darwin University (CDU). He has published extensively in the area of applied economics emphasizing the importance of economic contribution by humans rather than capital and finance. His work includes Silence in Organizations, Economic migration and formation of Diasporas, Economic pluralism, Refugee entrepreneurship and the intersections of multiculturalism and ethics.

References

Masurel, E., Nijkamp, P., Tastan, M. and Vindigni, G. (2002). Motivations and performance conditions for ethnic entrepreneurship. *Growth and Change*, 33(2), 238–260.

Pires, G. and Stanton, J. (2017). The articulation of ethnic entrepreneurship with ethnic marketing. *Paper presented at the 31st Business and Economic Society International Conference*, Crete (Greece), July 6–9.

Ram, M. (1994). Unravelling social networks in ethnic minority firms. *International Small Business Journal*, April–June, 12(3), 42–59.

Vemuri, S. (2015). Economics and diaspora. In T. Vekemans and N. Miletic (eds.), *Discovering Diaspora: A Multidisciplinary Approach*. Oxford: Inter-Disciplinary Press, pp. 24–33.

11 Product, Price, Place, Physical Evidence and Process

It is well documented in the marketing and psychology literatures that consumer attitudes and purchase intentions are influenced by ethnicity (Luedicke, 2011; Papadopoulos et al., 2008; Ouellet, 2007), with effects that help to predict and understand the decision-making process of ethnic consumers (Podoshen, 2009). Consumers sharing a similar ethnic background also share their consumption behaviours (El Banna et al., 2018; Balasubramanian and Herche, 1994), and, as discussed in Chapter 9 of this text, the sharing is extensive to consumers' long-term endorsement of community preferred suppliers.

The implication is that, as associations of self-ascribed and group recognized individuals sharing one ethnicity with a common cultural tradition and a sense of identity (Connor, 1978) minority ethnic groups offer potentially attractive opportunities for business that are sensitive to the ethnicity attributes binding the consumers making up the target market. Since these markets are protected by ethnicity-related entry barriers, built on culturally based tastes of ethnic minorities that, arguably, can be best served by co-ethnic businesses (Aldrich et al., 1985; Light, 1972), entry deterrence of competitors unable to overcome those barriers can lessen competitive pressures. Given ethnic minority businesses' embedding in their co-ethnic group, such businesses arise as particularly suited to take advantage of the emergent business opportunities.

Always acknowledging possible contextual effects, Chapters 5 and 10 of this text identified the challenge facing ethnic minority businesses as to devise ethnic marketing tactical activities which are ethnic sensitive and which focus on the establishment, maintenance and enhancement of desired long-term relationships with co-ethnic consumers.

This chapter discusses tactical activities for five of the elements of the marketing mix, namely product, price, place, physical evidence and process. Two other elements, promotion and personalization, are discussed in Chapter 12, while Chapter 13 accounts for people, including ethical behaviour and social responsibility.

The Product Element: Considering Tangibility and Perceived Risk

Ethnic minority consumers' behavioural uniqueness may involve choice difficulties that constrain their exchanges in the host country's markets. These include language difficulties and ensuing limited exposure to mass media; a lack of time, money and marketplace knowledge to search out and evaluate information about service-products and suppliers; and possible unfamiliarity with available brands as well as preference for familiar ethnic brands. From the business perspective, ability to reach these consumers may be limited by their own difficulties in understanding and communicating with different cultures, and by their possible unfamiliarity with ethnic communication networks (Laroche, Kim and Clarke, 1997; Kaufman, 1991). This converts into potential advantage for ethnic minority businesses targeting co-ethnic consumers.

Service activities are sufficiently different from tangible goods to justify research on how the differences may impact on service-product consumption by ethnic minority consumers. Consumption can be complicated by their restricted ability to read product literature and discomfort in consulting with service staff. Inexperience within the marketplace and differences in meanings and contexts are exacerbated by reduced service-product awareness due to perishability and, in comparison with mainstream consumers, increased perceived risk due to limited access to sources of information, more subjective assessment of value and quality and difficulty in participating in service-encounters.

The noted difficulties arguably lead to increased post-purchase evaluation, less information gathering from the front-stage, increased dependence on service providers, reduced incentive for extensive information search and to switch suppliers, and loyalty (Pires and Stanton, 2000). Implicitly, therefore, difficulties facing ethnic minority consumers and marketers trying to reach them may be a function of the degree of tangibility, greater for exchanges involving services rather than physical goods. But this is a conclusion that merits revisiting relative to the untested possibility that ethnicity can convert search and experience service-products into credence ones. For example, sardines and bottled water are tangible food items. Sardines imported from Portugal are better appreciated and more sought after by the Portuguese community in Australia. The community also remains supportive of an import co-ethnic business that distributes a variety of bottled water from Portugal.

Tangibility refers to the physical nature of the core product, the basic, generic central thing that is exchanged (Levitt, 1997). Goods may be displayed and examined by prospective purchasers often without interaction with the provider being necessary, providing the consumer "with the opportunity to make physical comparisons and to set standards on which to make purchase decisions" (Hartman and Lindgren Jr., 1993). In contrast, intangibility emphasizes services as performances resulting in experiences, so that a service may be argued "to have no existence apart from the interaction between the people, both provider and consumer, who experience the service together" (Friedman and Smith, 1993). People interactions reflect the inseparability characteristic of exchanges involving intangible service-products.

Service-products vary in their tangibility (Lovelock, 1996; Rothmell, 1966; Shostack, 1977), arguably in a continuum from highly tangible dominant to highly intangible-dominant (Zeithaml and Bitner, 2000). Whether the service-products are more or less difficult to evaluate by consumers is a quality inversely related to the dominance of their tangible element. Highly tangible service-products, such as groceries, are likely to be high in *search qualities* associated with some characteristic (e.g. appearance, colour or smell) that can be predetermined before purchasing takes place. Service-products that involve characteristics that can only be discerned after purchase or during consumption (e.g. taste and ease of handling) are likely to be high in *experience qualities* (Nelson, 1970). At the highly intangible end of the continuum, service-products may be impossible to evaluate even after consumption. Including activities (such as education, legal and medical services) involving a high degree of techno-professional specialization and expertise commonly out of reach to general consumers. These service-products are said to be high in *credence qualities* (Darby and Karni, 1973).

High tangibility offers consumers in general the ability to make physical comparisons across service-products, even if physical comparison may not always be sufficient to evaluate a complex product conclusively, or to choose between brands. If these consumers need to interact with co-ethnic service staff, as when learning how to use/consume an "ethnic" product, they may gain reassurance from peers as well as the added benefit from their ability to peruse appropriate service-product literature in their own language (Pires, Stanton and Stanton, 2004). Hence these consumers may experience lower perceived risk compared with what would be the case if interaction was with service staff without a shared ethnicity (Montoya and Briggs, 2013; Murray 1991).

From a business perspective, there may be a lower need for free trials or for "satisfaction or money back" guarantees. However, Montoya and Briggs (2013) show that

> shared ethnicity affects consumers' expectations of exchanging particularistic resources and receiving preferential treatment benefits (and) high levels of ethnic identification appear to promote in-group favoritism.
>
> (p 314)

Intangibility, personalization (referring to the social content between customer and service provider, discussed in Chapter 12) and the limited ability to replicate service performance associated with service-product heterogeneity all can be expected to limit ethnic minority consumers' objective ability to evaluate service-product quality (Mittal and Lassar, 1996). Hence, customer satisfaction and repeat patronage may be determined solely by the quality of the interaction during the personal encounter (Solomon et al., 1985, p. 100). For example, if evaluating quality for medical service-products is more difficult than for childcare service-products, there is a need for greater consumer perceived provider credibility in the first case, to ensure satisfying service-encounters.

The implication is that risk-reducing information by the business is likely to be highly valued, particularly for relatively intangible service-products, such that ethnic minority consumers may have no incentive to search for new information sources (or new suppliers) because to change partners is to reestablish risk (Bendapudi and Berry, 1997). It is thus justified to develop tactical activities focused on consumer perceptions regarding service quality and perceived value of a service-product. While ethnic minority consumers may rely on provider credibility as a major choice criterion, they are not passive when faced with poor service, inconvenience and/or overpricing.

Pires, Stanton and Stanton (2004)'s study of the Portuguese community in Sydney found that ethnic minority consumers value continuing relationships with suppliers, more so in the provision of service-products in the credence class. Habituation to the supplier is the most valued attribute in this class. But business attention to ensuring continued value creation also should strengthen relationships with consumers. For example, tactical activities that facilitate socialization between co-ethnic consumers within service delivery frontstages is recommended in relation to service-products high in experience qualities. This has been recognized as influencing customer relationship maintenance (Sheth and Parvatiyar, 1995), which is consistent with Brand and Cronin's (1997) observation that consumers of highly intangible service-products, high in credence qualities, tend to exhibit a great propensity to maintain long-term relationships with providers.

It is apparent that the discussion of tangibility fully supports the argument for tactical activities enacted by ethnic minority business to be embedded in a relational marketing environment, as discussed in Chapter 10. Tangibility matters: different service-products with different tangibility will have specific circumstances that need to be taken into account by providers in devising and implement tactical activities. Also, individual exchanges of service-products are not assessed in isolation but within a continuation of past exchanges likely to continue in the future (Bendapudi and Berry, 1997).

Approach to the Discussion of the Tactical Ethnic Marketing Mix

The tactical activities for each of the eight elements of the ethnic marketing mix to be deployed by ethnic minority business are included in

Chapters 11 to 13, one table for each element. The inclusions in these tables are neither arbitrary nor to be taken lightly. Rather, from a demand perspective, decisions on each activity need to be subject to careful analysis of the context characterizing the market(s) to be targeted, including information about:

- The entrepreneur's minority ethnic group of affiliation: socio-economic status, demographic and psychographic print, relevant regional characteristics of consumption in the country of provenance, the minority ethnic group's substantiality given that it is likely to be heterogeneous within itself (Kwok and Uncles, 2005), how close-knit the community is and factors of community distinctiveness relative to co-ethnic communities at distinct locations;
- Other minority ethnic groups co-located with the entrepreneur's group of affiliation: demographic and psychographic print, similarity in needs and wants across minority ethnic groups, relative substantiality, ethnic engagement;
- Other consumer groups that may offer targeting opportunities: demographics, substantiality, cross-target compatibility, group engagement.

From a supply perspective, the competitive environment needs to be well understood, both in terms of the range of service-products on offer and the characteristics of the direct suppliers—those who interact with consumers—independently of their association with the entrepreneur's co-ethnic group of affiliation. Particular attention should be given to learning from those suppliers endowed by community preference (see Chapter 9), particularly by recognizing the preferred suppliers to the community and the determinant factors of community preference.

Also relevant is an audit of community resources for each target market, including major gatekeepers, the range of service-products on offer and ethnic supplier networks. A minority ethnic group's ethnic resources can be an effective external indicator of group substantiality (Pires and Stanton, 2015, 2005).

Once the strategic objectives for identified target markets are identified, an ethnic minority business can proceed to consider the tactics to be deployed for achieving the objectives. This chapter first discusses product-related tactical activities.

Product

The product element refers to the core service-products that are offered to the market, augmented with value added features, branding and packaging as well as service and any warranties. Table 11.1 identifies product-related tactical activities, drawn from observation, own experience and from recommendations in the specialist literature. Given the importance

Table 11.1 Tactical Activities by Ethnic Minority Businesses—Product

---

Marketing Mix—Product Related Tactics

Consider the attributes of the value proposition that are best valued by ethnic consumers and relate that perception of value to consumers' strength of ethnic identification with the ethnic group. Research shows that the Hispanic community in the USA exhibited a direct relationship between ethnic identification strength and the likelihood of preferential consumption from co-ethnic service providers and for brands used by family and friends, with a lesser concern about economic value.

Consider evidence from the UK that that cultural differences do not explain preference for grocery brands, although ethnic minority consumers appear less concerned with country of origin than mainstream consumers.

Carry an appropriate range of ethnic products relevant to the specific community. Consider including other relevant and some mainstream products.

Sell branded products originating from country of origin.

Sell branded products specially developed for ethnic minorities in the host country.

Sell special pack sizes only suitable for consumption by ethnic minorities.

Sell product range unavailable via mainstream outlets.

Sell a range of famous and non-famous brands.

Consider any service-products characterized by credence attributes that may be embodied in the provider.

Consider opportunities to appeal to dissimilar markets, such as occasional customers from distinct consumer groups. This may involve the provision of exotic (from the mainstream perspective) service-products, of service-products from the country of origin of the minority ethnic group, as well as a range of convenience products sought after by customers in general.

---

of the nature of the service-product, reflected in the discussion of intangibility and perceived risk above, the table is conspicuous for the reduced number of entries, but this ensues from the attempt to identify types of activities that may be generalizable to a variety of contexts, rather than simply listing instances of activities deployed in very specific contexts.

The first entry refers to the effect of strength of ethnic consumer identification with a minority ethnic group in the preference for co-ethnic service providers and for brands used by family and friends, above economic value concerns. This finding was derived in the context of Hispanic communities in the USA (Donthu and Cherian, 1994) and may not apply in different contexts or over time. This is also the case of evidence from the UK—that cultural differences do not explain preferences for grocery brands, although ethnic minority consumers appear less concerned with country of origin than mainstream consumers (Omar, Hirst and Blankson, 2004). Both cases identify issues that are deemed sufficiently important to be given consideration by ethnic minority business in general, providing guidance on what the business should be taking into account when devising product-related tactical activities.

Most of ethnic minority businesses' product-related tactical activities in the table were identified by Jamal (2005) in the context of the UK. Attention is predominantly on the type of products to offer focusing on their ethnic nature as compared with mainstream products. Attention is also given to the consumer and product constellation, referring to the products co-ethnic consumers consume (Solomon and Buchanan, 1991) based on their emotional dispositions (Flight and Coker, 2016). Emphasis is given to making available an appropriate range of ethnic products relevant to the specific co-ethnic community, although also considering other relevant and some mainstream products (Jamal, 2005).

Accordingly, it is recommended that business should include branded products originating from the home country (Al Ganideh and Al Taee, 2012), products specially developed for ethnic minorities in the host country, including a range of famous and non-famous brands. Consideration should be given to a possible need for special pack sizes only suitable for consumption by ethnic minorities, as well as for a relevant range of products unavailable via mainstream outlets. The reasoning is to nurture consumer dependence by catering for the special needs of the targeted clientele, hence enhancing the relationship with the market.

A final entry in Table 11.1 may be particularly relevant in serving consumers who don't share the business ethnicity. For example, the provision of exotic (from the mainstream perspective) service-products, of service-products from the country of origin of the minority ethnic group, may appeal to consumers who don't share the business ethnicity, whether mainstream or similar-others (McClintock, Novie and Gebhardt, 2017; Parzer, Astleithner and Rieder, 2016; Aldrich and Waldinger, 1990).

Reflecting on the product-related activities, and similar to considerations of pricing tactics which are discussed next, it appears plausible to consider that technologic development, greater availability to all business and convergence across markets may have a role to play in the differentiation tactics available to of ethnic minority businesses. Even in the context of ethnic minority business, and to ethnic products in general, availability might depend more on computer literacy and on the ability to use the Internet, than on ethnic entrepreneurship related supply. Accordingly, Ulaga and Eggert (2006) report that product quality, delivery performance and economics have become only moderate supplier differentiators, price being the weakest, with service support and personal interaction benefits exhibiting a much stronger potential as core supplier differentiators. But, again, the matter of context cannot be set aside. That study addressed a business-to-business environment and more recent research in a business to consumer environment highlighted competitive pricing as the second most important ethnic-related attribute after delivery performance (Huang, Oppewal and Mavondo,

2013). As noted in Chapter 6, this is an area clearly requiring further research.

Price

Often related to the business position in the market, the price element in the marketing mix refers to the setting of prices for service-products on offer, including all the parts that make up overall cost. Table 11.2 lists price related tactical activities meriting consideration by ethnic minority businesses in targeting co-ethnic consumers. Again, most tactical activities in the table were identified by Jamal (2005) in the UK context.

Since minority ethnic groups can be expected to be heterogeneous within themselves a customer portfolio comprising different segments of co-ethnic consumers may result from the segmentation process and targeting decision. Presuming the requirements for effective market segmentation have been met, each segment that is selected for targeting requires a distinctive value proposition, and this may or may not involve distinct price related tactical activities, depending on the proposition attributes that are identified as important and as determinant, and on the business capabilities and competencies (Nagle and Müller, 2017).

The recurring recommendation in the specialist literature is that ethnic minority business should consider following a differentiated pricing strategy (Ibrahim and Galt, 2011; Blankson and Stokes, 2002), while generally keeping prices low, which is often the case for generic or unproven

Table 11.2 Tactical Activities by Ethnic Minority Businesses—Price

Marketing Mix—Pricing Related Tactics
Consider following a differentiated pricing strategy.
Keep the overall prices down.
Sell famous brands at a premium and non-famous brands at low prices.
Subject to reflecting additional value creation, premium pricing may be possible.
Use pricing as a promotional tool (cut prices on vegetables and fruit).
Take into account that research in Australia has found that ethnicity does not have a significant impact on responses to sales promotions.
For service-products in the search class, price needs to remain competitive, since consumers can easily shop around and compare essentially tangible service-products, even before they make a purchase.
Service-products in the credence class are complex and difficult to evaluate even after consumption. While this may suggest that price is much less important, this may not be the case because minority ethnic consumers condition their price evaluations in this class on their assessment of service quality. If performance is perceived positively, then price may not be a concern. If the performance is perceived negatively, then price provides an excuse for switching suppliers, even when the consumer lacks the technical expertise to assess performance quality.

service-products (Labrianidis and Hatziprokopiou, 2010; Ward, 2005; Aldrich and Waldinger, 1990). But it is also considered that premium pricing may be possible in the case of famous or well recognized and proven service-products or brands, provided the value proposition that is delivered reflects commensurate value creation. In any case, care needs to be taken with changes in the supplementary benefits surrounding the core product, such as price, particularly when seeking to maintain or enhance relationships with consumers for the long term, as is the case for ethnic minority business.

Charging different prices for equivalent value propositions, particularly when consumers share the same front-stage, is fraught with difficulty and can compromise trust and commitment, ultimately compromising loyalty (Han and Ryu, 2009). Hence, it is important to note that while it is recommended that ethnic minority businesses should consider using lower prices as a promotional tool, for example cutting prices of consumables such as vegetables and fruit, it has been found that at least in Australia ethnicity does not have a significant impact on responses to sales promotions (Kwok and Uncles, 2005). Hence, the effectiveness of price cutting as a tactical activity needs to be carefully assessed.

Amidst other important considerations such as reputation and conspicuous consumption of hedonic or utilitarian service-products (Dhar and Wertenbroch, 2000), pricing is necessarily dependent on the service-product itself so that intangibility and ease of quality assessment also need to be taken into account. Rather than the dollars involved, it is the perceived value that is perceived by consumers relative to competing offers that determines whether a price is high or low.

In the context of the Portuguese community in Sydney, Australia, Pires and Stanton (2000) provide insights on the implications of tangibility for pricing. In the case of complex, intangible-dominant service-products in the credence class, value is difficult to evaluate even after consumption. While this may suggest that price is much less important, this may not be the case because ethnic minority consumers condition their price evaluations in this class on their assessment of service quality. If performance is perceived positively, then price may not be a concern. If the performance is perceived negatively, then price provides an excuse for switching suppliers, even when the consumer lacks the technical expertise to assess performance quality.

In contrast, in the case of tangible dominant service-products in the search class it is expected that price needs to remain competitive because consumers might be able to easily shop around and compare essentially tangible service-products even before they make a purchase. Notwithstanding, as noted earlier in this chapter customer satisfaction and repeat patronage may be determined solely by the quality of the interaction during the personal encounter (Solomon et al., 1985, p. 100), rather than the tangible service-product per se.

Price is clearly a complex element in the marketing mix, depending on the service-product itself as well as on where it is delivered to consumers. At a minimum, price needs to take all costs into account, including those related to location.

Place

Place is a marketing tool that refers to how and where consumers and suppliers meet for business. It includes the physical location (such as via a shopfront, online or a distributor), delivery methods and even stock level management; however, these inclusions have been diluted to some extent by considering tactical activities related to people, physical evidence and process.

In the case of ethnic marketing, place is particularly important because it constrains and goes beyond transactional notions of convenience, involving stakeholder emotions and encompassing an "understanding" of the community, including ties to the home country, that may be difficult to grasp by outsiders to the ethnic community. This "understanding" is eloquently expressed in an article in National Geographic about Chinese individuals' attraction to New York's Chinatown as a community place, including individuals in the professions who have settled outside Chinese neighbourhoods. The Chinese are attracted to Chinatown

> to escape loneliness, to meet other Chinese people, to eat the best Chinese food, to remind themselves of where they came from. . . . Cultural pride is evident in Chinese Americans who live among non-Chinese neighbours . . . but come to Chinatown on weekends to give their children what they call "a Chinese experience. . . . It's nostalgic. You go even if you don't need anything, and you always pick up something that reminds you of home". . . . To keep their sense of the mother culture strong . . ., parents send their children to Chinese-language, or "Saturday" schools in Chinatown.
> (Swerdlow and Chang, 1998, pp. 64–71)

Place can be described as where the community happens. From a marketing perspective it is essentially where consumers and entrepreneurs who share their ethnicity come together, interact, transact and socialize, placing them at the marketers' reach for targeting purposes. Guided by ethnic sensitivity and relational imperatives, Table 11.3 lists place-related tactical activities meriting consideration by ethnic minority businesses in targeting co-ethnic consumers.

The attraction of the Chinese community to New York's Chinatown in the excerpt above strengthens the argument that it makes sense for ethnic minority businesses to locate within their community where their customers are, improving accessibility for both. Settling into the community by

Table 11.3 Tactical Activities by Ethnic Minority Businesses—Place

---

Place-Related Tactics

Place is particularly important for ethnic marketing practice because it constrains and goes beyond transactional notions of convenience, involving stakeholder emotions and encompassing an "understanding" of the community that may be difficult to grasp by outsiders to the ethnic community.

Ethnic minority businesses should consider locating within their co-ethnic community, given the group's extensive role on their viability at each stage of their development. Ethnic entrepreneurs are likely to derive from and remain entwined with their co-ethnic group, which also provides a market presumed to be substantial and stable over time.

Co-location with the target ethnic community may reduce communication and socialization deficits, as well as difficulties in earning a living. Self-employed ethnic entrepreneurs may take advantage of opportunities stemming from unmet demands of the co-ethnic group.

Locating near the ethnic community can be a source of access economies and competitive advantage for ethnic minority businesses based on birth-related attachment and belonging, a consideration consistent with use the theory of intercultural accommodation.

Co-location advantages can make all the difference. Some ethnic businesses are able to thrive by just "being there". Reportedly, 17 percent of Albanian businesses in Greece used no form of business promotion, simply locating their businesses in immigrant cultural centres.

Ethnic minority businesses are indicators of the existence of minority ethnic groups, and Minority ethnic groups signal the existence of affiliated ethnic minority business.

Location issues must take the line of business activity into account.

Separation from the co-ethnic group can dictate business demise, even in cases where businesses effectively deploy ethnic-sensitive tactical activities and establish successful relationships with their market. Alternative tactical activities need to be considered to defend relationship maintenance.

---

inexperienced co-ethnic consumers assists with eventual communication and socialization deficits. In addition to reducing cultural shock, the community may assist the settlers' need to earn a living, a view echoed by Zhou and Logan's (1989) reporting of thousands of ethnic jobs (such as jobs in ethnic food outlets) being provided by the Chinese enclave in New York City for Chinese immigrants. Reflecting Chinese society and organizations, ethnic jobs are arguably used to generate excellent relationships with customers, driving repurchase with a positive effect on customer relationship marketing (Liao, 2016).

Further to being a source of employment opportunities for co-ethnic individuals, minority ethnic groups also facilitate self-employment and entrepreneurship solutions (as discussed in Chapters 7 and 8 of this text) including business opportunities and the support needed to take advantage of the opportunities stemming from unmet co-ethnic group demands (Takyi and Boate, 2006).

Co-location within the ethnic group assists in the extensive role the group plays in the start-up and development phases of ethnic minority businesses and, crucially, in their ultimate viability. This is because the primary focus of these businesses is by definition the co-ethnic group itself, which is presumed to provide a stable and substantial market over time and without which the business might not survive due to declining sales (Komakech and Jackson, 2016).

There is evidence that being located near or within the co-ethnic community can be a source of access economies and competitive advantage for ethnic minority businesses, based on shared ethnicity, birth-related attachment and belonging (Du, 2017) and a consideration consistent with the theory of intercultural accommodation (Huang, Oppewal and Mavondo, 2013). Indeed, a study of Albanian minority business in Greece revealed that co-location is a substitute for business promotion, being sufficient for businesses to thrive by just "being there" (Piperopoulos, 2010).

The considerations surrounding place in the context of ethnic minority business are uncontested in the specialist literature, such that the existence of an ethnic community indicates that ethnic minority businesses can be expected to be found in its midst. Conversely, the existence of particular ethnic minority businesses is considered to signal the existence of a co-ethnic community. Such is the case of Warsaw, a Polish ethnic minority business in Ashton-under-Lyne, Manchester, UK. As noted by Bannister et al. (2016), the supermarket targets mainly Polish speakers, reflecting the owner's own language and the products it sells. The fact that a large Polish supermarket exists in the centre of Ashton-under-Lyne is indicative of a growing population of Polish residents in the area.

Location issues must take the line of business activity into account. While ethnic business as a rule locates within or in close vicinity with the co-ethnic milieu, it is not uncommon for businesses such as ethnic restaurants to break the rule, co-locating where similar establishments exist (Humphreys and Matti, 2018; Wang, 2013), often quite apart from the co-ethnic neighbourhood. There is also recent evidence of retail chains targeting ethnic markets and expanding into ethnic neighbourhoods of groups with less popular cuisines in New York, such as Caribbean, Indian and Korean (Somashekhar, 2018). However, these are special cases that can be justified by the nature of the service-product and its ability to appeal across markets, as well as related to competitive tactics seeking to attract a larger market (Chidambaram and Pervin, 2018; Thompson, 2010). In general, separation from the co-ethnic group can dictate business demise, as in the case of urban renewal in Toronto (Canada).

Urban renewal often drives away original residents, replacing them with higher income residents who can afford the new spaces, leading to gentrification. This was the case in a multicultural social housing neighbourhood in Toronto (Regent Park) where small ethnic retail grocery stores that supplied ethnic foods and items to the resident ethnic populations were excluded from the civic planning processes, being unable to compete for space in the new buildings. Conducted by Komakech and Jackson (2016), the qualitative study found that the resident population was supportive of these shops which provided culturally familiar items and offered a social credit scheme that recognized existing social relationships and allowed low-income residents to afford food and other amenities in a dignified manner and pay later, without penalty or interest. Yet, although the shops were trusted and provided valued cultural social spaces for ethnic identity formation and ethnic food security in an ethnic-sensitive manner, displacement from the renewed neighbourhood resulted in declining sales and loss of business, breaking the relationship and dictating their ultimate demise.

An implication from the study of ethnic minority businesses in Regent Park is that their demise happened irrespective of the ethnic-sensitive tactical activities they deployed, which generated favourable place identity for consumers, reflected in the congruency between a consumer's self-identity and a place and assessed by evaluating the ethnicity of employees and customers in a consumption setting (Rosenbaum and Montoya, 2007). The inference is that careful consideration must be given by ethnic minority businesses to their mixed embedding, accounting for the attitudes of the community at large, not only the co-ethnic community (Brown-Saracino, Thurk and Fine, 2008).

Ultimately, while consideration of place points to co-location as an almost unavoidable outcome from the process of formation of minority ethnic groups and ethnic minority businesses, analysis of context may reveal other tactical activities that can shore business activities and the maintenance of relationships with consumers for the long-term. For example, consideration of how and where consumers and suppliers meet for business includes traditional and online service scapes (Harris and Goode, 2010; Booms and Bitner, 1981, 1982) which can provide useful insights. Online service scapes are influenced by technologic development, greater availability to all business and convergence across markets, inviting perspectives of place being everywhere, but much more research is needed to fully understand related ethnic marketing and entrepreneurship effects. More is known about traditional service scapes, discussed in the next section dealing with tactical activities related to physical evidence, an element of the extended marketing mix.

Physical Evidence

Dominated by a significant mass of ethnic minority businesses, ethnic shopfronts, interesting landscapes, street furniture, spatial use patterns and people, ethnic neighbourhoods within culturally diverse cities provide consumers with rewarding cultural living experiences (Lam, 2001; Conzen, 1990), through their emersion on the neighbourhood's distinctive atmosphere, as in the cases of Chinatown, Little Italy, Latin Quarters, Klein Turkei and Koreatown, just to mention a few. They also represent the commodification and marketing of diversity (Rath, 2017).

One explanation for a neighbourhood's distinctiveness and appeal refers to the ethnic/foreign goods and services on offer, as well as different work practices and attitudes that give the place a particular socioeconomic identity, including a reputation for particular forms of doing business (Lagendijk et al., 2011). But the more general view recognizes the importance of the atmospherics (Ha and Jang, 2010; Kotler, 1973) of the neighbourhood and of the ethnic minority businesses within, for conveying subjective perceptions of familiarity to co-ethnic consumers and generating preference. For example, in restaurant settings, Turkish customers in Istanbul care particularly about service staff demeanour, facility aesthetics, layout, ambience, table setting and lighting (Tuzunkan and Albayrak, 2017). These are physical evidence cues that may help make sense of Turkish restaurants' physical environment within Turkish neighbourhoods. In general terms, ethnic minority businesses can influence consumer perceptions by using physical evidence-based tactical activities in their marketing mix.

Another physical evidence clue refers to front-stage staff, given that consumers regardless of their ethnicity prefer service staff of the same ethnicity (Baumann and Setogawa, 2015).

Understood as a visual metaphor that provides consumers with meaningful clues of the business itself, and of how it fits within the co-ethnic community, physical evidence refers to

> the environment in which the service is delivered and where the firm and customer interact, and any tangible components that facilitate performance or communication of the service.
>
> (Booms and Bitner, 1981)

Table 11.4 lists physical evidence related tactical activities meriting consideration by ethnic minority businesses in targeting co-ethnic consumers, most of which are self-explanatory.

The physical environment developed by ethnic minority business must be congruent with other elements of the marketing mix and may positively or negatively influence co-ethnic consumers' perceptions, with consumers feeling alien, excluded or unwelcome (Rishbeth, 2001). So the aim is to develop physical evidence cues that create an aesthetically pleasing environment or atmosphere, to assist consumers' favourable evaluation of the business and of its service-products before, during and after consumption (Ryu, Lee and Gon Kim, 2012). But care is required to

Table 11.4 Tactical Activities by Ethnic Minority Businesses—Physical Evidence

Physical (Tangible) Evidence Related Tactics
Put the welcome mat out (Tyler Morning Telegraph, Texas 3/3/2011).
Employ front-stage, bilingual, co-ethnic staff whenever possible. This helps co-ethnic customers to feel at home, facilitating communications. In the case of cross-cultural encounters in (Chinese) restaurants, for example, the clientele might expect employees to match the specialized food.
Also, similarity-attraction theory, involving homophily—the tendency of people to bond with others like themselves—and proximity—the tendency of people to bond with those nearby explain why ethnic minority consumers may be strongly predisposed to speciality shops and business establishments owned by members of their group of affiliation, and enter into personal relationships with (similar) shopkeepers (Parissis and Helfinger, 1993).
Whether co-ethnic employees are used or not, develop frontstages where members from your targeted minority ethnic group(s) feel welcome and comfortable doing business. This also requires:
1. Providing employees with extensive cultural training so as to develop their understanding of different groups' unique needs and perspectives, and 2. Using physical evidence to closely match customers' attributes. This is a very complex task to accomplish because the diverse clientele will possibly be sharing the frontstage, requiring well-developed interaction skills by personnel.
Increase visibility and achieve top of mind recognition by attending events of interest for the ethnic community, such as cultural events, feasts and festivals.
Beyond attending events, conspicuously get involved in and provide support to community events.
Engage with ethnic group related associations, social clubs and recognize group gatekeepers in general.
Create value for the community through conspicuous endorsements, sponsoring and scholarships.
Show commitment to the community by sponsoring and endorsing events over a significant period of time, such annual celebrations for number of years
Engage the community in business activities such as innovation drives, inviting community participation in regular focus groups seeking to improve service delivery to the group by better understanding the group's needs and wants.
Objective is to create a welcoming store atmosphere, but this cannot compromise perceptions of fair pricing (Huang, Oppewal and Mavondo, 2013)

ensure that store atmosphere is not perceived by co-ethnic consumers to compromise fair pricing (Huang, Oppewal and Mavondo, 2013).

The means to develop physical evidence cues are many and varied. The aesthetics and design of the premises, signs, symbols, artefacts, furnishing, lighting and decoration style; sounds like spoken language and music, scents, brochures, promotional materials, stationery, business cards, business vehicles, websites, blogs, social media and other forms of digital activity; service and support staff, business owner, the way personnel behaves and dresses and other customers visiting the premises, are just examples of physical elements of an ethnic shopfront that can be used to provide tangible clues of what the business represents and of the service-products it provides.

Conspicuous Commitment for the Long-Term

The underlining idea of the objectives to be achieved by tactically using physical evidence cues is for co-ethnic business to demonstrate a commitment to the relationship with the co-ethnic group that is sincere and for the long-term. In doing so, the end is to create and maintain an image as a good group member, in a way that is conspicuous to co-ethnic consumers without being construed as self-publicity, and through them to the group. Focus must be on augmenting the value creation to ethnic networks by contributing to the collective, heightening their demonstration of community citizenship. This involves ongoing and dependable engagement with the community, demonstrating a respectful understanding of co-ethnic group heterogeneity. Other relevant elements range from low employee turnover so the faces of the business remain familiar, to maintaining a preferred product mix, support for community activities and aspirations, such as funding of study scholarships, as well as care for how co-ethnic consumers participate in and experience the delivery of the business service-products—corresponding to the process element of the marketing mix discussed next. Other elements in the marketing mix, namely promotion, personalization and people are discussed in Chapters 12 and 13 of this text.

Process

The focus of the final element of the ethnic marketing mix discussed in this chapter refers to managing process related tactical activities, justified by service experiences perishability. In addition to adequately accounting for co-ethnic group needs, preferences and evaluative criteria when developing terms of exchange, ethnic minority business may develop service delivery systems designed to overcome logistic liabilities. Home delivery and pick-up (for possession processing service activities, such as car repair/detail, dry cleaning) or home delivery (for personal processing service activities, such as healthcare, hair care, financial planning) are some of many options.

Process refers to the activities, procedures, protocols and more by which service-products, including ideas, are eventually delivered to customers. As services are results of actions for, by or with customers, a process involves a sequence of steps and activities for achieving effective delivery, justifying care in adequately managing consumer expectations at each step and activity.

Table 11.5 lists a few process-related tactical activities meriting consideration by ethnic minority businesses in targeting co-ethnic consumers.

Table 11.5 Tactical Activities by Ethnic Minority Businesses—Process

---

Process-Related Tactical Activities

Value proposition: Primary focus is on the value that accrues to the co-ethnic group. Then, adjust by considering individual needs. Value is in your co-ethnic consumer's eyes.

Co-creation: Provide opportunities for co-ethnic consumers to decide on what service is provided and how.

Convenience: Provide home delivery where applicable.

Value creation process: Give emphasis to what your business contributes to your co-ethnic group, other than focusing on your own success.

Sobriety: Provide the means for your co-ethnic consumers to express their views about the business to other co-ethnic consumers, taking advantage of grassroots marketing.

Consistently act co-ethnic: Consider and implement tactics to ensure service delivery processes are consistent with acting in agreement with co-ethnic group expectations. People act in keeping with an ethnic identity. Arguably, "acting ethnic" is a collective performance, aimed not only at belonging to the group, but also as a means of maintaining and reproducing ethnic identity and asserting a legitimate alternative to the hegemonic identity (Kachtan, 2017; Tsuda, 2000).

Monitor consumer participation in service delivery.

Blueprint all delivery processes: As services are dynamic and experiential, service companies also use a blueprint method called "Service Blue Printing". This process-based method provides a better management of the service in the area of internal and external interaction, makes this transparent and ultimately this is implemented in practice (Bitner, Ostrom and Morgan, 2008).

The entries in the table should be understood as merely illustrative, given the strong link between business activities and associated processes, emphasizing the importance of context.

A brief discussion of the need to monitor co-ethnic consumer participation in service delivery processes assists in better understanding the issues involved. In addition to operational efficiency concerns in devising service delivery processes, ethnic minority businesses need to account for the specific behaviours, degree of effort and involvement, whether mental, physical and emotional, that relate to consumers' participation in the production and delivery of a service (Cermak, File and Prince, 1994). Customer participation can be high, medium or low (Bitner et al. (1997). It can involve technical qualities, referring to the resources (e.g. labour and knowledge) contributed by the customer, and functional (interactional) qualities, referring to how the customer behaves (including interpersonal aspects such as friendliness and respect) while participating (Ennew and Binks, 1999).

A crucial aspect to understand is that participation in service delivery can be valued either positively or negatively by consumers. For example, customer participation in healthcare decision-making may cause improved psychological well-being and greater satisfaction (McColl-Kennedy et al., 2012), while other customers may prefer to be told what to do. That is, customer participation can add or detract from the way customers assess a value proposition such that understanding how and why consumers participate in service delivery is a key factor in understanding value proposition creation, customer value creation and, ultimately, what contributes to competitive advantage (Pires, Dean and Rehman, 2015; Rehman, Dean and Pires, 2012), justifying its monitoring.

The primary focus is on processes that reflect cultural competency. Staying in the healthcare context, Reardon (2014) explains that providers need to look beyond overcoming language challenges and to consider other factors, such as social customs, attitudes toward medical care and non-verbal communication as key elements of cultural competency so as to better identify ethnic clients' needs. Focus should be on consumers' quality of life, making sure they are asked to engage with friendly service delivery processes that contribute positively to their well-being. This is the case of the user friendly, one-stop shopping place provided by Asian Human Services in Chicago, US, which sought to offer primary healthcare services but also mental health services, legal services, employment services, adult education programs and a charter school focused on the needs of immigrant and refugee children.

Ethnic minority businesses in healthcare may consider strengthening their relationship with co-ethnic consumers/patients by visiting them when justified, instead of always asking them to visit their surgery.

The next chapter discusses promotion and personalization tactical activities.

References

Aldrich, H., Cater, J., Jones, T., Mc Evoy, D. and Velleman, P. (1985). Ethnic residential concentration and the protected market hypothesis. *Social Forces*, 63(4), 996–1009.

Aldrich, H. and Waldinger, R. (1990). Ethnicity and entrepreneurship. *Annual Review of Sociology*, 16(1), 111–135.

Al Ganideh, S. and Al Taee, H. (2012). Examining consumer ethnocentrism amongst Jordanians from an ethnic group perspective. *International Journal of Marketing Studies*, 4(1), 48.

Balasubramanian, S. and Herche, J. (1994). Ethnicity and shopping behavior. *Journal of Shopping Center Research*, 1(1), 65–80.

Bannister, E., Hark, H., Joyce, L. and Portwood, A. (2016). *Multilingual Manchester's Linguistic Landscapes: A Study on the Use of Multilingual Signs for Businesses in Manchester*. The University of Manchester. Accessed 11/7/2018 at http://mlm.humanities.manchester.ac.uk/wp-content/uploads/2016/10/A-Study-on-the-Use-of-Multilingual-Signs-for-Businesses-in-Manchester.pdf

Baumann, C. and Setogawa, S. (2015). Asian ethnicity in the West: Preference for Chinese, Indian and Korean service staff. *Asian Ethnicity*, 16(3), 380–398.

Bendapudi, N. and Berry, L. (1997). Customers' motivations for maintaining relationships with service providers. *Journal of Retailing*, 73(1), 15–37.

Bitner, M., Faranda, W., Hubbert, A. and Zeithaml, V. (1997). Customer contributions and roles in service delivery. *International Journal of Services Industry Management*, 8(3), 193–205.

Bitner, M., Ostrom, A. and Morgan, F. (2008). Service blueprinting: A practical technique for service innovation. *California Management Review*, 50(3), 66–94.

Blankson, C. and Stokes, D. (2002). Marketing practices in the UK small business sector. *Marketing Intelligence & Planning*, 20(1), 49–61.

Booms, B. and Bitner, M. (1981). Marketing strategies and organization structures for service firms. In J. H. Donnelly and W. R. George (eds.), *Marketing of Services*. Chicago: American Marketing Association.

Booms, B. and Bitner, M. (1982). Marketing services by managing the environment. *Cornell Hotel and Restaurant Administration Quarterly*, 23(1), 35–40.

Brand, R. and Cronin, J. (1997). Consumer-specific determinants of the size of retail choice sets: An empirical comparison of physical good and service providers. *Journal of Services Marketing*, 11(1), 19–38.

Brown-Saracino, J., Thurk, J. and Fine, G. (2008). Beyond groups: Seven pillars of peopled ethnography in organizations and communities. *Qualitative Research*, 8(5), 547–567.

Cermak, D., File, K. and Prince, R. (1994). Customer participation in service specification and delivery. *Journal of Applied Business Research*, 10(2), 90–97.

Chidambaram, K. and Pervin, N. (2018). *Effect of Agglomeration in the Restaurant Industry*. aisel.aisnet.org

Connor, W. (1978). A nation is a nation, is a state, is an ethnic group is a. . . . *Ethnic and Racial Studies*, 1(4), 377–400.

Conzen, M. (1990). *The Making of American Landscape*. Boston: Unwin Hyman.

Darby, M. and Karni, E. (1973). Free competition and the optimal amount of fraud. *Journal of Law and Economics*, 16, 67–86.

Dhar, R. and Wertenbroch, K. (2000). Consumer choice between hedonic and utilitarian goods. *Journal of Marketing Research*, 37(1), 60–71.

Donthu, N. and Cherian, J. (1994). Impact of strength of ethnic identification on Hispanic shopping behavior. *Journal of Retailing*, 70(4), 383–393.

Du, H. (2017). Place attachment and belonging among educated young migrants and returnees: The case of Chaohu, China. *Population, Space and Place*, 23(1), e1967.

El Banna, A., Papadopoulos, N., Murphy, S., Rod, M. and Rojas-Méndez, J. (2018). Ethnic identity, consumer ethnocentrism, and purchase intentions among bi-cultural ethnic consumers: "Divided loyalties" or "dual allegiance"? *Journal of Business Research*, 82, 310–319.

Ennew, C. and Binks, M. (1999). Impact of participative service relationships on quality, satisfaction and retention: An exploratory study. *Journal of Business Research*, 46(2), 121–132.

Flight, R. and Coker, K. (2016). Brand constellations: Reflections of the emotional self. *Journal of Product & Brand Management*, 25(2), 134–147.

Friedman, M. and Smith, L. (1993). Consumer evaluation processes in a service setting. *Journal of Services Marketing*, 7(2), 47–61.

Ha, J. and Jang, S. (2010). Effects of service quality and food quality: The moderating role of atmospherics in an ethnic restaurant segment. *International Journal of Hospitality Management*, 29(3), 520–529.

Han, H. and Ryu, K. (2009). The roles of the physical environment, price perception, and customer satisfaction in determining customer loyalty in the restaurant industry. *Journal of Hospitality & Tourism Research*, 33(4), 487–510.

Harris, L. and Goode, M. (2010). Online servicescapes, trust, and purchase intentions. *Journal of Services Marketing*, 24(3), 230–243.

Hartman, D. and Lindgren, J., Jr. (1993). Consumer evaluations of goods and services: Implications for services marketing. *Journal of Services Marketing*, 7(2), 4–15.

Huang, Y., Oppewal, H. and Mavondo, F. (2013). The influence of ethnic attributes on ethnic consumer choice of service outlet. *European Journal of Marketing*, 47(5/6), 877–898.

Humphreys, B. and Matti, J. (2018). *The Spatial Distribution of Urban Consumer Service Firms: Evidence from Yelp Reviews*. SSRN Papers.

Ibrahim, G. and Galt, V. (2011). Explaining ethnic entrepreneurship: An evolutionary economics approach. *International Business Review*, 20(6), 607–613.

Jamal, A. (2005). Playing to win: An explorative study of marketing strategies of small ethnic retail entrepreneurs in the UK. *Journal of Retailing and Consumer Services*, 12(1), 1–13.

Kachtan, D. (2017). "Acting ethnic": Performance of ethnicity and the process of ethnicization. *Ethnicities*, 17(5), 707–726.

Kaufman, C. (1991). Coupon use in ethnic markets: Implications from a retail perspective. *Journal of Consumer Marketing*, 8(1), 41–51.

Komakech, M. and Jackson, S. (2016). A study of the role of small ethnic retail grocery stores in urban renewal in a social housing project, Toronto, Canada. *Journal of Urban Health*, 93(3), 414–424.

Kotler, P. (1973). Atmospherics as a marketing tool. *Journal of Retailing*, 49(4), 48–64.

Kwok, S. and Uncles, M. (2005). Sales promotion effectiveness: The impact of consumer differences at an ethnic-group level. *Journal of Product & Brand Management*, 14(3), 170–186.

Labrianidis, L. and Hatziprokopiou, P. (2010). Migrant entrepreneurship in Greece: Diversity of pathways for emerging ethnic business communities in Thessaloniki. *Journal of International Migration and Integration/Revue de l'integration et de la migration internationale*, 11(2), 193–217.

Lagendijk, A., Pijpers, R., Ent, G., Hendrikx, R., van Lanen, B. and Maussart, L. (2011). Multiple worlds in a single street: Ethnic entrepreneurship and the construction of a global sense of place. *Space and Polity*, 15(2), 163–181.

Lam, S. (2001). The effects of store environment on shopping behaviors: A critical review. *ACR North American Advances*. http://acrwebsite.org/volumes/8468/volumes/v28/NA-28

Laroche, M., Kim, C. and Clarke, M. (1997). The Effects of ethnicity factors on consumer deal interests: An empirical study of French- English- Canadians. *Journal of Marketing Theory and Practice*, 5(1), 100–111.

Levitt, T. (1997). What's your product and what's your business? In *Marketing for Business Growth*. New York: McGraw-Hill, p. 7.

Liao, K. (2016). Impact of traditional Chinese culture on business-to-business relationship marketing and service firm performance. *Journal of Business-to-Business Marketing*, 23(4), 277–291.

Light, I. (1972). *Ethnic Enterprise in America*. Berkeley: University of California Press.

Lovelock, C. (1996). *Services Marketing*, 3rd ed. New Jersey: Prentice Hall.

Luedicke, M. (2011). Consumer acculturation theory: (Crossing) conceptual boundaries. *Consumption Markets & Culture*, 14(3), 223–244.

McClintock, N., Novie, A. and Gebhardt, M. (2017). Is it local . . . or authentic and exotic? Ethnic food carts and gastropolitan habitus on Portland's eastside. *Food Trucks, Cultural Identity, and Social Justice: From Loncheras to Lobsta Love*, 15, 285.

McColl-Kennedy, J., Vargo, S., Dagger, T., Sweeney, J. and van Kasteren, Y. (2012). Health care customer value cocreation practice styles. *Journal of Service Research*, 15(4), 370–389.

Mittal, B. and Lassar, W. (1996). The role of personalization in service encounters. *Journal of Retailing*, 72(1), 95–109.

Montoya, D. and Briggs, E. (2013). Shared ethnicity effects on service encounters: A study across three US subcultures. *Journal of Business Research*, 66(3), 314–320.

Murray, K. (1991). A test of services marketing theory: Consumer information acquisition activities. *Journal of Marketing*, 55, 10–25.

Nagle, T. and Müller, G. (2017). *The Strategy and Tactics of Pricing: A Guide to Growing More Profitably*. Abingdon, UK: Routledge.

Nelson, P. (1970). Advertising as information. *Journal of Political Economy*, 81, 729–754.

Omar, O. E., Hirst, A. and Blankson, C. (2004). Food shopping behavior among ethnic and non-ethnic communities in Britain. *Journal of Food Products Marketing*, 10(4), 39–57.

Ouellet, J. (2007). Consumer racism and its effects on domestic cross-ethnic product purchase: An empirical test in the United States, Canada, and France. *Journal of Marketing*, 71(1), 113–128.

Papadopoulos, N., Laroche, M., Elliot, S. and Rojas-Méndez, J. (2008). Subcultural effects of product origins: consumer ethnicity and product nationality. In *Proceedings, 37th Annual Conference*, European Marketing Academy, Brighton, England, May 27, Vol. 30.

Parissis, M. and Helfinger, M. (1993). Ethnic shoppers share certain values. *Marketing (Maclean Hunter)*, 98 (January 11), 16.

Parzer, M., Astleithner, F. and Rieder, I. (2016). Deliciously exotic? Immigrant grocery shops and their non-migrant clientele. *International Review of Social Research*, 6(1), 26–34.

Piperopoulos, P. (2010). Ethnic minority businesses and immigrant entrepreneurship in Greece. *Journal of Small Business and Enterprise Development*, 17(1), 139–158.

Pires, G., Dean, A. and Rehman, M. (2015). Using service logic to redefine exchange in terms of customer and supplier participation. *Journal of Business Research*, 68(5), 925–932.

Pires, G. and Stanton, J. (2015). *Ethnic Marketing: Culturally Sensitive Theory and Practice*. Abingdon, UK: Routledge.

Pires, G. and Stanton, J. (2005). *Ethnic Marketing, Accepting the Challenge of Cultural Diversity*. London: Thomson Learning.

Pires, G. and Stanton, J. (2000). Marketing services to ethnic consumers in culturally diverse markets: issues and implications. *Journal of Services Marketing*, 14(7), 607–618.

Pires, G., Stanton, J. and Stanton, P. (2004). Tangibility consequences for ethnic marketing strategy. *Global Business and Economics Review*, 6(1), 38–54.

Podoshen, J. (2009). Distressing events and future purchase decisions: Jewish consumers and the Holocaust. *Journal of Consumer Marketing*, 26(4), 263–276.

Rath, J. (2017). *The Transformation of Ethnic Neighborhoods into Places of Leisure and Consumption*. San Diego: Centre for Comparative Immigration Studies, UC. https://escholarship.org/uc/item/5x63z3bn

Reardon, C. (2014). More than words: Cultural competency in healthcare. *Social Work Today*, 9(3), 12.

Rehman, M., Dean, A. and Pires, G. (2012). A research framework for examining customer participation in value co-creation: Applying the service dominant logic to the provision of living support services to oncology day-care patients. *International Journal of Behavioural and Healthcare Research*, 3(3–4), 226–243.

Rishbeth, C. (2001). Ethnic minority groups and the design of public open space: An inclusive landscape? *Landscape Research*, 26(4), 351–366.

Rosenbaum, M. and Montoya, D. (2007). Am I welcome here? Exploring how ethnic consumers assess their place identity. *Journal of Business Research*, 60(3), 206–214.

Rothmell, J. (1966). What is meant by services? *Journal of Marketing*, 30(4), 32–36.

Ryu, K., Lee, H. and Gon Kim, W. (2012). The influence of the quality of the physical environment, food, and service on restaurant image, customer perceived value, customer satisfaction, and behavioral intentions. *International Journal of Contemporary Hospitality Management*, 24(2), 200–223.

Sheth, J. and Parvatiyar, A. (1995). Relationship marketing in consumer markets: Antecedents and consequents. *Journal of the Academy of Marketing Science*, 23, 255–271.

Shostack, L. (1977). Breaking free from product marketing. *Journal of Marketing*, 41, 73–80.

Solomon, M. and Buchanan, B. (1991). A role-theoretic approach to product symbolism: Mapping a consumption constellation. *Journal of Business Research*, 22(2), 95–109.

Solomon, M., Surprenant, C., Czepiel, J. and Gutman, E. (1985). A role theory perspective on dyadic interactions: The service encounter. *Journal of Marketing*, 49, 99–111.

Somashekhar, M. (2018). Ethnic economies in the age of retail chains: Comparing the presence of chain-affiliated and independently owned ethnic restaurants in ethnic neighbourhoods. *Journal of Ethnic and Migration Studies*, 1–23.

Swerdlow, J. and Chang, C. (1998). New York's Chinatown. *National Geographic*, 58–77.

Takyi, B. and Boate, K. (2006). *Location and Settlement Patterns of African Immigrants in the US: Demographic and Spatial Context*. Lanham: Lexington Books, pp. 50–67.

Thompson, G. (2010). Restaurant profitability management: The evolution of restaurant revenue management. *Cornell Hospitality Quarterly*, 51(3), 308–322.

Tsuda, T. (2000). Acting Brazilian in Japan: Ethnic resistance among return migrants. *Ethnology*, 55–71.

Tuzunkan, D. and Albayrak, A. (2017). The importance of restaurant physical environment for Turkish customers. *Journal of Tourism Research & Hospitality* www.scitechnol.com/peer-review/the-importance-of-restaurant-physical-environment-for-turkish-customers-3yJe.php?article_id=4864

Ulaga, W. and Eggert, A. (2006). Value-based differentiation in business relationships: Gaining and sustaining key supplier status. *Journal of Marketing*, 70(1), 119–136.

Wang, Q. (2013). Beyond ethnic enclaves? Exploring the spatial distribution of Latino-owned employer firms in two US immigration gateways. *Journal of Urban Affairs*, 35(5), 569–589.

Ward, R. (2005). Economic development and ethnic business. In *Paths of Enterprise*. Abingdon, UK: Routledge, pp. 65–80.

Zeithaml, V. and Bitner, M. (2000). *Services Marketing: Integrating Customer Focus across the Firm*. Sydney: McGraw Hill.

Zhou, M. and Logan, J. (1989). Returns on human capital in ethnic enclaves: New York City's Chinatown. *American Sociological Review*, 809–820.

12 Promotion and Personalization

Focus on the promotional element of the marketing mix in this chapter is on its use in the targeting of minority ethnic groups by ethnic minority businesses, while taking into account that the meaning of communications with co-ethnics may be lost or even have negative effects if directed to other targets. Emphasis is also given to a preference for co-ethnic exchanges with communications in the mother language, although this preference does not imply ethnic minority consumers' inability to access and understand communications designed for other markets. Furthermore, ethnic minority business' marketing communications need to be integrated across media and in time and to account for the possibility of segments making up a heterogeneous minority ethnic group. Ultimately, communications need to support the establishment and enhancement of long-term relationships between ethnic minority businesses and their minority co-ethnic group by deploying a range of appropriate tactical activities.

In the context of a complex and dynamic communications environment, this chapter discusses elements of a communication strategy pertinent to developing an ethnic marketing approach by an ethnic minority business, focusing on the need to research and understand the preferred communication methods and media choices of a minority co-ethnic group.

The Promotional Element

This chapter outlines a basic model of the communication process. The elements of this process are then linked to the tools for effective marketing communications that are also relational. In communicating with ethnic consumers the sensitivity and focus of these tools is considered in terms of tactical activities appropriate to reaching a minority co-ethnic market and how to use communications with tailored messages to help retain co-ethnic consumers, once they have had a taste of the provider's value proposition.

Consistently tailoring the message to the audience, using the right media to deliver that message and ensuring it reaches the intended audience in a timely manner are communication requirements facing any business, even those deploying undifferentiated mass marketing tactics within a country. Effective communications are a key component of the marketing mix applied by any business to the targeting of its selected markets, including ethnic minority businesses.

While the focus of an ethnic minority business is, by definition, on fewer markets, even possibly a single one if the target minority co-ethnic group is perceived as homogeneous, developing effective and efficient marketing communications with co-ethnic minority consumers remains a challenging task. Particularly in the case of businesses managed by inexperienced ethnic entrepreneurs, some of which may lack the necessary business acumen, this challenge is augmented by the need to develop and implement communications that are both ethnic-sensitive and relational.

Serving Anyone That Comes Through the Door

Some may argue that the conceptualization of an ethnic minority business may be unrealistic because dependence on one narrowly defined minority ethnic group does not rule out the likelihood, in practice, of these businesses having mixed consumer portfolios and of this even being the norm. But it is the dependence on the group that matters.

Always subject to the ethnic entrepreneur's business objective, serving a minority ethnic group with an eye on establishing and nurturing a mutually advantageous long-term relationship is the primary strategic objective of the ethnic minority business. But this may be complemented by an essentially transactional, global-like approach. In this case, while no significantly differentiated tactics are objectively drawn for non-co-ethnic customers, their custom is facilitated and may even be encouraged.

Hence, it is not uncommon for ethnic minority businesses to display in some prominent place within their outlet multilingual signs with information about ethnic products they carry and how to use them, while also exhibiting a "we speak X, Y and Z languages" sign. Bannister et al. (2016) offers several examples of the communications of ethnic minority businesses in Ashton-under-Lyne, Manchester. Warsaw, for example, is a Polish business targeting mainly Polish speakers, but also welcoming local people who are interested in purchasing European foods, as made clear by the repetition of Polish signs in English (Bannister et al., 2016). The practice is richly illustrated in The Economist (2013) in the New York context.

The global-like transactional approach allows for some of the marketing mix (mostly the communication element) to be adjusted relative to the relational, ethnic-sensitive tactical activities deployed towards the co-ethnic group. Language is, perhaps, the most obvious element to adapt, with many ethnic entrepreneurs usually being able to make themselves more or less well understood, sometimes using a combination of words, images and gestures.

Rather than questioning the importance and adequacy of the narrow definition of an ethnic minority business in this text, pondering on its relaxation possibilities arguably reinforces and demonstrates its coherence. This is because the operationalization of the secondary market is not conducive to either sustainable competitive advantage or preference, mostly ruling out any relational objectives. Indeed, instead of drawing on shared ethnicity and affinity across consumers and suppliers, the focus of attraction may be the novelty of the ethnic product, if not the mere chance of the store being in the way of passers-by.

Overall, there is some justification to suggest that the approach adopted by ethnic minority businesses is often a mixed one, along a continuum from a relational ethnic-sensitive approach to an undifferentiated-transactional approach (Cui and Choudhury, 2002; Grönroos, 1991), under a dynamic environment umbrella.

Marketing Communications and Minority Co-Ethnic Groups

Ethnic minority businesses use marketing communications to enhance understanding of, association with and attitude and predisposition toward their brand and service-product. This requires attention to how the minority co-ethnic group works, both in terms of the communication tools and mix and the group's communication behaviour (Dhalla and Mahatoo, 1976), namely their media habits (such as readership of ethnic newspapers and magazines), attention paid and response to advertising of relevant product categories in various media and their decision-making processes; particularly to the relative importance of advertising versus recommendations received by word of mouth or from sales persons, the role of opinion leaders and perceptions of brands and providers on such attributes as competence and trust.

With such information on hand it is possible for ethnic minority businesses to devise a coordinated program of activities, often called integrated marketing communications (IMC) (Adcock et al., 1995). This is important because resources spent on isolated activities such as image building and brand building may be wasted and synergies lost in reaching the co-ethnic group.

The Challenges of a Dynamic Environment

Rapid and ongoing advances in information communication technologies (ICT) that are ubiquitous and general purpose justify differential adoption and usage by ethnic minority businesses and co-ethnic consumers, having a major impact on the development of marketing communications

(OECD, 2012). Reflecting their transformative impact on the way businesses and consumers interact with each other (APC, 2011, p. 74), peer-to-peer communications through web forums and social networking sites are freely accessible to all consumers, suppliers and institutions, facilitating and possibly influencing inter-communications.

Peer-to-peer communications have the potential to change the ways consumers interact and how they evaluate and conduct their exchanges, influencing their empowerment vis-à-vis suppliers (Fortin and Uncles, 2011), although it is not clear that this is always true for marketing communications involving minority ethnic groups. Indeed, while the collapse of print readership and plummeting advertising revenue of mainstream newspapers in many Western countries is universally recognized (Young, 2010; Omar, Hirst and Blankson, 2004), these behavioural changes are not glaringly evident in the case of the ethnic press, or in the social media interface of stakeholders bound by ethnicity.

The potential clearly exists for exposure by ethnic minority businesses and their target markets to economic and socio-cultural forces that potentially open their communication possibilities. For example, these business may be able to pursue transnational opportunities using social media (Wilding, 2007; Bryceson and Vuorela, 2002; Kloosterman and Rath, 2001), although the potential may be conditioned by differing stages in stakeholders' familiarity, competence and use of technologies, as well as by the communication resources available, local market conditions and the communication preferences of their market, which can be expected to change over time. It is, therefore, apparent that ethnic minority businesses need to develop their own understanding of how best to communicate with their co-ethnic consumers, with their co-ethnic group, and with parties in the co-ethnic business network, so as to develop appropriate relational ethnic-sensitive communication capabilities, hence long-term, in a constantly evolving environment.

Understanding Communication as Information Processing Activity

The importance of developing a considered communication approach for a particular culture is recognized by international marketers who are aware of the difficulties and pitfalls of communicating across cultural boundaries. If a person belonging to a minority ethnic group has adapted to the mainstream culture and understands a message in the mainstream language, this does not mean that this is the person's preferred way of receiving a message.

Effective communication needs to take into account all the elements of the communication process depicted in Figure 12.1.

Schramm (1971) depicts the communication process as an information processing activity that, in order to be successful, requires a shared orientation to certain signs or symbols, because the technology revolution has

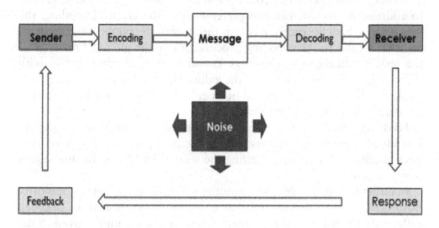

Figure 12.1 Elements of the Communication Process
Source: Schramm (1971).

changed the one-way nature of marketing communications and altered the nature of the relationship between businesses and any potential target market (Heo and Cho, 2009). Consequently, interactivity needs to be redefined more loosely as how a person or persons can influence or be influenced by a source (Florenthal and Shoham, 2010), and the concept of sender and receiver as well as the nature of information dissemination in the context of social media, when seeking to communicate with any group, has become immensely more complicated.

While the sender or source is the party sending the communication, both the targeting ethnic minority business and the targeted co-ethnic consumer can be involved in this role at some stage, requiring the business not only to be aware of its role as a sender but also to be aware of the ethnic consumer as a sender. This means taking steps to establish a means of communication with the co-ethnic group that co-ethnic consumers are comfortable in using. Nevertheless, peer-to-peer interactivity enables a wider community conversation and dialogue over which the business, as original sender, may have little control.

The receiver is the party receiving the message. Because the ethnic minority business seeks to develop a relationship with its co-ethnic group and affiliated consumers, an interactive two-way communication process will be required. While an individual ethnic consumer may be the recipient, substantiality in segmenting usually requires the business to pay attention to how the ethnic group rather than the individual perceives and receives a message. In turn, the business will need to provide channels and processes for it to receive and acknowledge communications from the group.

Message construction (encoding) and the medium of transmission need to address the sensitivities and preferences of the group. Decoding, the process by which the receiver assigns meaning to the symbols transmitted, must be similar to the encoding process, or else the intended message of the sender is likely to be distorted. Encoding is often ethnocentric, with the sender failing to understand the values and symbols of other cultures while decoding is inherently within a person's cultural context, providing a fertile field for misunderstanding.

Feedback and response are closely linked. Primarily, messages are intended to generate a response from a recipient, and this response feedback is critical to marketers, telling the sender if and how the message is being received.

In targeting a heterogeneous minority co-ethnic group, ethnic minority businesses need to understand that complex messages may be decoded differently by different sub-groups because of the meanings given to the encoded symbols, although this effect may be smaller than if distinct minority ethnic groups are involved. The use of photographs of personal images in a message, for example, can be used to interpret, abstract and activate readers' imaginations (Douglis, 2000). As well as what is photo-graphed, elements such as orientation to the camera, head cant, gestures and smiles become a part of a message that need to be conveyed across cultures, where different meanings may be attached to such depiction. In essence, photographs do not necessarily reflect how people behave but rather, how one thinks they behave (Anderson and Imperia, 1992). Both the encoder and decoder undertake their tasks based on their experiences and unless there is some overlap in experiences the message received by the decoder is likely to be different from that intended.

Further, in seeking to reach ethnic minority groups with their messages, co-ethnic businesses face considerable noise if they seek to use main-stream media because ethnic minority consumers can be expected to be subject to noisy communications being exposed to both mainstream and ethnic communications media. But the noise is likely to be much reduced when operating in the language of the minority ethnic group.

The Value Proposition

In order for a minority ethnic group to determine the value of a proposition on offer, a co-ethnic minority business must develop an effective communication strategy to attract and retain valued consumers via the group, before, during and after consumption. This requires:

> a substantial rethinking of marketing strategies and approaches . . . valuing these segments enough to learn about their needs, attitudes, culture, activities, heroes and lifestyles.
>
> (Swenson, 1990, p. 20)

Table 12.1 Communication Tactical Development Over Three Consumption Phases

Phase	Tactical Objectives
Pre-consumption	Addresses the problems that co-ethnic minority consumers may face initially when seeking to decide how to address a recognized need or want. The ethnic minority business 2-step decision is on how to best reach co-ethnic consumers (the media) with appropriate, relevant and attractive information about the value proposition (the message).
	Effective decision-making requires information about the important and determinant service-product attributes that are valued by the minority co-ethnic group. Generates realistic value promises to be met during the consumption phase.
Consumption	Deals with ensuring effective communications during consumption through effective service-encounters that deliver on the promises. Service encounter performance is commonly assessed based on five attributes, namely assurance, empathy, reliability, responsiveness, and tangibles.
Post-consumption	The main focus of the post-consumption phase is to produce a transformative experience, whereby interactions convert into relationships for the longer term. Satisfaction with the consumption experience can also justify positive feedback to the minority ethnic group, involving word-of-mouth recommendation of the supplier to similar-others.

Adapted from Walker (1995)'s model of service encounter satisfaction. See also Bigné, Mattila and Andreu (2008).

Ethnic minority businesses that are culturally sensitive and use their co-ethnic group's preferred media sources and etiquette are likely to offer a superior value proposition than their competitors. To better ensure the superiority of the value proposition, the inherent tactical activities needed to assist with consumers' understanding of the proposition and to address any discomfort with either the style and/or the means of communication are outlined in Table 12.1.

Drawing on Walker's (1995) model of service-encounter satisfaction, the table identifies three evaluative phases or stages: pre-consumption, consumption and post-consumption; each phase is briefly addressed below.

Newly arrived ethnic minority consumers may have communication difficulties in the host country language as well as limited market knowledge. On affiliation to a particular minority ethnic group they gain access to that group's resources and rely more on primary personal sources of information (Friedman and Smith, 1993). Addressing the *pre-consumption phase*, this justifies ethnic minority businesses deploying a relational communication approach, involving a decision on how to best reach co-ethnic consumers with appropriate, relevant and attractive information about the value proposition (Bolton et al., 2014). This is not an easy task to accomplish given the variety of media outlets that may exist. For example, Murray, Yu and Ahadi (2007) found 28 different media outlets targeting a rapidly growing, but still relatively small Korean community estimated to be less than 32,000 persons in British Columbia, Canada. The implication is that readership of the ethnic press by the group is likely to be fragmented, such that the questions of which media or medium, and which outlets to use to reach the minority ethnic group, remain as key research questions for any ethnic minority business.

During the *consumption phase* the onus is on how to communicate effectively through effective management of service-encounters so as to produce quality assessments that are perceived by consumers to deliver on the promises made by the selected business (which are drawn in the pre-consumption phase). This is a process commonly described in its narrow form to involve appropriate performance in terms of assurance, empathy, reliability, responsiveness and tangibles (Kassim and Asiah Abdullah, 2010; Furrer, Liu and Sudharshan, 2000; Parasuraman, Zeithaml and Berry, 1998).

An important aspect to decide in the *post-consumption phase* is how to generate repeat customers over time through carefully crafted co-ethnic consumer perceptions of continued value co-creation and barriers to exit, leading to a successful extended service encounter. It is a particularly important stage because it involves the process of providing feedback to the minority co-ethnic group (the recommendation source), often via word-of-mouth communicational exchanges with other ethnic minority consumers (Mangold and Faulds, 2009). It is also in this phase that recommendations to others are formed.

Typical Tactical Activities

Overall, ethnic minority businesses deploy a variety of tactical activities that make up their communications approach towards their selected target markets. Which activities are deployed, if any, always depends on business and marketing objectives, context, product type, time, and marketing strategies. Hence they may be thought of as typical rather than required.

The set of chosen activities and subsequent attention to their effects on the target market is focused on ensuring satisfactory service-encounters conducive to relationship maintenance or enhancement. Table 12.2 identifies many of the activities that are typically adopted by ethnic minority businesses targeting a market such as their minority co-ethnic group.

The table identifies ten activity types, with one or more entries for each type. Major attention is given to the choice of language and ethnic media, including social and outdoor media.

Table 12.2 Tactical Activities by Ethnic Minority Businesses—Promotion

Activity type	Typical Tactical Activity by Ethnic Minority Business
Language	Heavy use of ethnic language, accounting for market heterogeneity and level of literacy.
Ethnic media	Communication effectiveness in reaching and retaining a minority ethnic group varies with product class. Promotion of experience and credence service-products needs to use the group's ethnic networks (Pires, Stanton and Stanton, 2004; Pires, Stanton and Cheek, 2003).
	Heavy use of ethnic media, such as newspapers, magazines, radio and television; for food info. Often, communications name an employee recognizable by her/his "ethnic" name.
	Use print media promotions in migrant-focused newspapers periodicals to attract co-ethnics' and similar others' custom.
	More sophisticated forms of mass media promotion—TV, radio and Internet (website, newsletters) are relatively less used due to cost.
Word-of-mouth (WOM), social media	Encourage WOM about the business by fostering *controlled peer-to-peer communications*.
	Use WOM with friends and peers in social networks.
Outdoor media	Use leaflets and door-to-door drops.
Message consistency	Avoid cognitive dissonance by ensuring consistent messages and controlling for language issues.
	React to comments in social media, seeking to address eventual consumers' misunderstandings of the value proposition, hence averting dissonance from peer-to-peer communications.
	Seek professional support and avoid simple translation of communications across ethnic groups.
Message reach and content	Provide info about ethnic products and how they are used in a manner intelligible to all prospective customers, for example using multiple languages.
	Control for intra-ethnic group heterogeneity, without presuming that a particular promotional tool should work for everyone.
Appeal to ethno/ cultural emotions	Call to consumers emotions—e.g. we just won the World Cup, why wouldn't you prefer a French (service activity)?
Intercultural accommodation	Use ethnic attributes (*ethnic language, ethnic music, art, national flags, or other cultural symbols*) to increase similarity with the audience and ensure ongoing communication over time.

(*Continued*)

Table 12.2 Continued

Activity type	Typical Tactical Activity by Ethnic Minority Business
Grassroots/Viral marketing	Involves targeting a small group of consumers and persuading them to propagate the business message organically. Lower cost than broader marketing efforts, featuring low-cost and free campaigns, such as posting on social media or message boards, holding giveaways, contests and similar tactics. It takes advantage of existing social trends and gives audiences what they want.
Relational	Promote to the group, not to the individual consumer. *Reciprocity*—When appropriate recommend other ethnic minority businesses to customers, creating value to consumers through recommendations they can trust and demonstrating empathy, eliciting reciprocal behaviour by those businesses.

Language

Language takes a central place as an important facet of communication, largely anchoring most other tactical activities. Ethnic consumers who lack fluency in the host country's language and the opportunity to use their home country language face a loss of familiar benchmarks and may suffer various forms of cultural deprivation. Language contributes to individual well-being, and marketing communications in one's language can play a critical role in holding an ethnic consumer to a co-ethnic business. Following Jakobsen (1960), language proficiency allows six types of pleasure shared by ethnic entrepreneurs and their co-ethnic market, namely:

1. *Referential pleasure*: ability to express one's thoughts precisely and concisely;
2. *Expressive pleasure*: ability to articulate what one feels at any time;
3. *Conative pleasure*: the effect of own words on the receiving party;
4. *Phatic pleasure*: ability to start/maintain interaction rituals in strong cultural contexts;
5. *Meta-linguistic pleasure*: capacity to elicit, paraphrase, restate and finally to comment and amplify one's own discourse;
6. *Poetic pleasure*: ability to choose the message, its style, sounds, construction, meanings, images and sensations it conveys.

It is, therefore, not surprising that ethnic minority businesses heavily use their ethnic language and media, using simple word-of-mouth communications with friends, consumers and other businesses in the ethnic network (Chiswick and Miller, 1996), encouraging peer-to-peer communications under the control of the business (Dyer and Ross, 2003).

Media

Taking into account their market's level of literacy, a common practice is to advertise using the ethnic media (Deuze, 2006; Omar, Hirst and Blankson, 2004), using the ethnic language and with the particularity of recurringly naming some employee that can be recognized by consumers by her/his "ethnic" name. However, when seeking to attract other customers, some ethnic minority businesses use print media promotions in wider, migrant-focused newspapers and periodicals (Piperopoulos, 2010).

Ethnic radio is widely used in many culturally diverse countries—such as Australia, Canada, France, Germany, Kenya, Mexico, South Africa, United Kingdom and the United States—having the power to valorize and cultivate ethnic differences (Derderian, 2013; Kijana, 2012; Echchaibi, 2011; Mhlanga, 2010; Cohen, 2003; Carlson, 1997; Vargas, 1995), helping to sustain ethnic identification in a multicultural context (Jeffres, 2000). Radio stations dedicated to the minority ethnic group of affiliation are used very often by ethnic minority businesses, attracting a large part of the group constituency as listeners and as participants and diffusing extensive information about businesses which are a source of sponsorship (Jamal, 2005; Deshpandé and Stayman, 1994; Deshpande, Hoyer and Donthu, 1986). More sophisticated forms of mass media promotion such as TV, mainstream radio and the Internet (website, newsletters) are relatively less used due to cost (Piperopoulos, 2010).

Message

At the level of the message to be conveyed, consistency, reach and content are the concern. Consistency seeks to foster correct understanding, including taking steps to avoid cognitive dissonance by using professional translation of messages and addressing any consumer misunderstanding of the value proposition. Messages are on occasion enriched by emotional involvement enhanced with oral pleasure elements (such as ethnic language, ethnic music and other cultural symbols, such as the presence of the home country flag), all of which may assist with intercultural accommodation (Huang, Oppewal and Mavondo, 2013; Usunier, 1998). Appealing to ethnic/cultural emotions is also important: sponsoring community events, such as the broadcast of sports events and giving consideration to any merchandising materials for their ethnic-related suitability, since imitating other businesses' tactics may not be advisable.

Effective Ethnic Communication—More Than Just Language

Communication encompassing language is therefore much more than the development of a functional ability to operate in any particular society.

Individuals deprived of the opportunity to express fully what they mean may experience deprivation. The pleasure of hearing or speaking the home country language can provide a pleasurable experience and the capacity of a provider to offer that experience (perhaps because that is where other members of the group also meet) is a strong retention weapon.

Marketing communications towards an ethnic group must involve more than just using the group's preferred language, and ethnic minority businesses have a variety of elements at their avail, some of which are likely to be more successful than others. Together with the effective delivery of other elements in the marketing mix and consistent with the information in Table 12.1, the right choices of communication style and communication media are needed for these business to effectively attract their co-ethnic consumers and to eventually earn their preference and that of their minority co-ethnic group. Constituting effective barriers to entry for other businesses, it is this preference that sustains ethnic minority business development and consolidation, as well as the achievement of a preferred supplier status discussed in Chapter 9.

Nevertheless, successful performance at the level of the co-ethnic group cannot be seen as indicative of successful communications with consumers in other markets, with distinct ethnicities. Research about the communicational needs and preferences in those markets is required, and the deployment of ethnic-sensitive communication strategies can be expected to be more difficult with a lack of shared ethnicity, all of which supports the claim that achieving a preferred supplier status will be more challenging.

Intra-Ethnic Group Segmentation: Communicating in "Portinhol"

Are the segmentation strategies deployed by businesses to the whole of a host country transferable to minority ethnic groups within that country? Beyond issues related to segment substantiality inadequacies (Pires, Stanton and Stanton, 2011), the same strategies would require the same demographic and lifestyle profiles, as well as similar acculturation paths to the host country. Over time, different acculturation paths, or different stages in the same path, correspond to different consumer groups based on different needs, wants and preferences, including with relation to communications.

Greater competence in a host country's language increases with length of stay and reflects in an increased use of host language marketing communications (Miglietta and Tartaglia, 2009). Nevertheless, even those who are fluent in one language may face difficulty when communicating in a different language. This is the case, for example, of some Portuguese individuals attempting to communicate in Spanish, who end up expressing themselves in "portinhol" (Kid, 2013). The phenomenon is far from atypical of ethnic minorities who congregate in a host country, and its recurrence is not uncommon (Klimpfinger, 2009).

Nevertheless, it has also been argued that, in certain situations, combining two languages is better than the use of only one, perhaps promoting intelligibility among the speakers (Bhatia, 1992); for example, the case of mixing two languages—English and Cantonese—by social community groupings in Hong Kong, was described as either *expedient*, that is, pragmatically motivated, or *orientational*, that is, socially motivated (Luke, 1998). There is no reason, then, to rule out a tactical mixing of languages in marketing communications by ethnic minority businesses however challenging this might be.

Whether language proficiency and purity mean a liking or preference for marketing communication in that language is an issue. Even at the narrow level of one minority co-ethnic group, intra-group heterogeneity may mean that a promotional tool that works for some doesn't work for others, justifying a need for primary research by the business about the different communicational preferences within the group so as to develop marketing communications that will effectively reach specific segments within a minority ethnic group.

Different acculturation levels may justify differences in the desire for communications in the host country language, in the language of the country of provenance or somewhere in-between, as in the cases of "portinhol" and "English-Cantonese". Given the allegedly limited skills-set available to ethnic entrepreneurs, co-ethnicity may be insufficient to warrant effective communications, when seeking to reach an ethnic group.

Communicating to Reduce Perceived Risk

The influence of ethnicity creates a group profile made out of behaviours, ideas and beliefs with which group members are comfortable and consider "proper" or the right way (Brislin, 1981). This distinctiveness can be enhanced by communication complexity, given by the degree of reliance on non-verbal cues (Weiss and Stripp, 1998). After a relationship has developed with a particular co-ethnic business, barriers to switching may be created because communication complexity may discourage further search. Barriers arise because consumers are attracted to and stay with a co-ethnic business due to the link between communication difficulties and perceived risk when dealing with non-co-ethnic businesses. Familiarity and satisfaction with established and complex communication processes increases the perceived risk of switching.

It is important to recall here that, as earlier discussed in Chapter 5 dealing with ethnic loyalty, the role of the minority ethnic group in reaching individual co-ethnic consumers must be addressed by co-ethnic businesses in considering the marketing communication approach to be adopted. While the aim is to cause a response from individual co-ethnic consumers, this is done by focusing on the co-ethnic group, often using the groups' communication networks, such that the ethnic group acts as a reference group. It is the group's endorsement that leverages the business to the group's constituency (Macchiette and Roy, 1992), capitalizing on group members' goodwill towards stakeholders with a shared ethnicity.

From a perceived risk perspective, initial interaction with co-ethnic businesses depends on the consumer's inexperience in the new market-place and on the quality of the long-term relationship of the business with the co-ethnic group, drawing from its collective experience. That is, the minority ethnic group does not react to individual negative exchanges in isolation (which may be blamed on the ethnic consumer), rather it sees them as a continuation of successful past exchanges with group members likely to continue in the future (Cronin et al., 1997). Hence, ethnic consumers depend on their ability and easy communications with their peers, often using word-of-mouth, as a preferred source of perceived risk-reducing market information. This dependence influences the maintenance of customer relationships with preferred suppliers (Sheth and Parvatiyar, 1995) as discussed in Chapter 9.

Word-of-Mouth

Word-of-mouth communications emerge as the most important source of risk-reducing information (Lutz and Reilly, 1974; Sheth and Venkatesan, 1968), with an emphasis on opportunities for clarification and feedback. Word-of-mouth is particularly valued by ethnic minority consumers when conveyed by family and friends as well as opinion leaders and reference group members (Hofstede, 2001), credible for their independence from suppliers and for their previous use of the service-product. In the case of inexperienced ethnic minority consumers, reliance may be on word-of-mouth sourced from their co-ethnic group.

Summing up, belonging to co-ethnic group is not enough; it is necessary to be seen to belong. Individual ethnic consumers must exhibit needs and preferences *mostly* coincidental with those of the co-ethnic group, as well as similar evaluative criteria before and after consumption. It is this requirement that ensures that the minority ethnic group is perceived by ethnic minority businesses as sufficiently, internally homogeneous and its consumption behaviour predictable.

The implication is that inexperienced ethnic minority consumers are likely to obtain consumption information from peers more knowledge-able about the marketplace. A recommendation from peers is likely to be adopted because it reduces perceived risk, while the positive or negative experiences feedback to the group, reinforcing or weakening group preference. Recommendation by peers is, therefore, attractive to ethnic minority businesses.

Grassroots/Viral Marketing

Another typical, tactical activity is for ethnic minority businesses to draw on the likelihood that recommendations from peers are more trusted thus more likely, accepting grassroots or viral marketing activities (Wilson et al., 2013; Southwell et al., 2010; Bush et al., 2004; Makuni, 2001). Accordingly, ethnic minority businesses seek to target a small group of co-ethnic consumers and persuade them to propagate the business message organically to their peers and to their co-ethnic group. These activities are likely to cost less than broader marketing efforts, featuring low-cost and free campaigns such as posting on social media or message boards, holding giveaways and contests. It takes advantage of existing social networks and market trends.

Because of the interlinking of individual consumers within the co-ethnic group, the process of supplier selection can lead to ethnic minority consumers depending on a few ethnic minority businesses bearing the group's imprimatur of enhanced perceived credibility. As explained in Chapter 9, customer satisfaction and a low incentive to switch promote these businesses to a preferred supplier status for both individual consumers and their co-ethnic group, a process that fosters ethnic loyalty.

Relational Communications for Ethnic Loyalty

The link between ethnic consumers and their co-ethnic group supports a long-term relationship with ethnic minority businesses who have achieved a preferred supplier status. Provided the consumer's experiences are positive, this converts into positive feedback to the co-ethnic group and providers remain credibile. Inexperienced ethnic consumers benefit from the referral and support of the co-ethnic group through lower perceived risk and because they become important to co-ethnic businesses through their identification with their co-ethnic group.

Continued group membership requires conformance to the group's values and attitudes. Switching their allegiance attracts economic, social and psychological costs arising from no longer partaking in Oliver (1999)'s "village envelopment" (see Chapter 5). The bottom line, however, is that the social benefits foregone from moving outside the village, including the loss arising from the ease and satisfaction of communicating with co-ethnic peers and eventual barred access to the co-ethnic networks, are ex post and not necessarily apparent to consumers deciding to switch. Hence, ensuring that co-ethnic consumers remain loyal also requires consideration of communications to be used by co-ethnic businesses.

The major advantage for ethnic minority businesses may be that ease or comfort in communicating may be valued by co-ethnic consumers. Oral pleasure may substitute for the sensory deprivation that characterizes cultural shock, contributing to a preference for a co-ethnic supplier, even in cases where consumers have achieved a considerable degree of proficiency in the host country's language (Miglietta and Tartaglia, 2009). The assumption is that ethnic-related attributes contribute positively to the perceived attractiveness of the business, which suggests that proper care should be taken in communicating their position as a co-ethnic business. Using the preferred ethnic language and being involved socially and through participation and sponsorship in community events (Rosenfeld, 2008; Holland and Gentry, 1999; Schneider, 1990) are recurring themes on how to build and improve those communications, but even more important is developing a relationship with the co-ethnic group because it is this that provides the social context that is valued by the individual co-ethnic consumers. Hence the typical tactical activity of promoting to the co-ethnic group rather than to the individual, noted in Table 12.2.

Co-Ethnic Business-to-Business Cooperation

Mostly missing from the specialist literature is the role of co-ethnic business-to-business cooperation within ethnic networks, although the importance of the potential cooperation between co-ethnic businesses in the ethnic network is recognized. For example, it is argued that beyond the benefits from the direct relationships between suppliers in the ethnic network, it is through these relationships that ethnic minority businesses learn about potential customers and suppliers and can develop relationships with them such that the network is a platform for building bridges to new opportunities (Tian et al., 2018).

These growth opportunities can assist an ethnic minority business domestically and in its eventual internationalization, justifying reciprocal behaviours between co-ethnic suppliers. Where appropriate, reciprocity principles support recommendation of peer co-ethnic minority businesses to customers, creating value to consumers through recommendations they can trust and demonstrating empathy both with consumers' needs and wants (Yamagishi, 2003); hence, eliciting reciprocal behaviour by the recommended co-ethnic minority businesses (Bouckaert and Dhaene, 2004).

Reflection on the various tactical activities typical of ethnic minority businesses invites consideration of the effect of personalization, the 8th element of the marketing mix, in successful relational ethnic marketing by ethnic minority businesses. While it is clear that co-ethnic group perceptions are the real focus of attention, it is the understanding and satisfaction of the specifics of co-ethnic consumer needs by the business that flows back to the group, one consumer at a time. Personalization is briefly discussed in the last section of this chapter.

The Personalization Element

Interaction with an ethnic minority business provides co-ethnic consumers with the opportunity to not only make their needs and preferences known to the business but also to share additional personal information. Businesses may use such information for better tailoring their value proposition, enhancing their relational value propositions. To the extent that the cultural awareness and sensitivity of the business leads to responsiveness, customization and personalization may ensue. This involves adjusting the value proposition so that it provides a better match for the particular needs of each customer (Hartman and Lindgren Jr., 1993) as well as converting the commercial interaction into a de facto social interaction (Mittal and Lassar, 1996). Both foment co-ethnic consumer dependence on the preferred ethnic minority business (Bowen and Jones, 1986).

Value similarity and similarity-attraction theory explain why ethnic minority consumers may be strongly predisposed to business establishments owned by members of their co-ethnic group and to enter into personal relationships with the co-ethnic personnel in those businesses (Parissis and Helfinger, 1993). The importance of the "personal" factor justifies further elaboration in considering human resource skills.

'Personalization' refers to the social content of interaction between employees and customers. It is distinct from customization and responsiveness, both of which can be offered with total lack of personalization. If there is a human encounter in a business transaction, the manner in which an ethnic minority business relates to their co-ethnic customers can be expected to contribute significantly to business success. Personalization is the reason why customers in general, not only ethnic minority consumers, seek familiar, likeable, friendly businesses.

Table 12.3 identifies the typical tactical activities (and ways of doing things) to take into account in devising relational value propositions towards minority ethnic consumers.

The general thrust of the entries in Table 12.3 is on the choice of ethnic language and ethnic media, including social ethnic sensitivity, affording importance, respect and relevance to the individual ethnic minority consumer without jeopardizing the importance of other co-ethnic consumers and of the co-ethnic group, and duly recognizing group gatekeepers.

Learning, memorizing, recalling and using proper consumers' names, recognizing consumers social standing, memorizing past exchanges with the consumer, such as asking questions about their holidays, their children (and remembering their names) are meaningful activities in the tactical personalization process. Operationalization of these activities may involves the adoption of a "system for remembering", keeping in mind

Table 12.3 Tactical Activities by Ethnic Minority Businesses—Personalization

---

Personalization-Related Tactics

Focus is on ethnic sensitivity, affording importance, respect and relevance to the individual consumer without jeopardizing the importance of the group.

Recalling and using proper consumer names, recognizing their social standing, memorizing past exchanges with the customer, such as asking questions about their holidays, their children (and remembering their names). This involves the adoption of a "system for remembering", keeping in mind that differential treatments delivered and valued by some may create resentment in others.

Demonstrate an interest in the customers' activities that are in the community domain.

Do not confuse ethnic identity for membership of an aggregate of ethnic group. Two Hispanic stakeholders from different origins may perceive themselves as the same in a mainstream context, but quite distinct from each other in a Hispanic context.

Recognize group gatekeepers.

---

that differential treatments delivered by the business will be valued by some, with or without the conspicuous element (Locander, 2015; Atwal and Williams, 2009), but the same delivery may create feelings of resentment or discomfort on others (Nakano, MacDonald and Douthitt, 1995).

Ethnic minority consumer interaction with an ethnic minority business can be intra- or extra-role. Extra-role interactions involve social bonds that may develop outside the business relationship. For example, ethnic minority consumers interact with peers in social or sporting activities organized by community social clubs. Some of these fellow members may be the travel agent or the electrician preferred by the community. Indirect social interaction may also occur through business links to individuals (as in the case of a doctor that has treated a family over the years) or with institutions that the customer identifies with (such as the community church).

The influence of family, friends and reference groups on purchase behaviour and relationship maintenance is well documented in the consumer behaviour literature (Sheth and Parvatiyar, 1995; Childers and Rao, 1992). Hence, the operationalization of personalization tactics also includes the display of genuine interest in the consumer's activities (those that are known to the community), demonstrating involvement with the community.

Ultimately, personalized interactions may provide customers with social support consisting of social interactions which offer psychological comfort and elation to a person. Support outcomes can range from alleviation of mild boredom to ventilation of anxiety or personal thoughts, confirmation of personal opinions, receiving comfort in grief or the satisfaction of being liked.

Simultaneity/Inseparability as a Vehicle for Responsiveness and Personalization

Simultaneity (and inseparability) implies that service-products are often produced and consumed at the same time, and that the consumer is often an active participant in the performance resulting from the production process. As a performance that results in a service experience, intangible-dominant service-products may be argued *"to have no existence apart from the interaction between the people, both provider and consumer, who experience the service together"* (Friedman and Smith, 1993). This consumer-supplier interaction provides ethnic minority consumers with the opportunity to make their individual needs and preferences known to co-ethnic businesses. Hence, depending on business responsiveness, inseparability provides the opportunity to match co-ethnic consumer's particular needs more closely, by adjusting the service-product (Hartman and Lindgren Jr., 1993).

Inexperienced ethnic minority consumers with communication difficulties may be challenged in situations where their needs and preferences have to be unambiguously transmitted to suppliers, often in the presence of others (Hui and Bateson, 1991). The consumption of intangible-dominant service-products may be particularly challenging because of these consumers' perceived or real difficulties both in explaining their needs and in responding to what may be required of them during their participation or co-creation in the production process. These difficulties have two important outcomes. One is that consumers may apportion part of the blame for service failure resulting from incorrectly provided instructions or faulty participation (Dunn and Dahl, 2012; Harris, Mohr and Bernhardt, 2006; Rebecca, Gwinner and Su, 2004). The other refers to the opportunity that is created for the co-ethnic business to create value for consumers through personalization—the social content between consumer and supplier (Minkiewicz, Evans and Bridson, 2014; Mittal and Lassar 1996)—encouraging co-ethnic consumer loyalty. As noted earlier in this chapter, this is because of an increased opportunity cost of switching suppliers and because the social interaction is, in itself, a possible retention motive (Rohm and Swaminathan, 2004).

Conclusion

The importance of developing marketing communications focused on the minority ethnic group is underpinned by functional elements of communicating and by the psychological pleasure that co-ethnic consumers may receive from engaging in communications using their native language.

The process model of communication was briefly explained and used to elaborate the main elements of communication that need to be addressed by an ethnic minority business seeking to reach a co-ethnic group. Taking advantage of the ease of encoder and decoder use of language and symbols with which both are familiar for establishing and enhancing a relationship with the target group, use of the relevant ethnic media and the reduced noise levels can also facilitate businesses accessing the co-ethnic group.

While a common language, familiarity with coding and decoding symbols, use of co-ethnic media and possibly less noise effects, facilitate communications between ethnic minority businesses and their minority co-ethnic group, a well-designed, integrated marketing communications plan is required. Given the relatively closed nature of the minority ethnic group and the dependence on the recommendation-feedback mechanism, the generation of positive word of mouth is even more crucial than in cross-cultural environments.

Integrated marketing communication is needed to ensure consistent and coherent use of particular marketing communication activities to achieve a purposeful dialogue with the co-ethnic group. Selecting the most effective communication tools depends on an understanding of the group's communications behaviour with respect to media habits, advertising responsiveness and the group's decision-making process.

Communication tactics must be built into the value proposition offered by the ethnic minority business because these tactics can offer various forms of pleasure to co-ethnic consumers, including personalization benefits. But the underlying focus of the adopted communication approach is the co-ethnic group, not the individual consumer, because the group acts as a reference and social agent for the individual.

Understanding preferences for marketing communications in either home country or host country languages is complex. Some individuals may prefer the host country language, others the home country. The use of host country language may be expected to involve the use of cultural values from the home country.

The next chapter examines the people element of the augmented marketing mix, together with issues of ethics and social responsibility.

References

Adcock, D., Bradfield, R., Halborg, A. and Ross, C. (1995). *Marketing Principles and Practice*, 2nd ed. London: Pitman.

Anderson, C. and Imperia, G. (1992). The corporate annual report: A photo analysis of male and female portrayals. *The Journal of Business Communications*, 22(2), 113–128.

APC: Australian Government Productivity Commission (2011). *Economic Structure and Performance of the Australian Retail Industry*. Productivity Commission Inquiry Report No. 56, November.

Atwal, G. and Williams, A. (2009). Luxury brand marketing: The experience is everything! *Journal of Brand Management*, 16(5–6), 338–346.

Bannister, E., Hark, H., Joyce, L. and Portwood, A. (2016). *Multilingual Manchester's Linguistic Landscapes: A Study on the Use of Multilingual Signs for Businesses in Manchester.* The University of Manchester. Accessed 11/7/2018 at http://mlm.humanities.manchester.ac.uk/wp-content/uploads/2016/10/A-Study-on-the-Use-of-Multilingual-Signs-for-Businesses-in-Manchester.pdf

Bhatia, T. (1992). Discourse functions and pragmatics of mixing: Advertising across cultures. *World Englishes,* 11(2–3), 195–215.

Bigné, J., Mattila, A. and Andreu, L. (2008). The impact of experiential consumption cognitions and emotions on behavioral intentions. *Journal of Services Marketing,* 22(4), 303–315.

Bolton, R., Gustafsson, A., McColl-Kennedy, J., Sirianni, N. and Tse, D. (2014). Small details that make big differences: A radical approach to consumption experience as a firm's differentiating strategy. *Journal of Service Management,* 25(2), 253–274.

Bouckaert, J. and Dhaene, G. (2004). Inter-ethnic trust and reciprocity: Results of an experiment with small businessmen. *European Journal of Political Economy,* 20(4), 869–886.

Bowen, D. and Jones, G. (1986). Transaction cost analysis of service organization-customer exchange. *Academy of Management Review,* 11(2), 428–441.

Brislin, R. (1981). *Cross-Cultural Encounters.* New York: Pergamon Press.

Bryceson, D. and Vuorela, U. (2002). *The Transnational Family: New European Frontiers and Global Networks.* ecsocman.hse.ru.

Bush, I., Damminger, R., Daniels, L. and Laoye, E. (2004). Communication strategies: Marketing to the "majority minority". *Concept,* 28.

Carlson, A. (1997). A geographical analysis of America's ethnic radio programming. *The Social Science Journal,* 34(3), 285–295.

Childers, T. and Rao, A. (1992). Influence of familiar and peer-based reference groups on consumer decisions. *Journal of Consumer Research,* 19 (September), 198–211.

Chiswick, B. and Miller, P. (1996). Ethnic networks and language proficiency among immigrants. *Journal of Population Economics,* 9(1), 19–35.

Cohen, E. (2003). Voices of our land: Ethnic radio and the complexity of diasporic practices in multicultural Australia. *Humanities Research,* 10(3), 125–148.

Cronin, J., Brady, M., Brand, R., Hightower, R., Jr. and Shemwell, D. (1997). A cross-sectional test of the effect and conceptualization of service value. *Journal of Services Marketing,* 11(6), 375–391.

Cui, G. and Choudhury, P. (2002). Marketplace diversity and cost-effective marketing strategies. *Journal of Consumer Marketing,* 19(1), 54–73.

Derderian, R. (2013). Broadcasting from the Margins: Minority ethnic radio in contemporary France. In *Post-Colonial Cultures in France.* Abingdon, UK: Routledge, pp. 115–130.

Deshpande, R., Hoyer, W. and Donthu, N. (1986). The intensity of ethnic affiliation: A study of the sociology of Hispanic consumption. *Journal of Consumer Research,* 13(2), 214–220.

Deshpandé, R. and Stayman, D. (1994). A tale of two cities: Distinctiveness theory and advertising effectiveness. *Journal of Marketing Research,* 57–64.

Deuze, M. (2006). Ethnic media, community media and participatory culture. *Journalism,* 7(3), 262–280.

Dhalla, N. and Mahatoo, W. (1976). Expanding the scope of segmentation research. *Journal of Marketing*, 40, 34–41.

Douglis, P. (2000). Photojournalism: telling it like it is. *Communication World*, 17 (February), 44–47.

Dunn, L. and Dahl, D. (2012). Self-threat and product failure: How internal attributions of blame affect consumer complaining behavior. *Journal of Marketing Research*, 49(5), 670–681.

Dyer, L. and Ross, C. (2003). Customer communication and the small ethnic firm. *Journal of Developmental Entrepreneurship*, 8(1), 19.

Echchaibi, N. (2011). *Voicing Diasporas: Ethnic Radio in Paris and Berlin between Cultural Renewal and Retention*. New York: Lexington Books.

The Economist (2013). We speak your language: The elaborate multilingualism of New York on display, January 25. Accessed 4/2018 at www.economist.com/johnson/2013/01/25/we-speak-your-language

Florenthal, B. and Shoham, A. (2010). Four-mode channel interactivity concept and channel preferences. *Journal of Services Marketing*, 24(1), 29–41.

Fortin, D. and Uncles, M. (2011). The first decade: Emerging issues of the twenty-first century in consumer marketing. *Journal of Consumer Marketing*, 28(7), 472–475.

Friedman, M. and Smith, L. (1993). Consumer evaluation processes in a service setting. *Journal of Services Marketing*, 7(2), 47–61.

Furrer, O., Liu, B. and Sudharshan, D. (2000). The relationships between culture and service quality perceptions: Basis for cross-cultural market segmentation and resource allocation. *Journal of Service Research*, 2(4), 355–371.

Grönroos, C. (1991). The marketing strategy continuum: Towards a marketing concept for the 1990s. *Management Decision*, 29(1).

Harris, K., Mohr, L. and Bernhardt, K. (2006). Online service failure, consumer attributions and expectations. *Journal of Services Marketing*, 20(7), 453–458.

Hartman, D. and Lindgren, J., Jr. (1993). Consumer evaluations of goods and services: Implications for services marketing. *Journal of Services Marketing*, 7(2), MCB University Press, 4–15.

Heo, J. and Cho, C.-H. (2009). A new approach to target segmentation: Media-usage segmentation in the multi-media environment. *Journal of Targeting, Measurement and Analysis for Marketing*, 17(3), 145–155.

Hofstede, G. (2001). *Culture's Consequences*, 2nd ed. Thousand Oaks, CA: Sage.

Holland, J. and Gentry, J. (1999). Ethnic consumer reaction to targeted marketing: A theory of intercultural accommodation. *Journal of Advertising*, 28(1), 65–77.

Huang, Y., Oppewal, H. and Mavondo, F. (2013). The influence of ethnic attributes on ethnic consumer choice of service outlet. *European Journal of Marketing*, 47(5/6), 877–898.

Hui, M. and Bateson, E. (1991). Perceived control and the effects of crowding and consumer choice on the service experience. *Journal of Consumer Research*, 18(2), 174–184.

Jakobsen, R. (1960). Closing statement: Linguistics and poetics. In T. A. Sebeok (ed.), *Style in Language*. Cambridge, MA: MIT Press, pp. 350–357.

Jamal, A. (2005). Playing to win: An explorative study of marketing strategies of small ethnic retail entrepreneurs in the UK. *Journal of Retailing and Consumer Services*, 12(1), 1–13.

Jeffres, L. (2000). Ethnicity and ethnic media use: A panel study. *Communication Research*, 27(4), 496–535.

Kassim, N. and Asiah Abdullah, N. (2010). The effect of perceived service quality dimensions on customer satisfaction, trust, and loyalty in e-commerce settings: A cross cultural analysis. *Asia Pacific Journal of Marketing and Logistics*, 22(3), 351–371.

Kid, K. (2013). *Inferno*. mundouniversitario.pt

Kijana, E. (2012). A general assessment of the independent ethnic radio broadcasting stations in Kenya. *International Journal of Business and Social Science*, 3(8).

Klimpfinger, T. (2009). "She's mixing the two languages together": Forms and functions of code-switching in English as a Lingua Franca. *English as a Lingua Franca: Studies and Findings*, 348371.

Kloosterman, R. and Rath, J. (2001). Immigrant entrepreneurs in advanced economies: Mixed embeddedness further explored. *Journal of Ethnic and Migration Studies*, 27(2), 189–201.

Locander, D. (2015). The role of guilt and shame on conspicuous consumption. In *Marketing Dynamism & Sustainability: Things Change, Things Stay the Same. . . .* Cham: Springer, pp. 826–826.

Luke, K. (1998). Why two languages might be better than one: Motivations of language mixing in Hong Kong. *Language in Hong Kong at Century's End*, 145–159.

Lutz, R. and Reilly, P. (1974). An exploration of the effects of perceived social and performance risk on consumer information acquisition. In Scott Ward and Peter Wright (eds.), *NA—Advances in Consumer Research, Volume 01*, Ann Abor, MI: Association for Consumer Research, pp. 393–405.

Macchiette, B. and Roy, A. (1992). Affinity marketing: What is it and how does it work? *Journal of Product and Brand Management*, 2(1), 55–67.

Makuni, T. (2001). The marketing of tourism for ethnic minorities. *Travel & Tourism Analyst* (1), 77–89.

Mangold, W. and Faulds, D. (2009). Social media: The new hybrid element of the promotion mix. *Business Horizons*, 52(4), 357–365.

Mhlanga, B. (2010). The ethnic imperative: Community radio as dialogic and participatory and the case study of XK FM. *The Citizen in Communication*. University of Hertfordshire Research Archive.

Miglietta, A. and Tartaglia, S. (2009). The influence of length of stay, linguistic competence and media exposure in immigrants' adaptation. *Cross-Cultural Research*, 43, 46–61.

Minkiewicz, J., Evans, J. and Bridson, K. (2014). How do consumers co-create their experiences? An exploration in the heritage sector. *Journal of Marketing Management*, 30(1–2), 30–59.

Mittal, B. and Lassar, W. (1996). The role of personalization in service encounters. *Journal of Retailing*, 72(1), 95–109.

Murray, C., Yu, S. and Ahadi, D. (2007). *Cultural Diversity and Ethnic Media in BC: A Report to Canadian Heritage Western Regional Office*. Burnaby, BC: Centre for Policy Studies on Culture and Communities School of Communication, Simon Fraser University.

Nakano, N., MacDonald, M. and Douthitt, R. (1995). Toward consumer well-being: Consumer socialization effects of work experience. *New Dimensions of Marketing/Quality-of-Life Research*, 151–175.

OECD (2012). *The Impact of Internet in OECD Countries*. OECD Digital Economy Papers No. 200, OECD Publishing.

Oliver, R. (1999). Whence consumer loyalty. *Journal of Marketing*, 63, 33–44.

Omar, O., Hirst, A. and Blankson, C. (2004). Food shopping behavior among ethnic and non-ethnic communities in Britain. *Journal of Food Products Marketing*, 10(4), 39–57.

Parasuraman, A., Zeithaml, V. and Berry, L. (1998). Alternative scales for measuring service quality: A comparative assessment based on psychometric and diagnostic criteria. In *Handbuch Dienstleistungsmanagement*. Wiesbaden: Gabler Verlag, pp. 449–482.

Parissis, M. and Helfinger, M. (1993). Ethnic shoppers share certain values. *Marketing (Maclean Hunter)*, 98 (January 11), 16.

Piperopoulos, P. (2010). Ethnic minority businesses and immigrant entrepreneurship in Greece. *Journal of Small Business and Enterprise Development*, 17(1), 139–158.

Pires, G., Stanton, J., and Cheek, B. (2003). Identifying and reaching an ethnic market: Methodological issues. *Qualitative Market Research: An International Journal*, 6(4), 224–235.

Pires, G., Stanton, J. and Stanton, P. (2011). Revisiting the substantiality criterion: From ethnic marketing to market segmentation. *Journal of Business Research*, 64(9), 988–996.

Pires, G., Stanton, J., and Stanton, P. (2004). Tangibility consequences for ethnic marketing strategy. *Global Business and Economics Review*, 6(1), 38–54.

Rebecca, Y., Gwinner, K. and Su, W. (2004). The impact of customer participation and service expectation on Locus attributions following service failure. *International Journal of Service Industry Management*, 15(1), 7–26.

Rohm, A. and Swaminathan, V. (2004). A typology of online shoppers based on shopping motivations. *Journal of Business Research*, 57(7), 748–757.

Rosenfeld, R. (2008). Cultural and heritage tourism. *Municipal Economic Tool Kit Project*. Available at www.researchgate.net/profile/Raymond_Rosenfeld/publication/237461371_CULTURAL_AND_HERITAGE_TOURISM/links/540f3e580cf2df04e75a2ab7.pdf

Schramm, W. (1971). The nature of the communication process between humans. In W. Schramm and D. Roberts (eds.), *The Process and Effects of Mass Communication*. Urbana, USA: University of Illinois Press, pp. 1–53.

Schneider, J. (1990). Defining boundaries, creating contacts: Puerto Rican and polish presentation of group identity through ethnic parades. *The Journal of Ethnic Studies*, 18(1), 33.

Sheth, J. and Parvatiyar, A. (1995). Relationship marketing in consumer markets: Antecedents and consequents. *Journal of the Academy of Marketing Science*, 23, 255–271.

Sheth, J. and Venkatesan, M. (1968). Risk-reduction processes in repetitive consumer behavior. *Journal of Marketing Research*, 307–310.

Southwell, B., Slater, J., Rothman, A., Friedenberg, L., Allison, T. and Nelson, C. (2010). The availability of community ties predicts likelihood of peer referral for mammography: Geographic constraints on viral marketing. *Social Science & Medicine*, 71(9), 1627–1635.

Swenson, C. (1990). Minority groups emerge as major marketing wedge. *Management Review* (May), 24–26.

Tian, Y., Nicholson, J., Eklinder-Frick, J. and Johanson, M. (2018). The interplay between social capital and international opportunities: A processual study of international "take-off" episodes in Chinese SMEs. *Industrial Marketing Management*, 70, 180–192.

Usunier, J. (1998). Oral pleasure and expatriate satisfaction: An empirical approach. *International Business Review*, 7, 89–110.

Vargas, L. (1995). *Social Uses and Radio Practices: The Use of Participatory Radio by Ethnic Minorities in Mexico*. Boulder, CO: Westview Press.

Walker, J. (1995). Service encounter satisfaction: Conceptualized. *Journal of Services Marketing*, 9(1), 5–14.

Weiss, S. and Stripp, W. (1998). Negotiating with foreign business persons. In S. Niemeier, C. Campbell and R. Driven (eds.), *The Cultural Context in Business Communication*. Amsterdam: John Benjamin's Publishing Company.

Wilding, R. (2007). Transnational ethnographies and anthropological imaginings of migrancy. *Journal of Ethnic and Migration Studies*, 33(2), 331–348.

Wilson, J., Belk, R., Bamossy, G., Sandikci, Ö., Kartajaya, H., Sobh, R., . . . Scott, L. (2013). Crescent marketing, Muslim geographies and brand Islam: Reflections from the JIMA Senior Advisory Board. *Journal of Islamic Marketing*, 4(1), 22–50.

Yamagishi, T. (2003). The group heuristic: A psychological mechanism that creates a self-sustaining system of generalized exchanges. In *Proceedings of the Santa Fe Institute Workshop on the Coevolution of Institutions and Behavior*.

Young, S. (2010). The Journalism "crisis" Is Australia immune or just ahead of its time? *Journalism Studies*, 11(4), 610–624.

13 People, Ethics and Social Responsibility

The focus of discussion on the importance of people to ethnic marketing is foremost a human resources problem that may hinder the adoption of ethnic marketing strategies due to limited cross-cultural business skills tied to deficient understanding of ethnic markets. Mostly underpinned by cross-cultural perspectives, the argument is that businesses in general tend to deal with these problems by undertaking cultural awareness/diversity training as a means for managing cultural differences.

Alternatively, or in addition to cultural awareness/diversity training, there are instances where businesses elect to employ ethnic staff as a means of overcoming skills shortages. However, these hiring tactics may be counterproductive, being viewed by some as potentially discriminatory for favouring one group to the detriment of another, unless based on an unlikely in-depth understanding of the diversity of the business' customer base and their specific service and communication preferences (Bendick Jr., Egan and Lanier, 2010).

This chapter deals with people-related tactical activities deployed by ethnic minority businesses. By definition of an ethnic minority business, their dependence is on the targeting of a minority co-ethnic group. While this does not rule out other target markets, whether other minority ethnic groups or even the mainstream community, the main focus of business is the co-ethnic group. Implicit in this context is the knowledge that entrepreneurs have of their group and their shared ethnicity. While this may not suffice for effectively competing against other peer businesses, it is presumed to contribute to competitive advantage vis-a-vis non-co-ethnic businesses.

Following from the discussion in Chapter 9, attention is first given to ethnocentrism within national boundaries, seeking to comprehend the underpinnings of business and consumer dependence on their minority ethnic group of affiliation.

Ethnocentrism Within National Boundaries

Cultural distortions, like other perceptual mechanisms, are important because there is no clear dividing line between image and reality: the

> *reality of our strategic world is inextricably interconnected with our man-*
> *ner of conceiving it.*
>
> (Booth, 2014, p. 9)

Typically involving in-group favoritism (Hammond and Axelrod, 2006), ethnocentrism is an exemplary socio-psychological phenomena of a cultural distortion and a recurring theme in international business, arising in the discussion of strategy formulation (the strategy works successfully in my home market, and it should work in foreign markets), in marketing (if the marketing mix worked at home, it should work abroad) and in human resource management (why should the workforce practices and training be any different to those at home?). One way to think of ethnocentrism is as referring to feelings of group centrality and superiority (Sumner, 1906)

Awareness of "ethnocentrism"- the tendency to refer spontaneously to one's own values and ways of thinking by drawing from one's own ethnic or cultural group—can lead to disinterest, feelings of cultural superiority and cultural biases when making business decisions (Usunier and Lee, 2009) in a cross-cultural setting. The main premise of an ethnocentric way to see the world is that societies place their own group at the centre of that world, perceiving and interpreting other societies within their own frames of reference, and invariably judging them as inferior (Booth, 2014); that is, "(t)he 'we' group is characterized by feelings of superiority and pride, while the 'others' group is perceived as inferior" (Siamagka and Balabanis, 2015, p. 68).

In a domestic environment, studies of ethnocentrism mostly focus on the feelings of immigrants towards the products of their host country. In the case of Asian immigrants in the USA, the finding was that perceived ethnicity and acculturation play an important role in influencing ethnocentric feelings towards the host country, reflected in attitudes and behavioural intentions toward products made in the USA (Watchravesringkan, 2011).

One argument is that when home and host countries represent significantly different degrees of economic advancement, both ethnocentric and non-ethnocentric immigrants generally favor the products of the more advanced country (Zolfagharian, Saldivar and Sun, 2014). This would presumably favour a preference for the host country products since immigrants are generally presumed to look for a better life in a better place.

However, the findings are inconclusive because the role of acculturation and product type remain somewhat nebulous for their effect on ethnic consumers' relative preferences for ethnic products and for mainstream products. For example, Marques, Yzerbyt and Leyens (1988) considered in-group heterogeneity and identified the Black Sheep Effect, addressing judgments about likeable and unlikeable in-group members versus out-group members, finding more extreme judgments by in-group members. Another example is a recent study of second-generation Turkish immigrants in the Netherlands—the children of immigrants who were born and bred in the Netherlands. This study found that acculturation and ethnic identification were important predictors of both consumer ethnocentrism and consumer disidentification, the latter referring to consumer repulsion towards Turkey negatively affecting the purchase of products made in that country or by businesses in that country (Josiassen, 2011). While somewhat startling in its finding of consumer repulsion to their ancestor's place of birth, it certainly is not clear how generalizable this finding is. More research is needed.

The above studies are only meant as examples of the research interest generated in this area, which nevertheless remains immature. Without questioning these or other contributions, much more needs to be discovered about consumer ethnocentrism (and disidentification), given that it is a complex multi-dimensional construct encompassing five dimensions (explained in Table 13.1)—namely ethnocentric prosociality, ethnocentric cognition, ethnocentric insecurity, ethnocentric reflexiveness and ethnocentric habituation (Siamagka and Balabanis, 2015). All have

Table 13.1 The Dimensions of Consumer Ethnocentrism

Ethnocentric Dimensions	Description
Prosociality	Home country's interests take precedence over a person's self-interest, embracing helping co-ethnic individuals without expectation of reward (Powers and Hopkins, 2006).
Cognition	The world is interpreted from the ethnic group's point of view (Applebaum, 1996), biasing beliefs and views about other countries and their products, and encouraging the perpetuation and persistence of false stereotypes (Tiedens and Linton, 2001).
Insecurity	Heightened perception of threat from foreign products (Shimp and Sharma, 1987) increases own group identity and cohesion (Grant, 1993), leading to an intensified attempt to defend the in-group (Bizumic et al., 2009) by supporting domestic products from the home country.
Reflexiveness	Many ethnocentric tendencies are often unconscious and automatically activated (MacDonald, 2006), so the consumer is unaware of the interpretive bias of the information and cannot try to change it to a more socially acceptable one (Bargh, 1989).
Habituation	Consumer ethnocentrism is learned from an early age (Shimp and Sharma, 1987) and the combination of two ethnic identities (alias *partial acculturation*) in the immigrant group does not eliminate the development of ethnocentrism (Zolfagharian, Saldivar and Sun, 2014), being higher for those who adopt a dual ethnic identity, such as Asian-Americans (Watchravesringkan, 2011).

implications for ethnic minority consumers and for ethnic minority businesses affiliating actively to a minority ethnic group, as eloquently indicated by the continued resilience and increasing importance afforded to minority ethnic groups within culturally diverse societies (Jamal, Peñaloza and Laroche, 2015; Pires and Stanton, 2015b).

While an ethnocentric approach may be successful, a prior requirement for this choice is cultural awareness (Bonvillian and Nowlin, 1994), which involves being aware of how another person's acculturation affects one's behaviour, and self-awareness of how one's own culture affects one's behaviour. The increasing visibility of minority ethnic groups, particularly in the USA but also in Australia, the UK and throughout Europe, has heightened business awareness of the opportunities offered by "new" markets based on multiple ethnicities within national borders. Yet, the perceived effectiveness of the increased multicultural marketing efforts to take advantage of those opportunities were estimated at only four of each ten cases.

Targeting ethnic markets is clearly challenging for all businesses, not the least because of the cultural differences that may need to be understood and effectively bridged if the aim is to establish relationships with consumers in these markets, as endorsed in this text. But the argument here is that if an ethnic minority business can target a co-ethnic audience and talk to it in its own language and in its own ways, then it can create a special bond with that audience that is not available to non-co-ethnic businesses (Hotchkiss, 1996). Overcoming the cultural challenge requires staff with a variety of skills and competencies (see Table 13.2 for an explanation), namely: interpersonal skills, linguistic ability, cultural curiosity, tolerance for uncertainty and ambiguity, flexibility, patience and respect, cultural empathy, strong sense of self and sense of humor (Schneider and Barsoux, 2003, pp. 190–195), while operating effectively in the local language and culture may also be important (LNTO, 2000).

The ability to deploy suitable, ethnic-sensitive tactical activities can result in competitive advantage (Emslie, Bent and Seaman, 2007; Cui and Choudhury, 2002; Cui, 1997), but the needed skills and competencies ensure that the cultural challenge is also a challenge for human resource management.

Human Resource Management (HRM) is the term used to describe formal systems devised for the management of people within an organization, involving the staffing (recruitment and hiring), deployment and management of the organization's employees (defining/designing work, employee compensation and benefits). Its purpose is to maximize the productivity of an organization by optimizing the effectiveness of its employees, covering the broad tasks of managing employee assignments and opportunities, competencies, ethical behaviours and motivation (Schuler and Jackson, 2007). It is important in the present context

Table 13.2 Expatriate Skills Required to Function Effectively

Interpersonal skills	The ability to form relationships.
Linguistic ability	Since having total command of the other language may not be feasible and may be less important than trying to develop a feel for what matters to others.
Cultural curiosity	Genuine interest in other cultures.
Tolerance for uncertainty and ambiguity	Information is often insufficient, unreliable and conflicting.
Flexibility	In responding to customer needs and preferences.
Patience	Learning new ways of doing things takes time; indeed, different cultures may hold distinct horizons.
Respect	Non-ethnocentric approach.
Cultural empathy	Focused learning and a non-judgmental approach.
Strong sense of self	Allows for cross-cultural interaction without losing one's identity.
Sense of humor	As a mechanism for coping with a sometimes hostile and always different environment, and for relationship building.

Adopted from Pires and Stanton (2015b)

because business demand for the skills and competencies that facilitate effective communication and interaction with ethnic communities can be expected to influence the criteria that are used in employee selection, as well as the need for, extent and nature of employee training.

Dealing With Cultural Distance

Within any country and any industry, businesses need to train their employees in a variety of areas but, compared with internally oriented areas of specialization, this need may be more pressing in areas involving interactional exchanges with the market. Organizational culture and sub-altern aspects such as service-delivery performance, handling complaints, service recovery and ethical behaviour are just examples that assume particular importance when the strategic focus is on the development and implementation of relational ethnic-sensitive tactical activities.

Staff of ethnic minority businesses need to be prepared to handle enquiries, interact and arrive at an understanding with their co-ethnic consumers within a competitive environment, which implies that consumers have a choice. Hence, understanding consumers' needs and to know how to interact effectively with them while addressing those needs is an important aspect of human resource management and employee training,

However, while formal training programs that foster cultural sensitivity and acceptance of different ways of doing things at country level are widely practiced by businesses that use an expatriate workforce (Harvey and Moeller, 2009; Littrell et al., 2006), such programs are usually focused on alleviating cultural shock effects (Usunier and Lee, 2009; Oberg, 1960), centred on expatriate employees' adaptation to a new mainstream culture, and much less likely to focus on the characteristics of any one specific minority ethnic group. They are, therefore, much less likely to be attractive to ethnic minority businesses, and to be seen as crucial by entrepreneurs for assuring their businesses' effective performance. This is corroborated in Australia by the findings of a report on energy consumption by ethnic minority consumers and businesses, which recommended the recruitment and training of bilingual educators in the languages of the ethnic communities to deliver information sessions on energy markets, demand side participation and hardship assistance (EEC, 2012)

Learning to accept and understand that cultural differences exist can help individuals reduce own discomfort and to better adapt to a new cultural environment (Pires, Stanton and Ostenfeld, 2006). Although essential, this is just the first step in understanding all that needs to be known about a minority ethnic group, with its cultural traits, values, gatekeepers, networks and other specifics required to power effective business performance that eventually meets with group preference.

The lack of group specific training programs can be explained by the minority status of the group in focus, justified both by a lack of critical mass to attract training providers, and by uncertain demand for the training, given the financial and time costs involved. Notwithstanding, while the consequences of a lack of training programs specific to a minority ethnic group are likely to be greater for non-co-ethnic businesses, such as mainstream businesses, due to the greater cultural distance (Chen et al., 2010; Harrison and Peacock, 2009; Hofstede, 1983), ethnic minority businesses may also suffer from the lack of formal business training programs for ethnic entrepreneurs.

The absence of formal training programs for ethnic minority businesses needs to be managed by suitably trained ethnic entrepreneurs, who then need to select the right employees and to train them to ensure they have the right skills and competencies, coaching them to perform effectively (Berg and Karlsen, 2012; Hameed and Waheed, 2011).

Summing up:

1. Different countries will offer ethnic entrepreneurs more—as in the case of the UK (Hussain and Matlay, 2007; Basu, 2004), or less, as in Australia (Collins, 2003)—business support and training programs;

2. Employee selection may involve a process with greater complexity for these businesses because prospective employees are often family members (possibly without the required skills), co-ethnic individuals, similar-others and, perhaps less often, individuals from the dominant group;
3. Given a possible lack of formal cultural training about the specific minority ethnic group, training is often on-the-job, with or without supervision; field training/coaching by the entrepreneur requires skills, which may be limited as per point 1 above;
4. While the main focus of an ethnic minority business is on the co-ethnic minority ethnic group, other ethnic groups and the mainstream cannot be excluded from day-to-day operations, with encounters taking place in the presence of each other.

There is, therefore, no apparent reason why the skills explained in Table 13.2 would not apply here. In fact, those skills may be more strongly required given a perceived power shift from the customer to the supplier, and the high probability that customers from different minority ethnic groups may be in each other's presence when interacting with an ethnic minority business.

The implication is that, while ethnic minority business dependence is necessarily on the co-ethnic group of affiliation, cross-cultural interactions cannot be excluded, adding to the complexity in dealing simultaneously with different cultures, although this difficulty may be moderated if:

*   It is accepted that all consumers try to fit, to some extent, with the mainstream way of doing things, thus providing a shared base for consumption behaviour and facilitating employees' performance (Anthias and Cederberg, 2009); and
*   In the case of highly intangible service activities' instances of business failure, simultaneity and inseparability in service-encounters may help reduce the negative implications for business through the partial appropriation by customers of the responsibility for poor interactions.

Notwithstanding, a common way adopted by business in general in dealing with exchanges involving cultural distance issues is to reduce the distance by employing individuals that identify themselves with the target minority ethnic group (Hou, 2009; Aldrich and Waldinger, 1990). Together with the skills required to manage cross-cultural differences, language and cultural differences between businesses and consumers within a host country result in different vocabularies for the interpretation of things and different behaviours in consumption. Employing co-ethnic labour reduces cross-cultural communication issues.

Cultural Distance Is Not All About Language

A common language and intracultural understanding may facilitate interactions and agreement with co-ethnic minority consumers, reducing transaction costs (eventually making new business opportunities viable) and fostering business relationships, leading to enhanced competitiveness. But reducing cross-cultural communication problems goes beyond differences in written and spoken languages.

At the service-encounter level, co-ethnic employees may assist with face-to-face interactions, reducing differences in verbal and non-verbal behaviours. Verbal behaviour involves what we say and how we say it, relating to accent, tone of voice, volume of voice, rate of speech and slang. Non-verbal behaviour involves what we say when we are not talking, including "body language" such as eye contact and ways of showing respect, "object language" such as dress codes and ornaments; "communication style" or how we prefer to express ourselves, such as ways of getting our point across and assumptions about ways of speaking and interacting with each other; and perhaps critically, values, attitudes and prejudices.

Values, attitudes and prejudices are the most complex aspects of non-verbal language because they relate to an individual's deep beliefs and feelings about their own identity, about the world and about how they evaluate other people (Martin and Nakayama, 2013; Australian Multicultural Foundation, 2010; Argyle et al., 1970), including matters of ethics.

Communication, including language skills and cultural understanding, are fundamental internal elements in the process of defining organizational capabilities necessary for ascertaining customer needs and preferences and, ultimately, for achieving competitive advantage. But while the need for these competencies is generally understood and enacted by business, context and intra-group heterogeneity of the target group involving individual acculturation differences also play an important role in determining how to proceed.

The marketing literature offers abundant evidence of attempts by mainstream businesses to reach ethnic communities with problematic translations of mainstream advertising and stereotyping of those communities. For example, in the broadly defined Hispanic market in the U.S., the cardinal rule appears to be the provision of customer service in Spanish. Hence the report that, in predominantly Hispanic areas, over 90 percent of the customer service personnel of Coral Gables Federal, a financial institution serving central and southern Florida Markets, spoke Spanish (Holliday, 1993). Given the language and cultural diversity of the Hispanic market, cultural misunderstandings are not surprising.

Language Preference Matters

Shanmuganathan, Stone and Foss (2004) noted that 60 percent of Hispanic-Americans preferred to speak Spanish, compared to only 21 percent who preferred to speak English. Similarly, a majority of integrated

Chinese-Americans still preferred to use Chinese when communicating with each other, while Indians (from Asia) were comfortable communicating in English. In Australia, a study of culturally and linguistically diverse energy consumers in households and in ethnic-specific businesses found a preference for receiving information about energy usage, costs and savings in their home language, together with assistance in understanding different types of contracts and how to reduce or conserve energy (EEC, 2012). The implication is that, even if consumers are bilingual and effective users of the mainstream language, there are reasons for business and government to use the ethnic language instead.

> Speak the language, get the business.
>
> (Pollock, 1993, p. 13)

The suggestion is that, while communicating in the mainstream language might be adequate, businesses may need to go beyond "adequate". Communicating in the ethnic language earns respect and attention. For example, there are many Hispanics in the USA who speak Spanish as well as English. However, if a business communicates with these consumers in Spanish (particularly their kind of Spanish), there is an emotional attachment as well as a moral obligation in operation:

> (T)here is a company that is trying to reach me in a way I see as positive. Therefore, I want to do business with them.
>
> (Hotchkiss, 1996, p. 31)

Generally speaking, businesses that show their sensitivity towards ethnic minority consumers by communicating in their language may be rewarded with their custom (Medcalf, 1993). This sensitivity may be heightened if the use of the ethnic language is complemented by ethnic employees who are aware of the customer's cultural makeup, and by their involvement with the minority group. Notwithstanding, the question of how to bridge the cultural distance separating general businesses and ethnic consumers goes well beyond language and language preference, remaining an area for ongoing research much facilitated in the case of ethnic minority businesses.

Typical Tactical Activities Deployed by Ethnic Minority Businesses

Following the European Commission (2008), the typical ethnic minority business is likely to be a micro business owned and managed by a male ethnic entrepreneur with few employees, if any, operating in areas of business with low entry barriers and requiring low skill requirements. Low entry barriers mean that the business is vulnerable to price competition, by other co-ethnic entrepreneurs, by ethnic minority businesses affiliated to other ethnic groups, and by business in general. But a main reason is also a lack of differentiation expertise—by entrepreneur and employees—which explains labour intensive production, long working hours and low wages, as well as lower turnover and lower profit than typical businesses without the ethnic connotation. Asian shopkeepers, for example, are noted for their "commendable industriousness" working 80 hours a week and ignoring the toll this takes on them as human beings (Jones and Ram, 2012; Ram, Jones and Edwards, 2007).

Congruent with discussions in previous chapters of this text, there is somewhat limited research on tactical activities deployed by ethnic minority businesses given the variability in understanding what a minority business is, and the relative concentration of focused research in just a few countries, such as the UK. However, it is possible to propose that many ethnic minority businesses follow a typical path from their start-up to the outgrowth threshold that highlights the people side of the business, where ceasing to be dependent on a minority co-ethnic group dictates their loss of an ethnic connotation.

In the first instance, newly arrived migrants join a minority co-ethnic group, gaining access to its networks. In this process they may gain employment in existing co-ethnic minority businesses in a process that also provides them with opportunities to learn on the job and access to business contacts, to role models and to the consumer community with which some may develop professional and social relationships. This process can provide a way into an ethnic minority business of their own, drawing on co-ethnic peers as a means of reciprocating the benefits gained from the co-ethnic group (Yamagishi, 2003). The discussion that follows provides commentary relevant to Table 13.3.

The Choice of People to Employ

Ethnic minority businesses may be created in the first place to take on opportunities available in the co-ethnic market(s). This involves identifying what the unfulfilled needs and wants of that market are and sensing (more than recognizing based on experience) an ability to satisfy those needs and wants. Often the business objectives of earning a living and/or achieving family employment and/or or enhancing the entrepreneur's social status are pursued through marketing strategies focused on responding effectively and efficiently to the unfulfilled needs and wants (Benavides-Velasco, Quintana-García and Guzmán-Parra, 2013). Amongst the tactical activities adopted to aptly satisfy consumers' demand is the employment of people capable of more easily establishing relationships with the target market.

Given the need for the business to understand the cultural nuances of the group, when group needs and wants cannot be addressed solely by the entrepreneur, demand for co-ethnic labour will be created. That demand may be met by the entrepreneur's family members, or by individuals recruited from

Table 13.3 Tactical Activities by Ethnic Minority Businesses—People

Typical People-Related Tactical Activities

Employing co-ethnic staff (including family members)	Makes the business more similar to the target audience, providing a sense of belonging and of contributing to the welfare of the group (consistent with the theory of intercultural accommodation).
	Using family and co-ethnic staff may lead to competitive advantage and growth due to lower recruitment and payroll costs. Co-ethnic labour may work for less if they have an illegal status and/or are unable to secure other employment.
	Recruiting co-ethnic staff who are knowledgeable about the products being supplied. Service differentiation happens if customers are informed on the products and on their usage.
	Objective may be to take advantage of co-ethnic markets, targeting their demands and creating demand for co-ethnic employees who understand the group's culture. Demand may be met by family members, or by co-ethnic individuals.
Staff ethnicity, development and growth	Independent of own ethnicity, consumers prefer co-ethnic service staff. This justifies employing mainstream staff when the host country is seen as a growth market for the business.
	There is an inverse relationship between growth and proportion of co-ethnic or family employees in the UK.
Use family members as formal/informal workforce	Can make the difference vis-a-vis other types of business, but it can be a bad thing, given reports of underpayment for long hours of work. Growth can be restrained by nepotism in selection/promotion decisions and low productivity.
	Assuring family employment or enhanced social status may be important key performance indicators in entrepreneur's/ ethnic minority business' key business objectives.
Recruitment	Using ethnic networks as the main yet informal recruitment source of co-ethnic and loyal employees reduces economic risks. Ethnic networks may perform better than formal recruiting sources, yielding a more stable and productive workforce.
Training	Develops skills, changes attitudes and directly influences growth, contributing to increased sales, effective team building, improved quality standards and a stronger new organizational culture. However, ethnic entrepreneurs usually recruit their employees from family and from their co-ethnic group using informal practices.
	Businesses may face problems with on the job management training, skills acquisition, and reliance on family and co-ethnic labour, justifying a formal recruitment approach.
Competitive advantage	May derive from the exploitation of unskilled co-ethnic labour ready to work for less, or from nepotism in recruitment.
	Staff cultural diversity can increase competitiveness, in expanding to other minority ethnic groups' markets.

the target market, commonly co-ethnic individuals (Light and Gold, 2000). Depending on the target market, individuals affiliated with other minority ethnic groups and even mainstream individuals may be recruited.

Employing Family Members

Using family members as a formal/informal workforce can make a competitive difference vis a vis other types of business (Danes et al., 2008; Olson et al., 2003) due to lower recruitment and payroll costs.

While family members may be willing to work for less, they may contribute highly to the success of the business by working more hours and, especially due to their eventual ability to advise consumers on the service-products offered by the business and on how to use those products. Similar to non-family co-ethnic employees, this type of enhanced service provided to consumers may convert into a differentiator factor, reducing business exposure to price-based competition.

The downside from employing family members (and co-ethnic individuals), however, is reflected in many reports of unethical practices of underpayment for very long hours worked by co-ethnic and family employees. Ethnic minority business growth can be restrained by nepotism in selection and in promotion decisions (Noon, 2007; Bates, 1994). Furthermore, research (in the UK) has found indications of an inverse relationship between ethnic minority business growth and the proportion of co-ethnic or family employees (Basu, 1998).

Employing Co-Ethnic Staff (Other Than Family Members)

Similar to employing family, using co-ethnic staff may lead to competitive advantage and growth potential due to lower recruitment and payroll costs, but also has ethical downsides that may involve work exploitation. Co-ethnic labour may work longer for less (Anderson, 2010; Kassim, 2001), even more so if they have an illegal status and/or are unable to secure other employment.

Recruitment of co-ethnic staff is particularly justified as a tactical activity if the staff is knowledgeable about the ethnic products being supplied. Their ability to inform customers about the products and to advise on their use may be a source of effective service differentiation that reduces business exposure to price-based completion, an important aspect to consider in competitive markets.

Employing Staff That Share Their Ethnicity With the Target Market

The proposition that most people will willingly gravitate toward community groups with traits similar to their own is explained by the combination of similarity-attraction theory, social identity theory and self-categorization theory. A large body of literature in interpersonal relationships has established that similar-others are more attractive, liked better and more trusted compared to dissimilar others. Attitudinal and value similarity promote trust toward the other (Dwyer, Schurr and Oh, 1987). Accordingly, interaction is easier and less cognitively challenging with others who have similar experiences, attitudes, activities or values.

Accordingly, employing people that share their perceived and self-ascribed ethnicity with the market targeted by an ethnic minority business assists in making the business more similar to the consumers in that market, potentially causing a sense of belonging for the supplier and the consumer that may reflect on comfortable easy communications and negotiations. Provided the manager and service employees are able to service consumers in an ethnic sensitive way, for example, by using the ethnic language, demeanour and ways of doing things, this can be expected to reflect on the value proposition perceived by consumers making up the market.

This approach towards recruiting contributes to the welfare of the market, as proposed by the theory of intercultural accommodation (Huang, Oppewal and Mavondo, 2013), and can be a possible source of competitive advantage by the business because, independent of the entrepreneur's own ethnicity, consumers prefer co-ethnic service staff (Baumann and Setogawa, 2015). However, this may be counterproductive if there is a lack of fit between the employee's culture and that of the employer, leading to the suggestion by Schneider and Barsoux (2003) that ethnic minority businesses need to consider how well the employee will relate to the employer and with employees from distinct ethnic groups, how well and how easily the employee will socialize and what specific training will be required.

Overall, ethnic minority businesses targeting minority ethnic groups other than their own can employ non-co-ethnic staff who share their ethnicity with the target market, as in the case of an Italian business targeting consumers in the Greek ethnic group. This also justifies employing mainstream staff when the mainstream market is seen as a growth market for the business.

Using Ethnic Networks for Recruiting Consumers and Suppliers

Ethnic entrepreneurs often seek to take advantages of business opportunities offered by perceived unmet demands within their co-ethnic group. Affiliation with the group provides access to the group's ethnic networks. Social and business networks can thus become a source of co-ethnic employees, who come with recommendations by the group (Bloch and McKay, 2015; Patacchini and Zenou, 2012).

Business networks, including preferred suppliers to the co-ethnic group, are a further source of advice and recruitment, preferably consensual, as well as a tactical preferred source of supply (Kim, 1999). This is because employees recruited from within the business network may be already experienced in the socialization process with consumers in the group, offering the additional advantage to the new employer of a proven, ethnically sensitive delivery of service.

Barring adversarial recruitment practices, the business network may recognize the cooperative behaviour of the ethnic minority business. When this converts into recommendation to their own customer base, it provides a platform for the ethnic minority business to strengthen its own customer base, as well as enhance its standing in the co-ethnic social network.

In addition to providing access to co-ethnic employees, hence presumed to require less training to minimize cultural distance reflected in ethnic-sensitive service delivery, using ethnic networks as the main yet informal recruitment source of co-ethnic and loyal employees reduces economic risks.

Finally, employing from within the co-ethnic group implies offering employment opportunities to co-ethnic individuals. This can reverberate positively with the group, enhancing the standing of the business within the community and strengthening promotion to a preferred supplier status as a good community member.

Overall, the conclusion is that ethnic networks may perform better than formal recruiting sources for ethnic minority businesses, yielding a more stable and productive workforce (Brüderl and Preisendörfer, 1998) and strengthening the standing of the business within the co-ethnic social and business community. Nevertheless, minority ethnic groups should not be seen as closed enclaves, rather contributing together with other similar groups to the cultural diversity of cities and of countries. The implication is that individuals who can demonstrate ethnically sensitivity skills are also coveted by businesses seeking to target culturally diverse populations within large cities, such as London, Sydney and New York (Ortlieb and Sieben, 2013; Lee and Nathan, 2010), hence competing with ethnic minority businesses. Ethnic sensitivity skills are clearly valued by ethnic minority businesses, and should attract appropriate rewards for employees and employers.

Ethnic Sensitivity Skills Training

As detailed in Table 13.3, training employees develops skills, changes attitudes and directly influences growth (Basu and Goswami, 1999), contributing to increased sales, effective team building, improved quality standards and a stronger, new organizational culture (Daniels, 2003). However, ethnic minority businesses usually recruit their employees from family and from their co-ethnic group using informal practices.

Difficulty in accessing relevant, ethnic sensitive training geared to individual minority ethnic groups explains why co-ethnic businesses often expect their employees to learn on the job, a practice that also reduces substantial training costs (Wood and Mallinckrodt, 1990). This also may explain that these businesses are generally geared towards the recruitment of family labour and co-ethnic employees via informal sources, namely their social and business networks (Waldinger, 2005).

On the job management training and skills acquisition as well as reliance on family and co-ethnic labour may be the source of problems for ethnic minority businesses, particularly those in the start-up phase (European Commission, 2008). While the answer to these problems may be the adoption of a formal recruitment and training approach, the necessary resources and mechanisms may be lacking given the specificity of minority ethnic groups and what ethnic-sensitive practices entail.

Management Training and Skills Acquisition

Given that ethnic minority consumers identify with their co-ethnic group, an ethnic minority business faces reduced complexity in the management of cultural differences arising from possible group heterogeneity, when compared with the difficulties faced by outsider businesses.

However, when targeting outside the co-ethnic group, ethnic minority businesses face greater difficulties in managing cultural differences, whether they simply ignore the differences or adopt a standard or global approach to dealing with cultural differences or attempt to develop cultural competencies either by employing bilingual ethnic employees or through appropriate skills training of existing co-ethnic employees. Following Pires and Stanton (2015a), the contextual embedding of the ethnic minority business needs to be taken into account, including the number of minority ethnic groups to be targeted, the current stock of skills within the business, the degree of competition and barriers to entry, the availability of suitable bilingual employees, the relative importance of the ethnic market in the overall market of the business and the resources available to the business.

But the complexity involved in diversity training cannot be over emphasized. Employees need to feel that they are freely choosing to be non-prejudiced, not that they have that imposed on them. As noted by Rock and Grant (2017),

> When people perceive one another as members of the same in-group, racial bias (. . .) tends to melt away. Thus, the way to increase inclusion in the workplace is to make everyone feel like they're part of the same team.
>
> (p. 11)

Finally, an important aspect to take into account is that it is the business as a whole that needs to learn and operationalize the necessary skills to successfully satisfy customer needs and preferences in alternative cultural markets, not individual employees.

People Tactics for Competitive Advantage

Competitive advantage may be relatively easy to achieve by ethnic minority businesses, when they achieve the special status of preferred supplier to their co-ethnic group. However, achieving a preferred supplier status depends on the value proposition offered by the business which encapsulates a variety of tactical activities, of which "people" is a major one. As an element of the marketing mix, the role played by people with soft ethnic-sensitive skills is crucial to an ethnic minority business' ability to ensure positive and productive interactions with co-ethnic customers, without questioning the contribution derived from other elements in the marketing mix.

Given the shared ethnicity and small cultural distance between the ethnic minority business and the co-ethnic group on which it depends, it should be expected that managing any minor ethno-cultural differences related to group heterogeneity may be relatively easy when compared with operations across ethnic groups. Hence, provided ethnic minority businesses remain focused on their co-ethnic group and are able to defend against the poaching of their best employees by businesses focusing on culturally diverse markets, co-ethnic employees can increase the ability to compete and to achieve competitive advantage.

This premise, however, is challenged when ethnic minority businesses attempt to grow outside the boundaries of the co-ethnic group. Whether expansion is into other minority ethnic groups' markets or into the mainstream, ability to compete will depend on employee cultural diversity (Smallbone, Bertotti and Ekanem, 2005), as reflected in their service delivery practices. For example, there is no clear reason to argue that Chinese employees who are highly proficient in serving the Chinese minority ethnic group will be equally proficient serving the Japanese minority ethnic group instead.

Finally, various aspects of ethical practices by ethnic minority businesses were alluded to. For example, it was noted that the employment of family members and, in some cases, co-ethnic staff may be disruptive to ethnic minority business growth, hence to competitive advantage. While it may be the lure of competitive advantage that explains attempts to exploit unskilled co-ethnic/family labour ready to work for less, the likelihood is that these practices, together with unethical practices of nepotism in recruitment and selection, may reduce productivity and expose the business to competitors (Dhaliwal, 2008).

Indeed, opportunistic practices such as work exploitation by requiring family and co-ethnic labour to work longer for less (Anderson, 2010) may be incidentally justified by eventually precarious business contexts. Occasionally, such practices may even be assessed positively as altruistic by the community, as in the case of the employment of co-ethnic individuals unable to secure other employment (whether with legal or illegal status in the host country). However, there is no evidence that nepotism, discriminatory work advancement and underpayment practices (Noon, 2007) can be expected to meet with positive assessments by the co-ethnic community for the longer term implied in the deployment of relational business approaches.

Given other ethics-related practices discussed in Chapter 11, such as unfair premium pricing at community events, supply of ethnic products of poor quality and general over-promising may not always be distinct from fair pursuance of opportunities in serving co-ethnic minority groups, so their possibly negative repercussion cannot be overlooked. For example, it is widely accepted that black, Asian and minority ethnic female entrepreneurs are subject to more discrimination, also reflected in a lack of business and social support (Carter et al., 2015; Davidson, Fielden and Omar, 2010; Collins and Low, 2010; Pearce, 2005)

Reflecting the sparse attention given to issues of social responsibility and ethics in a small business context (Worthington, Ram and Jones, 2006), this chapter concludes with a brief appraisal of those issues in the context of ethnic marketing relevant to ethnic minority businesses, largely drawing from Pires and Stanton (2002, 2015b).

Ethnic Minority Business: Ethics and Social Responsibility

> *(T)rying to do the right thing when marketing to ethnic minorities, is the risk of causing offence to others when a well-meaning campaign is poorly targeted.*
>
> Chankon Kim

Drawing on Vitell, Rallapalli and Singhapakdi (1993), ethnic marketing ethics is understood as referring to the nature and grounds of moral judgments, standards and rules of conduct relating to ethnic marketing decisions and ethnic marketing situations. This allows for decisions and situations inherent to business-to-consumer (B2C), administration/government to consumer (A/G2C) and, indeed, business-to-business (B2B) environments.

The importance of issues of ethnic marketing ethics and social responsibility has been highlighted by relatively recent research in the marketing literature (Jamal, Peñaloza and Laroche, 2015; Pires and Stanton, 2015b, 2002; Cui and Choudhury, 2002; Cui, 1997). Including discussions of social responsibility usually limited to A/G2C perspectives, examination is overwhelmingly focused on issues of ethics related to the targeting/non-targeting of vulnerable consumers affiliated with minority ethnic groups (Andreasen and Manning, 1990), or some aggregate of these groups (such as Hispanics, African-Americans and Asian-Americans). The context of that research is, invariably, on business and Government behaviour in the B2C domain and typically limited to the examination of cross-cultural aspects.

An extensive multi-disciplinary search for literature largely met with silence on matters of social responsibility and ethical behaviour involving ethnic minority businesses either as a perpetrator or as a recipient. Urged by the identification of important and enduring issues of ethical concern in the discussion of the importance of people in ethnic minority businesses' marketing mix, ethics is the mainstay of the discussion concluding this chapter.

Statement of Ethics, American Marketing Association (AMA)

As stewards of society in creating, facilitating and executing the transactions that are part of the greater economy, businesses are responsible for the deployment of marketing activities toward multiple stakeholders (e.g. customers, employees, investors, peers, channel members, regulators and the host community) in a way that is subject to professional ethical norms and values. In order to establish terms of reference for the discussion of ethnic minority business ethics, reliance is on the Statement of Ethics endorsed by the American Marketing Association (AMA, 2018), reproduced in Table 13.4 for easy reference.

Values represent the collective conception of what communities find desirable, important and morally proper, also serving as the criteria for evaluating our own personal actions and the actions of others (AMA, 2018). While all businesses are presumed to strive to make decisions

Table 13.4 Ethical Norms and Values for Ethnic Minority Business (AMA, 2018)

Ethical Norms and Values to be Considered by Ethnic Minority Business	
Norms	1. Do no harm—Consciously avoid harmful actions or omissions by adopting high ethical standards and adhering to all applicable laws and regulations. 2. Foster trust—strive for good faith and fair dealing so as to contribute towards exchange process efficacy and avoid deception in product design, pricing, communication and delivery of distribution. 3. Embrace ethical values—Building relationships and enhancing consumer confidence in the integrity of the business by affirming these core values: honesty, responsibility, fairness, respect, transparency and citizenship.
Values	Represent the collective conception of what communities find desirable, important and morally proper.
Honesty: Be forthright in dealings with stakeholders	Involves offering products of value that do what we claim in our communications; stand behind our products if they fail to deliver their claimed benefits; honour all commitments and promises.

(Continued)

Table 13.4 Continued

Ethical Norms and Values to be Considered by Ethnic Minority Business	
Responsibility: Avoid using coercing any stakeholders	Acknowledge social obligations to stakeholders from increased marketing/economic power; recognize commitment to vulnerable market segments (e.g. children, seniors, market illiterates, the economically impoverished) who may be disadvantaged; considering environmental stewardship in decision-making.
Fairness: Balance justly the needs of the buyer with the interests of the seller.	Involves representing products in a clear way in selling, advertising and other forms of communication (avoiding false, misleading and deceptive promotion); rejecting manipulative sales tactics that harm customer trust; refusing price fixing, predatory pricing, price gouging or "bait-and-switch" tactics; avoiding knowing participation in conflicts of interest; and protecting the private information of customers, employees and partners.
Respect: Acknowledge the basic human dignity of all stakeholders	Valuing individual differences and avoiding stereotyping customers or depicting demographic groups (e.g. gender, race, sexual orientation) in a negative or dehumanizing way; listening to customers' needs and making all reasonable efforts to monitor and improve their satisfaction; making every effort to understand and respectfully treat buyers, suppliers, intermediaries and distributors from all cultures; acknowledging contributions by others (e.g. consultants, employees and co-workers) to marketing endeavours; and treating everyone, including competitors, as we would wish to be treated.
Transparency: Create a spirit of openness in marketing operations	Striving to communicate clearly with all constituencies; accepting constructive criticism from customers and other stakeholders; explaining and taking appropriate action regarding significant product or service risks, component substitutions or other foreseeable eventualities that could affect customers or their perception of the purchase decision; disclosing list prices and terms of financing as well as available price deals and adjustments.
Citizenship: Fulfil economic, legal, societal and philanthropic responsibilities	Striving to protect the ecological environment in the execution of marketing campaigns; giving back to the community through charitable donations and volunteerism; contributing to the overall betterment of marketing and its reputation; and urging supply chain members to ensure that trade is fair for all participants, including producers in developing countries.

guided by those values regardless of the context, there are particular values that have greater resonance for ethnic minority businesses given their focus on minority ethnic groups and the objective of developing long-term relationships with the minority ethnic group through relational tactical activities extended to co-ethnic consumers. The various values are briefly discussed below.

"Honesty" involves protecting the value proposition that stimulates and anchors consumer loyalty (see Chapter 5). Together with matters of consumer advocacy in marketing, honouring all promises and commitments made to consumers is fundamental for anchoring loyalty (Chelminski and Coulter, 2011; Urban, 2005). This involves recognizing consumers' needs and the business' ability to deliver what is required.

'Responsibility' involves recognizing consumer vulnerability and possible dependence, contributing positively to their socialization, while being proactive in assuring environmental leadership. Instances of advocacy in the realm of social responsibility range from programs aimed at improving energy consumption by ethnic consumers by seeking to better understand the experiences and concerns of culturally and linguistically diverse energy consumers in households and in ethnic-specific businesses in Australia (EEC, 2012); to assistance with healthcare plans (Health Reform, 2014) and promotion of pro-consumer policy helping consumers be heard by those in power (Consumeraction, 2013) in the USA; as well as the promotion of dialogue between stakeholders in advocating for the respect of consumers' basic rights in Mauritius (http://cap-mauritius.org/).

"Fairness" refers to co-development of the value proposition in a way that accounts for the mutual benefits that must accrue both to the business and the customer without compromising consumer privacy.

"Respect" is a core element of cross-cultural and ethnic sensitivity competency training concerned with valuing individual differences and avoiding stereotyping, even when the drive is for building substantial market segments in the case of internally heterogeneous minority ethnic groups. An *ethnic stereotype* exists when ethnic minority consumers are perceived and treated by others in terms of a generalized and often idealized notion of the minority ethnic group they affiliate with, rather than in terms of specific profiling of the group (Hamilton, 1979). Respect also involves exercising a reasonable effort to listen to all stakeholders and to monitor and improve their satisfaction on an ongoing basis, treating everyone to the same standard desired for the business itself.

"Transparency" means keeping open communication channels with all stakeholders, accepting constructive criticism and assuring that consumers know all they need to know in order to defend their own interests. Finally, "citizenship" recognizes that the business is embedded and responsible for the upkeep of the minority ethnic group of the host country and of the ecological environment. As a good citizen, an ethnic minority business may give back to the community through donations, sponsoring and similar activities. Good citizenship combines with social responsibility and is fundamental in firming a position as a preferred supplier.

Disadvantage, Vulnerability and Poor Business Practices

Examining social responsibility and ethics issues related to ethnic marketing at any level can benefit from clearly distinguishing general considerations of business ethics, "what is good" related to business practice (Seelye and Wasilewski, 1996), from poor business practice (as contrasted with unethical behaviour) and social responsibility (what is "good" for society in general, present and future).

The distinction between ethics and social responsibility may be easier to operationalize in the case of ethnic minority businesses given their shared ethnicity with their target market, although market heterogeneity may be a complicating factor. This is because a business needs to define a level of "what is good" that balances own goals, customers' needs and those of society in general (Pires and Stanton, 2002), thus respecting their primary function as providers of a service to their customers (Buchholz and Rosenthal, 2000). Notwithstanding, dependence on the co-ethnic marketing group does not impede exploration of opportunities focused on other minority groups, the mainstream or even external markets. Clearly, operationalization is more complex in these cases because distinct cultures lead to eventual lack of alignment of the notion of "what is good" across cultures (Kotler et al., 1998, p. 833; Sarwono and Armstrong, 1998).

Adapted to the present context from a critical review of the relevant literature, Table 13.5 reports ethics and social responsibility issues associated with ethnic marketing targeted to co-ethnic minority consumers by ethnic minority businesses.

Often noted in the literature for their vulnerability and disadvantaged status vis-a-vis the mainstream population, consumers within heterogeneous minority ethnic groups may suffer from inequalities in the marketplace (Wolburg, 2005; Brenkert, 1998). Ethnic minority consumers, particularly early in their settlement within a host country, may have limited market knowledge about what is available, where and for how much, as well as about market "do's and don'ts", reflected in poor socialization. This may lead to newcomers being perceived as disadvantaged with their vulnerability exploited through deceptive practices by both ethnic minority businesses and businesses in general (Kotler et al., 1998; Moore-Shay, 1996), clearly a matter of concern for ethnic marketing ethics.

New arrivals in the host market often rely on referral or recommendation by similar-others they trust (Frable, Platt and Hoey, 1998)—eventually their minority ethnic group of affiliation, particularly when market inexperience and communication difficulties limit the number and range of accessible secondary sources—as a means to reduce vulnerability to deceptive practices (Pires and Stanton, 2000) and lessen the effects of cultural shock (Oberg, 1960). Notwithstanding, there is a continued perception of vulnerability and disadvantage, perhaps explained by incongruent stereotyped conceptualizations reflective of cultural sensitivity limitations and based on early information impervious to subsequent evidence, or epistemic freezing (Kruglanski and Freund, 1983).

Table 13.5 Ethical and Social Responsibility—Ethnic Minority Businesses

Consumer preference for a co-ethnic supplier may defer, at least temporarily, the acquisition of market information. While consumption from a supplier preferred by the co-ethnic group may be effective and efficient, it may be below optimal since alternative supplier options may not be tested.

Failure to correct for imperfect market socialization mechanisms which can increase the power of the business over inexperienced co-ethnic consumers.

Combined with failure to correct for imperfect market socialization mechanisms, consumer preference for a co-ethnic supplier may lead to a stagnant ethnic business network and, ultimately, to a closed ethnic enclave situation, resulting in ineffective and inefficient business practices.

Failure to accommodate ethnic minority consumers' wants due to cultural sensitivity limitations may cause loss of self-esteem and contribute to cultural shock (Oberg, 1960; Usunier and Lee, 2009).

Failure to satisfy "real" needs and wants in order to pursue desired business outcomes may result in misallocation of resources. This is also a social responsibility issue related to the principle of economic efficiency (Kotler et al., 1998).

Discrimination against smaller segments within the ethnic group on presumed substantiality grounds, may involve the deliberate distortion of businesses' primary function of providing a service (Buchholz and Rosenthal, 2000), as well as poor business practices, reflecting poorly on consumers' feedback to the group.

Breach of ethnic sensitivity through undesired targeting of smaller segments within the ethnic group as a separate market.

Discrimination against smaller segments within the ethnic group by providing inadequate, insufficient, misdirected and/or misinterpretable information. Similar to principle of consumer education and information (Kotler et al., 1998) and a recurring issue in healthcare (Grier and Kumanyika, 2008).

Unfair use of fine print in contracts and use of legalese to take opportunistic advantage of ethnic minority consumers' market inexperience.

Adoption of an *etic* approach towards ethnic minorities' need for culturally sensitive therapies when an *emic* approach is justified (Hall, 2001).

Social responsibility issues such as the failure to translate public interest information about the value proposition (e.g. non-smoking campaigns, medical information and product information).

Considerations about ethnic group substantiality, sometimes perpetuated by a lack of objective information and by the perception of poor returns to the business, may lead to eventual failure to focus on the needs and wants of some sub-segments, including the provision of market information that could enable neglected segments to look for solutions in an informed way. In situations of racial discrimination, as discussed below for the Indian community in the United States, consumer disadvantage may ensue (Grier, Williams and Crockett, 1996). While exposure to a multicultural experience may have ameliorative effects through epistemic unfreezing (Tadmor et al., 2012), deception and discrimination remain important ethics issues involving ethnic minority consumers.

From a social responsibility perspective, failure by ethnic minority businesses to focus on the needs and wants of some ethnic minority consumer segments may lead to dual misallocation of resources, with failure to satisfy "real" needs and over-marketing due to overestimation of the size of the minority ethnic group as a whole resulting in increased costs for the group (Fisher et al., 1999), for the business and for society as a whole. Some of the potential consequences listed in Table 13.5 may result mostly from poor business practices, in which case the resulting ethics/ social responsibility issue is present but is not deliberate. Nevertheless, the targeting of minority ethnic groups by ethnic minority businesses may involve deliberately unethical actions as well as actions intrinsically unethical.

Adapted from Cui (1997) Table 13.6 identifies five areas of potential ethical failure by ethnic minority business, namely: inadvertent

Table 13.6 Areas of Potential Ethical Failure by Ethnic Minority Business

Description	
Inadvertent stereotypes	Refers to situations of increased participation by some consumers (e.g. Buddhists) from that group in advertising to co-ethnic consumers, with messages that are stereotypical and do not reflect the diversity of the ethnic group as a whole. This is often the case of communications involving African Americans in the USA (Craemer, 2011);
Biology and Genetics	Refers to the use of superficial or exaggerated physical or biological attributes of different segments within a minority ethnic group, possibly suggesting that those segments may be inferior or that ethnic minority consumers are inferior;
Nature of the product	Refers to the target marketing of a community with negative, inferior or harmful products, such as ethnic products of unknown brands sourced from the country of provenance;
Redlining	Refers to the selection/exclusion of segments of the community based on racial lines. It can be perceived as *implicit discrimination* (Bertrand, Chugh and Mullainathan, 2005), and extended to the *symbolic racism* concept of whites versus blacks (McConahay and Hough Jr, 1976). Also similar to *consumer racism*, with significant negative effects for minority-owned business performance (Ouellet, 2007);
Ethnocentric bias	Questions whether fundamental principles of marketing based on research of the minority ethnic group as a whole, such as in the case of the Indian community, can be generalized to all segments in the community.

Source: Adapted from Cui (1997)

stereotypes, biology and genetics, nature of the product, redlining and ethnocentric bias.

From an outset where all ethical and social responsibility implications related to socio-economic activity apply equally to all minority ethnic group affiliates, issues of inadvertent stereotypes, and biology and genetics may not apply in the context of a homogeneous minority ethnic group. However, even those issues may apply in situations of inner-minority ethnic group heterogeneity. A major example is the Indian community in the USA, comprising 2.4 million Indian immigrant residents in 2015. The community grew more than eleven-fold, up from just 12,000 in 1960, and it is second only to the Mexican community (Zong and Batalova, 2017). Comprising Hindus, Christians, Muslims, Sikhs, Jains, Buddhists, Parsis and Indian Jews, the Indian community is far from homogeneous, as clear in the excerpt below:

> My doctor is a Kiwi, but Ella goes to an Indian medical doctor. Her dentist is also an Indian. So the cultural dilution may be important. If you come from a strong ethnic background it may be different. In our case, it's not strong because Ella comes from a different part of India. Her house would be 3,000 kilometers from my house. So her culture is very different from my culture. We would eat fish every day. They would eat fish maybe once in a year.
>
> Very different food habits in India. If we were both from the same community then we would have been maybe much stronger in those ethnic similarities. Also the Gods we believe in are also different. They come from the same family of Gods but the prime God in our part of the world is different to the prime God in their part of the world . . . so there is a big difference . . . the way we look at life is very different to the way they look at life. In fact where I come from they look at life in education. From where they come from they look at life in more in material terms. These are very different outlooks and the consequence is that our kids don't have a very strong stamp of that thinking in them.
>
> (Kamal Ghose)

Applied to the Indian community, the practice of ethnic minority business based on the unrealistic homogeneity of the community may be questioned, based on all five areas of possible ethical failure. *Redlining*, for example, refers to the selection/exclusion of segments within a heterogeneous ethnic minority group (such as the Indian community) by ethnic minority business based on racial lines. It can be perceived as *implicit discrimination* if the business is not aware of its practice (Bertrand, Chugh and Mullainathan, 2005). It is also similar to *consumer racism*, a measure of consumer judgments of, and willingness to buy, ethnic products that are perceived as being made by selected or excluded segments, with significant negative effects for minority-owned business performance (Ouellet, 2007).

In the case of ethnocentric bias, the ethical concerns derive from the development of marketing programs towards the co-ethnic group as a whole, hence ignoring the specific needs and wants of segments within the group.

Other issues that may arise from unethical targeting of ethnic minority consumers by ethnic minority businesses are reported in Table 13.7, involving stereotyping, incorrect ascriptions to the community, exclusion, racial discrimination, privacy concerns, dumping of products, alienation of trusted sources, price discrimination, bribes and behaviours that are opportunistic and/or discriminatory (Davidson, Fielden and Omar, 2010; Aldrich and Waldinger, 1990). An example in the literature refers to the targeting of tobacco and alcohol-related products to minority ethnic groups, sometimes understood as racist behaviour (Moore, Williams and Qualls, 1996).

A notable feature of Table 13.7 is its inclusion of issues related to actions enacted by businesses directed to consumers, strictly a B2C environment, albeit intertwined at times with A/G2C aspects relevant to social responsibility. Given the active participation of ethnic minority consumers and businesses in the host country's marketplace not only as consumers and users of social products but also as producers and retailers, functions usually in the B2B domain, focus on only the B2C environment is, on ethical grounds, hazardous. This is more so in the present context given the role played by ethnic business networks in the day-do-day life and resilience of minority ethnic groups.

For example, dependence on existing preferred suppliers to the community during the start-up phase of a business may be rewarded with reciprocal behaviour to the otherwise unjustified exclusion of competitors, hence possibly adulterating market mechanisms. This defies compliance of the "Respect" value discussed above—the need to "make every effort to understand and respectfully treat buyers suppliers, intermediaries and distributors from all cultures" (AMA, 2018), implicitly recognizing responsibility for ethical responsible behaviour along the whole of the supply chain.

Table 13.8 provides a preliminary review of ethical considerations on ethnic marketing ethics in a B2B context, involving at least one ethnic business.

Acknowledging that business environments are often subject to written norms and regulations, ethical behaviour by embedded ethnic minority businesses is guided by what is legal and what is illegal, as well as by unwritten rules of conduct that, inherently unethical as they may be, are sometimes perceived as characteristic of the normal way of doing business. For example, the potential for bribery practices within the B2B ethnic marketing context is justified by such practices being deemed as common in international/cross-cultural marketing (Dunfee et al., 1999),

Table 13.7 Consequences From Unethical Targeting of Ethnic Minority Consumers by a Co-Ethnic Minority Business

	Description
Alienation	Of trusted sources, potential gatekeepers to the minority ethnic group and affiliated ethnic minority consumers, through bribes or similar practices (Varner and Beamer, 1995; Fadiman, 1986), e.g. leading to preferred supplier status independent of performance.
Consumer privacy infringement	Since consumers' right to be left alone includes unwanted marketing solicitations. For example, personal data ethically collected by business or government into a database—respecting ethnic minority consumers' autonomy, informed consent and freedom to withdraw—that may or not be passed to other marketers (Fisher et al., 1999; Smith, 1994).
Deception	By deliberate omission of information or use of small print in contracts (Fair Trading, 2013). Also related to *bad faith*, which involves intentionally misleading someone or undertaking an agreement without any intention of fulfilling its provisions (Borgerson and Schroeder, 2002).
Emotional damage to ethnic minority consumers	• Due to *stereotyping, incorrect ascription, discrimination,* etc., by ethnic minority businesses when appearance, country of birth, neighbourhood of residence, etc., wrongly suggest affiliation to a minority ethnic group (Cocchiara and Quick, 2004). • By businesses and government using collective stereotypes, ascription, etc., when consumers are affiliated to a minority ethnic group. Similar to *inadvertent bias* (Cui, 1997) and *implicit bias* (Greenwald and Krieger, 2002) or prejudice (Rudman et al., 1999).
Dumping	Of lower quality, unsuccessful, defective, untried products on inexperienced and resource-poor ethnic minority businesses. There may be an element of danger.
Exclusion	Of ethnic minority consumers from minority ethnic group affiliation when an affiliation exists (Pires and Stanton, 2002).
Opportunistic behaviour	Due to deliberate overpricing or limiting access to services in order to capitalize on market inexperience and communication difficulties.
Price discrimination	Relative to prices set for segments in the same ethnic group (even if price matches perceived net value).
Preferential/ discriminatory behaviours on ethnic grounds	• When considering recruitment of employees. • When considering employment conditions and advancement for certain employees, such as family employees, based on ethnic grounds.
Racial discrimination	Of ethnic minority consumers, similar to *redlining* (Cui, 1997) and extensive to *symbolic racism* (McConahay and Hough Jr, 1976).

Source: Adapted from Pires and Stanton (2015b)

Table 13.8 Preliminary Considerations of Ethics and Social Responsibility in the B2B Domain Involving an Ethnic Minority Business

Description	
Bribery	Accepting bribes or requesting extraordinary compensation when allocating contracts to ethnic-related business. Explained using social contracts theory (Dunfee, Smith and Ross, 1999).
Deception	By deliberate omission of information or use of small print in contracts with ethnic minority businesses (Fair Trading NSW, 2013).
Dumping	Of lower quality, unsuccessful, defective, untried products on inexperienced and resource-poor ethnic minority businesses. There may be an element of danger.
Price discrimination	Relative to prices set for the mainstream or for other ethnic communities (even if price matches perceived net value).
Opportunistic behaviour	• Due to deliberate overpricing or limiting access to services in order to capitalize on lack of market experience and communication difficulties; • *By other ethnic minority businesses in the ethnic business network* due to deliberate overpricing or limiting access to services in order to capitalize on lack of market experience and communication difficulties.
Preferential or discriminatory behaviours	• In banking and financing—limited ethnic minority businesses' access to resources at start-up and at times of crisis, such as access to small business loans (Manneh, 2011), extra requirements for collateral before getting loans (Ekwulugo, 2013) and general access to banking services (Allawas, 2013); • In designing the terms of, adjudicating and managing contracts.
Respect issues	Due to dependence on existing preferred suppliers to the community during the start-up phase of a business may be rewarded with reciprocal behaviour to the otherwise unjustified exclusion of competitors, hence possibly adulterating market mechanisms.
Resource misallocation	*By ethnic minority businesses* due to a lack of mainstream audience appeal and reliance on preferential behaviour from within their ethnic network, such that best price is not a priority (Allawas, 2013).

Source: Adapted from Pires and Stanton (2015b).

justifying the upkeep of a "Bribe Payers Index" (The Economist, 2011). An argument can be made that, since a home culture has predictable effects on managerial decision-making (Tse et al., 1988), similar effects apply within a B2B ethnic marketing domain (Armstrong, 1996).

As social outsiders within a host country, ethnic minority businesses may experience deficits in wealth, in valid educational credentials, in lobbying power and influential contacts. To compensate for these deficits and to overcome political and economic obstacles they face, businesses use personal networks, family and co-ethnic labour, building special relationships and delivering special services, supporting ethnic associations, paying penalties and seeking protection from governments officials and owners outside their ethnic communities through bribery (Waldinger et al., 1990). As stated by Aldrich and Waldinger (1990),

> Government is dealt with by ethnic owners in much the same way that non-ethnic owners always have: bribery, paying penalties, searching for loopholes, and organising protests.
>
> (p. 131)

Justified by what is "known" to actually happen in markets, the Business Marketing Association (New York City) has a Code of Ethics discouraging bribery and practices such as disparaging a competitor's products unfairly, and encouraging treating suppliers equitably (BMA, 2013).

Objection to the noted, almost exclusive examination of ethical issues in the B2C domain, also extends to ethical implications of C2C communications, including the fair or unfair preference for particular ethnic minority businesses and potential influence on exchanges within other environments. These are created by exposure to structural change in information and communication technologies (ICT) and convergence capabilities which support C2C communications.

Exposure to ICT-Based Structural Change

Changes in marketing activity related to consumer-based communication and accessibility issues for ethnic minority businesses from a perspective of ethics and social responsibility are barely covered in the relevant literature. Notwithstanding, the verified importance of this exposure within ethnic markets strengthens the call by Pires and Stanton (2015b) for further research, since minority ethnic groups and their affiliated consumers and businesses are empowered to independently satisfy their unique demands, at least for some types of goods and services. This may result in a widening of the gap between consumers' wants and suppliers' offers, inviting examination of associated ethics and social responsibility issues (Pires, Stanton and Rita, 2010).

The question is whether ethnic minority businesses strengthen their position in the market due to the wider access to alternative suppliers, or whether their ability to benefit is impaired, at least to a greater extent than competitors' ability, by their deficits in wealth, in valid educational credentials, in lobbying power, in influential contacts and in access to banking and financing. To presume that all ethnic minority businesses benefit from the same accessibility as competitors, or that they are likely to become equally proficient in communicating in the language of the web does not appear a sensible presumption from the outset, given all the known vulnerabilities related to the cultural, language and digital divides (Pires and Aisbett, 2003).

Inequitable ICT-driven gains may contribute to market imbalances, with implications for social responsibility. This may require more Government support for ethnic minority businesses, including proficiency in ICT and, unavoidably, proficiency in English, still the common language of the Internet.

Flexibility and Evolutionary Dynamism

Ethnic minority businesses may benefit from ICT-based flexibility to interact with consumers and suppliers in tactical ways that duly takes into account aspects of ethics and social responsibility. Pires and Stanton (2015b) recommend examining the potential for the operationalization and implementation of glocalized marketing programs, both within multi-ethnic domestic markets and for minority ethnic communities with multi-locations globally. However, it is unrealistic to consider that only ethnic minority businesses adapt to the evolution of the internet, or that this adaptation will be positive, given the multi-level embedding of ethnic minority businesses. Some questions that need answers and are examined for their implications for ethical behaviour and social responsibility include:

- Can ethnic minority businesses benefit from the potential of robotics?
- Can the use of substitutes for humans able to replicate human actions meet the need for bilingual employees recruited from the co-ethnic group or family?
- Can greater accessibility allow ethnic minority businesses to go beyond their outgrowth threshold?
- Can ICT and robotics dictate the demise of ethnic minority businesses because any business will be able to woo co-ethnic minority consumers with effective and efficient ethnic-sensitive strategies?

Summary

Attention in this chapter was first given to people as an element of the marketing mix, highly relevant to the tactical activities deployed by ethnic minority businesses. The importance of people was strongly highlighted, but a number of issues of ethics and social responsibility were discovered. Drawing on Pires and Stanton (2015b), attention thus focused on providing an updated perspective of the ethical and social responsibility issues impacting ethnic minority business, necessarily spreading to ethnic marketing as a whole, culminating in a brief discussion of issues emanating from the internet revolution.

It is apparent that the dynamic nature of the capabilities currently becoming available to ethnic minority businesses is grounded on continuous ICT-based innovation that demands capabilities that are both flexible and dynamic, justifying continuous examination. However, ICT-based innovation does not question the tenet that ethnic communities are socially determined. The internet revolution has been ongoing, yet the digital divide remains a reality across and within countries, remaining a real matter of social justice and social responsibility and justifying continued intervention by government.

Clearly, the impact of government policies on immigrants can affect the opportunities available to start a business or the types of businesses that may be started. Some nations require a person to be a resident in order to start a business and it may be extremely difficult, or take many years for an immigrant to obtain their citizenship. Many communities have zoning and ordinances which prohibit certain types of businesses from operating or which dramatically increase the start-up costs for a business in order to comply with the local regulations (Waldinger et al., 1990; Min and Bozorgmehr, 2003).

On a global scale, there are marked differences in the public policies and strategies that countries have adopted to deal with immigrants and refugees, either political or economic. Over the past 60 years, the United States of America has consistently shown a positive stance, while European nations have dithered on the fence at times aggressively "recruiting" immigrants and, more recently, enacting legislation to curb major influxes and/or hinder economic incorporation (Hollifield, 1994).

While research points to the myriad of difficulties encountered by both illegal and legal immigrants in terms of "language barriers, cultural differences, rising competition, racial segregation, taxes and money problems" (Nam and Herbert, 1999, p. 341), immigrant tenacity has delivered positive returns in both struggling and booming economies as well as contributing to the emerging global economy.

> In the beginning I worked in a small firm producing plastic flowers . . . Then we managed . . . to get a license for being street vendors . . . and we have worked, together with my husband, as street vendors at open markets, feasts, such things.
>
> (Hatziprokopiou, 2003, p. 1041)

Issues of environmental conditions favourable to the growth of ethnic marketing are discussed in the next chapter.

References

Aldrich, H. and Waldinger, R. (1990). Ethnicity and entrepreneurship. *Annual Review of Sociology*, 16(1), 111–135.

Allawas, J. (2013). Hispanic emarketing in a B2B Environment. *Advertising & Marketing Review*. Accessed 23/07/2018 at www.ad-mkt-review.com/public_html/docs/fs076.htmled

AMA: The American Marketing Association's (2018). *Statement of Ethics*. Accessed 20/7/2018 at www.ama.org/AboutAMA/Pages/Statement-of-Ethics.aspx

Anderson, B. (2010). Mobilizing migrants, making citizens: Migrant domestic workers as political agents. *Ethnic and Racial Studies*, 33(1), 60–74.

Andreasen, A. and Manning, J. (1990). The dissatisfaction and complaining behavior of vulnerable consumers. *Journal of Consumer Satisfaction, Dissatisfaction and Complaining Behavior*, 3, 12–20.

Anthias, F. and Cederberg, M. (2009). Using ethnic bonds in self-employment and the issue of social capital. *Journal of Ethnic and Migration Studies*, 35(6), 901–917.

Applebaum, B. (1996). Moral paralysis and the ethnocentric fallacy. *Journal of Moral Education*, 25(2), 185–199.

Argyle, M., Salter, V., Nicholson, H., Williams, M. and Burgess, P. (1970). The communication of inferior and superior attitudes by verbal and non-verbal signals. *British Journal of Social and Clinical Psychology*, 9(3), 222–231.

Armstrong, R. (1996). The relationship between culture and perception of ethical problems in international Marketing. *Journal of Business Ethics*, 15(1), 1199–1208.

Australian Multicultural Foundation (2010). *Managing Cultural Diversity Training Program Resource Manual*. Carlton South, Victoria, Australia: Australian Multicultural Foundation,.

Bargh, J. (1989). Conditional automaticity: Varieties of automatic influence in social perception and cognition. In J. S. Uleman and J. A. Bargh (eds.), *Unintended Thought*. New York: Guilford Press, pp. 3–51.

Basu, A. (2004). Entrepreneurial aspirations among family business owners: An analysis of ethnic business owners in the UK. *International Journal of Entrepreneurial Behavior & Research*, 10(1/2), 12–33.

Basu, A. (1998). An exploration of entrepreneurial activity among Asian small businesses in Britain. *Small Business Economics*, 10(4), 313–326.

Basu, A. and Goswami, A. (1999). South Asian entrepreneurship in Great Britain: Factors influencing growth. *International Journal of Entrepreneurial Behavior & Research*, 5(5), 251–275.

Bates, T. (1994). Social resources generated by group support networks may not be beneficial to Asian immigrant-owned small businesses. *Social Forces*, 72(3), 671–689.

Baumann, C. and Setogawa, S. (2015). Asian ethnicity in the West: Preference for Chinese, Indian and Korean service staff. *Asian Ethnicity*, 16(3), 380–398.

Benavides-Velasco, C., Quintana-García, C. and Guzmán-Parra, V. (2013). Trends in family business research. *Small Business Economics*, 40(1), 41–57.

Bendick, M., Jr., Egan, M. and Lanier, L. (2010). The business case for diversity and the perverse practice of matching employees to customers. *Personnel Review*, 39(4), 468–486.

Berg, M. and Karlsen, J. (2012). An evaluation of management training and coaching. *Journal of Workplace Learning*, 24(3), 177–199.

Bertrand, M., Chugh, D. and Mullainathan, S. (2005). Implicit discrimination. *American Economic Review*, 95(2), 94–98.

Bizumic, B., Duckitt, J., Popadic, D., Dru, V. and Krauss, S. (2009). A cross-cultural investigation into a reconceptualization of ethnocentrism. *European Journal of Social Psychology*, 39(6), 871–899.

Bloch, A. and McKay, S. (2015). Employment, social networks and undocumented migrants: The employer perspective. *Sociology*, 49(1), 38–55.

BMA (2013). *Code of Ethic*. Accessed 22/7/2018 at www.marketing.org/i4a/pages/index.cfm?pageid=5279

Bonvillian, G. and Nowlin, W. (1994). Cultural awareness: An essential element of doing business abroad. *Business Horizons* (November–December), 44–51.

Booth, K. (2014). *Strategy and Ethnocentrism*. Routledge Revivals. Abingdon, UK: Routledge.

Borgerson, J. and Schroeder, J. (2002). Ethical issues of global marketing: Avoiding bad faith in visual representation. *European Journal of Marketing*, 36(5/6), 570–594.

Brenkert, G. (1998). Marketing and the vulnerable. *Business Ethics Quarterly*, 1, 7–21.

Brüderl, J. and Preisendörfer, P. (1998). Network support and the success of newly founded business. *Small Business Economics*, 10(3), 213–225.

Buchholz, R. and Rosenthal, S. (2000). Ethics, economics, and service: Changing cultural perspective. In *Proceedings, Seventh Annual International Conference Promoting Business Ethics*. New York: St John's University, pp. 9–16.

Carter, S., Mwaura, S., Ram, M., Trehan, K. and Jones, T. (2015). Barriers to ethnic minority and women's enterprise: Existing evidence, policy tensions and unsettled questions. *International Small Business Journal*, 33(1), 49–69.

Chelminski, P. and Coulter, R. (2011). An examination of consumer advocacy and complaining behavior in the context of service failure. *Journal of Services Marketing*, 25(5), 361–370.

Chen, G., Kirkman, B., Kim, K., Farh, C. and Tangirala, S. (2010). When does cross-cultural motivation enhance expatriate effectiveness? A multilevel investigation of the moderating roles of subsidiary support and cultural distance. *Academy of Management Journal*, 53(5), 1110–1130.

Cocchiara, F. and Quick, J. (2004). The negative effects of positive stereotypes: Ethnicity-related stressors and implications on organizational health. *Journal of Organizational Behavior*, 25(6), 781–785.

Collins, J. (2003). Cultural diversity and entrepreneurship: Policy responses to immigrant entrepreneurs in Australia. *Entrepreneurship & Regional Development*, 15(2), 137–149.

Collins, J. and Low, A. (2010). Asian female immigrant entrepreneurs in small and medium-sized businesses in Australia. *Entrepreneurship and Regional Development*, 22(1), 97–111.

Consumeraction (2013). *Advocacy & Media*. Accessed 22/7/2018 at www.consumer-action.org/about/articles/advocacy_media

Craemer, T. (2011). Preventing inadvertent stereotyping in the racial gap literature. *APSA 2011 Annual Meeting Paper*. Accessed 22/7/2018 at http://papers.ssrn.com/sol3/papers.cfm?abstract_id=1901764

Cui, G. (1997). Marketing strategies in a multi-ethnic environment. *Journal of Marketing Theory and Practice*, 5(1), 122–134.

Cui, G. and Choudhury, P. (2002). Marketplace diversity and cost-effective marketing strategies. *Journal of Consumer Marketing*, 19(1), 54–73.

Danes, S., Lee, J., Stafford, K. and Heck, R. (2008). The effects of ethnicity, families and culture on entrepreneurial experience: An extension of sustainable family business theory. *Journal of Developmental Entrepreneurship*, 13(3), 229–268.

Daniels, S. (2003). Employee training: A strategic approach to better return on investment. *Journal of Business Strategy*, 24(5), 39–42.

Davidson, M., Fielden, S. and Omar, A. (2010). Black, Asian and minority ethnic female business owners: Discrimination and social support. *International Journal of Entrepreneurial Behavior & Research*, 16(1), 58–80.

Dhaliwal, S. (2008). Business support and minority ethnic businesses in England. *Journal of Immigrant & Refugee Studies*, 6(2), 230–246.

Dunfee, T., Smith, N. and Ross, W., Jr. (1999). Social contracts and marketing ethics. *Journal of Marketing*, 63(3), 14–32.

Dwyer, F., Schurr, P. and Oh, S. (1987). Developing buyer-seller relationships. *Journal of Marketing*, 51(2), 11–27.

The Economist (2011). Bribe payers index: International back scratching-corruption in the Public and Private sectors go together. Accessed 22/7/2018 at www.economist.com/blogs/dailychart/2011/11/bribe-payers-index

ECC: Ethnic Communities Council (2012). *Experiences of Energy Consumption for Culturally and Linguistically Diverse (CALD) Communities*, March. Accessed 22/7/2018 at www.eccnsw.org.au/Documents/FinalCALDReport_31May.aspx

Ekwulugo, F. (2013). Ethnic minority businesses: Challenges and agenda for research. *Enterprise Matters eMagazine*. Accessed 22/7/2018 at www.isbe.org.uk/EthnicMinorityBusinesses

Emslie, L., Bent, R. and Seaman, C. (2007). Missed opportunities? Reaching the ethnic consumer market. *International Journal of Consumer Studies*, 31(2), 168–173.

European Commission (2008). Supporting entrepreneurial diversity in Europe-ethnic minority entrepreneurship/migrant entrepreneurship: Conclusions and recommendations of the European commission's network "ethnic minority businesses". *Enterprise and Industry Directorate-General*. ec.europa.eu/DocsRoom/documents/2365/attachments/1/translations/en/.../pdf

Fadiman, J. (1986). A traveler's guide to gifts and bribes. *Harvard Business Review*, July–August, 122–136.

Fair Trading, NSW Government (2013). Accessed 21/7/2018 at www.fairtrading.nsw.gov.au/Consumers/Contracts/Unfair_contract_terms.html

Fisher, J., Garrett, D., Cannon, J. and Beggs, J. (1999). Problem businesses: Consumer complaints, the better business bureau, and ethical business practices. In *Marketing and Public Policy Conference Proceedings*, Vol. 9. Chicago, IL: American Marketing Association, pp. 69–72.

Frable, D., Platt, L. and Hoey, S. (1998). Concealable stigmas and positive self-perceptions: Feeling better around similar others. *Journal of Personality and Social Psychology*, 74(4), 909–922.

Grant, P. (1993). Ethnocentrism in response to a threat to social identity. *Journal of Social Behavior and Personality*, 8(6), 143.

Greenwald, A. and Krieger, L. (2002). Implicit bias: Scientific foundations. *California Law Review*, 94(4), 945–967.

Grier, S. and Kumanyika, S. (2008). The context of choice: Health implications of targeted food and beverage marketing to African Americans. *American Journal of Public Health*, 98(9), 1616–1629.

Grier, S., Williams, J. and Crockett, D. (1996). Racial discrimination as a consumer disadvantage? The marketplace experiences of Black men. In R. P. Hill and C. R. Taylor (eds.), *Proceedings Marketing and Public Policy Conference*, Vol. 6. AMA, p. 131.

Hall, G. (2001). Psychotherapy research with ethnic minorities: Empirical, ethical, and conceptual issues. *Journal of Consulting and Clinical Psychology*, 69(3), 502–510.

Hameed, A. and Waheed, A. (2011). Employee development and its affect on employee performance a conceptual framework. *International Journal of Business and Social Science*, 2(13). http://ijbssnet.com/journals/Vol._2_No._13_Special_Issue_July_2011/26.pdf

Hamilton, D. (1979). A cognitive attribution analysis of stereotyping. In L. Berkowitz (ed.), *Advances in Experimental Social Psychology*, Vol. 12. New York: Academic Press.

Hammond, R. and Axelrod, R. (2006). The evolution of ethnocentrism. *Journal of Conflict Resolution*, 50(6), 926–936.

Harrison, N. and Peacock, N. (2009). Cultural distance, mindfulness and passive xenophobia: Using Integrated Threat Theory to explore home higher education students' perspectives on "internationalisation at home". *British Educational Research Journal*, 36(6), 877–902.

Harvey, M. and Moeller, M. (2009). Expatriate mangers: A historical review. *International Journal of Management Reviews*, 11(3), 275–296.

Hatziprokopiou, P. (2003). Albanian immigrants in Thessaloniki, Greece: Processes of economic and social incorporation. *Journal of Ethnic and migration Studies*, 29(6), 1033–1057.

Health Reform (2014). Accessed 22/7/2018 at www.healthreform.ct.gov/ohri/lib/ohri/work_groups/equity_access/2014-09-18/presentation_fontanella_oha_09182014.pdf

Hofstede, G. (1983). National cultures in four dimensions: A research-based theory of cultural differences among nations. *International Studies of Management & Organization*, 13(1–2), 46–74.

Holliday, K. (1993). Reaching ethnic markets. *Journal of Bank Marketing* (February), 35–37.

Hollifield, J. (1994). Immigration and republicanism in France: The hidden consensus. *Controlling Immigration: A Global Perspective*, 143–175.

Hotchkiss, D. (1996). Weaving cultural sensitivity into marketing. *Journal of Bank Marketing*, 28 (June), 26–33.

Hou, F. (2009). Immigrants working with co-ethnics: Who are they and how do they fare? *International Migration*, 47(2), 69–100.

Huang, Y., Oppewal, H. and Mavondo, F. (2013). The influence of ethnic attributes on ethnic consumer choice of service outlet. *European Journal of Marketing*, 47(5/6), 877–898.

Hussain, J. and Matlay, H. (2007). Vocational education and training in small ethnic minority businesses in the UK. *Education+ Training*, 49(8/9), 671–685.

Jamal, A., Peñaloza, L. and Laroche, M. (eds.) (2015). *The Routledge Companion to Ethnic Marketing*. Abingdon, UK: Routledge.

Jones, T. and Ram, M. (2012). Revisiting. . . Ethnic-minority businesses in the United Kingdom: A review of research and policy developments. *Environment and Planning C: Government and Policy*, 30(6), 944–950.

Josiassen, A. (2011). Consumer disidentification and its effects on domestic product purchases: An empirical investigation in the Netherlands. *Journal of Marketing*, 75(2), 124–140.

Kassim, A. (2001). Trans-national migration within and among. In *AUSLEA 2001 Proceedings: ASEAN Universities Student Leaders Conference*. Universiti Malaysia Sabah, p. 59.

Kim, D. (1999). Beyond co-ethnic solidarity: Mexican and Ecuadorean employment in Korean-owned businesses in New York City. *Ethnic and Racial Studies*, 22(3), 581–605.

Kotler, P., Armstrong, G., Brown, L. and Adam, S. (1998). *Marketing*. Sydney: Prentice Hall.

Kruglanski, A. and Freund, T. (1983). The freezing and unfreezing of lay-inferences: Effects on impressional primacy, ethnic stereotyping, and numerical anchoring'. *Journal of Experimental Social Psychology*, 19, 448–468.

Lee, N. and Nathan, M. (2010). Knowledge workers, cultural diversity and innovation: Evidence from London. *International Journal of Knowledge-Based Development*, 1(1–2), 53–78.

Light, I. and Gold, S. (2000). *Ethnic Economies*. San Diego: Academic Press.

Littrell, L., Salas, E., Hess, K., Paley, M. and Riedel, S. (2006). Expatriate preparation: A critical analysis of 25 years of cross-cultural training research. *Human Resource Development Review*, 5(3), 355–388.

LNTO (Languages National Training Organisation) (2000). *Business Communication across Borders: A Study of Language Use and Practice in European Companies* (S. Hagan, ed.). London: Centre for Information on Language Teaching and Research.

MacDonald, K. (2006). Psychology and White ethnocentrism. *Occidental Quarterly*, 6(4), 7–46.

Manneh, S. (2011). New consumer bureau could especially protect ethnic communities. *New America Media*, News Report, September. Accessed 23/7/2018 at http://newamericamedia.org/2011/09/new-consumer-bureau-stalled-by-gop-could-especially-protect-ethnic-communities.php#

Marques, J., Yzerbyt, V. and Leyens, J. (1988). The "black sheep effect": Extremity of judgments towards in-group members as a function of group identification. *European Journal of Social Psychology*, 18(1), 1–16.

Martin, J. and Nakayama, T. (2013). *Intercultural Communication in Contexts*. New York, NY: McGraw-Hill.

McConahay, J. and Hough, J., Jr. (1976). Symbolic racism. *Journal of Social Issues*, 32(2), 23–45.

Medcalf, L. (1993). A creative mosaic. *Marketing (Maclean Hunter)*, 98 (July 19), 13.

Min, P. and Bozorgmehr, M. (2003). United States: The entrepreneurial cutting edge. *Immigrant Entrepreneurs: Venturing Abroad in the Age of Globalization*, 17–37.

Moore, D., Williams, J. and Qualls, W. (1996). Target marketing of tobacco and alcohol-related products to ethnic minority groups in the United States. *Ethnicity and Disease*, 6, 83–98.

Moore-Shay, E. (1996). The lens of economic circumstance: How do economically disadvantaged children view the marketplace? In R. P. Hill and C. R. Taylor (eds.), *Proceedings, Marketing and Public Policy Conference*, Vol. 6. AMA, p. 132.

Nam, Y. and Herbert, J. (1999). Characteristics and key success factors in family business: The case of Korean immigrant businesses in metro-Atlanta. *Family Business Review*, 12(4), 341–352.

Noon, M. (2007). The fatal flaws of diversity and the business case for ethnic minorities. *Work, Employment and Society*, 21(4), 773–784.

Oberg, K. (1960). Cultural shock: Adjustment to new cultural environments. *Practical Anthropology*, 7(4), 177–182.

Olson, P., Zuiker, V., Danes, S., Stafford, K., Heck, R. and Duncan, K. (2003). The impact of the family and the business on family business sustainability. *Journal of Business Venturing*, 18(5), 639–666.

Ortlieb, R. and Sieben, B. (2013). Diversity strategies and business logic: Why do companies employ ethnic minorities? *Group & Organization Management*, 38(4), 480–511.

Ouellet, J. (2007). Consumer racism and its effects on domestic cross-ethnic product purchase: An empirical test in the United States, Canada, and France. *Journal of Marketing*, 71(1), 113–128.

Patacchini, E. and Zenou, Y. (2012). Ethnic networks and employment outcomes. *Regional Science and Urban Economics*, 42(6), 938–949.

Pearce, S. (2005). Today's immigrant woman entrepreneur. *The Diversity Factor*, 13(3), 23–29.

Pires, G. and Aisbett, J. (2003). Macro issues in electronic commerce: The cultural divide. *Global Business & Economics Review*, 5(2), 369–390.

Pires, G. and Stanton, J. (2015a). *Ethnic Marketing: Culturally Sensitive Theory and Practice*. New York City, NY, USA: Taylor and Francis.

Pires, G. and Stanton, J. (2015b). Revisiting ethnic marketing ethics. In *The Routledge Companion to Ethnic Marketing*. Abingdon, UK: Routledge, pp. 327–342.

Pires, G. and Stanton, J. (2002). Ethnic marketing ethics. *Journal of Business Ethics*, 36(1–2), 111–118.

Pires, G. and Stanton, J. (2000). Marketing services to ethnic consumers in culturally diverse markets: Issues and implications. *Journal of Services Marketing*, 14(7), 607–618.

Pires, G., Stanton, J. and Ostenfeld, S. (2006). Improving expatriate adjustment and effectiveness in ethnically diverse countries: marketing insights. *Cross Cultural Management: An International Journal*, 13(2), 156–170.

Pires, G., Stanton, J. and Rita, P. (2010). Assessing relevancy of ICT driven consumer empowerment for business. *Global Business & Economics Anthology*, 2(1), 293–302.

Pollock, J. (1993). Ethnic marketing: The new reality. *Marketing (Maclean Hunter)*, 98 (July 19), 13–19.

Powers, T. and Hopkins, R. (2006). Altruism and consumer purchase behavior. *Journal of International Consumer Marketing*, 19(1), 107–130.

Ram, M., Jones, T. and Edwards, P. (2007). Staying underground: Informal work, small firms and employment regulation in the UK. *Work and Occupations*, 34, 290–317.

Rock, D. and Grant, H. (2017). Is your company's diversity training making you more biased? *Strategy + Business*, 88 (Autumn). strategy+business.com

Rudman, L., Greenwald, A., Mellott, D. and Schwartz, J. (1999). Measuring the automatic components of prejudice: Flexibility and generality of the implicit association test. *Social Cognition*, 17(4), 437–465.

Sarwono, S. and Armstrong, R. (1998). Cross-microcultural business ethics: Ethical perceptions differences in marketing among ethnic microcultural groups in Indonesia. In J.-C. Chebat and A. B. Oumlil (eds.), *Proceedings Multicultural Marketing Conference*. Montreal: AMS, pp. 80–86.

Schneider, S. and Barsoux, J. (2003). *Managing across Cultures*, 2nd ed. Harlow, England: Prentice Hall.

Schuler, R. and Jackson, S. (2007). *Strategic Human Resource Management*, 2nd ed. Wiley.

Seelye, H. and J. Wasilewski (1996). *Between Cultures: Developing Self-Identity in a World of Diversity*. Chicago, IL: NTC Publishing Group.

Shanmuganathan, P., Stone, M. and Foss, B. (2004). Ethnic banking in the USA. *Journal of Financial Services Marketing*, 8(4), 388.

Shimp, T. and Sharma, S. (1987). Consumer ethnocentrism: Construction and validation of the CETSCALE. *Journal of Marketing Research*, 24 (August), 280–289.

Siamagka, N. and Balabanis, G. (2015). Revisiting consumer ethnocentrism: Review, reconceptualization, and empirical testing. *Journal of International Marketing*, 23(3), 66–86.

Smallbone, D., Bertotti, M. and Ekanem, I. (2005). Diversification in ethnic minority business: The case of Asians in London's creative industries. *Journal of Small Business and Enterprise Development*, 12(1), 41–56.

Smith, H. (1994). *Managing Privacy: Information Technology and Corporate America*. UNC Press Books.

Sumner, W. (1906). Folkways: A study of the sociological importance of usages. In *Manners, Customs, Mores, and Morals*. Boston, MA: Gin and Company.

Tadmor, C., Hong, Y., Chao, M., Wiruchnipawan, F. and Wang, W. (2012). Multicultural experiences reduce intergroup bias through epistemic unfreezing. *Journal of Personality and Social Psychology*, 103(5), 750–772.

Tiedens, L. and Linton, S. (2001). Judgment under emotional certainty and uncertainty: The effects of specific emotions on information processing. *Journal of Personality and Social Psychology*, 81(6), 973–988.

Tse, D., Lee, K., Vertinisky, I. and Wehrung, D. (1988). Does culture matter? A cross-cultural study of executives' choice, decisiveness, and risk adjustment in international marketing. *Journal of Marketing*, 52(4), 81–95.

Urban, G. (2005). Customer advocacy: A new era in marketing? *Journal of Public Policy & Marketing*, 24(1), 155–159.

Usunier, J. and Lee, J. (2009). *Marketing across Cultures*. Pearson Education Limited.

Varner, I. and Beamer, L. (1995). *Intercultural Communication in the Global Workplace*. Chicago, IL: Irwin McGraw-Hill.

Vitell, S., Rallapalli, J. and Singhapakdi, A. (1993). Marketing norms: The influences of personal moral philosophies and organizational ethical culture. *Journal of the Academy of Marketing Science*, 21, 331–337.

Waldinger, R. (2005). 12 Networks and niches: The continuing significance of ethnic connections. *Ethnicity, Social Mobility, and Public Policy: Comparing the USA and UK*, 342.

Waldinger, R., Ward, R., Aldrich, H. and Stanfield, J. (1990). *Ethnic Entrepreneurs: Immigrant Business in Industrial Societies*. University of Illinois at Urbana-Champaign's Academy for Entrepreneurial Leadership Historical Research Reference in Entrepreneurship.

Watchravesringkan, K. (2011). Exploring antecedents and consequences of consumer ethnocentrism: Evidence from Asian immigrants in the US. *International Journal of Consumer Studies*, 35(4), 383–390.

Wolburg, J. (2005). Drawing the line between targeting and patronizing: How "vulnerable" are the vulnerable? *Journal of Consumer Marketing*, 22(5), 287–288.

Wood, P. and Mallinckrodt, B. (1990). Culturally sensitive assertiveness training for ethnic minority clients. *Professional Psychology: Research and Practice*, 21(1), 5.

Worthington, I., Ram, M. and Jones, T. (2006). Exploring corporate social responsibility in the UK Asian small business community. *Journal of Business Ethics*, 67(2), 201–217.

Yamagishi, T. (2003). The group heuristic: A psychological mechanism that creates a self-sustaining system of generalized exchanges. In *Proceedings of the Santa Fe Institute Workshop on the Coevolution of Institutions and Behavior*.

Zolfagharian, M., Saldivar, R. and Sun, Q. (2014). Ethnocentrism and country of origin effects among immigrant consumers. *Journal of Consumer Marketing*, 31(1), 68–84.

Zong, J. and Batalova, J. (2017). Indian Immigrants in the United States. *Spotlight*, August 31. Accessed 21/7/2018 at www.migrationpolicy.org/article/indian-immigrants-united-states?gclid=EAIaIQobChMI7fDYio2w3AIVBLTtCh0gkwewEAAYASAAEgJ9U_D_BwE

14 Environmental Forces, Ethnic Marketing and Ethnic Entrepreneurship

The growth of ethnic marketing in any specific country faces very different opportunities and threats because, as discussed in previous chapters, individuals' ethnic identity and their ties to their minority ethnic group are shaped by their experiences in the home country and with the relevant minority ethnic group, as well as their wider acculturation experiences in the host country.

As discussed in Chapter 3 and Table 3.2, a five-category grouping of the relevant forces shaping a chosen acculturation path—namely society of origin, society of settlement, moderating factors prior to acculturation, group acculturation and moderating factors during acculturation) was provided by Berry and Sam (1997), with examples of relevant variables. Two aspects need further elaboration. One refers to the impact of government policies in the society of settlement on how a person's ethnic identity evolves; the other refers to the moderating factors during acculturation, influencing a chosen acculturation path. Elaboration is needed because how these variables evolve has a direct bearing on the growth of ethnic marketing.

The purpose of this chapter is to discuss how host country environmental conditions shape the growth and practice of ethnic marketing and ethnic entrepreneurship. We show that the interaction occurring between government policies (such as immigration policy, attitudes to immigration and to particular ethnic groups or phenotypes) and the factors moderating the acculturation process, creates the environment within which ethnic groups and their networks form. Which acculturation paths are followed influences how closed or open a minority ethnic group becomes, its accessibility as a market, as well as employment and business opportunities. Specifically, we show how the environment for ethnic marketing and ethnic entrepreneurship changes, depending on the migration policies of the host country and how these policies extend to the treatment of any migrant groups seeking to express their ethnic identity.

The Political Environment

Stated bluntly, the political environment of a country determines whether marketers can practice ethnic marketing and whether ethnic entrepreneurs will be more or less restricted in businesses venturing and in their growth opportunities by focusing on a marginalized ethnic group or be able to more easily participate and expand into wider markets. More than discourse that may be uttered by the rulers of the day, more or less reflective of the general attitudes towards immigration, the major effect comes from the policies that are in place.

The borders of many nation-states have evolved to encompass people who claim a distinct ethnicity from either the majority population or other minorities. The degree of freedom given to such groups to maintain and grow their group identity will also determine the potential for ethnic marketing to have a useful role. The diverse political systems of nation-states, as well as their current ethnic diversity and approaches to inward and outward migration, ensure widely different environments confronting ethnic marketers. In countries such as Malaysia and South Africa, for example, the political conditions for ethnic marketing to be practiced using ethnic media and ethnic networks differs from countries that seek to repress ethnic minorities or to deliberately acculturate (or even assimilate) them to a mainstream culture.

Then there are countries that have instituted immigration policies that may permit immigrant entry regardless of their country of origin or ethnicity. Economic and political disruption following the Second World War revived the growth of immigration to traditional host counties such as the USA, Canada and Australia. This has been followed in the late twentieth century by a widening globalization process with ongoing immigration to a much wider array of Western and non-Western nations, constituting both intended permanent migration and intended temporary migration of workers and refugees seeking either work or refuge.

Immigration policy is a political decision often driven by socioeconomic goals but within this group of recipients, largely Western and Latin American nations, political conditions will differ widely in terms of permitting or encouraging ethnic groups to grow and thrive and thus for ethnic marketing to flourish. Even within liberal-democratic countries, the political environment can provide very different alternative scenarios for ethnic marketing, as examples in this chapter will illustrate.

Ethnicity, Migration and the Future of Ethnic Marketing

In 1985, Yinger called attention to

> the near universality of multiethnicity in contemporary states, the persistence—culturally and structurally-of the ethnic factor, contradicting modernization and Marxist theories.

(p. 151)

Destruction of the myth of the cultural homogeneity of many Western nation-states precedes the onset of the "age of migration" (Castles and

Miller, 2003). This is an age that continues into the twenty-first century, characterized by very large and diverse kinds of migration movements, and with larger and more culturally diverse numbers of source and host countries involved than in the nineteenth and most of the twentieth century.

These international population movements can be expected to feed a growing ethnic diversity in many destination countries, raising a host of issues that are increasingly covered by researchers in the political, socio-economic, health, entrepreneurship and labour studies areas. For marketers, the growing percentage of foreign-born population occurring in nearly all OECD economies, reflected in the Table 14.1 below, raises a conundrum of how best to understand and meet the needs and wants of a growing population with distinct cultural backgrounds and of ethnic groups emerging within the borders of many advanced economies, given that migration may not only increase the heterogeneity of the marketplace but also strengthen and increase the importance of marketing to particular groups.

Table 14.1 shows the growth in the percentage of the foreign-born population in selected OECD countries over the 20-year period from 1995 to 2015. Very few of the member countries had either a constant or decreasing percentage of foreign-born population over this period, but we see rapid growth in some European countries moving into the

Table 14.1 Foreign-Born Residents to Total Population, Selected OECD Economies (Percentage of Growth Rate)

OECD Economy	1995	2000	2005	2010	2015
Australia	22.3 (1991)	23.3 (1996)	24.1	26.5	28.0
Austria	5.9	9.0	14.5	15.4	28.0
Belgium	9.1	9.0	12.0	14.9	16.6
Canada	16.1 (1991)	17.4 (1996)	18.7	19.9	20.3
France	6.3	n.a.	11.3	11.7	12.3
Germany	8.8	8.8	12.8	13.2	14.2
Hungary	n.a.	1.4	3.3	4.4	5.1
Italy	1.4	1.7	n.a.	9.7	9.9
Netherlands	8.1	9.1	10.6	11.2	12.2
New Zealand	n.a.	16.2 (1996)	20.3	21.6	24.5
Spain	0.7	1.3	11.0	14.3	13.2
Sweden	n.a.	10.5	12.5	14.8	17.1
UK	3.2	3.4	9.2	11.3	13.9
USA	7.9	8.8	12.1	12.9	13.5

Sources: OECD International Migration Outlook 2017, Annex A.4; OECD Trends in International Migration, 2000.

Note: Early data for 1995 and 2000 varies in sources between countries due to differing data sources; n.a. = Data not available twenty-first century. Traditional nineteenth century host nations continue to receive large inflows, but traditional emigrant nations are seeing growing ethnic minorities, both through the formation of the EU and through migration from poorer to richer nations. Not only are these cross-border flows diverse in terms of ethnicity, but also in intended purpose and skill composition, encompassing permanent and temporary movements of variable duration, movement of the highly skilled and educated as well as the less skilled, taking advantage of the emergence of globalizing labour markets and shortages in some regions.

What are the implications for ethnic marketing and entrepreneurship? Does this growing diversity within nation-states presage increased opportunities for ethnic entrepreneurship and for marketing practice? Here, the answers are clouded by uncertainties emerging over migration and the effects of ethnic groups on the social fabric of nations when emphasis is given to ethnicity. Government policies toward large migration flows and toward ethnic groups seeking to maintain or construct their ethnic identity appear to vary considerably between and within nations depending on political discourse. The future of ethnic entrepreneurship and ethnic marketing is tied to which political discourse will dominate.

As ethnic groups are already present in many of these economies, preceding the contemporary growth of migration flows currently occurring, and as ethnicity and ethnic identity tend to persist and often grow stronger when faced with attempts to suppress such identity (Vertovec and Wessendorf, 2010, p. 7), we need to distinguish between the effects of government policies on entrepreneurship and marketing to ethnic groups instead of seeking to apply ethnic marketing when seeking to market to an ethnic group, regardless of the political and social context.

Ethnic entrepreneurship and marketing to an ethnic group will tend to persist and develop wherever groups of people sharing a common ethnic identity co-locate in sufficient numbers to meet the conditions discussed in Chapters 4 and 11 for sustainable and profitable segmentation. Entrepreneurs, usually from within the group, will recognize unfulfilled opportunities and will use whatever possible marketing tools are available to them to try to take advantage of those opportunities by meeting the inherent needs and wants. However, the more constrained ethnic entrepreneurs and marketers in general are, in using all the marketing apparatus of the modern economy to reach such groups, the more ethnic entrepreneurship and ethnic marketing—the approaches outlined in this book—will also be constrained.

Ethnic marketing requires that ethnic groups be readily identifiable. If national policies reject the concept of different ethnic groups residing within the one nation-state, not counting their presence or main localities of residence, marketing to the ethnic group by necessity of the lack of identifiability reverts to grassroots and community-based approaches, if it happens at all. If the ethnic group is small relative to other groups, some governments that gather such data may still ignore smaller groups, conveying an invisibility that will limit ethnic marketing (Pires and Stanton, 2002), irrespective of the group's unique demands. Notwithstanding, this effect is much attenuated in the case of an ethnic minority business targeting their co-ethnic group.

If governments restrict or hinder the development of ethnic media or the use of languages preferred by individual ethnic groups, perhaps by driving the use of mainstream media and not addressing practically the need for cultural diversity in media, again ethnic marketing by dissimilar others is unlikely to reach its communication objectives.

Government policies shape how the mainstream and other groups perceive each other. Policies that engender antipathy by the mainstream to campaigns targeting minorities will also restrict the growth of ethnic marketing as mainstream marketers weigh up the costs of alienating one group at the expense of another. Something as simple as the decision of governments to collect data on whether residents ascribe to a particular ethnicity, as well as the way in which this question is phrased in a Census, can frame policy decisions that render some groups invisible, while setting in train forces for the emergence of pan ethnic groups.

In general, a liberal and democratic approach will enable all residents to express their identity and associate with those of like identity within the constraints of the nation's core values. As such, ethnic marketing by all business is also free to develop and to focus on reaching ethnic groups without hindrance to the communication channels used and without repercussions from mainstream consumers.

Western and other democracies have taken to the reawakening (in countries where several co-resident ethnic groups have been an historical reality) or growth (where post-war immigration has been ongoing) of ethnic identity in very different ways, leading to the curtailment of ethnic entrepreneurship and marketing in some and to their growth in others. Accordingly, ethnic minority business and practices of marketing to ethnic groups have also been shaped by these differing environments.

Implications From Differences in Immigration Policies and Acculturation

Several different acculturation paths immigrants may seek to follow were discussed in Chapter 3. The path chosen is shaped as much by the host country environment as by the past circumstances of the immigrant.

Berry and Sam (1997) defined integration as a process where individuals seek to maintain the cultural identity of their ethnic heritage while embracing part of the cultural identity of the host culture. Host country policies that assist immigrants to settle in that country, while recognizing and perhaps supporting their desires to retain or choose their ethnic identity over time, are more likely to lead to an environment where ethnic network ties can be developed and maintained with less overt hostility from those in the mainstream who support assimilation strategies, especially if civil rights protections are in place. As such, countries that seek to provide policies that support multicultural practices within their borders are likely to be more conducive to ethnic entrepreneurship and to the practice of ethnic marketing.

One incomplete but useful measure of differences in this multicultural environment between predominantly Western countries is The Multiculturalism Policy Index (or MCP Index). Distinguishing between indigenous minorities and more recent immigrant ethnic minorities, the Index examines policies and actions in 21 primarily Western liberal-democratic countries from 1980 to 2010, in terms of the extent to which they go beyond the non-discriminatory protection of traditional individual rights of citizenship to also provide some additional form of public recognition, and support or accommodation for ethnic minorities to maintain and express their distinct identities and practices. This recognition and support for a multicultural society, if accepted by all its citizens, is likely to provide an environment within which ethnic networks can form and strengthen and ethnic marketing can be freely practised.

The construction of The MCP index is explained in more detail on its site, but the essence of the approach is to ascertain if countries have implemented policies that could be considered accommodating to ethnic minorities in the retention of their ethnic identity, as opposed to policies seeking to assimilate or marginalize ethnic minorities, or taking no policy actions.

The MCP Index monitors 8 indicators of actions likely to be conducive to the growth of a multicultural society, shown in Table 14.2.

Most indicators are assessed in terms of whether there is evidence that the indicator has been met either in full, partially, or not at all. While it is possible to contest both the limited scope and subjectivity of the methodology, the approach does highlight wide differences among developed economies in their willingness to accommodate the migrant inflows that have been occurring.

Table 14.2 Indicators of Multiculturalism

The MCP Index: Indicators of Multiculturalism

---

1. Affirmation of multiculturalism at a governmental level and the existence of structures to implement this policy in consultation with ethnic communities;
2. **The adoption of multiculturalism in the school curriculum;**
3. The inclusion of ethnic representation in public media or media licensing;
4. Exemptions from dress codes (either by statute or court cases);
5. Allowing of dual citizenship;
6. The funding of ethnic group organizations or activities;
7. The funding of bilingual education or mother-tongue instruction;
8. Affirmative action for disadvantaged immigrant groups.

Table 14.3 Multiculturalism Policies for Immigrant Minorities Summary Scores from 1980, 1990, 2000 and 2010

	Total Score			
	1980	*1990*	*2000*	*2010*
Australia	5.5	8	8	8
Austria	0	0	1	1.5
Belgium	1	1.5	3.5	5.5
Canada	5	6.5	7.5	7.5
Denmark	0	0	0	0
Finland	0	0	1.5	6
France	1	2	2	2
Germany	0	0.5	2	2.5
Greece	0.5	0.5	0.5	2.5
Ireland	1	1	1.5	4
Italy	0	0	1.5	1.5
Japan	0	0	0	0
Netherlands	2.5	3	4	2
New Zealand	2.5	5	5	6
Norway	0	0	0	3.5
Portugal	0	1	3	3.5
Spain	0	1	1	3.5
Sweden	3	3.5	5	7
Switzerland	0	0	1	1
United Kingdom	2.5	5	5	5.5
United States	3.5	3	3	3

Source: Multiculturalism Policy Index, www.queensu.ca/mcp/, accessed April 22, 2018.

Measured at decade intervals, Table 14.3 reveals Australia and Canada as the leaders in moving to a benign multicultural environment, but it also picks up other countries clearly moving towards a more accommodating posture. In 1980, only two of the 21 countries met five of the eight indicators, rising to seven in 2010. Unsurprisingly, three of the five (Australia, Canada and New Zealand) are countries who have actively pursued long-term, permanent immigration (Clydesdale, 2008), whereas many of the others have been either the recipient of intended temporary migration, perhaps due to the opening of European borders, or to resettlement resulting from the post-war contraction of the European colonial system.

Nevertheless, surprising anomalies exist between Western and Northern European countries. Sweden and Finland, for example have moved more rapidly towards multicultural accommodation than Denmark, while among the three large European economies of France, Germany and the UK, the latter appears to have followed a different path. The

Table 14.4 Liberal Democracies Grouped by Immigration History

Immigration History		Illustrative Countries
Longstanding "countries of immigration" (Duncan, 2006)	Immigration grew during the nineteenth century and continuing into the twenty-first century	Australia Canada New Zealand USA
Past major emigration countries	Becoming large immigration countries in the late twentieth and twenty-first centuries	Germany, Italy, UK Netherlands, Spain; also France as a colonizer but not as a large emigration country
Past colonized countries	With long-standing established ethnic groups from past migrations and with little recent inflow from past sources that recognize their ethnic diversity	South Africa and Malaysia

USA, although a country welcoming immigration for a long time, shows little recognition of its growing cultural diversity, policy wise. Our contention, that marketing to ethnic groups by mainstream business is conditioned by a country's' socio-economic environment, would suggest obstacles facing ethnic marketing in many of these countries. We turn to trying to better understand why.

Rather than using Table 14.3 to categorize countries for further examination, we look at their immigration policies—whether they have actively sought to grow their economies seeking either or both permanent and temporary migrants, or whether migration has been the reluctant consequence of adjustments in European borders, or past colonial history.

Most liberal democracies can be divided into three broad groups in terms of their immigration history. Their past colonial role (colonizer or colonized) and/or whether they were either predominantly emigration or immigration countries provides a simple but useful basis for grouping them, whilst acknowledging some differences between countries of immigration in terms of the receptivity of the host country populations not only to migrants in general but to specific ethnic groups. Table 14.4 provides detail on the three groups. Each group is discussed below.

Longstanding Countries of Immigration

Australia, Canada, New Zealand and the United States continue to host large immigrant populations, both permanent and temporary. Australia, Canada and New Zealand prioritize skilled immigrants. In contrast, the United States (US) prioritizes family immigrants (Australian Government, Productivity Commission, 2016).

Australia, Canada and New Zealand use a points-based system to select most of their permanent skilled immigrant intake. Prospective immigrants are required to fill out expressions of interest, and points are awarded for a number of characteristics that can include age, educational attainment, work experience, host country language proficiency and having a job offer. In theory, this system can lead to emigrants from a wide array of countries but, clearly, countries where these skills are in excess supply with consequent downward pressures on the returns to these skills, will tend to emerge as source countries, as in the case of the recent prominence of countries such as India and the Philippines in migration flows to Australia.

While the USA system is essentially non-discriminatory by country (restrictions based on race and ancestry were abolished with the introduction of the Immigration and Nationality Act 1965 (Australian Government, Productivity Commission, 2016)), there is a quota system based on migrants from the eastern hemisphere and the western hemisphere. Such quotas tend to give a weighting to the western hemisphere out of proportion to the number of countries and populations classed as eastern hemisphere. Accordingly, this is likely to be reflected in stronger flows from Latin America.

We use Australia as an example in this group. It has had and continues to have, probably the "more expansive" and ongoing immigration program of the four countries (Ongley and Pearson, 1995) regardless of labour market conditions. It also has the highest percentage of foreign-born population and a longstanding although changing espousal by successive Federal Governments of a "multicultural policy" but still continues to lead The MCP Index (as shown in Table 14.2).

Australian Migration Policy Sketch

Current Policy Towards Permanent Immigration

It is necessary to distinguish policy towards immigrants seeking long-term residency from policy towards other categories, including "temporary" flows of immigrants (excluding tourists) coming under various visa arrangements, such as student visas. Many of these may later transition to permanent residents (Australian Government, Productivity Commission, 2016).

Current policy towards immigrants seeking long-term residency, or intended permanent migration, has transitioned, especially since the late 1940s, from a country of origin focus to one based on a skills-based points system, regardless of country. This transition has increased Australia's cultural diversity, particularly away from western and southern European sources towards the inclusion of immigrants from many Asian nations, as partly reflected in Table 14.5.

Nevertheless, Australia is still a country with a dominant Anglo-Celtic majority with many small ethnic groups. Table 14.6 shows the top 10 countries by place of birth in 2016. These countries account for only

Table 14.5 Top 10 Countries of Birth of Immigrants, Australia Selected Censuses

Rank	1901	1981	1991	2001	2011
1	UK	UK	UK	UK	UK
2	Ireland	Italy	New Zealand	New Zealand	New Zealand
3	Germany	New Zealand	Italy	Italy	China
4	China	Yugoslavia	Yugoslavia	Vietnam	India
5	New Zealand	Greece	Greece	China	Italy
6	Sweden & Norway	Germany	Vietnam	Greece	Vietnam
7	India	Netherlands	Germany	Germany	Philippines
8	USA	Poland	Netherlands	Philippines	South Africa
9	Denmark	Malta	China	India	Malaysia
10	Italy	Lebanon	Philippines	Netherlands	Germany

Prior to the 1954 Census, persons recorded as born in Ireland included persons born in the Republic of Ireland and Northern Ireland.

Source: Productivity Commission 2016, Migrant Intake into Australia, Inquiry Report No. 77, Canberra.

Table 14.6 Estimated Foreign-Born Resident Population, Australia Top 10 Countries of Birth—30 June 2016(a) (b) (c)

Country of Birth	No. Persons	Percent of Australian Population
UK, CIs & IOM(d)	1,198,000	5.0
New Zealand	607,200	2.5
China(e)	526,000	2.2
India	468,800	1.9
Philippines	246,400	1.0
Vietnam	236,700	1.0
Italy	194,900	0.8
South Africa	181,400	0.8
Malaysia	166,200	0.7
Germany	124,300	0.5
Total		16.4

(a) Estimates are preliminary—see paragraph 9 of the Explanatory Notes.
(b) Top 10 countries of birth excluding Australia.
(c) All population figures presented in this table are rounded. Estimates of the proportion of the Australian population are based on unrounded numbers.
(d) United Kingdom, Channel Islands and Isle of Man.
(e) Excludes SARs and Taiwan.

Source: ABS, 3412.0—Migration, Australia, 2015–16

16.4 percent of the Australian population while another 10 percent is made up of a very large group of countries, each contributing less than 0.5 percent to the total population.

These figures of overseas-born by nation-state understate the complexity of ethnic diversity. Table 14.7 below uses an Australian 2016 census

Table 14.7 Australia: Census 2016 Languages Spoken at Home—Leading Countries in Each Group Only

Northern European Languages		Southern European Languages	
Dutch	33,835	French	70,873
English	17,020,417	Greek	237,588
German	79,353	Italian	271,597
Other Northern		Maltese	31,987
European Languages	75,845	Portuguese	48,853
		Spanish	140,817
		Other Southern European Languages	142614
Total	*17,209,450*	*Total*	*802,675*
Eastern European Languages		Southwest and Central Asian Languages	
Croatian	56,885	Arabic	321,728
Macedonian	66,019	Persian	
Polish	48,083	(excluding Dari)	58,313
Russian	50,314	Turkish	58,355
Serbian	53,801	Other	138,325
Other	97,447		
Total	*372,549*	*Total*	*576,721*
Southern Asian Languages		Southeast Asian Languages	
Bengali	54,566	Filipino	71,220
Gujarati	52,888	Indonesian	67,891
Hindi	159,652	Tagalog	111,273
Malayalam	53,206	Thai	55,444
Nepali	62,005	Vietnamese	277,400
Punjabi	132,496	Other Southeast Asian	
Sinhalese	64,612	languages	117,257
Tamil	73,161		
Urdu	69,293		
Other Southern Asian languages	164,227		
Southern Asian languages	*800,758*	*Total*	*700,335*

Table 14.7 Continued

Eastern Asian Languages		Australian Indigenous Languages	
Cantonese	280,943	*Total*	64,762
Japanese	55,966	*Other Languages*	
Korean	108,997		
Mandarin	596,711	*Total*	*211,713*
Other East Asian		Inadequately described	12,847
languages	54,081	Not stated or unclear	1,509,829
Total	*1,096,698*		
Total	**23,401,892**		

Source: ABS, Census (2016): Languages Spoken at Home.

question to show the preferred spoken languages of the Australian resident population. National groups such as Indian and Chinese hide the ethnic diversity existing within such nation-states, indicated by this table, taking into account not only first but subsequent generations. Given such diversity and the potentially small size of many groups, ethnic marketing will need to be shaped to the challenges of this diversity.

Australian Multicultural Policy

The growing ethnic diversity of the Australian population was an unintended outcome of a pursuit for population growth that was driven by the economic and security concerns of the Second World War. As traditional Anglo-Celtic and then Northern European immigration sources diminished with post-war economic recovery in Europe, primarily economic pressures to maintain high immigration intakes led to a gradual dismantling of a racially based migration policy known as the White Australia Policy (Australia, Department of Home Affairs, Fact Sheet 8, undated).

A wider, skills-based approach was implemented over time (mainly a series of steps between 1957 and 1973) which tended to be non-discriminatory with respect to country of origin, thus encouraging immigration initially from other parts of Europe and then spreading to Asian and Middle Eastern sources. Explicit policy recognition of this growing diversity was absent for approximately the first three decades of rapid immigration growth, the implicit belief apparently being that which seemed to prevail in the USA, that new migrants would be assisted to assimilate by encouraging English language skills and movement into the workforce (Australia, Department of Immigration and Citizenship, Fact Sheet 6, Canberra, 2011).

A change from decades of conservative government in 1973 saw the term "multiculturalism" officially used. At a ceremony proclaiming the Racial

Discrimination Act 1975, the Prime Minister referred to Australia as a "multicultural nation". The first national multicultural policies, focused on government programs and services for migrants, were implemented in the succeeding conservative government in 1978 (Australia, Department of Immigration and Citizenship, Fact Sheet 6, Canberra, 2011).

The return of non-conservative government saw the setting up in 1987 of an Office of Multicultural Affairs within the Department of Prime Minister and Cabinet, advising the Prime Minister directly on issues relating to Australian multicultural society. One of the defining outputs from that Office was the *National Agenda for a Multicultural Australia* (Office of Multicultural Affairs, 1989). In this influential paper, multiculturalism was seen as a policy for managing the consequences of cultural diversity, in the interest of the individual and of society as a whole, expressed in terms of three dimensions, namely cultural identity, social justice and economic efficiency.

Cultural identity (the right of all Australians, within carefully defined limits, to express and share their individual cultural heritage, including their language and religion) and social justice (the right of all Australians to equality of treatment and opportunity and the removal of barriers of race, ethnicity, culture, religion, language, gender or place of birth) provide the critical foundations for ethnic groups to grow. However, the constraint of "defined limits" is the area that remains contentious for multiculturalism, not only in Australia but other liberal-democratic societies.

The Agenda also sought to set the boundaries to multiculturalism in general terms:

- Multicultural policies are based upon the premise that all Australians should have an overriding and unifying commitment to Australia, to its interests and future first and foremost;
- Requires all Australians to accept the basic structures and principles of Australian society (the Constitution and the rule of law, tolerance and equality, Parliamentary democracy, freedom of speech and religion, English as the national language and equality of the sexes);
- Requires acceptance of the right of others to express their views and values.

Subsequent Australian governments of both conservative and non-conservative persuasion have largely endorsed similar policies (The People of Australia: Australia's Multicultural Policy, 2011; Multicultural Australia, 2018) with relatively small changes in emphasis, such as in terms of citizenship requirements and English language tests (accessed April 2018 at (www.homeaffairs.gov.au/trav/life/multicultural/australias-multicultural-policy-history).

In such an environment, minority ethnic groups have been able to develop network structures around ethnic community organizations (such as social and sporting clubs) and organized business groups and ethnic media (radio stations, press and community television). Ethnic community organizations are encouraged and supported at various government levels.

An important component of the sustenance and continued growth of minority ethnic groups is the Australian school education system, where a state-based, public education system competes with a private (religious and non-religious) system. Federal government aid to the private system is significant and subject to schools meeting a range of educational commitments. This can include infrastructure and recurrent support for schools supported by minority ethnic groups.

Hence, minority ethnic group members have an impetus to co-locate in close geographical proximity, and the social capital will tend to attract and hold many successive generations. Because of such policies it is little surprise that The MCP Index scored Australia highest in terms of policies designed to recognize, accommodate and support ethnic minorities, should they choose to retain their ethnic identity (The Multiculturalism Policy Index, www.queensu.ca/mcp/, April 22, 2018).

Canada, New Zealand and the USA

While a non-discriminatory immigration by country approach is common to all three countries, recognition of multiculturalism in terms of minority ethnic groups residing within a country is probably most explicit in Canada and Australia. The Canadian Multiculturalism Act (Canada, Minister of Justice. 1988) sought to enshrine similar freedoms for minority ethnic groups to retain and practice their beliefs, as afforded to Australian ethnic minorities.

New Zealand provides an illustration of how the existing host country population mix can hinder or slow down a move to a multicultural approach. While successive governments have gradually acted in terms of many of the eight indicators of multiculturalism (early in Table 14.2), the process has been complicated because of the need to maintain the indigenous rights of the Maori (Spoonley, 2006, 2015; also Spoonley et al., 2005).

New Zealand migrant flows were far more culturally homogenous until the 1950s. While Australia and Canada were moving towards multiculturalism during the 1970s, New Zealand was more focused on bi-culturalism, needing to work around the rights and protection of its First People, the Maori. In turn, this has hindered legislative moves towards multiculturalism such that, as noted by the MCP Index, although multiculturalism appears in New Zealand's discourse and rhetoric, it is not affirmed through any constitutional, legislative or parliamentary instruments.

USA

The USA remains the leading country of immigration by numbers. Like Australia, Canada and New Zealand, those who freely migrated mainly came from West European sources, with later waves from a wider group of European countries and, more recently, predominantly Hispanic language sources. Its sourcing of migrants, as with the other three countries, tended to be discriminatory between countries. It was only in 1965 that the discriminatory national origins quota system, and remaining restrictions on Asian immigration as well as the numerical limits imposed in the 1920s, were overcome (Zolberg, 2006).

Alba (2005) argues that receiving populations impose a social distinction with immigrants along the lines of religion, population and race as well as other variables. His distinction between blurred and bright boundaries facing immigrant groups appears to apply most strongly to racial phenotypes and more lately, religion. Whether an ethnic group boundary is either blurred or bright is particularly relevant to explaining why some minority ethnic groups have been able to retain a strong group identity, albeit in changing form over time, while other groups seem to have assimilated into the "melting pot" of Americanization. Zolberg (2006) cites examples of forceful assimilationist strategies including the development of patriotic school curricula and the imposition of citizenship requirements for a variety of both local and Federal jobs and licences.

Both World Wars, but especially the second, added to these pressures where military service, universal in the Second World War, legitimized their membership in the "American nation" (Zolberg, 2006). However, as Alba (2005) notes, the assimilation of various European ethnic immigrant groups into the American mainstream was largely because of the porous boundaries of the mainstream culture, allowing for the incorporation of cultural elements brought in by immigrant groups, leading to a composite mainstream culture. Largely excluded from this process were particular phenotypes. Spanish speaking Puerto Ricans who migrated to the mainland were more able to resist because they were "American", while Mexicans faced either blurred or bright boundaries, mainly dependent on their phenotype (Alba, 2005). These exclusions in some ways paved the way for the rapid growth of Spanish language users in the USA.

For several decades the pattern of immigration into the USA has been a similar experience to the other three countries in this group: the intake is culturally diverse and no longer European dominated; immigrants initially cluster geographically; and their residential preferences are urban or city localities (Pearson and Hanlin, 2006). These trends assist new arrivals in affiliating with similar-others on arrival with access to the social capital of the minority co-ethnic group networks. As such, this appears an environment conducive to the development of ethnic minority business and to using ethnic marketing to reach such groups. However, the environment for ethnic marketing differs from others in this group because, of the four countries, there is far less government involvement and resources in the settlement process. The MCP Index criteria show that there is a lack of legislative recognition of multiculturalism although there exists civil rights and affirmative action legislation designed to assist minorities as well as females. A Department of Justice based Community Relations Service arising from the 1964 Civil Rights Act acts more as a conciliator among ethnic groups.

Skirting around a precise definition of what he means by "integration", Duncan (ch. 4, 2006) argues that, while the U.S. government has no policies or programs for immigrant integration, the outcomes are not too different from those in countries where there are multicultural policies. However, as just noted, over the long immigration history of the country there have been ongoing societal and economic pressures for many to "assimilate" as well as the exclusion of some based on their phenotype, that lead to different outcomes in how groups interact and network. Pearson and Hanlin (2006) argue that some groups have become alienated from each other, including those who share a common history of social oppression, such that the issue of diversity is never far from public consciousness.

Returning to Chapter 4 and section 4.3 of this book, panethnicity can be seen as a response to the American socio-economic environment, reflected in the Census-based ascription of broad groups, and the coalescing of smaller minority groups to attract scarce resources. While the country is open to the use of ethnic marketing, the context of its use needs to recognize the growth of panethnicity as well as assimilationist pressures which have tended to encourage communications and targeting strategies either along panethnic lines, or mainstream marketing using different phenotypes to stress inclusivity. Neither approach constitutes ethnic marketing.

Past Major Emigration Countries

Similar to several other European countries, Germany, France and the UK have seen large inflows of immigrants arising from both an increasing post-war economic prosperity and the accompanying demand for labour and, in the case of the UK and France, the inheritance of a decolonization legacy. The three countries are used here to examine the opportunities and hurdles to ethnic marketing because each has reacted differently to the growing ethnic diversity within their borders.

In terms of the adoption of multicultural policies or government support for multicultural practices, the UK has been far more active than either Germany or France, as reflected in The MCP Index values for the three (Table 14.3). How each country views immigrants arriving to its shores provides the basis for this difference.

Germany

Significant differences in the migration policies of Germany and France help explain differences in their approach to the treatment of ethnic minority groups and what may or may not be acceptable in terms of ethnic marketing.

Quite a lot has been written on the post-war migration to Germany, with the "temporary" immigration of Turkish workers and the subsequent attempts of successive German governments to "integrate" (term usually undefined) them into the German nation, often being the focus (Gumus, 2016; Aybek, 2012; Klusmeyer and Papademetriou, 2009; Alba, 2005). This focus obscures other streams of migration that have also occurred and the differences in treatment of the different groups, leading to the classic conditions for the creation of outgroups.

Intended short-term labour migration commenced in the mid-1950s, as some labour shortages started to appear in the then West Germany. Turkish migrant workers then grew rapidly in numbers during the 1960s after the signing of an agreement between the two governments, though this involved two year contracts, and contained no family reunification process. Considerable movement of Turkish workers and families occurred over the succeeding decades even after the programs ceased. That is, many migrants returned to their homeland while others visited and returned to Germany, keeping ties with their homeland, including through marriage and family resettlement (Aybek, 2012).

Other waves of immigrants from Eastern Europe and Russia came later who were subsequently accepted as ethnic Germans, while others successfully fled communist East Germany. However, guest workers and their descendants, as well as asylum seekers were treated differently in terms of their legal standing (Klusmeyer and Papademetriou, 2009), with Turkish temporary migrants and their children precluded from pathways to citizenship until very recently.

The MCP Index states that immigration to Germany is a "highly politicized" issue, most likely because of popular perceptions that is not an "immigration country". Gumus (2016) argues this is because Germany defines its national community in terms of ethnicity and, therefore, welcomes re-settlers as Germans returning to the fatherland, but regards settled foreigners as aliens. Denial of the immigration situation, especially that temporary migrants had turned into permanent residents, was officially maintained by the German Federal government until 1998.

Aybek (2012) argues a second era commenced around 2000 with policy initiatives that accepted Germany was de-facto a country of immigration. These included initiatives for the entry of the highly skilled, and the amendment of the citizenship law through the adoption of the Immigration Act in 2005. At the same time, there was and continues to be, considerable debate about the limiting of migration and integration processes, the latter emphasizing German language proficiency. However, Gumus (2016) argues that while integration policies now potentially include access to the benefits of the German welfare state, this is undermined due to a restrictive naturalization program. Further, as Alba (2005) notes, in Germany the religion of the Turkish minority creates a bright boundary. It is reinforced by the barriers to citizenship for the second generation that existed before 2000 because those changes affected only those born starting in 2000, meaning the majority of second-generation Turkish adults were still precluded from becoming German citizens. Thus, recognition of past and current migration as permanent and the development of integration policies do not extend to an acceptance that Germany is a multicultural country (The MCP Index).

German Policies Facilitating/Hindering Multiculturalism

While immigrants with a regular residence status are encouraged to integrate, those with a so-called "tolerated" status are discouraged as the ultimate goal is to see them return to their country of origin (The MCP Index, citing Cyrus and Vogel, 2005). Thus, although education is a state responsibility in Germany, compulsory schooling is generally neither offered to children of refugees whose residence status is considered "tolerated" but insecure and temporary, nor to the children of undocumented migrants (The MCP Index citing Miera, 2008). A lack of intercultural education and recognition of cultural diversity within schools reinforces a mono-cultural approach detrimental to multicultural acceptance (The MCP Index). In terms of tolerance to different rites and customs, The MCP index notes differences between states and also ongoing debate over permitting teachers to wear the hijab, permission for Muslim and Jewish students to observe religious holidays and other customs.

Media, consisting of public and private broadcasters, has the potential to be more diverse. Larger cities offer radio channels broadcasting in foreign languages, and public broadcasters produce some programs that target ethnic minorities and are broadcast in various foreign languages (The MCP Index citing Wagner and Blumenreich, 2009).

A National Integration Plan (Bundesregierung, 2007) recognizes migrant associations are needed for the development and delivery of integration and immigration policies. While umbrella-type organizations deliver the bulk of social welfare programs, welfare associations play a significant role, including some immigrant associations. That is, they receive public funds to deliver some integration programs (The MCP Index citing Cyrus and Vogel, 2005). Immigrant associations are growing and commonplace as funds are provided to support and promote immigrant integration (The MCP Index citing Bundesregierung, 2007).

Embassies or governments of the countries that commonly provided guest workers have offered mother-tongue language courses in Germany on the assumption that the immigrants would eventually return to their countries of origin. As migrants have remained in Germany, this has led some states to prohibit mother-tongue instruction because it is viewed as a hindrance to integration (The MCP Index citing Miera, 2008).

France

It is in some ways a paradox that, approaching from two very different perspectives in terms of the acceptance of immigrants, France and Germany have very similar positions in terms of how their governments view multiculturalism and respond to the growth of cultural diversity arising from the large, late twentieth century migrant inflows.

Although interrupted by wars during the nineteenth and twentieth centuries, France has a long history of inward migration accompanying its industrialization. These immigrants have, until the post-colonial era, been mainly from surrounding countries; they have been integrated into French society—where integrated in this context appears to mean a loss of their ethnic identity and assimilation into French mainstream culture (Martin, 1994; Gumus, 2016), as opposed to our use of the term (Berry and Sam, 1997).

Citizenship paths for immigrants and children of immigrants born in France are far less restrictive than Germany (Martin, 1994). Gumus (2016) relates this back to the French Revolution and a universalist view of citizenship, with no differences or exceptions between citizens. Hence, Gumus (2016, p. 57) argues that

> (t)he French have always been reticent about the use of ethnic categories. Republican ideology is based on principles of civic citizenship and equal individual rights for all. The recognition of cultural difference or ethnic communities in unacceptable.
>
> (p. 57)

A similar point is made by The MCP Index, which cites Article 1 of the French constitution (1958) to the effect that there shall be equality before the law without distinction of origin, race or religion. This has been interpreted as affirmation that France does not recognize ethnic, religious, linguistic or other minorities (The MCP Index citing Delvainquière, 2007). Unsurprisingly, French law prohibits the collection of data on race or ethnic origin. In addition, schools are seen as a core institution for the integration of immigrants and their children; the French school system makes very few provisions for ethnic or cultural minorities; for example students are banned from the public wearing of clothing which manifest their religious faith, such as the hijab or turban (Gumus, 2016, The MCP Index).

Similar to Germany, The MCP Index notes steps to accommodate ethnic differences occurring, especially with the growth of the Maghrebian population from North Africa. France's *Law on Association*, which was originally passed in 1901, was extended in 1981 to immigrants and the foreign-born, giving them the right to establish associations under certain conditions with respect to French laws and values, including French cultural identity. Ethnic minority organizations have since grown.

In terms of media, the relative absence of minorities on mainstream television and radio has spurred the development of ethnic media (The MCP index citing Schuerkens, 2005). As in Germany, there is considerable resistance to ethnic minority groups developing or maintaining their ethnic identity. Unlike Germany, this is based on a universal citizenship model. However, in both cases, the religion of either the Turkish migrants and descendants in the case of Germany or Maghrebian migrants and descendants in France, creates a bright ethnic boundary (Alba, 2005) that tends to create marginalization rather than integration, using the Berry and Sam (1997) definition of the term. Similarly, the practice of ethnic marketing is hindered, not only by the lack of data collected by government on ethnic minorities but also by rejection that France is a multicultural nation.

United Kingdom

The UK also became a favoured country of immigration during the 1950s. Almost as an anomaly, the collapse of the empire and the expansion of the Commonwealth of Nations gave freedom of entry to the United Kingdom to all Commonwealth citizens including most of its former colonies in Asia, Africa and the Caribbean, which remained in the Commonwealth (Coleman, 1995). The opportunity for migration from these generally low-income, relatively less developed economies into the UK was quickly recognized and acted upon. As many residents from the UK took up opportunities to migrate to the old Commonwealth in search of better living standards, opportunities for employment in lower paying, relatively unskilled occupations opened up to immigrants from the new Commonwealth. (Choudhary, 2014; Coleman, 1995).

From the perspective of successive UK governments, this migration was unplanned and unanticipated. Citing various sources, Choudhary (2014) argues these were sojourners, intended temporary migrants seeking to improve their economic position and then returning home, as well as longer-term settlers also planning to return to their homeland on retirement; that is, each shared a common myth of return to their homeland.

Although coming from very different cultures and countries, they were distinctive in a "White" United Kingdom. Combined with the lack of skills held by many and the subsequent low-status work many had to pursue, social and economic segregation tended to interact, creating ethnic urban communities in the major cities.

As the UK sought to restrict immigration occurring from mainly the new Commonwealth (Commonwealth Immigration Act, 1962) those who had intended to return to their homeland, even for temporary visits such as for marriage, had to make a decision whether to remain in the UK, spurring family migration (Choudhary, 2014) and entrenching the growth of ethnic communities within major cities.

Another consequence of the UK policy was that, given the scope of the former colonies, migration was more diverse. In combination with the later opening of borders to fellow EU states, a more multicultural UK emerged compared with either France or Germany. While the UK Census collects ethnicity statistics, its collection obscures this diversity. While based on self-ascription, the available ethnic group classifications are restricted and are primarily country and region based. Hence, differences are obscured within the Indian category, African Blacks or Caribbean Blacks, by way of example of the aggregations used.

One consequence of this restriction is the tendency to aggregate ethnic groups for policy purposes, again changing the dynamics of minority group formation with a tendency towards panethnicity, as in the USA. Based on the 2011 Census, no particular non-White minority groups stand out in size, with the Indian nationality group being slightly larger (2.5 percent) than the Pakistani (2.0 percent) followed by "Black Africans" and "Black Caribbean" (U.K., Office of National Statistics, 2012), suggesting the need for a multicultural policy approach.

The addressing of multicultural issues in the UK is more advanced than either France or Germany (see Table 14.3), although, while multiculturalism is recognized as a demographic fact, policies to address this diversity are expressed in terms of building cohesion and integration (The MCP Index). The schooling system includes both public and private schools but a government requirement is that schools have a duty to promote community cohesion in addition to recognizing diversity, human rights and equity. Unsurprisingly, exemptions for dress codes exist, including headwear. Complimentary ethnic schools exist based on language, ethnic group or religion but are increasingly self-funded (The MCP Index).

As an open society, ethnic media is available from abroad, assisted by home country governments or home country organizations. Within the UK, there is a strong ethnic media both in print and digitally (Georgiou, 2002). In terms of public broadcasting, programming is expected to reflect the cultural diversity of the UK. A 1983 report by the Commission for Racial Equality, entitled *Ethnic Minority Broadcasting*, encouraged networks to look more seriously at media content in order to reflect a multi-racial society. Retention of ethnic identity is also facilitated by a relatively benign dual citizenship law. One can acquire UK citizenship without renouncing the original one. Ethnic networks and minority ethnic groups are free to form and are widespread. At various times they have been able to bid for funds, for example, to promote their cultural festivals (The MCP Index).

In summary, compared with Germany and France, the UK presents a more supportive environment for ethnic minority groups to network and seek to retain their group identity. As noted in a path breaking study by Heath and Demireva (2014), there is strong evidence this relatively more benign policy approach has led to minority ethnic groups integrating into UK society, using the Berry and Sam definition of the term. That is, they have sought to maintain an ethnic identity consistent with recognizing the value of participating within the UK polity rather than seeking separation, or marginalization. Ethnic marketing practice is therefore likely to face less social resistance from the mainstream and should be able to employ the full arsenal of ethnic marketing communications that is increasingly available to marketers.

The Potential for Ethnic Marketing in Other Environments

South Africa

Very few nation-states of any significant territorial and/or population size can deny they contain ethnic minority groups, in many cases in spite of long histories of deliberately trying to assimilate such groups. For ethnic marketing opportunities we have focussed on liberal democracies which also have primarily market-based economies, because these conditions enable businesses to more clearly assess the costs and benefits of targeted marketing of ethnic minority groups within a transparent legal framework without repercussions from the state, given that many nation-states still repress ethnic minorities. While we have focussed on two groups of liberal democracies with very different immigration patterns, there are other emerging markets for ethnic marketing where current immigration is less active but past immigration has led to very multicultural nations. South Africa and Malaysia are two examples but the purpose here is to bring out how political and social conditions may hinder ethnic marketing, focussing on South Africa.

The role of the political environment in shaping the environment for ethnic marketing is evident in the changes that have occurred in post-apartheid South Africa. In terms of the phenotype categories used to describe the population of South Africa, pre-1991, four major categories were distinguished: "Black Africans", currently accounting for about 80 percent of the total population, is itself an aggregate of different ethnic and tribal groups. This category increasingly can be seen as pan ethnic as urbanization and industrialization leads to a loss of tribal connection. "Whites", who now account for approximately 9 percent of the population, again derive from past disparate European sources but are primarily either Dutch or Anglo-Celtic. Descendants from past Indian subcontinent migration, *"South African Indians"* account for around 2 percent and "Coloureds", those of mixed White and Black descent, account for 9 percent. Although the South African law of racial categories has been abolished, many South Africans still view themselves according to these categories, although religion, languages as well other cultural practices, vary across all four groups. Adding to this complexity has been a post-apartheid influx of immigrants from surrounding, generally poorer countries (especially with political and civil unrest in many of these countries) who have been the subject of exclusion (Tsheola, 2015).

The ascendancy of the African National Congress to government in 1994 saw a strong emphasis on seeking to unify the nation whilst recognizing the cultural diversity and protection of minorities in the transition to a democracy with an open franchise. One of the consequences of these negotiations was the recognition of 11 official languages although Henrard (2003) noted that, less than a decade on, official use of English was becoming ascendant.

Racial segregation previously practiced was removed but a right for students to receive instruction in their language of choice was also inserted which has tended to assist minority ethnic groups to maintain their identity. Unlike Australia or other traditional immigration countries, where immigrant groups can choose an acculturation path maybe towards integration with the mainstream culture or to separate etc., the South African option is that of longstanding settled groups retaining their indigenously formed ethnic values and traditions whilst subscribing to an emerging concept of South African nationhood. Major income and wealth disparities within the country exist between groups, with income disparities most marked in the largest group, the "Blacks" (Wesso and Robertson, 2015), adding to the difficulties of using ethnic marketing as opposed to socio-economic variables.

Media diversity has grown in the move to democracy. The government-run public broadcaster continues, but as Duncan (2016) notes, community media has expanded. Television stations increased from seven to 100 between 1991 and 2010, and the number of radio stations from 34 to 138. The major newspapers are largely English language, but community press is often in the preferred ethnic language (Duncan, 2016). In summary, one can see potential for ethnic marketing in South Africa because there are officially no policy restrictions in recognizing and responding to this cultural diversity. However, with a lower level of development and with major impediments arising from what appears to be a more fragmented social environment than in other countries examined in this chapter, there are more challenges to the effective use of ethnic marketing.

Conclusion

In Chapter 1 of this book we observed that marketing to ethnic minority groups has taken several different names and different approaches. While it may be the case that this sometimes reflects idiosyncrasies and misunderstandings by marketers of the markets they are seeking to target, a more general reason may well be because of the different environmental forces at work in different national markets.

In this chapter we have focussed on the political environment—the effects of national differences in immigration and integration policies— in encouraging or discouraging marketing (particularly by mainstream business) that targets minority ethnic groups. The impact of such policies will also extend to ethnic entrepreneurship and minority ethnic business but probably with distinct effects. While policies that result in the marginalization of minority ethnic groups may create less employment opportunities with the mainstream economy and more self-employment of settlers, they may also lead to tight ethnic networks that encourage the formation of minority ethnic businesses established to meet the needs of a small market that is alienated from the mainstream. But marginalization also means that these businesses' opportunities for growth outside the co-ethnic minority group may also be restricted. The political and economic context clearly matter (Razin, 2002)

Policies towards permanent immigration have been largely non-discriminatory in terms of country selection, and more skills-based oriented in countries such as Canada and Australia, attracting migrants with a high degree of human capital. Within these countries, a pro-multicultural approach has enabled new arrivals to relatively, freely develop their ethnic identity and their links to persons of similar ethnic identity, leading to resilient ethnic groups with strong social networks that have assisted the settlement of new immigrants both in terms of employment and creation of ethnic minority businesses.

Instead of marginalization, which may be a consequence of policies that seek to assimilate or discourage the practice of one's ethnic identity, a multicultural policy approach as engaged in by these countries has encouraged integration, enabling ethnic social networks where bridges can be built across minority ethnic groups and with the mainstream. From a marketing perspective, such ethnic markets will be more open to targeting by mainstream and ethnic minority businesses, while ethnic entrepreneurs commencing from within their own ethnic group should have more opportunity to grow beyond that group. Nevertheless, unless carefully managed, a multicultural policy can generate reactions that can inhibit both ethnic marketing and the expansion of ethnic minority business beyond co-ethnic markets:

> Emphasizing the value of ethnic diversity can have the unfortunate side effect of amplifying . . . tribal tendencies. Studies have shown that when countries pursue multiculturalism policies, many people become more racist and more hostile toward immigrants.
>
> (Rock and Grant, 2017, p. 11)

Policy attitudes towards the acceptance of ethnic minorities have many unintended consequences. The policies themselves can influence the recognition and collection of data on ethnic minorities within a country, with statistical groupings used to distribute social resources or to report social and economic data by "ethnic group". When very broad groupings are used this can encourage panethnic groups. Such groupings can also influence businesses' and marketers' perceptions about the strength and cohesiveness of the market created by such grouping, leading to marketing strategies that are less effective in meeting the needs of specific minorities.

What is needed is a set of policy instruments that enables pertinent support to be given to different minority ethnic groups and to their affiliated businesses (Ibrahim and Galt, 2003). Alternatively, seeking to ignore the existence of ethnic minority groups, assuming assimilation is the only acculturation path, can lead to their marginalization and invisibility. In both alternatives, ethnic marketing and ethnic small business opportunities can be impeded by lack of accurate information about ethnic groups, their size and resilience.

Other environmental forces also impact on both the desirability of ethnic marketing and how it will be practiced. Economic and technology forces are drivers of globalization, influencing labour migration and interaction between different cultures. The increasing global ubiquity of digital technologies can affect acculturation paths in many different ways. In one sense, ethnic networks can be more readily maintained in spite of geographical distance perhaps helping in bonding to the home country culture, but studies of immigrant youth also suggest that in their more ready access to local, transnational and global youth cultures, what emerges from the process is unpredictable (D'Haenens, Koeman and Saeys, 2007; Razavi, 2013). That is, it is also possible the internet and the growth of social media may weaken ethnic identity, fostering hybridity and bi-culturalism (Bauhn and Tepe, 2016). Returning to the role of host country policies, we can also observe how governments, resolute in their opposition to how such technologies are used to build social networks and ties they do not approve of, can take actions to control their use to communicate with like-minded individuals, but that clearly means a departure from the principles of liberal democracy.

The liberal democracies discussed in this chapter contained governments that accepted they were multicultural nation-states as well as those who have resisted accepting what appears to be a reality. Ethnic marketing faces less resistance when governments are supportive of integration, where ethnic minorities can retain their group networks and the social and economic support this often entails. Even when ethnic group differences are very pronounced, marketers need to look at the wider picture of economic inequalities and political stability, before determining an ethnic marketing route.

References

Alba, R. (2005). Bright vs. blurred boundaries: Second-generation assimilation and exclusion in France, Germany, and the United States. *Ethnic and Racial Studies*, 28(1), 20–49.

Australian Bureau of Statistics (ABS) Catalogue 3412.0. *Migration, Australia, 2015–16*. Accessed 23/4/2018 at www.abs.gov.au/AUSSTATS/abs@.nsf/mf/3412.0/

Australian Bureau of Statistics (ABS) (2017). *2071.0 Census of Population and Housing: Reflecting Australia-Stories from the Census, 2016-Cultural Diversity*, Table 12. Language Spoken at Home by State and Territory of Usual Residence, Count of persons—2016(a). Accessed 18/4/2018 at www.abs.gov.au/ausstats/abs@.nsf/mf/2071.0

Australian Government, Department of Home Affairs (undated). *Fact Sheet 8, Abolition of the 'White Australia' Policy*. Canberra. Accessed 4/2018 at www.homeaffairs.gov.au/about/corporate/information/fact-sheets/08abolition

Australian Government, Department of Home Affairs (2018a). *The People of Australia: Australia's Multicultural Policy*, 2011. Accessed 4/2018 at www.homeaffairs.gov.au/trav/life/multicultural/australias-multicultural-policy-history

Australian Government, Department of Home Affairs (2018b). *Multicultural Australia*. Accessed 4/2018 at www.homeaffairs.gov.au/trav/life/multicultural/australias-multicultural-policy-history

Australian Government, Department of Immigration and Citizenship (2011). *Australian Immigration Fact Sheet 6. Australia's Multicultural Policy*. Canberra. Accessed 4/2018 at www.immi.gov.au/media/fact-sheets/06australias-multicultura

Australian Government, Productivity Commission (2016). Migrant *Intake into Australia*. Inquiry Report No. 77. Accessed 23/4/2018 at www.pc.gov.au/inquiries/completed/migrant-intake#report

Aybek, C. (2012). Politics, symbolics and facts: Migration policies and family migration from Turkey to Germany. *Perceptions*, 17(2), 37.

Bauhn, P. and Tepe, F. (2016). Hybridity and agency: Some theoretical and empirical observations. *Migration Letters*, 13(3), 350–358.

Berry, J. and Sam, D. (1997). Acculturation and adaptation. *Handbook of Cross-Cultural Psychology*, 3, 291–326.

Bundesregierung, D. (2007). *The National Integration Plan: New Paths, New Opportunities*. Berlin: Press and Information, Office of the Federal Government. Accessed 26/8/2010 at www.bundesregierung.de/Content/DE/Publikation/IB/Anlagen/ib-flyernip-englisch-barrierefrei,property=publicationFile.pdf

Canada, Minister of Justice (1988). *Canadian Multiculturalism Act*. Accessed 18/8/2018 at http://laws—lois.justice.gc.ca/eng/acts/C—18.7/

Castles, S. and Miller, M. (2003). *The Age of Migration: International Population Movements in the Modern World*. New York: The Guilford Press.

Choudhary, S. (2014). Political colonization of multi-ethnic Britain: A study of Indian Diaspora, Diaspora. *Studies*, 7(2), 100–120.

Clydesdale, G. (2008). Business immigrants and the entrepreneurial nexus. *Journal of International Entrepreneurship*, 6(3), 123–142.

Coleman, D. (1995). International migration: Demographic and socioeconomic consequences in the United Kingdom and Europe. *The International Migration Review*, 29(1), 155–190.

Commonwealth Immigration Act (1962). Accessed 18/8/2018 at https://web. archive.org/web/20110927012831/www.britishcitizen.info/CIA1962.pdf

Cyrus, N. and Vogel, D. (2005). Germany. In Jan Niessen, Yongmi Schibel and Cressida Thompson (eds.), *Current Immigration Debates in Europe: A Publication of the European Migration Dialogue*. Dusseldorf and Brussels: Migration Policy Group. Accessed 26/8/2010 at www.migpolgroup.com/public/docs/141.EMD_Germany_2005.pdf

Delvainquière, J. (2007). Country profile, France. *Council of Europe/ERICarts: Compendium of Cultural Policies and Trends in Europe*. Accessed 4/3/2010 at www. culturalpolicies. net

D'Haenens, L., Koeman, J. and Saeys, F. (2007). Digital citizenship among ethnic minority youths in the Netherlands and Flanders. *New Media Society*, 9, 278–299.

Duncan, H. (2006). Immigrant integration and social capital, chapter 4. In R. Lewis (ed.), *Multiculturalism Observed: Exploring Identity*. ASP. ProQuest Ebook Central. Accessed 4/2018 at http://ebookcentral.proquest.com/lib/uwsau/detail.action?docID=3115865

Duncan, J. (2016). Pluralism with little diversity: The South African experience of media transformation, chapter 13. In P. Valcke, M. Sükösd and R. Picard (eds.), *Media Pluralism and Diversity*. Houndmills, UK: Palgrave Macmillan.

Georgiou, M. (2002). Mapping minorities and their media: The national context-the UK. *London: London School of Economics*. Accessed 15/3/2018 at www. lse.ac.uk/media@lse/research/EMTEL/minorities/papers/finlandreport.doc

Gumus, Y. (2016). What explains differences in countries' migration policies? *International Journal of Research in Business and Social Science (2147–4478)*, 4(1), 51–65.

Heath, A. and Demireva, N. (2014). Has multiculturalism failed in Britain? *Ethnic and Racial Studies*, 37(1), 161–180.

Henrard, K. (2003). Post-apartheid South Africa: Transformation and reconciliation. *World Affairs*, 166(1), 37–57.

Ibrahim, G. and Galt, V. (2003). Ethnic business development: Toward a theoretical synthesis and policy framework. *Journal of economic issues*, 37(4), 1107–1119.

Klusmeyer, D. and Papademetriou, D. (2009). *Immigration Policy in the Federal Republic of Germany*. New York: Berghahn Books.

Martin, P. (1994). Comparative migration policies. *The International Migration Review*, 28(1), 164–171.

Miera, F. (2008). Transnational strategies of Polish migrant entrepreneurs in trade and small business in Berlin. *Journal of Ethnic and Migration Studies*, 34(5), 753–770.

The Multiculturalism Policy Index [The MCP Index] (Multiculturalism Policy Index). Accessed 22/4/2018 at www.queensu.ca/mcp/

OECD (2017). *International Migration Outlook 2017*. Paris: OECD Publishing. Accessed 20/3/2018 at http://dx.doi.org/10.1787/migr_outlook-2017-en

OECD (2001). *Trends in International Migration, Annual Report, 2000*. Paris: OECD.

Office of Multicultural Affairs, Department of the Prime Minister and Cabinet (1989). *National Agenda for a Multicultural Australia, Sharing our Future*. Canberra: Australian Government Publishing Service.

Ongley, P. and Pearson, D. (1995). Post-1945 international migration: New Zealand, Australia and Canada compared. *The International Migration Review*, 29(3), 765–786.

Pearson, F. and Hanlin, E. (2006). Managing diversity: The evolving American experience, chapter 8. In R. Lewis (ed.), *Multiculturalism Observed: Exploring Identity*. ASP, ProQuest Ebook Central. Accessed 4/2018 at http://ebookcentral.proquest.com/lib/uwsau/detail.action?docID=3115865

Pires, G. and Stanton, J. (2002). Ethnic marketing ethics. *Journal of Business Ethics*, 36(1–2), 111–118.

Razavi, M. (2013). *Navigating New National Identity Online: On Immigrant Children, Identity & the Internet*. Thesis submitted to the Faculty of the Graduate School of Arts & Sciences, Georgetown University, USA.

Razin, E. (2002). Conclusion: The economic context, embeddedness and immigrant entrepreneurs. *International Journal of Entrepreneurial Behavior & Research*, 8(1/2), 162–167.

Rock, D. and Grant, H. (2017). Is your company's diversity training making you more biased? *Strategy + Business*, 88 (Autumn). strategy+business.com

Schuerkens, U. (2005). Active civic participation of immigrants in France. *Country Report prepared for the European Research Project Oldenburg 2005*.

Spoonley, P. (2015). A political economy of labour migration of New Zealand. *New Zealand Population Review*, 41, 169–190.

Spoonley, P. (2006). He iwi tahi Tatou? Policy in a diverse New Zealand. *Canadian Diversity*, 5(1), 64–67.

Spoonley, P., Peace, R., Butcher, A. and O'Neill, D. (2005). Social cohesion: A policy and indicator framework for assessing immigrant and host outcomes. *Social Policy Journal of New Zealand: Te Puna Whakaaro* (24), 85–110.

Tsheola, J. (2015). Xenophobic societal attitudes in a "new" South Africanism: Governance of public perceptions, national identities and citizenship. *The Journal for Transdisciplinary Research in Southern Africa*, 11(4) (December), Special edition, 232–246.

United Kingdom, Office of National Statistics (2012). *Ethnicity and National Identity in England and Wales*, 2011. Accessed 27/4/2018 at www.ons.gov.uk/peoplepopulationandcommunity/culturalidentity/ethnicity/articles/ethnicityandnationalidentityinenglandandwales/2012-12-11

Wagner, B. and Blumenreich, U. (2009). Country profile—Germany. *Compendium of Cultural Policies and Trends in Europe*. 11th ed. Updated August 2009. Brussels: Council of Europe. Accessed 23/10/2018 at www.culturalpolicies.net/web/profiles-download.php?pcid=1140

Vertovec, S. and Wessendorf, S. (eds.) (2010). *Multiculturalism Backlash: European Discourses, Policies and Practices*. Abingdon, UK: Routledge.

Wesso, A. and Robertson, R. (2015). Assessing consumer behavior in diverse markets, the South African experience. *I-Manager's Journal on Management*, 10(1), 1–8.

Yinger, J. (1985). Ethnicity. *Annual Review of Sociology*, 11, 151–180.

Zolberg, A. (2006). The changing nature of migration in the 21st century: Implications for integration strategies, chapter 2. In R. Lewis (ed.), *Multiculturalism Observed: Exploring Identity*. ASP.

Index

Note: Page numbers in italics indicate figures; page numbers in bold indicate tables.

Printed in the United States
by Baker & Taylor Publisher Services